First Kings of Europe

From Farmers to Rulers in Prehistoric Southeastern Europe

First Kings of Europe

From Farmers to Rulers in Prehistoric Southeastern Europe

Edited by Attila Gyucha and William A. Parkinson

UCLA Cotsen Institute of Archaeology Press

THE FIELD MUSEUM OF NATURAL HISTORY

Edited by R. Neil Hewison
Design and layout by Doug Brotherton

A copublication between The Field Museum of Natural History and
The Cotsen Institute of Archaeology at UCLA.

First Kings of Europe Exhibition Venues:

Institute for the Study of the Ancient World at New York University, New York, NY, USA
September 21, 2022 through February 19, 2023

Field Museum of Natural History, Chicago, IL, USA
March 31, 2023 through January 28, 2024

Canadian Museum of History, Gatineau, Quebec, Canada
April 4, 2024 through January 19, 2025

Library of Congress Cataloging-in-Publication Data:

Identifiers: LCCN 2021005793 | ISBN 9781950446247 (Hardback) | ISBN 9781950446254 (Adobe PDF)
LC record available at https://lccn.loc.gov/2021005793

Contents

Contents

Figures

Preface

T HIS BOOK IS A COMPANION to the *First Kings of Europe* exhibition that, with a tremendous amount of help from a great deal of friends and colleagues, we have developed over the course of the past five years. For nearly a quarter of a century, we have been running international, collaborative research projects—shoulder-to-shoulder and trowel-to-trowel—to explore early agricultural societies in southeastern Europe. We have long discussed how wonderful it would be to present the marvelous archaeological heritage of southeastern Europe to a North American audience. With both of us living in Chicago for several years, where hundreds of thousands of people with roots in the Balkans and neighboring regions live and cherish their origins and traditions, we felt it was the right time to try to make this happen; it was an ambitious, albeit daunting, task that the Field Museum, where we both worked, was uniquely positioned to carry out.

We needed a compelling conceptual framework for the exhibition. The fundamental question was how to showcase and promote southeastern European archaeological heritage using a storyline that is both accessible and relevant to the modern world. We ended up with a narrative that is familiar to many but which also challenges people to think about how the world came to be the way it is. We all know what kings and queens are in modern societies, and especially in European history, but how did these political and economic inequalities and hierarchies start and develop in ancient times? How did the emergence

of these inequalities go hand-in-hand with positions of leadership and, eventually, the emergence of royal monarchs? We decided to tether these questions to four themes—technology and craft production, trade and exchange, warfare and conflicts, as well as ceremonies and rituals—to approach these questions using the rich material culture from across southeastern Europe. In 2017, the exhibition was formally approved by the Field Museum. The following years took us on an unbelievable adventure, including many rounds of artifact selection, design, and development, and fruitful collaborations with dozens of museums. We had the once-in-a-lifetime opportunity to work with amazing colleagues from eleven countries who helped us make this unprecedented exhibition happen, and we are thrilled to be able to work with them to write several books that will make sure the exhibition will not be forgotten as soon as it is over.

This book is the product of a multi-year collaboration between the authors and illustrators, the Field Museum, the UCLA Cotsen Institute of Archaeology, and us as editors. In addition to a foreword and an introductory chapter that provide the conceptual groundwork, the book also includes nine essays written by outstanding scholars from ten countries, most with active, long-term research programs in southeastern Europe. The chapters explore a range of themes related to the evolution of hierarchy and leadership from the Neolithic to the Iron Age in the region.

The primary audience for this book is the general public and we have tried to produce a richly illustrated volume written in accessible language. At the same time, we also hope the book will be used by scholars who will appreciate a synthetic monograph that brings together diverse materials—and ideas—between two covers.

Acknowledgments

WE ARE INDEBTED to everyone who has contributed to this book, which is the first of a set of books that complement the *First Kings of Europe* exhibition. We include additional acknowledgments for those who participated in the exhibition in the second volume. We are particularly grateful to the authors for their dedication, superb work, and the endless patience they demonstrated during the course of the—sometimes painful—editing process. We believe that their chapters will help promote the uniquely rich archaeological heritage of southeastern Europe to the world. Our special thanks go to Dr. Gary M. Feinman of the Field Museum for writing the foreword to this volume.

We thank the many people and numerous institutions from Europe who facilitated our access to their museum collections and assemblages for photography or made their own personal or archival photographs available for publication. Although they are credited in the figure captions, we also want them to know how much we truly appreciate their help in making this a beautiful book.

We also thank Jill Seagard for her tremendous assistance with the illustrations in this book, and Ferenc Paár and Erica Lynn Rodriguez for making the wonderful maps. Ádám Vágó took several road trips throughout southeastern Europe to take the amazing photographs for both the book and the exhibition.

We also thank John Papadopoulos (Department of Classics, University of California Los Angeles) and Chris Scarre (Archaeology Department, Durham University) who commented on an earlier version of the manuscript. Their suggestions helped us improve the quality of this book.

During the editing process, we worked closely with Randi Danforth and Neil Hewison at the UCLA Cotsen Institute of Archaeology Press. Thank you, Randi and Neil, for your fantastic work and stamina!

We also want to thank our colleagues at the Field Museum who have worked tirelessly for years on this project, especially Jaap Hoogstraten, Susan Neill, Tom Skwerski, Janet Hong, Ryan Schuessler, and Tiffany Charles. The project was funded in part by a grant from the National Endowment for the Humanities (2020 Exhibitions: Implementation Program; William A. Parkinson, Project Director; Attila Gyucha, Co-Primary Investigator; *First Kings of Europe: The Emergence of Hierarchy in the Prehistoric Balkans*), and we are grateful to our colleagues, Deborah Bekken, Pamela Clayburn, Lisa Niziolek, and Kathryn Harris, for helping prepare the proposal and process the grant. The project also received a generous grant from the America for Bulgaria Foundation, and we thank Karin Victoria and Darren Incorvaia for their assistance in preparing the proposal. We also thank the former president and CEO of the Field Museum, Richard Lariviere, and his successor, Julian Siggers, as well as former chief marketing officer, Ray DeThorne, for their support of this ambitious project.

Finally, we want to thank our families, Dani, Betsy, Josie, and Sadie, for their constant support not only for this project but also for all the other insane projects we do that take us away from them for long periods of time. We recognize that we can only pull off hairbrained ideas like this because you support us and our crazy careers! Thank you!

Contributors

János Angi
Déri Museum, Hungary

Corina Borş
Department of Archaeology,
National History Museum of Romania

János Dani
Department of Archaeology,
Déri Museum, Hungary

Peter Delev
Faculty of History, St. Kliment Ohridski
University of Sofia, Bulgaria

Gary M. Feinman
Negaunee Integrative Research Center,
Field Museum of Natural History, USA

András Füzesi
Department of Archaeology,
Hungarian National Museum, Hungary

Michael L. Galaty
Museum of Anthropological Archaeology
and Department of Anthropology,
University of Michigan, USA

Florin Gogâltan
Institute of Archaeology and History of
Art and Babeş-Bolyai University,
Cluj-Napoca, Romania

Attila Gyucha
Department of Anthropology,
University of Georgia, USA

Eleonora Petrova Mitevska
Directorate for Protection of Cultural Heritage,
Republic of North Macedonia

Jovan D. Mitrović
Department of Archaeology,
National Museum of Serbia, Serbia

Goce Naumov
Center for Prehistoric Research and
Department of Archaeology,
Goce Delčev University,
Republic of North Macedonia

William A. Parkinson
Negaunee Integrative Research Center,
Field Museum of Natural History
and Department of Anthropology,
University of Illinois at Chicago, USA

Hrvoje Potrebica
Department of Archaeology,
University of Zagreb, Croatia

Andrijana Pravidur
Department of Archaeology,
National Museum of Bosnia and Herzegovina

Bianca Preda-Bălănică
Department of Cultures,
University of Helsinki, Finland

Pál Raczky
Institute of Archaeology,
Eötvös Loránd University, Hungary

Botond Rezi
Department of Archaeology,
Mureş County Museum, Romania

Rudenc Ruka
Prehistory Department,
Institute of Archaeology, Albania

Gábor V. Szabó
Institute of Archaeology,
Eötvös Loránd University, Hungary

János Gábor Tarbay
Department of Archaeology,
Hungarian National Museum, Hungary

FOREWORD

From Farmers to Kings

Gary M. Feinman

I T IS MY GREAT PLEASURE to have the opportunity to write the foreword to this volume, giving me a role, albeit minuscule, in the collaborative endeavor that has resulted not merely in this book but the *First Kings of Europe* exhibition, which this collection contextualizes and celebrates. Cooperation, even if only over several years—the time that it has taken to implement this project—is never easy. And so, I applaud the editors, the contributors, and the entire production team that built the *First Kings of Europe* exhibition, and everyone involved in this international effort for their fruitful achievements, which realized both this unique, multinational exhibition and the accompanying volumes.

Royalty, a highly institutionalized mode of governance, like other modes of leadership, implies at least a degree of interpersonal interaction and cooperation. Leaders or rulers cannot exist without followers.[1] And institutionalized leadership, more than contingent or situational headship, tends to require closer, more enduring ties. If the institutionalization of leaders requires the transfer or allocation of resources (such as tax or tribute), as it often does, then affiliates and/or followers are requisite.

Why do we have leaders? Why and how do their relations with followers vary across space and over time? And why are specific modes or lineages of leadership often ephemeral? In global history, lineal lines of familial rule rarely have lasted more than a few generations. Across world history, dynasties tend to be measured in centuries. Even if we look at modern nations, how many of them (very few, in fact) have kept relatively consistent borders or modes of governance longer than a millennium?

To address these questions, we first have to consider human social networks, interpersonal affiliations, and our ability as a species to form groups.

Humans have an exceptional capability to cooperate (behaviors that deliver benefits to other individuals or are advantageous to both actor and recipient) with unrelated individuals at scales not found in any other animal.[2] But, as a species, we also are selfish and competitive, especially when resources are involved.[3] Human cooperation is contingent, strategically situational.[4] Our cooperative arrangements are impermanent, somewhat ephemeral, even those that are relatively small in size.[5] Furthermore across time, human social formations and networks tend to be open, not tightly bounded.[6] As a consequence, leaders and governance, ever reliant on followers and the resources and labor that they provide, also are subject to uncertainty across deep time.

In the remainder of this essay, I consider why in so many regions of the world, as described for southeastern Europe, we see the institutionalization of leadership in conjunction with (or shortly following) the transition to increasingly settled lifeways and the advent of more permanent communities. Yet, globally, although the advent of institutionalized forms of leadership often temporally has corresponded with the formation of larger, more sedentary settlements, the nature of that leadership and associated modes of governance is often markedly variable. Across the world, leadership, monumentality, and inequality correlate in distinct ways. Likewise, sequences of change and the role of new technologies in these shifts vary from place to place and historical case to case. For example, metallurgical innovations were integral to the processes associated with the development of rulers and inequality in Europe. Yet metal was a non-issue in pre-Hispanic Mesoamerica until much later; it was not employed until long after both the rise of cities and the institutionalization of powerful rulers in that region.[7]

Leadership, Scale, and Community

A general relationship between the size of human social groupings and the complexity of political organization has long been recognized.[8] Across time and cross-culturally, the larger the scale of permanent human aggregations and political units, the more levels or tiers of governance tend to be present.[9] And yet, even though this association is broadly presumed and expected, the relationship between these two variables, aggregate size and political complexity, weakens when one focuses down on narrower population ranges.[10] There is no simple threshold or magic number at which human groupings change organizationally in uniform ways. Larger aggregations generally entail greater governmental complexity, but such changes take different forms and shift at variable rates.

This general relationship has a basis in human cognitive capability, interpersonal interaction, and the sustenance of cooperative arrangements. For mobile hunter–gatherers, networks of social relationships generally are dispersed, open, ephemeral, and changing with regularity as groups and individuals split apart and nucleate. But the most stable unit is small, made up of close kin, affines, and those who are proximate, all of whom have in-depth knowledge of each other.[11] These individual relations tend to be face-to-face, personal, and biographical.[12] Yet hunting and gatherer groupings are not purely egalitarian, as inequities are often manifest along the lines of age, sex, and ability.[13] Likewise, especially during aggregational episodes, leaders and ritual specialists may arise, but their roles tend to be situational, ephemeral, and not institutionalized or heritable over time.[14]

Globally, there is ample evidence that the transition from mobile lifeways to more permanent settlements precipitated demographic growth,[15] although the specific suite of causal factors may not be uniform. With more permanent settlements and the cleared areas and tended fields that entailed householder labor and resource investments or sunk costs,[16] departure from settled communities (fissioning) became a less viable option than in more mobile networks. Larger, denser settlements have wide-ranging implications[17] for human social networks. As community size increases arithmetically, the potential number of interpersonal interactions expands exponentially.[18] The abandonment of fission–fusion mobility in the shift to habitual co-residence in larger aggregations exacerbates social stresses, and these have to be met coincidently with economic adjustments and changes in resource procurement, storage, risk cycles, and travel times.[19] With seasonal and temporal fluctuations, no longer could network size map directly on resource availability.[20]

Michael Smith sees "the concentration of formerly dispersed people into villages, towns, and cities" as "one of the most consequential processes" in human history.[21] He also rightly notes that although scholars across the social sciences view this process as a critical transition, there are disparities in framing, with some focused on scalar costs and others on the benefits.[22] Such scalar increases have been widely discussed in the anthropological literature, albeit referenced under various terms, including "scalar stress,"[23] "social stress,"[24] "communications stress,"[25] "intracommunity conflict,"[26] and "density-dependent conflict."[27] These approaches emphasize how greater settlement densities and interaction foment shifts in organizational complexity.

At the same time, researchers in economics and geography emphasize the positive effects of "energized crowding,"[28] where in larger and denser settlements, increases in face-to-face social interaction provoke technological innovation, accelerated transfers of knowledge, and economic growth.[29] The properties of social networks are non-linear, so settlement expansion foments exponential changes in the use of space, comprehension of information, productivity, and labor divisions. These processes did not begin at the onset of cities but materialized when people aggregated in permanent co-resident communities; subsequently they were scaled up as further nucleation occurred.

With co-residence in larger, denser settlements, not only the number but also the nature of social ties change. The burdens of sustaining and servicing social relationships strain time and energy budgets, increasing demand on memory and social cognition.[30] The specific scope of human cognitive capabilities is individually variable, and there is debate over precise capacities.[31] But there is little disagreement over the fact that constraints do exist and that they range around no more than several hundred associations.[32] Thus, once proximate social networks exceed that size, the nature of relations shift[33] so that ties with close affiliates (biographical) differ from those farther afield (categorical, role-based).

Similar differences in interpersonal ties were present in mobile networks as well, but there the option to fission could diminish stresses. Furthermore, the proportion of people linked through weak ties[34] would become much greater as settlements expanded. The size of networks and communities may grow, and still endure, only if individuals are able to cope not merely with increasingly large sets of social ties but also with a lesser familiarity with an expanded set of contacts. The ability to stabilize weak ties represents an important adjustment for human existence in larger social formations that offsets the cognitive, temporal, and energetic costs of processing greater quantities of social information and large sets of interpersonal relationships.[35] As the scale of population concentrations grows, interactions are mediated less by in-depth mutual knowledge and more by symbols linked to place and status, by social role.[36]

The integration of relational networks, some with weak ties and others with strong ties, allows communities to grow and expand rather than break apart. Shared ritual practices, and the associated material culture, can help scaffold and affirm weak ties, just as drinking, feasting, and reciprocal exchanges may solidify less intimate relations.[37] As the size of social affiliations scale up, there are collective challenges/opportunities to integrate and cooperate with people who were outside the sphere of regular, intimate interaction.[38] For sustainability, the potential disruptions of fissioning, distrust, and free-rider problems had to be managed and avoided, while collective action problems, such as defense, had to be faced.

Social and economic axes of horizontal complexity can foster cooperation and collective action in communities and closely linked social networks that range up to two to three thousand people in size (although hierarchical structures can be present), but above that scale, supra-household leadership (vertical complexity) generally is found.[39] For mobile foragers, the larger the camp sizes, the more dispersed they tend to be, thereby minimizing interpersonal interactions and the chances of dispute. However, in sedentary communities, with more institutionalized bases for dispute resolution, larger communities tend to be settled more densely.[40]

Of course, horizontal affiliations do not disappear and tend to be maintained through neighborhood organizations, dyadic exchanges, sodalities, and other socioeconomic interactive modes. Thus, in large groups, most, if not all, individuals actually have multiple social affiliations. In many regions, vertical complexity (differential power, leadership, and levels of decision making above domestic units) develop shortly after (or even at the time of) the transition to sedentism. When human groupings become very large, cooperation may take place between individuals who may not share a common language and are not known to each other through either direct social knowledge or reputation. These factors all greatly enhance opportunities for free-riding and individual agency in more impersonal social interactions.[41]

In large human groupings, leader–follower relations are a key dynamic[42] that is instrumental to the nature of cooperation and its maintenance over time.

These dialectical relations take a range of forms that can entail greater or lesser degrees of cooperation and differential degrees of concentrated power and wealth.[43] Leadership and governance vary from more collective forms characterized by shared power, social contracts, high degrees of cooperation, and rules of law to more autocratic forms typified by unchecked power and principals, inequitable distribution of wealth and services, the rule of men, and lesser degrees of cooperation. More autocratic forms of rule tend to be fiscally financed by funding sources that are easier to monopolize, while more collective modes of governance, with more distributed power, wealth, and voice, tend to rely on exactions of taxes and labor from subalterns.[43] Although ritual is universal in human groupings,[44] ritual practices vary in nature dependent on the scale of human groupings and how they are organized/governed.[45] Likewise, the nature of leadership and governance is closely related to where and how resources and labor are allocated, and so to the relative degrees to which defensive walls, princely graves, palaces, and/or temples tend to be built. Are investments made in monuments to glorify and legitimize the powerful few or is infrastructure built in ways that potentially benefit the broader community?

Europe's First Kings and Their Predecessors

Using the conceptual perspective outlined above, I highlight key observations by the contributors to this volume that serve to question and force us to reconsider how we view the processes leading up to the emergence of Europe's first kings and the presumptions we make when we conceptualize the human past more generally. Traditionally, discourses on history have focused on grand, rather categorical narratives that tend to privilege uniform step-like modes of change across homogeneous epochs, such as the Bronze and Iron Ages. These accounts tend to stress unilinear sequences, in which technology is positioned as the key driver (such as the Agricultural Revolution). A further presumption is that change is frequently generated through population replacements or external contact/diffusion, whereby isolated, homogeneous local populations are inspired or overrun by foreign migrations or outside influences that introduce a new set of normative practices. The findings presented in this collection offer the foundations for a new frame and a re-visioning of the past, one that stresses processes, rather than unilineal sequences, of change, variation across time and space, and a greater understanding of scale and historical openness of human social networks (see Chapter 4, this volume).[46]

From the perspective of process (and given the discussion above), the correspondence of sedentary communities with the advent of early indications of leadership and inequality across southeastern Europe is not surprising. Yet, as many of the chapters in this volume elaborate, this transition did not occur in lockstep across the region. For example, the transition to farming in regions where earlier sedentary foragers resided prior to the introduction of grains varied from those previously occupied by more mobile peoples (see Chapter 3, this volume).[47] Likewise, the earliest exploitation of copper occurred during the Neolithic in the Balkans, not during the Copper Age (see Chapter 2, this volume). Although larger, more permanent communities emerged temporally in conjunction with inequalities in burial goods in some southeastern European locations, there is little indication that leadership and hierarchical forms of governance were institutionalized for extended periods. At many of the larger Neolithic period sites described in this volume, a major focus of collaborative labor was the construction of earthen settlement mounds and surrounding enclosures and moats, all of which provided defense, a benefit to most householders (see Chapters 1 and 2, this volume).

Across most of southeastern Europe, shifts during the Bronze Age corresponded with the institutionalization of leadership, which generally took an exclusionary form[48] in which leadership was centered in patrilines (see Chapters 4 to 7, this volume). Select male burials, placed in association with earthen mounds, as well as inequities in the domestic distribution of exotic and other wealth items, serve as indicators of growing inequality. The bases of leadership and power were underpinned by the control of metal trade and leadership in war, which likely resulted in booty that could be distributed selectively to allies and kin. Spectacles, performances staged for wide audiences to show off elite regalia studded with metal, were staged to dazzle and legitimize the power of leaders (see Chapter 1, this volume).[49] The relative positioning of different Bronze Age settlements in the larger macroregional networks of trade was a basis for differentiation in the size of communities, the monumentality of their associated earthen structures, and the relative power of leaders. Propinquity to transport nodes, for example, along river junctions, enhanced the ability of certain leaders to concentrate economic wealth and political clout.

The importance of the Bronze Age metal trade across southeastern Europe and beyond serves as a critical reminder of how European communities from the Neolithic on were never isolates, but they always were part of larger networks in which people and goods moved.[50] For the most part, these were not complete demographic replacements but the consistent mobility of individuals and households migrating for economic, marriage, security, alliance, or other reasons.[51] Whether we consider the movements from the eastern steppe during the transition from the Copper Age to the Bronze Age (for example, see Chapters 4 and 6, this volume) or links to the Mediterranean world in the Iron Age (for example, see Chapters 8 to 10, this volume), these long-distance links did not promote large-scale shifts in the extant cultural traditions engaged in these networks.

Finally, it is important to recognize the importance of the new data and perspectives offered here to debates that extend beyond Europe's past. As noted earlier, the circulation of metals, which were so central to the emergence of inequality in southeastern Europe, had very different roles in other regions of the globe where there were no pre-modern Copper, Bronze, or Iron Ages, but inequalities, urbanism, markets, and concentrations of power were well manifest.

As a final observation, most early forms of leadership in southeastern Europe, which encompassed the archetype of pre-industrial democracy (Classical Athens), tended to be, in marked contrast, autocratic. Yet, just as distributed power and muted inequalities were not unique to Europe or Athens in the pre-modern world,[52] governance in ancient Europe was more frequently autocratic than democratic. At the same time, it is enlightening, and perhaps a bit heartening, to recognize that modes of governance are not culturally bound. So, globally, the rise of democratic governance in ancient Athens from more autocratic roots and traditions is not a singular case.[53]

Notes

1 Ahlquist and Levi 2011.

2 Melis and Semmann 2010.

3 Carballo 2013; Carballo et al. 2014.

4 Blantont and Fargher 2016:31–32.

5 Blanton and Fargher 2016:40.

6 Feinman and Neitzel 2019; Lesser 1961; Sterelny 2019.

7 Blanton et al. 1993.

8 Carneiro 1967; Ember 1963; Kosse 1990; Lekson 1985; Naroll 1956.

9 Feinman and Neitzel 1984; Johnson 1982.

10 Feinman 2013:39–40; Johnson 1982:391.

11 Apicella et al. 2012.

12 Coward and Gamble 2008.

13 Cashdan 1980; Flanagan 1989.

14 Feinman 1995; Flannery 1972.

15 Bandy and Fox 2010; Bellwood and Oxenham 2008.

16 Janssen et al. 2003.

17 Birch 2013; Smith 2019.

18 Coward and Dunbar 2014; Johnson 1982.

19 Pool 2012.

20 Coward and Dunbar 2014.

21 Smith 2019:37.

22 Smith 2019.

23 Bandy 2004; Johnson 1982.

24 Düring 2013.

25 Fletcher 1995.

26 Ur 2014.

27 Birch 2013.

28 Kostof 1991:37.

29 Bettencourt 2013; Ortman and Coffey 2017; Smith 2019.

30 Roberts 2010.

31 Dunbar 2011.

32 Sutcliffe et al. 2012; Wellman 2012.

33 Coward and Dunbar 2014.

34 Granovetter 1973; Granovetter 1983.

35 Coward and Dunbar 2014.

36 Sterelny and Watkins 2015.

37 Adler 1989; Adler and Wilshusen 1990; Coward and Dunbar 2014; Nettle and Dunbar 1997.

38 Coward and Dunbar 2014; Dunbar 2013.

39 Bernard and Killworth 1973; Feinman 1998; Feinman 2013; Feinman and Neitzel 1984.

40 Lobo et al. 2019.

41 Blanton and Fargher 2013:102.

42 Blanton and Fargher 2008; Blanton and Fargher 2016; Feinman 2012; Feinman and Carballo 2018; Renfrew 1974.

43 Blanton and Fargher 2008; Blanton and Fargher 2016.

44 Rappaport 1971:23.

45 Feinman 2016.

46 Furholt 2019.

47 Tringham 2000.

48 Blanton et al. 1996.

49 Feinman 2016.

50 Sherratt 1993.

51 Furholt 2018; Mittnik et al. 2019.

52 Blanton and Fargher 2008; Feinman and Carballo 2018; Feinman and Nicholas 2016.

53 Blanton and Fargher 2008.

The Evolution of Leadership and Inequality in Southeast European Prehistory

CHAPTER 1

INTRODUCTION

From Farmers to Rulers in Prehistoric Southeastern Europe

Attila Gyucha and William A. Parkinson

MAGES OF KINGS and queens pervade Western history and thought—from the ancient legendary tales of Arthur and Guinevere to Anna and Elsa in Disney's *Frozen*—the history of Europe is replete with depictions of royal families and stories of their successes as well as lessons to be learned from their failures. Some of the earliest recorded stories in Europe, the Homeric epic poems, tell the tales of powerful kings who waged wars alongside gods, fighting for honor and territory, and sometimes tragically dying for love. Even the roots of Western democracy in the Classical world are intimately intertwined with tyrants and kings; the reforms of Cleisthenes, which in 508 BC established a secure democratic footing for the Greek city-state of Athens, were only adopted in response to the overthrow of the tyrant king Hippias by the Spartan king Cleomenes I.[1] Kings, queens, princes, and princesses are ingrained into Western systems of history, government, politics, economics, and even children's books.

We know what kings and queens are, but where did they come from? This is the story of the *First Kings of Europe* exhibition, and of this book. Our story begins during the Neolithic period, in a time before kings, when prehistoric farmers lived in what is today the Balkan Peninsula in southeastern Europe (Figure 1.1). And it ends with the kings of the Iron Age whose names we know from ancient written sources, such as Seuthes III, Odrysian king of Thrace, and Dromichaetes, king of the Getae, who went head-to-head with Lysimachus, a successor of Alexander the Great who proclaimed himself king of Thrace, Asia Minor, and Macedon in 305 BC.

This story of the emergence of Europe's first kings unfolded geographically between Central Europe and Southwest Asia, where similar, dynamic social processes transformed societies, albeit at different chronological tempos. Indeed, by the time the first Neolithic farmers arrived in southeastern Europe toward the end of the seventh millennium BC, their ancestors in Southwest Asia had been living in sedentary villages, cultivating domestic crops, like wheat and barley, and herding animals, like sheep and goats, for thousands of years.

Conversely, although farming started later in southeastern Europe than it did in Asia Minor and the Near East, this part of Europe was in many respects precocious compared to the rest of the continent (Figure 1.2). After spreading quickly from the Aegean to the Carpathian Basin at the end of the seventh millennium BC, a settled, agricultural way of life took over two thousand years to spread throughout the rest of Europe, eventually arriving in Great Britain and Ireland during the beginning of the fourth millennium BC. By the time the first Neolithic farming groups arrived in the British Isles, the

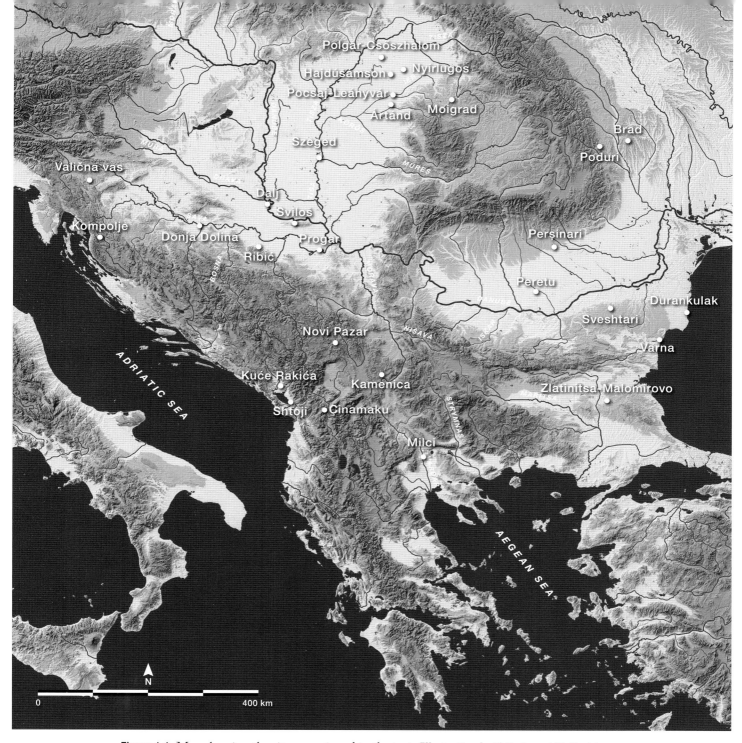

Figure 1.1. Map showing the sites mentioned in the text. *Illustration by F. Paár and E. Rodriguez.*

Neolithic period in southeastern Europe had been over for a thousand years; the Copper Age elites of the Varna necropolis in present-day Bulgaria with sumptuous funerary assemblages of copper axes, gold scepters, carnelian beads, and *Spondylus* shell bracelets had been buried hundreds of years before, and their shining flash of ostentatiousness lost forever.

This geographic context of southeastern Europe—between Europe and Asia, constantly negotiating between the two continents—continued to have a significant impact on the trajectory of major prehistoric social changes. Horses, which first were domesticated on the Eurasian steppe, became a necessity for Bronze Age warriors in the Balkans who were desperate to control intercontinental trade routes that provided them access to the tin they needed so metal smiths could cast the extravagant bronze weapons that represented their high status. Across the Black Sea and through the Aegean, the emergent elite in the Late Bronze Age of the Balkans traded with groups like the Mycenaeans and Hittites who already had well-established, centralized political and economic systems. Although their societies were not equal in terms of political and economic complexity, the Bronze Age Balkan warrior who was buried with a Mycenaean sword in his arms held an elite status and authority the likes of which few of his countrymen had ever seen; he was a part of a world they were not.

Similarly, the Iron Age aristocrats of the Balkans exhibited their wealth and status through the conspicuous display of symbols and objects that epitomized their close ties to other distant aristocrats—in Persia, Greece, and Etruria, among others. The aristocrat who was buried in Ártánd in Hungary with a bronze *hydria* made by master craftsmen in Sparta, in southern Greece, demonstrated, quite literally, the extent of their family's reach and power. Similarly, many of the extravagant drinking rituals that characterized Thracian feasting and funerary ceremonies incorporated the use of a variety of ostentatious drinking vessels bearing symbols and figures from Greek and Persian mythology. Even the ceremonies themselves can be traced to foreign traditions—such as the Greek feasting tradition (*symposium*) and the kinds of elaborate ancient funerary ceremonies described by Homer.

In this introductory chapter, we outline, in very broad strokes, the various social processes that came into play as the small, egalitarian farming villages of prehistoric southeastern Europe transformed over time into hierarchical, centralized states—the first tribal kingdoms in Europe. This transformation did not happen quickly or simultaneously; it unfolded over several thousand years as different regions underwent their own trajectories of social change. During this time, there were numerous technological innovations and adoptions, including significant advances in metalworking, transportation, and agriculture. There were also migrations of different groups into and out of the area, which, along with the emergence of expanded transportation networks as a result of the horse, the wheel, and the thirst for exotic goods, like amber, led to an increasingly interconnected and more complicated world.

Within this changing world, leaders emerged. Some of these leaders were ephemeral; quickly replaced, removed from office, or killed. Other leaders were more successful and managed to convert their fragile hold of power into something more long-lasting that could be passed down along blood lines. Some of those who were fortunate enough to inherit power were able eventually to consolidate their control over increasingly larger areas, creating the earliest states in the continent. But as leaders became rulers, and rulers became kings and queens, more people also became disenfranchised, with fewer opportunities to climb up the social ladder. This is the paradox of increasingly 'complex' political forms: social inequalities go hand-in-hand with more powerful, centralized systems of political organization. Not always, but usually, more powerful leaders lead to more social inequities.

Inequality and Leadership in Human Societies: How Did We Get Here?

Political and economic inequalities currently are the highest they have been during the entirety of the human experience on the planet. In 2018, Oxfam reported that 82 percent of all wealth created in 2017 went to the top one percent, while the bottom 50 percent saw no increase at all. That same year, a mere eight individuals owned as much combined wealth as half of all humankind.[2] The *First Kings of Europe* exhibition explores how we got to this point by focusing on the early emergence of social and economic inequalities in prehistoric southeastern Europe.

The question of whether inequality is inherent to the human condition has been wrestled with since the Classical period (see Foreword, this volume).[3] The issue re-emerged during the Enlightenment, when Jean-Jacques Rousseau famously questioned the morality of inequality.[4] More recently, anthropologists, sociologists, and historians have developed methods for measuring the extent of inequalities in the modern world that permit comparisons between societies, both ancient and modern.[5]

The striking Oxfam figures make no sense for a mammal species that evolved by overcoming—and actively suppressing—the social dominance hierarchies that predominate in other primate societies.[6] In a vicious world filled with large carnivores during the Pliocene and Pleistocene epochs, hominins and human ancestors survived by developing cultural practices that permitted them to cooperate and outcompete stronger species. Cooperation in human societies was successful only because our ancestors were able to suppress the, perhaps innate, tendencies toward social dominance, which in other primates is based primarily on biological sex and age. By working together, as communities, humans were able to exploit and colonize even the harshest, most unpredictable, marginal environments in the world. But even tens of thousands of years after modern humans had spread throughout the world, the hunters and gatherers of the Pleistocene and early Holocene did not develop social institutions based on social hierarchies.

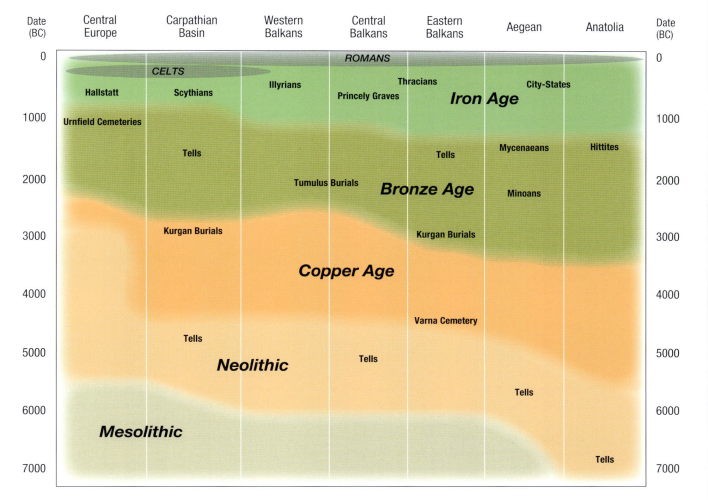

Figure 1.2. Later prehistoric chronology of southeastern Europe and neighboring regions.
Illustration by W.A. Parkinson and A. Gyucha.

This started to change in different parts of the world as people began to settle down into permanent, sedentary, farming villages. In some areas, such as in specific parts of prehistoric Mesoamerica, economic and political hierarchies occurred quickly, within a few generations after the establishment of the first sedentary agricultural villages. In other parts of the world, such as in southeastern Europe, it took several thousand years for social inequalities to become institutionalized and accepted as part of a new worldview within which political and economic strata were perceived as inevitable and 'normal.'

Along with the long-term development of political and economic inequalities, different forms of leadership became institutionalized within human societies. During the Pleistocene and throughout much of the Holocene, political organization in so-called 'egalitarian,' mobile hunting and gathering societies was based largely upon sharing and cooperation, with specific cultural traditions, such as resource pooling and redistribution, that limited the development

of durable vertical hierarchies. This changed with the formation of sedentary farming villages, when hierarchical positions of leadership in some societies became embedded in hereditary lines. When it became institutionalized, hierarchical leadership spread quickly, resulting eventually in the emergence of centralized, autocratic states with established, durable, bureaucratic systems. This change in political and economic organization—from basically egalitarian social systems with very limited vertical hierarchy to those with extremely rigid social stratification—is one of the most significant developments during the course of human existence on the planet.

Adapting Charles Darwin's influential theory of biological evolution, nineteenth-century scholars, such as Lewis Henry Morgan, Herbert Spencer, Edward Burnett Tylor, and Émile Durkheim, attempted to model the changes in economic and political organization within human societies according to progressive evolutionary stages.[7] These models, though teleological and sometimes overtly racist, were explicit attempts to explain the variations exhibited in human social organization that had been documented ethnographically and archaeologically.

During the twentieth century, cultural anthropologists, such as Elman Service, Marshall Sahlins, and Morton Fried, revisited the concept of cultural evolution, albeit with a more nuanced understanding of cultural change that was based not upon the successive progression through evolutionary stages but rather upon how the social organization of cultures within specific regions changed over time.[8] Morgan's global model of humanity's progressive evolution from barbarism to civilization was recast as a more nuanced attempt to model change within specific cultural trajectories based on changes in specific political and economic institutions. Rather than simply applying Darwinist concepts directly to cultural change, the so-called 'neo-evolutionary' perspective drew heavily from early twentieth-century concepts in biology, such as ecology. Within this framework, societies were viewed as cultural systems that adapted to their environmental and social contexts over time. The inevitability of progression that was presumed within nineteenth-century models of cultural evolution was replaced instead by a consideration of the various internal and external factors that encouraged or caused the emergence of hierarchical societies, such as 'chiefdoms' and 'states.'

These 'neo-evolutionary' models that were developed by twentieth-century cultural anthropologists became central themes during the development of anthropological archaeology, especially in the United States. Many models for the evolution of leadership in human societies derived from this broader theoretical background, which focused on how individual leaders, such as 'big men,' became 'chiefs' and eventually 'kings.'[9]

Frustration with the typological rigidity of the neo-evolutionary framework's almost exclusive focus on individual hierarchical leadership began to emerge toward the end of the twentieth century, with some calling for models that could accommodate more variability in the various forms of leadership exhibited within different human societies.[10] Central to the issue was the gradual understanding that the archaeological record preserved an astonishingly more robust range of variability in social organization than the ethnographic and ethnohistoric records. This led to some

proposing concepts such as 'heterarchy' that attempted to recognize that leadership roles could sometimes be held not only by individuals but also by groups of individuals.[11] Others proposed a model that included modes of social orientation that took into account whether the nature of leadership and hierarchy within different societies was concentrated more in individuals (network mode) or groups (corporate mode; see Foreword, this volume).[12] More recently, these debates have been reconsidered in light of 'collective action theory.'[13] Adapted from other social sciences, collective action theory, as it relates to hierarchy and leadership, considers the negotiation between leaders and followers, especially with regards to decision-making input. If a leader is interested in securing the long-term durability and sustainability of a political and economic system, then the populace needs to be given input into how the system functions. Although more cumbersome and less efficient, at least from a decision-making perspective, collective decision-making generally results in more durable and stable political and economic forms of organization. Relinquishing, even if only some, decision-making authority also can be risky for leaders, especially in fragile, nascent political and economic systems.

The Emergence of Leadership and Inequality in Southeastern Europe

Prehistoric southeastern Europe is an ideal context for exploring the relationship between leadership and inequality, despite the fact that most people associate this part of the world, and especially Classical Greece, with the origins of democracy and Western civilization. Although a form of democratic governance was practiced in ancient Athens, it was in fact a notable exception within the broader geographic and temporal context of the area. European societies, from the end of the Neolithic to the twentieth century, were, almost without exception, much more autocratic. Focusing on the evolution of inequality and leadership in southeastern Europe over the course of about 5,500 years, from the Neolithic through the Copper Age and Bronze Age to the Iron Age, enables us to explore the wide range of leadership strategies and techniques that were employed in different societies as they abandoned more egalitarian forms of social organization in favor of more centralized, hierarchical systems of governance.

Prior to 2,500 years ago, written records are lacking throughout most of southeastern Europe, therefore the archaeological record offers the sole source for addressing these issues. We have identified four themes that are helpful for exploring the emergence of communities with increasingly complex political and economic inequalities in southeastern Europe: technology and craft production, trade and exchange, conflicts and warfare, and rituals and ceremonies.

Technology and Craft Production

The control of production and distribution of different technologies, such as metallurgy, and different crafts, such as ceramic production, was a tool that was wielded by emergent elites as they gained, maintained, and consolidated their power.[14] In ancient Europe, technological innovations facilitated the development of increasingly sophisticated ways of securing social and political power. The elite frequently used the craft products and the people who made them to enforce and promote the ideological narratives to justify and maintain inequalities. This often happened forcibly, through the use of weaponry, but sometimes also voluntarily through the use of artwork and prestige goods. Metallurgy, and particularly the control of metal resources and technology, was critical in this respect from the Copper through the Iron Ages.[15]

Trade and Exchange

The control of long-distance trade and exchange came to be concentrated in the hands of a few individuals, and was a major source of prestige and wealth accumulation throughout prehistory.[16] In addition to the exchange of raw materials and goods, the circulation of ideas also played a significant role in the emergence of elite status, as technological and social innovations were instrumental in the continuous rejuvenation of the elites' social and economic superiority.[17] Maintaining networks was key to maintaining security and stability, and the regular demonstration of connections with other territories contributed substantially to elevated social status in prehistoric communities.[18]

Conflicts and Warfare

Violent conflicts and warfare frequently played a central role in the development of social stratification in ancient societies.[19] Although the form and scale of intergroup conflicts in prehistory varied, the skills leaders demonstrated in battle were paramount in establishing and reinforcing their prestige and status.[20] Leaders also controlled the redistribution of the spoils of war, and this likely occurred frequently in prehistory. While conflicts and warfare directly benefited successful leaders, various societal benefits also extended to other members of these societies, including access to land, raw materials, and trade opportunities. Participating in conflicts also helped reinforce group identities and solidify social bonds. Therefore warfare was also important for achieving and sustaining social cohesion within prehistoric societies.[21]

Rituals and Ceremonies

Public rituals and ceremonies are cohesive social mechanisms that frequently were used in prehistory to establish, reinforce, and challenge social and political structures.[22] Ceremonial gatherings, which varied in degree of inclusivity and exclusivity, were prominent arenas for social competition and were used actively by the elite to display their wealth and justify their privileged status.[23] These gatherings were also ideal occasions for negotiating and manipulating social and political roles for the lesser elite. Individuals and groups frequently took advantage of ceremonies to showcase links with powerful ancestors and/or supernatural forces to legitimate their differential statuses. In addition to public ceremonies, the more personal and intimate contexts of funerals were also important venues for manifesting and promoting differences between lineages and other groups in attendance.[24]

Leadership, Power, and Inequality in Prehistoric Southeastern Europe

The Age of Farmers: The Neolithic

The first farmers from the Near East migrated into Europe during the first half of the seventh millennium BC, bringing the know-how of agricultural practices to the continent. During the Neolithic, most communities in southeastern Europe lived in small, egalitarian farming villages.[25] Institutionalized vertical hierarchies that would have permitted individuals—or individual families—to assume positions of power through birth right were not common.[26] Instead, social statuses and political ranks regularly were achieved throughout one's lifetime, not ascribed at birth.

Inequalities within Neolithic farming villages were based typically on age, gender, and personal skills (see Chapter 3, this volume).[27] This is especially evident in the differential treatment of select Neolithic indi-

Figure 1.3. Ceramic altar with goat heads, vicinity of Szeged, Hungary. Middle Neolithic, 5300–5200 BC. Hungarian National Museum, Budapest. *Photo by Á. Vágó.*

viduals during mortuary rituals. As a result, mortuary studies provide important insight into the origins of these incipient forms of social differences. For example, a female burial from the Late Neolithic site of Polgár-Csőszhalom in Hungary (see Figures 3.14 and 3.15, this volume) includes many objects made of *Spondylus* shell from the Adriatic or Aegean Sea.[28] The presence of these exotic goods, acquired through long-distance trade, demonstrates their importance in the establishment and expression of social differences.

Rituals in the Neolithic permitted people to communicate with their ancestors and other supernatural forces to ensure the continued success of the harvest and the longevity of the community.[29] Compelling objects related to these rituals are the face pots, figurines, and altars, which reflect regional and shifting traditions throughout the Balkans (Figure 1.3). Some ceremonies were held in domestic settings, as indicated by ritual objects that frequently are found inside and outside of Neolithic houses (Figure 1.4), while others took place in spatially demarcated areas in the villages. These more inclusive events, which might have related to long-lasting traditions, such as communal feasts and harvest festivals, would have served to promote group cohesion and identity. But these same occasions would also have provided contexts for different groups to compete with one another.

The Age of Leaders: The Copper Age

Technological innovations, in particular the spread of metallurgy, triggered fundamental changes in economic and political organization in southeastern Europe during the fifth millennium BC.[30] During this era, trade in metals, including copper and gold, created new interregional networks that fed increasing social inequalities.

The famous Varna necropolis in Bulgaria illustrates this trend spectacularly. The excavations of almost three hundred burials yielded more than three thousand gold artifacts (a total of more than 6 kg), 160 copper tools, *Dentalium* and *Spondylus* shell ornaments, and hundreds of other objects produced by highly skilled craft specialists (Figure 1.5).[31] The majority of these finds were found in a small number of graves, providing the first unambiguous mortuary evidence for stark social and economic differentiation and status competition between individuals and groups in southeastern Europe.[32] One single burial, Grave 43, contained more gold than has been found from the rest of the world for the mid-fifth millennium BC. Forty-three graves contained no human remains and are referred to as 'cenotaphs;' some of these were

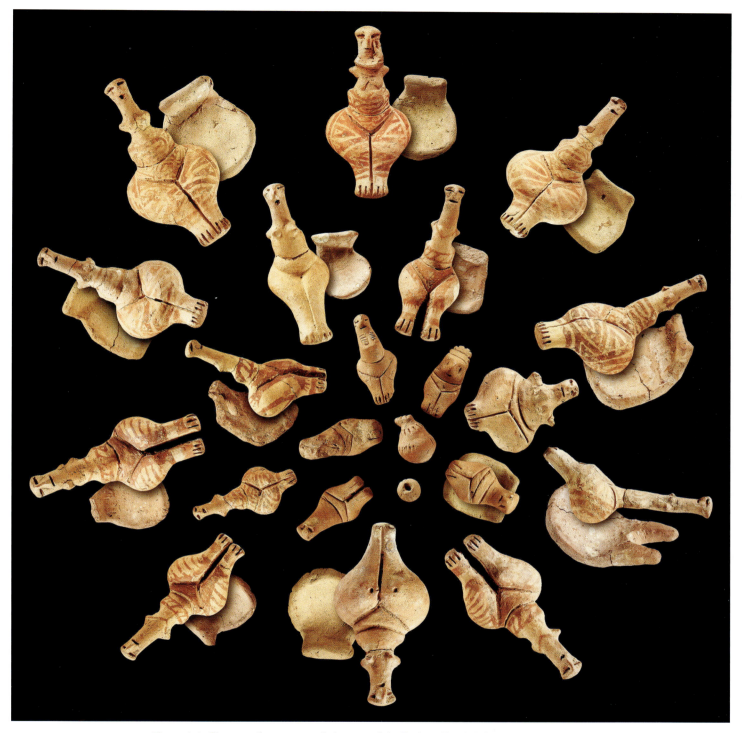

Figure 1.4. Ceramic figurines and chair models, Poduri-Dealul Ghindaru, Romania. Late Neolithic, 4900–4750 BC. Neamț County Museum Complex, Piatra Neamț. *Photo by Á. Vágó.*

laid out as burials without skeletons, a few with clay masks in the place of the head.

The cemetery was discovered by accident during a construction project in 1972, and since its discovery, the site has been the subject of much scholarly discussion because it reflects such an unprecedented accumulation of valuable materials (such as gold, copper, exotic beads, and shells) and symbols (for example, scepters, axes) that clearly are associated with hierarchy and status all in one place (Figure 1.6). The mortuary patterns suggest that people buried in the cemetery—or in the case of the cenotaphs, people who died elsewhere and were memorialized in the cemetery—were being recognized for the achievements they carried out throughout their lifetime. This elaborate

Figure 1.5. Gold bull-shaped appliqués, Grave 36, Varna, Bulgaria. Late Copper Age, 4600–4400 BC. Varna Regional Museum of History. *Photo by Á. Vágó.*

marking of achieved status, especially with massive quantities of gold, copper, and other exotic materials, became more frequent during later periods but remains truly exceptional for the Copper Age.

These clear indicators of status and, presumably, competition between different lineages, become even more exceptional when the broader context of the cemetery itself is considered. Cemeteries were themselves novel social arenas that had been rare prior to the Copper Age in the region. During the Neolithic, most burials occurred within settlements, not as stand-alone features in the landscape. But during the Copper Age, cemeteries that were used many times by multiple villages began to function as regional stages for elaborate funerary performances. Demographically, only a small percentage of the regional population were afforded the honor of being buried in cemeteries like Varna, suggesting yet another level of social differentiation at the regional scale.

Although we may never understand all the nuanced complexities of social competition and display that came into play during the funerary rituals that

Figure 1.6. Gold scepters, bracelets, and appliqués, Grave 36, Varna, Bulgaria. Late Copper Age, 4600–4400 BC. Varna Regional Museum of History. *Photo by Á. Vágó.*

Figure 1.7. Hoard of gold, copper, and deer canine artifacts, Brad, Romania. Early Copper Age, 4200–4050 BC. Neamț County Museum Complex, Piatra Neamț. *Photo by Á. Vágó.*

occurred at Varna (and other nearby sites, like Durankulak) during the Copper Age, one of the most striking aspects is how short-lived this social experiment in emerging hierarchy was, at least from an archaeological perspective. Radiocarbon dates indicate that the Varna cemetery was used for approximately a century,[33] and after this brief period of fluorescence, nothing approached the complexity of burial rituals and conspicuous funerary display at Varna throughout southeastern Europe until the Bronze Age.

In addition to burials at cemeteries like Varna, other indicators of the accumulation of wealth into the hands of a few are the first large caches of copper and gold objects that were ritually buried in displays of conspicuous consumption (Figures 1.7 and 1.8).[34] The consistency of the kinds of objects in these caches, called 'hoards,' indicates that they were not buried to be hidden, like pirate treasures. Instead, they were buried in an intentional, ritualized manner during

the course of ceremonies where competition for status was a primary motivation. In the course of ceremonies, the early leaders of the Copper Age also displayed some common status symbols, including specific copper axe types and anthropomorphic pendants, that were manufactured and understood in the same way over a large geographic area. The anthropomorphic pendants were the first widely produced and circulated gold objects, and they occur in abundance in the Varna cemetery as well (Figure 1.9).

Southeast European Copper Age communities came into contact with nomadic groups of the Eurasian steppe region. An early phase of interaction in the final centuries of the fifth millennium BC is well illustrated by artifacts from the Balkans that were used as status markers in the steppe, such as zoomorphic stone scepters (see Figure 4.2, this

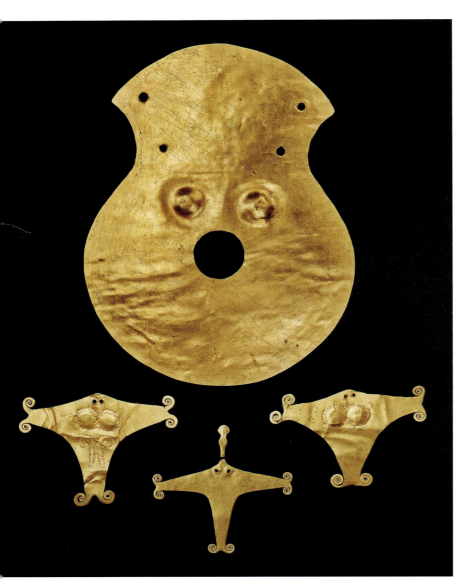

Figure 1.8. Gold anthropomorphic pendant and appliqués, Moigrad, Romania. Middle Copper Age, 4000–3500 BC. National History Museum of Romania, Bucharest. *Photo by Á. Vágó.*

volume). New migrant groups arrived in southeastern Europe from the steppe zone in significant numbers during the transition between the Copper and Bronze Ages, at the turn of the fourth and third millennia BC. Their leaders were commemorated and buried in monumental burial mounds, or *kurgans*, that still dot the landscapes of the eastern Balkans and the Great Hungarian Plain (see Figures 4.3 and 6.2, this volume). In addition to the height of these kurgans, variation in funerary practices and the number and quality of grave goods testifies to differences in status among the interred individuals (see Chapters 4 and 6, this volume).[35]

The Age of Chiefs: The Bronze Age

From the early third millennium to the beginning of the first millennium BC, the Bronze Age saw the regular emergence of hereditary chiefs who lived in fortified settlements with retinues of craftsmen and traders.[36] By controlling the production, distribution, and redistribution of specialized craft goods and agricultural products, their status in many regions became institutionalized and endured, in some cases, for generations. This is the era of the first complex societies with marked hereditary social inequality, at least in some parts of southeastern Europe.

Figure 1.9. Gold anthropomorphic pendant, Progar, Serbia. Middle Copper Age, 4000–3500 BC. Archaeological Museum in Zagreb. *Photo by Á. Vágó.*

Figure 1.10. Ceramic wagon model, Pocsaj-Leányvár, Hungary.
Early Bronze Age, 2100–1900 BC. Déri Museum, Debrecen. *Photo by Á. Vágó.*

Bronze metallurgy, incorporating alloys of copper and tin, required more sophisticated technological skills than copper smelting. While copper ore sources occur locally, tin comes from much farther afield, perhaps as far away as Cornwall and Afghanistan. The widespread distribution of bronze demonstrates that an intercontinental exchange system linked Bronze Age villagers.[37] Standardization of some artifact types, including copper ingots, indicates the regular exchange not only of traded goods but also ideas between chiefs and traders.

Long-distance exchange systems of the Bronze Age were composed of many interconnected regional systems, at the focal points of which were chiefs who benefited the most from the intensified interactions.[38] Concurrent advances in horse gear and chariotry

promoted these interactions. The regular appearance of horse cheek pieces made of antler and ceramic wagon models demonstrate these developments and the importance of travel for the elite—literally and into the afterworld (Figure 1.10). In addition to trade of raw materials and finished goods, knowledge transfer also occurred between regions, and was distributed by traveling chiefs, traders, artisans, and warriors. Sets of commonly held beliefs among various cultural groups also spread over large geographic areas. These common beliefs are materialized in the archaeological record, for example, by newly appearing ceramic figurines with similar shapes and motifs that were

Figure 1.11. Ceramic figurine, Dalj, Croatia. Middle Bronze Age, 1700–1400 BC. Archaeological Museum in Zagreb. *Photo by Á. Vágó.*

produced throughout the northern part of southeastern Europe (Figure 1.11). Through trade contacts, symbols from farther regions were also incorporated into local elite ideologies. Excellent examples include the violin-shaped ceramic figurines from Kuće Rakića in Montenegro and Shtoji in Albania (Figure 1.12), which mimic similar figurines from the Cycladic islands of the Aegean, where they were always made of marble.[39] Imitations of technology also include the widespread distribution of Mycenaean-type weaponry throughout southeastern Europe, including swords and daggers.[40] These artifacts allow dazzling insights of how the more politically precocious cultures of the eastern Mediterranean affected status representation in the Balkans and neighboring regions during the Bronze Age.

Hoards and burials provide us with a great deal of information concerning social organization, status display, and elite ceremonies.[41] Although the practice of burying valuables had begun in the Copper Age, hundreds of hoards have been recovered from southeastern Europe that date to the Bronze Age.[42] Some may have been votive offerings to deities, testifying to wealth sacrifice and conspicuous consumption. Others contain a variety of bronze weapons, including

Figure 1.12. Set of ceramic figurines, Shtoji, Albania. Early Bronze Age, 2800–2500 BC. Archaeological Museum in Tirana. *Photo by Á. Vágó.*

Figure 1.13. Bronze sword with engraved motifs, Hajdúsámson, Hungary. Middle Bronze Age, 1700–1600 BC. Déri Museum, Debrecen. *Photo by Á. Vágó.*

the first metal helmets, swords, axes, and spearheads, and may be associated with ceremonial rituals related to wars or battles[43]—the beginning of the tradition of 'burying the hatchet' (see also Chapter 5, this volume). In addition to hoards, burials with weapons also signal that, along with hierarchical political systems, a new elite class of warriors emerged across many regions of southeastern Europe around the middle of the second millennium BC.[44] A warrior-cult developed during this later stage of the Bronze Age, and the related

objects frequently display artistic craftsmanship through complex, engraved motifs on shields, swords, and axes (Figure 1.13). These elaborate motifs were visible only close up, and thus these assemblages are indicative of more exclusive ceremonies as arenas of competition among the members of the warrior elite. The consumption of alcoholic beverages was also an

Figure 1.14. Bronze situla with stylized waterbird motif, Nyírlugos, Hungary. Late Bronze Age, 1000–900 BC. Déri Museum, Debrecen. *Photo by Á. Vágó.*

Figure 1.15. Gold daggers, Perşinari, Romania. Middle Bronze Age, 1700–1600 BC. National History Museum of Romania, Bucharest. *Photo by Á. Vágó.*

integrated part of these exclusive gatherings, as illustrated by sets of bronze drinking vessels buried after ceremonies (Figure 1.14).

Performances staged for a large audience to exhibit elite regalia were held regularly for the first time in the Bronze Age. During the later phase of the period, the elevated social status of the elite in these inclusive assemblies was expressed by objects that would have been striking for the viewers, such as gold and silver ceremonial weapons that were completely useless in combat (Figure 1.15), and oversized, exquisite jewelry (Figure 1.16). The bronze and gold, the rich decoration, and the incorporation of exotic materials would have exemplified the economic and political clout of the bearer. Many of these artifacts were worn by females, demonstrating the active participation of women in elite display and competition within Bronze Age societies.

The Age of Rulers: Iron Age

Rigid social stratification and stark inequalities spread throughout southeastern Europe during the Early Iron Age.[45] From the beginning of the first millennium until the third century BC, the archaeological record shows the emergence of increased political regionalization and groups with collective identities marked by distinct practices and material culture. Many of these polities were controlled by warrior–rulers and, in some cases, they transformed into complex chiefdoms and centralized, bureaucratic states.[46] Several of these rulers' names and achievements were recorded in ancient Greek, and later Roman, accounts. These written sources indicate that, in addition to other groups to the south, such as Paeonians, Dardanians, and Macedonians, groups known as Illyrians predominantly inhabited the western and Thracians the eastern part of the central Balkan Peninsula (see Chapters 8 to 10, this volume). Beginning in the fourth century BC, the adoption and intermingling of Greek and Celtic culture and genes, processes known as Hellenization and Celtization, unfolded in many regions of southeastern Europe, and the entire political setting transformed fundamentally during the Roman expansion from the late third century BC onward.

Bronze jewelry and tools continued to be produced in the Iron Age, but advances and innovations in pyrotechnology also resulted in the mastery of iron-working techniques. Unlike tin, which was necessary for alloying bronze and had to be acquired from distant sources, iron ore was widely available throughout southeastern Europe. During the Iron Age, the control of iron production became critical for those vying for economic and political control.

Figure 1.16. Bronze fibula, Sviloš, Serbia. Late Bronze Age, 1300–1100 BC.
Archaeological Museum in Zagreb. *Photo by Á. Vágó.*

The social and economic development of south-eastern European Iron Age societies was linked to developments in neighboring regions. Although researchers frequently describe these interregional relations as a World System dominated by 'high cultures' in the Aegean, Asia Minor, and the Italian Peninsula,[47] these connections can be better understood within a framework of interdependence and competition as major forces driving socioeconomic changes.

From the eighth century BC onward, interactions were common between the rulers, trading elite, and military aristocracy of tribal polities in the Balkans and the ancient Mediterranean states.[48] Control of iron mining and trade, which included agricultural products and other precious minerals (such as silver), was a significant source of wealth and political power for Illyrian chiefs. In addition, access to iron ores allowed for the production of weapons in large quantities for a large number of warriors, contributing to frequent warfare among these societies. Illyrian rulers regularly waged wars against Greek territories to the south and provided various Greek city-states with mercenaries. These specialized fighters with new weaponry, the leaders of which formed a strong military aristocracy, brought back the spoils of war and commonly embraced elite symbols that were used in the Mediterranean (Figure 1.17; see Chapter 9, this volume).[49]

Regalia deposited in the burials of this military and political elite reflect these multifold and complex interactions. From the early first millennium BC, the

Figure 1.17. Bronze helmet, Çinamaku, Albania. Late Iron Age, 500–400 BC.
Archaeological Museum in Tirana. *Photo by Á. Vágó.*

Figure 1.18. Bronze situla, Valična vas, Slovenia. Middle Iron Age, 400–300 BC. National Museum of Slovenia, Ljubljana. *Photo by T. Lauko.*

Figure 1.19. Amber breast ornament, Kompolje, Croatia. Early Iron Age, 600–400 BC. Archaeological Museum in Zagreb. *Photo by Á. Vágó.*

Figure 1.20. Bronze scepter with 'Macedonian' bronzes, Grave 111, Milci, North Macedonia. Early Iron Age, 700–650 BC. National Institution Museum–Gevgelija. *Photo by B. Husenovski.*

Figure 1.21. Gold pendants and pectoral, Novi Pazar, Serbia. Early Iron Age, 550–450 BC. National Museum of Serbia, Belgrade. *Photo by Á. Vágó.*

practice of burying members of elevated social status under earthen mounds re-emerged in southeastern Europe—only this time people were buried not under earthen kurgans but in mounded tumuli.[50] The largest concentration of these 'princely graves' is found in Illyrian territories, for example, in the Glasinac region of Bosnia and Herzegovina (see Figures 9.11 and 9.12, this volume).[51] The fusion of local and Mediterranean systems of status display is apparent in these elite burials. Farther north, elite members of Veneti communities along the northwestern Adriatic shore were buried with status items manufactured in Etruscan-style and adopted or imported from central and northern Italy (Figure 1.18).

Marked differences in material culture as they relate to status display also characterized the Iron Age groups of the western and central Balkans. Several scholars have attempted to link these regional differences in material culture to specific ethnic groups.[52] In addition to the representatives of an Illyrian group called the Autariatae on the Glasinac plateau, other examples of regionalization in elite display include Iapoda objects, such as exquisite bronze head ornaments

and amber breast ornaments (Figure 1.19).[53] Probably the best example of regionally specific traditions exemplified in material culture are the so-called 'Macedonian' bronzes, including composite pendants and belts, which were possibly associated with the Paeonian tribe (Figure 1.20; for a further discussion of 'Macedonian' bronzes, see Chapter 2, this volume).[54]

The importance of females in the tribal aristocracy of the Early Iron Age is represented by splendid assemblages from various parts of the Balkans.[55] In addition to archaeological evidence such as the burials at Novi Pazar in Serbia, Milci in North Macedonia, and Donja Dolina in Bosnia and Herzegovina (Figure 1.21; see also Chapters 2 and 9, this volume), we even know the name of an Illyrian queen.

The northern part of southeastern Europe witnessed the influx of steppe people, presumably Cimmerians and Scythians, from the ninth century BC onward.[56] Similar to groups from the steppe during the transition from the Copper to the Bronze

Figure 1.22. Bronze hydria, Ártánd, Hungary. Middle Iron Age, 700–500 BC. Hungarian National Museum, Budapest. *Photo by Á. Vágó.*

Ages, these horse riders introduced new material culture, particularly weaponry and steppe-type horse gear, and some of these objects became integrated into elite representations across southeastern Europe. These groups, after securing control in the eastern Carpathian Basin, traded horses with the Etruscans and Greeks through the Veneti. Some artifacts, such as the aforementioned large bronze hydria (wine vessel) from Ártánd in Hungary made in a Spartan workshop, may illustrate the circulation of royal diplomatic gifts of precious foreign import goods (Figure 1.22).

The ceremonies and performances and the related paraphernalia in various regions of southeastern Europe evoked an array of worldviews and narratives. Like the burial practices, these narratives oftentimes provide links to Mediterranean, including Greek and Etruscan, traditions. For example, a unique stone urn from Ribić in Bosnia and Herzegovina depicts libation ceremonies widely practiced in the Greek world and known from, among others, Homer's epic poems (Figure 1.23). Similarly, a stone relief from Kamenica in Kosovo shows a funerary wailing scene that also occurs on Greek Geometric Period monumental *kraters* (funerary vases; Figure 1.24). Local elements tend to co-occur with foreign ones on these

Figure 1.23. Stone funerary urn, Ribić, Bosnia and Herzegovina. Early Iron Age, 600–300 BC. National Museum of Bosnia and Herzegovina, Sarajevo. *Photo by Á. Vágó.*

Figure 1.24. Stone funerary relief, Kamenica, Kosovo. Late Iron Age or Hellenistic Period, 500–100 BC. National Museum of Kosovo, Prishtina. *Photo by Á. Vágó.*

objects, demonstrating that the elites integrated foreign mythologies, practices, and narratives into local traditions to display, maintain, and manipulate their social status.

In the eastern Balkan Peninsula, the fusion of local and foreign traditions brought about the emergence of the unique Thracian material culture and art.[57] This art was commissioned by the political elite and, as a result, it concentrated on the expression of a royal ideology. Elite material culture, indicated by signature metal artifacts made of gold and silver, reflects this ideology. These spectacular Thracian assemblages were manufactured for royal family members of the numerous kingdoms that developed across Thrace from the sixth to the third century BC (see Chapter 10, this volume).[58]

The most exquisite manifestations of elite culture in Thrace are royal tombs, such as the Sveshtari tomb in Bulgaria, that signified the sociopolitical status of the deceased in their degree of architectural elaboration as well as the quantity and quality of grave goods they contained (see Figure 10.5, this volume).[59] According to Xenophon, during the course of aristocratic burials, feasts that included competitive games as well as wine-drinking were held to honor the dead. The elaborate nature of these feasts is reflected in sets of bronze and silver gilt tableware from royal tombs and many hoards found in Bulgaria and southern Romania (Figure 1.25).

Following Bronze Age traditions in the region, a warrior ideology dominated the Thracian worldview;[60] however, the symbols changed during the Iron Age as new sets of horse gear and weapons were produced for the warrior elite. The rulers utilized lavishly decorated artifacts, such as gilded silver greaves, helmets, and gold wreaths (Figure 1.26), to demonstrate their wealth, power, and status.

Figure 1.25. Silver and gilded silver human head, helmet, and phialae, Peretu, Romania. Late Iron Age, 500–400 BC. National History Museum of Romania, Bucharest. *Photo by Á. Vágó.*

Conclusions

From the first egalitarian farming communities in the Neolithic to the emergence of hierarchical kingdoms in Iron Age Thrace, six millennia of prehistory saw increasing differentiation between the rich and the poor, the haves and the have-nots, the kings and the commoners. Nevertheless, this process was not linear, steady, and uninterrupted. Some societies resisted and regulated the emergence of inequalities and hierarchies and chose to maintain more egalitarian settings and more collective forms of governance. Other societies experimented with and oscillated between different forms of hierarchical or collective systems over time (see Foreword, this volume).

As a result, during most of this time, the nature of power tended to be fragile, vulnerable, and tenuous. In some cases, ambitious leaders successfully managed to develop an array of creative solutions to persuade people to embrace their superiority. Over time, these

Figure 1.26. Gold wreath, Zlatinitsa-Malomirovo, Bulgaria. Late Iron Age, 375–325 BC.
National Museum of History, Sofia. *Photo by Á. Vágó.*

leaders were able to pass their political and economic power down to their descendants and extend it to their supporters—their priests, generals, and kin. By the Iron Age, many parts of southeastern Europe were dominated by societies with stratified social classes—one was born as king or commoner.

To sustain the dominance of the few over the many, sophisticated power techniques were required, and the archaeological heritage of prehistoric southeastern Europe illustrates a wide range of the techniques that were employed. The control of the circulation of precious materials and goods as well as the control of venues and courses of rituals were instrumental in securing prestige and status starting in the Neolithic.

Technological innovations were promoted by the accumulation of wealth through surplus from agricultural and trade activities, and, along with control over craftsmanship, they began to play an important role in the development of social hierarchies beginning in the Copper Age. The emergence of formal elites coincided with recurrent technological innovations particularly in weaponry, horse breeding and equipment, and chariotry in the Bronze Age. This is when the elites of southeastern European societies became plugged into the rest of the world. New forms of interactions evolved through regular travel, diplomacy, and warfare, resulting in novel ideas related to the material expression of social and political status. The demonstration of power and the means of the manipulation of the masses were mastered during the Iron Age. New elite ideologies, narratives, and related art were used to promote the legitimacy of the elite, giving rise to increasingly more elaborate, and more ostentatious, objects displayed for the public over the course of lavish ceremonies and rituals.

Structure of the Book

We were honored to have Gary M. Feinman write the Foreword to this book, in which he discusses the broader, cross-cultural anthropological issues raised in the chapters and in the *First Kings of Europe* exhibition. As an archaeologist who explores the evolution of complex societies in other parts of the world—primarily in Mesoamerica and in China—Feinman places the themes raised throughout the book into a broader social framework of our general understanding of the emergence of leadership and hierarchy within human societies. He also discusses how the trajectory of social change in southeastern Europe can inform our understanding of similar processes elsewhere in the world, noting that the role of metals, which were so central to many of the social developments that occurred in European prehistory, were not critical commodities in other social contexts, such as in Central and South America, where similar inequalities and complex political systems evolved.

In the following chapter (Chapter Two), Goce Naumov and Eleonora Petrova Mitevska conclude the first section of the book, which focuses on the general issues of the evolution of leadership and inequality in southeastern Europe. With a primary focus on the central and southern Balkans, their chapter provides an overview of how the main social changes that characterized the emergence of increasingly hierarchical societies are reflected in architecture, mortuary practices, and artifact typologies from the Neolithic to the Iron Age.

The next section of the book, Section II, concentrates on the Neolithic and Copper Age. In the first chapter of that section (Chapter Three), Attila Gyucha, William A. Parkinson, András Füzesi, and Pál Raczky explore the spatial and social organization of three important Late Neolithic large sites on the Great Hungarian Plain in the Carpathian Basin. They note that although there were striking similarities in material culture between these contemporaneous sites,

which each emerged as a center within its own region, the settlement biographies indicate that their communities each developed their own local forms of economic and political organization. This kind of regional variability characterizes many aspects of society in southeastern Europe throughout prehistory—connected, but still differentiated.

Chapter Four by János Dani, Bianca Preda-Bălănică, and János Angi explores the impact migrant populations from the steppe region had on the emergence of a new elite culture in the Carpathian Basin and several regions of the Balkans during the transition between the Copper and Bronze Ages. These impacts and influences on material culture and burial traditions in many ways laid the foundation for many of the changes that occurred later, during the Bronze Age.

In the Bronze Age section, Section III, Gábor V. Szabó and Botond Rezi (Chapter Five) discuss the traditions associated with the deposition of metal hoards over the course of the Bronze Age in the Carpathian Basin and Transylvania. Through a detailed discussion of some of the most compelling and interesting hoards in Europe, which number more than twelve thousand in this period, Szabó and Rezi discuss the rituals associated with hoard deposition, as well as their implications for understanding hierarchy within the chiefly societies of the Bronze Age.

Florin Gogâltan and Corina Borş then examine how recent investigations of settlement layouts on the "eastern frontier" of the Carpathian Basin reflect different aspects of Bronze Age hierarchical social organization (Chapter Six). By tracking the diachronic evolution of burial mounds, settlements, and mega-forts, Gogâltan and Borş demonstrate how these monumental constructions reflect the emergence of more hierarchical, centralized political and economic communities throughout the Bronze Age and into the Early Iron Age.

The final chapter in this section (Chapter Seven), by János Gábor Tarbay and Jovan D. Mitrović, explores the objects and ideology associated with the warrior persona that characterized a new class of elites in southeastern Europe during the Late Bronze Age. Building on the previous chapter, which focused on settlements, Tarbay and Mitrović focus on the artifacts that were used to promote the warrior ideology that prevailed during the Late Bronze Age. They discuss how the weaponry associated with Balkan warriors can inform us about the trade networks and hierarchical relationships that characterized social organization during the period.

The final section of the book, Section IV, begins with Michael L. Galaty and Rudenc Ruka's consideration of how the tribal kingdoms of the region were differentially organized during the Iron Age prior to Roman conquest (Chapter Eight). Incorporating both archaeological and ancient historical sources into their discussion, Galaty and Ruka demonstrate how various historical processes, such as Hellenistic Greek colonization along the Adriatic coast, influenced the trajectories of different communities throughout the Iron Age.

The next chapter (Chapter Nine), by Hrvoje Potrebica and Andrijana Pravidur, explores the unique relationship between Iron Age elites in the Balkans and their contemporaries in Central Europe. Focusing on the lavish Iron Age cemeteries of the central and western Balkans, Potrebica and Pravidur discuss how the regional elite were connected physically—through trade—and symbolically—through ideology—to the broader European world.

The book concludes with a discussion by Peter Delev about the emergence of Thracian kingdoms and their relationship to other societies known from Antiquity (Chapter Ten). Delev synthesizes copious amounts of archaeological and ancient references to paint a clear picture of how the kings of ancient Thrace—literally at the edge of history—lived, ruled, and died.

Notes

1   Cleomenes I instituted an oligarchy led by Isagoras in 510 BC that was upended by the reforms of Cleisthenes in 508 BC.

2   Oxfam 2018.

3   Grossano 2017.

4   Rousseau 1754.

5   E.g., Baldus 2017; Scheidel and Freisen 2009; Smith et al. 2018.

6   Knauft 1991.

7   Trigger 2006.

8   Richerson and Boyd 2005.

9   Flannery and Marcus 2012.

10 Feinman and Neitzel 1984.

11 Ehrenreich et al. 1995.

12 Blanton et al. 1996.

13 Blanton and Fargher 2008.

14 Earle 1997.

15 Kienlin 2015b; Kristiansen 1998.

16 Earle and Kristiansen 2010.

17 Johnson and Earle 1987.

18 Dillian and White 2010.

19 Guilaine and Zammit 2005; Turchin 2011.

20 Keeley 1997.

21 LeBlanc 2003.

22 Wason 1994.

23 Flannery and Marcus 2012.

24 Parker Pearson 2003.

25 Bailey 2000; Chapman 1989.

26 Müller et al. 2015.

27 Porčić 2019.

28 Raczky and Anders 2017.

29 Chapman 2000; Whittle 2018.

30 Kienlin 2008; Radivojević et al. 2010.

31 Ivanov and Avramova 2000.

32 Chapman 1991; Renfrew 1986; Slavchev 2008.

33 Chapman et al. 2007; Higham et al. 2019.

34 E.g., Chernakov 2018; Heeb 2014.

35 Dani and Horváth 2012; Govedarica 2004; Heyd 2011.

36 Earle 2002; Kristiansen 1998.

37 Alexandrov et al. 2018; Kristiansen 2018a; Pare 2000.

38 Harding 2000; Kristiansen and Larsson 2005.

39 Govedarica 2016b.

40 Bouzek 1994.

41 Bradley 2015; Gori 2014.

42 Hristova 2018; König 2004; Mozsolics 2000.

43 Szabó 2019b.

44 Harding 2007; Jung 2018.

45 Collis 1984; Kristiansen 1998.

46 Delev 2014; Wilkes 1996.

47 Beaujard 2010; Kristiansen 1998.

48 Potrebica 2008.

49 Wilkes 1996.

50 Babić 2002; Palavestra 1998.

51 Čović 1987b.

52 Bouzek 1974; Vasić 1991.

53 Babić 2001.

54 Chausidis 2017.

55 For a more detailed discussion, see Stapleton 2014.

56 Bouzek 1983; Kemenczei 2009.

57 Fol and Marazov 1977; Valeva et al. 2015.

58 Martinez et al. 2015.

59 Valeva 2015.

60 Fol et al. 2000; Stoyanov 2015d.

CHAPTER 2

Social Change and Elites in the Prehistoric Central and Southern Balkans

Goce Naumov and Eleonora Petrova Mitevska

T HE CENTRAL AND SOUTHERN Balkans played a significant role in the introduction and development of social complexity in Europe. This is indicated by buildings, burials, and artifacts. During the Neolithic period, the first glimpses of communal differences appeared and eventually developed into tribal elites and hierarchical tribal kingdoms in the Chalcolithic (Copper Age), Bronze Age, and Iron Age (see also Chapter 1, this volume). These prehistoric stages witnessed a variety of technological, economic, and social changes that permitted the advancement and differentiation of individuals and groups. They distinguished themselves from one another by decorated structures, prestigious objects, and lavish funerary rituals that signified the different statuses or roles they held in society. In this chapter, we provide an overview of these changes from the end of the seventh to the middle of the first millennium BC, focusing specifically on the central southern parts of the Balkans (Figure 2.1).

Social Diversity in the Neolithic

Even though archaeologists traditionally describe the early farming societies of southeastern Europe as more or less egalitarian, the increased significance of specific individuals and groups is already evident during the Neolithic in North Macedonia, Bulgaria, Albania,

Greece, and Serbia. Excavations in these countries have provided important information about ceramic artifacts, daub structures, and varying preferences in burial practices that demonstrate the social complexity of the first farmers in the region.

The introduction of agriculture led to crucial changes in the social structure of communities in the Balkans that started to plant cereals and herd domesticated animals.[1] For the first time, resources were produced and managed, creating a surplus of goods and a large quantity of reserves. In addition to being able to settle down in areas with fertile fields and pastures for longer periods of time, the accumulation of reserves also initiated a novel notion of property. There is no evidence for the emergence of durable, institutionalized social inequality in the Neolithic, but archaeological research in the Balkans indicates that there were some differences between specific social groups within and between settlements (see also Chapter 3, this volume). This can be observed in the production of clay objects (such as pottery, figurines, and models), daub structures (such as bins, ovens, and granaries), and even in the defensive systems (such as ditches and palisades) built around these early farming villages.

One of the most obvious clues for the accumulation of stored reserves is the construction of daub structures for the storage of cereals.[2] The majority of Neolithic houses in the Balkans have ovens made of clay or hearths for cooking, but there are not many that have installations intended for cereal storage. The sites of

Figure 2.1. Map showing the sites mentioned in the text. *Illustration by F. Paár and E. Rodriguez.*

ALBANIA:
1 Barç
2 Kamnik
3 Kuçi i Zi
4 Maliq
5 Pazhok
6 Vajzë
7 Vodhinë

BULGARIA:
8 Ai Bunar
9 Borovo
10 Drama
11 Durankulak
12 Golyamo Delčevo
13 Hotnitsa
14 Kovačevo
15 Ovčarovo
16 Panagyurishte
17 Pernik
18 Polkovnik Taslakovo
19 Promachon-Topolnica
20 Provadia
21 Rogozen
22 Slatina
23 Sozopol
24 Usoe
25 Varna

GREECE:
26 Aravissos
27 Delphi
28 Dimini
29 Dimitra
30 Dodona
31 Kastanas
32 Makriyalos
33 Mandalo
34 Olympia
35 Rachmani
36 Sindos
37 Vardarophtsa
38 Vergina

KOSOVO:
39 Pećka Banja

NORTH MACEDONIA:
40 Amzabegovo
41 Brod
42 Bučim
43 Crnobuki
44 Demir Kapija
45 Dimov Grob
46 Dzuniver
47 Gorna Porta
48 Govrlevo
49 Klučka-Hipodrom
50 Kravari
51 Krušeanska Čuka
52 Lisičin Dol
53 Madjari
54 Marvinci
55 Milci
56 Petilep
57 Porodin
58 Prilep
59 Prisad
60 Saraj
61 Štip
62 Šuplevec
63 Tetovo
64 Trebenište
65 Visoi
66 Veluška Tumba
67 Vodovratski Pat
68 Vrbjanska Čuka
69 Zelenikovo
70 Živojno
71 Zović

ROMANIA:
72 Cernavodă
73 Gumelniţa
74 Salcuţa
75 Sultana
76 Vidra

SERBIA:
77 Atenica
78 Belovode
79 Bubanj
80 Gomolava
81 Jarmovac
82 Lepenski Vir
83 Novi Pazar
84 Petrova Crkva
85 Pločnik
86 Rudna Glava
87 Vinča

Figure 2.2. Daub granary structure, Vrbjanska Čuka, North Macedonia. Early Neolithic, ca. 6000 BC. *Adapted from Naumov et al. 2017:Figure 15.*

Slatina in Bulgaria and Kamnik in Albania have large, quadrangular granaries in the dwellings where the communities stored their crops.[3] The granary in Vrbjanska Čuka in North Macedonia is approximately 4 m across with lateral bins for processing cereals (Figure 2.2).[4] It also has massive clay appliqués on the walls, identical to those that also occur on small clay tablets, indicating the symbolic importance of the granary and the close relationship between economy, status, and religion during the Neolithic. With regard to decorated daub structures, the oven from

Figure 2.3. Excavation at the Neolithic tell of Vrbjanska Čuka,
North Macedonia. The boxes indicate structures and major features within the
structures. *Modified from Naumov 2020:Figure 7.11 by J. Seagard.*

Zelenikovo in North Macedonia also should be mentioned due to its specific decorative design.[5] It has several rows of a deeply incised zig-zag pattern on the wall of the platform used for bread preparation.

Similar massive clay installations in Neolithic buildings are rare, and the same designs have not been found at other sites in the same region, or even elsewhere on the settlements where these installations were found. Consequently, they are exceptional in the Balkans, and imply particular groups or individuals that were associated with the deposition of cereal reserves, its processing, and distribution. This may be regarded as an indication of social hierarchy, although it is difficult to substantiate whether these

constructions were related to private possessions or if they signal the distribution of cereals at the scale of entire village communities.

At Vrbjanska Čuka, other buildings also have large daub structures related to the processing of cereals and the preparation of bread. These are much larger and more solid than those at other Neolithic sites in the Pelagonia region, in the southwestern part of North Macedonia, or in the region of Macedonia as a whole.[6] These architectural features demonstrate that Vrbjanska Čuka was a center for cereal storage, processing, and distribution. It most likely had a privileged status compared to other contemporaneous villages in its respective region (Figure 2.3). Geomagnetic prospection identified a large ditch encircling this site (Figure 2.4).[7] Similar ditches are uncommon at neighboring Neolithic sites, suggesting that they were associated

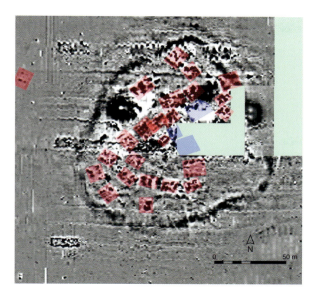

Figure 2.4. Results of magnetometric prospection at the Neolithic tell of Vrbjanska Čuka, North Macedonia. The red and blue boxes indicate Neolithic structures, the green boxes represent areas destroyed in the 1970s. *Modified from Naumov et al. 2018b:Figure 18b by J. Seagard.*

Figure 2.5. Ceramic painted vessel, Veluška Tumba, North Macedonia. Early Neolithic, 6000–5800 BC. Institute for Protection of Cultural Heritage and Museum–Bitola. *Photo by F. Kondovski.*

with the security of the inhabitants and their property at Vrbjanska Čuka. In the later stages of the Neolithic, and particularly during the succeeding Chalcolithic, ditches became more frequent across the Balkans; these are periods when conflicts intensified.[8] So far, evidence for violent conflicts in the Neolithic Balkans is meager, although projectile points were found in the walls of Dimini in Greece, indicating the siege of that settlement. Nevertheless, as in the Neolithic societies of central and western Europe,[9] violence as a result of emerging social differences likely occurred among the early farmers of southeastern Europe.

In addition to these specific daub structures and the spatial organization of settlements, the material culture of Neolithic villages also demonstrates social differences and the emphasis on local identities in these early agricultural communities. Ceramic vessels were decorated with distinct designs, and in the Early Neolithic, almost each region had its own particular painted designs on pottery (Figure 2.5). It is difficult to demonstrate whether pottery indicated social differences within the same settlement, but the regional differences in ceramic designs suggest that individual villages had different economic levels or at least different notions of communal identity that likely was based on the accumulation of goods and their distribution.[10]

Human and zoomorphic representations, possibly associated with status, were created by the agricultural communities in the Balkans. Some animal figurines depict vessels on their back for transporting supplies (Figure 2.6). These are rare artifacts on Neolithic sites, including those from Porodin in North Macedonia and Vinča in Serbia, and it appears that only a few

Figure 2.6. Ceramic zoomorphic figurine, Porodin, North Macedonia. Early Neolithic, 6000–5800 BC. Institute for Protection of Cultural Heritage and Museum–Bitola. *Photo by F. Kondovski.*

families had them in their houses.[11] Regarding human representations, the anthropomorphic house models from across Macedonia are among the most impressive Neolithic findings (Figure 2.7). These models were massive clay lanterns and likely represented particular individuals associated with the history of

Figure 2.7. Ceramic anthropomorphic house model, Govrlevo, North Macedonia. Early Neolithic, 6000–5800 BC. Museum of the City of Skopje. *Photo by Á. Vágó.*

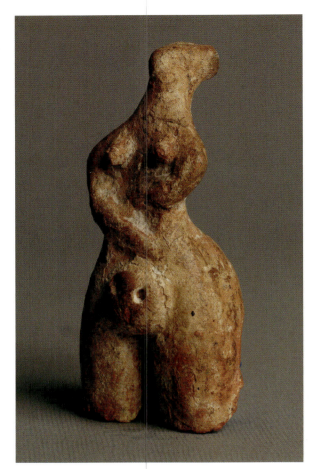

Figure 2.8. Ceramic anthropomorphic figurine, Veluška Tumba, North Macedonia. Early Neolithic, 6000–5800 BC. Institute for Protection of Cultural Heritage and Museum–Bitola. *Photo by F. Kondovski.*

specific houses or households. Alternatively, these objects also may have symbolized entire household communities that were significant for village communities.[12] Human figurines from elsewhere in the Balkans also indicate social differentiation because some are more decorated than others or have specific ornaments on their bodies (Figure 2.8).

Personal adornments, including jewelry, were depicted on these figurines. As they were infrequent objects, these bracelets, necklaces, and pendants made of bone and shell were indicators of particular statuses within the communities. Some ornaments were made of marine shells that were transported to the continental Balkans from the sea, and because they were difficult to obtain, they likely had a high value.[13] Nevertheless, most of the Neolithic burials from the region do not contain jewelry.

Regarding burials, not everyone received the privilege to be interred within the confines of settlements. Intramural funerary rituals were common across the Neolithic Balkans; however, only a few, selected community members were buried inside the villages, next to, or beneath, the dwellings.[14] This selection does not seem to have been based on economic status, but most likely had more to do with the symbolic potential of the deceased. Infants, children, and women frequently were buried in Neolithic villages, as suggested by the excavations at Amzabegovo in North Macedonia, Kovačevo in Bulgaria, Lepenski Vir in Serbia, and many other sites throughout the Balkans.[15] These individuals may have

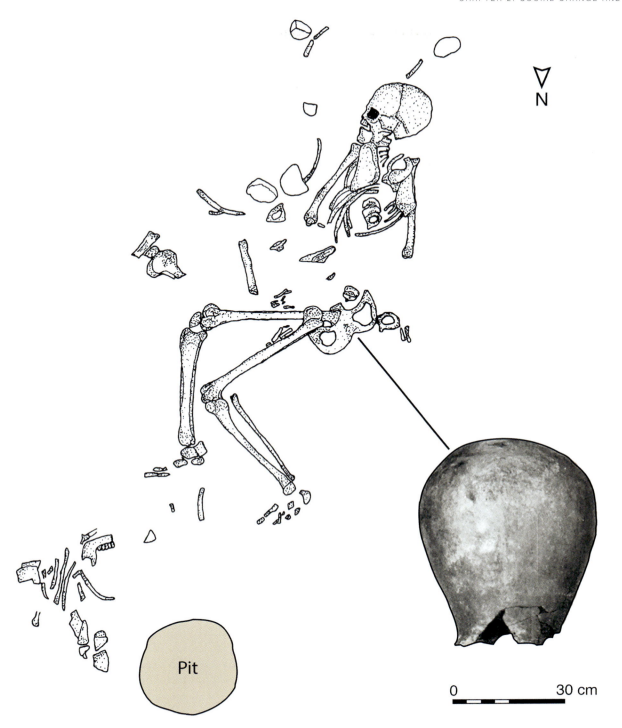

Figure 2.9. Adult burial above vessel with
infant remains, Amzabegovo, North Macedonia.
Early Neolithic, 6200–6000 BC.
*Modified from Naumov
2015b:Figure 4 by J. Seagard.*

contributed substantially to the continuity of the
community, and therefore, after their death, they were
symbolically placed within their own villages. Children
were involved in the economy from a young age, and
the future maintenance and increase of family goods
and wealth would be their responsibility. Consequently, they were buried in the immediate vicinity of
dwellings in order to symbolically assure their continued presence in the society (Figure 2.9).

Metals, Salt, and Burials
in the Chalcolithic

For many decades, it was thought that metal in Europe appeared in the Chalcolithic period for the first time. But recent research demonstrates that the earliest larger-scale exploitation and processing of copper ore occurred during the Late Neolithic. Contemporaneous important sites include Belovode and Pločnik in Serbia, Amzabegovo and Dzuniver in North Macedonia, and Usoe and Promachon-Topolnica in Bulgaria where extractive metallurgy was practiced.[16] At the end of the Neolithic, various, significant shifts took place in the lives of Balkan farming communities, and alongside the production of copper objects, changes occurred in pottery and figurine styles as well as in the spatial organization of villages. The pottery became darker and frequently was decorated with incisions, figurines became much more frequent and more intensively decorated in several regions of southeastern Europe, and settlements often were established on hills, many with ditches as defensive features.

These changes took place as a result of internal transformations within Neolithic societies and gradually led to a period that in different parts of the Balkans is called the Chalcolithic, the Eneolithic, or the Copper Age, reflecting the increased degree of copper production. In many regions, the range of exploited resources became broader, resulting in the emergence of elites and an increase in the number of people who controlled the circulation of valuable materials, such as salt, and the production and exchange of prestige goods, especially those made of copper and gold.

The copper mines at Pločnik, Rudna Glava, and Jarmovac in Serbia, Ai Bunar in Bulgaria, and Bučim in North Macedonia provided new sources of wealth. Large copper axes, for example those from Varna, Golyamo Delčevo, and Polkovnik Taslakovo in Bulgaria, Kravari in North Macedonia, and Dimini in Greece, were used more as status symbols rather than as weapons in combat.[17] Along with copper beads, sheets, plates, rings, and various pendants, axes were a feature commonly associated with the emergent elite in the Chalcolithic Balkans. They were worn or utilized during a variety of social and religious performances.

In addition to copper ornaments and scepters, decorative items made of gold were also used to strengthen the impression of wealth and power during the fifth millennium BC. These artifacts were found as burial deposits in necropoleis, such as Varna, Hotnitsa, and Durankulak in Bulgaria, Gumelnița, Vidra, and Sultana in Romania, and Dimitra and Aravissos in Greece. The majority of individuals buried in these cemeteries were male, and larger amounts of grave goods tend to be associated with them. In addition, cenotaphs—that is, graves without skeletons that contain only grave goods—also occurred in this period.[18]

With regard to resources and products related to wealth and power, salt also must be considered.[19] Although it was mined and consumed already during the Neolithic, salt became a significant exchange material in the Chalcolithic, as indicated by the site of Provadia in Bulgaria. The excavator argued that this site was a regional center for salt production and distribution, and that it was associated with the extremely rich elites buried in the nearby Varna necropolis (see Chapter 1, this volume). These elite members are thought to have controlled the distribution of salt—one of the most crucial ingredients in human and animal diet.[20] Due to its importance, Provadia was fortified, as were many Chalcolithic sites in the region. In general, defensive structures became more common in this period throughout the Balkans, as indicated by enclosures at Golyamo Delčevo and Ovčarovo in Bulgaria, Gumelnița and Salcuța in Romania, Gomolava and Bubanj in Serbia, Krušeanska Čuka in North Macedonia, and Makriyalos and Mandalo in Greece.[21]

These fortified settlements with walls, palisades, and ditches protected not only resources but also the people living at the sites—and the emerging elites in particular. Burials with gold and copper grave goods indicate social differentiation among the inhabitants of these villages.[22] The prestige objects from Chalcolithic necropoleis are associated mainly with males, highlighting their role within social hierarchy. Conversely, there are only a few male representations among the numerous figurines produced in this period. Most figurines depict female individuals, many with incised decoration and a few with holes for attaching or detaching heads, such as those found at Cernavodă in Romania, Krušeanska Čuka, Crnobuki, and Šuplevec in North Macedonia, Maliq in Albania, and Rachmani

Figure 2.10. Stone scepter with animal head, Šuplevec, North Macedonia. Middle Chalcolithic, 4300–4200 BC. Institute for Protection of Cultural Heritage and Museum–Bitola. *Photo by Á. Vágó.*

in Greece. Their decorations, as well as the removable and modifiable heads, apparently demonstrate various statuses that women had in Chalcolithic societies.[23] It is debated whether these statuses were associated with the economic role of women or whether they were more closely related to the symbolic roles that women held in the great variety of rituals performed within their households and villages.

Scepters as status indicators also should be discussed briefly. These stone artifacts, which sometimes depicted horses, have been found in several sites across Southeast Europe, including Salcuța in Romania, Sozopol and Drama in Bulgaria, and Šuplevec in North Macedonia (Figure 2.10). They were inserted into a wooden or bone handle, and indicated their owners' economic or ritual significance (for further discussions of these objects, see also Chapters 4 and 6, this volume).[24] The horse was domesticated in the Chalcolithic and was introduced to the Balkans from the Eurasian steppes as a novel means of power. Simultaneously, the horse was idealized and considered a significant economic symbol due to its role in transportation and ability to speed up travel, but also because the horse literally raised those who rode them above the masses.

Tribal Elites in the Bronze Age

The last waves of Indo-European migrations that marked the Early Bronze Age in the Balkans bore obvious signs of hierarchy, signified by burials under mounds (for an overview of this process, see Chapter 4, this volume). At the end of the Early Bronze Age, at Barç, Pazhok, and Vodhinë in Albania, these tumuli were characterized by the centrally positioned grave of the founder of a family or a lineage. Additional family or lineage members later were interred radially around this central burial. This points to the strengthened role of a tribal elite.[25]

Burials under tumuli continued into the Middle Bronze Age in the southern part of the central Balkans. Graves in Albania dating to this period, approximately 1500 BC, have strong analogies with the Middle Helladic period and the Late Helladic I period in Greece. These connections are demonstrated by grave goods, including a sword of Mycenaean

Figure 2.11. Bronze and Iron Age burials under a tumulus, Visoi, North Macedonia. *Photo: Institute for Protection of Cultural Heritage and Museum–Bitola.*

origin excavated at Pazhok. The Middle Bronze Age is best represented by sites in central and southern Albania, including the mound burials at Pazhok, Vodhinë, and Vajzë as well as the tumuli of the Maliq group in southeastern Albania.[26] The burial mounds in Greece from the Early Helladic III (2200–2000 BC), Middle Helladic (2000–1550 BC), and the Late Helladic I (1500–1400 BC) periods share many common elements with the tumuli in southern Albania from the same era.[27]

Macedonia saw cultural stagnation during the Middle Bronze Age, but the Vardar Valley, represented by the sites of Vardarophtsa and Kastanas, had some influence from the north. Considering present-day Serbia, the Early Bronze Age cultural group of Belotić-Bela Crkva is associated with the Vatin cultural group of the Middle Bronze Age (1600–1300 BC). Also, the burial mounds from the region of Metohija demonstrate close cultural relations with those of the west Serbian variant of the Vatin group.[28] Finally, Thrace can be attributed to the Middle Bronze Age chronology of Asia Minor, and did not have direct connections with cultural groups in the central Balkans.

The burial assemblages of this era are indicative of hierarchical relations among tribal lineages, wealth differences between them, and the significance of imported weapons for the tribal leaders. In regions settled by Indo-Europeans, this period also saw the emergence of Indo-Europeanized indigenous elements.

During the Late Bronze Age and the Transitional Period to the Iron Age, the territories on the periphery of the Mycenaean civilization in Greece, including Macedonia, were also influenced by Balkan and Lower Danube cultural complexes. Impacts from the south and north are reflected by burial deposits dating to the Transitional Period.

In Pelagonia, burials in a tumulus have been found only at Visoi, where the central grave was, most probably, much older than the additional interments (Figure 2.11). It contained a skyphos and a labrys-shaped bronze razor. Other vessels similar to Mycenaean pottery of the Late Helladic IIIC period in Greece (1200–1075 BC) also have been found elsewhere in Pelagonia (Figure 2.12). The labrys-shaped razor, however, is characteristic for central Europe, and dates to the twelfth century BC. Such objects have been recovered exclusively from the graves of tribe founders, and they illustrate the significance of these leaders who, although they did not have regal authority, had sufficient power to rule tribes. Dating also to the Transitional Period, several cist graves have been excavated in Pelagonia, in the vicinity of Prilep, some of them of gigantic proportions. These graves are not associated with tumuli but are individual burials belonging to the Late Helladic IIIB–IIIC period. They contained swords from the Catling 1 and Catling 2 groups, as well as a Neuzingen-type sword from central Europe, typical for the Bronze Age C and D periods (1300–1200 BC). These weapons, used for conquering territories and controlling populations, clearly signify that important leaders were interred in these graves.[29]

Figure 2.12. Ceramic Aegean-style vessel, Brod, North Macedonia. Late Bronze Age, 1200–1100 BC. Institute for Protection of Cultural Heritage and Museum–Bitola. *Photo by F. Kondovski.*

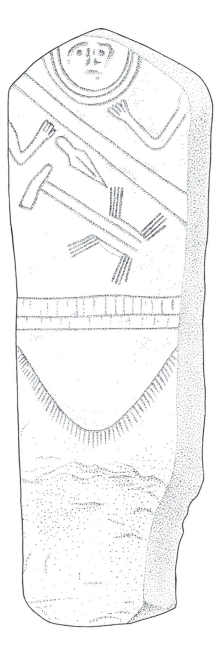

Figure 2.13. Stone funerary stele, Dimov Grob, North Macedonia. Late Bronze Age, 1200–1100 BC. *Modified from Mitevski 1995:Figure 7 by J. Seagard.*

Across Macedonia, in the upper and central flow of the Vardar River, many weapons have been recovered from burials dating to the Late Bronze Age and the Transitional Period, indicating the emergence of a powerful military class within the tribal communities of this region. It is presumed that from around 1250 BC onward, a Paeonian population inhabited this area. The Paeonian tribe eventually evolved into a tribal kingdom in what is now North Macedonia and Bulgaria during the first millennium BC (see Chapter 9, this volume).

At the sites of Vodovratski Pat and Dimov Grob in North Macedonia, many cist graves were excavated in which, except for short daggers, no weapons were found. However, at Dimov Grob, weapon finds were supplemented by a stone stele of a warrior in full military equipment, indicative of a high-ranking military leader (Figure 2.13). The stele features ornaments on the garments and on a part of the armament, rendered in bas relief. The find, which most probably dates to the twelfth century BC, bears resemblance to a stele from the fifth century BC discovered in the vicinity of Pernik in Bulgaria, in the territory of the Paeonian tribe of the Laeaei. The Pernik stele is coarsely manufactured and trapezoid in shape, and depicts a warrior with ornaments on his garments and weapon. It is assumed that this stele represents a Laeaeian ruler. During this period, the Laeaei minted coinage, yet another indicator of new economic and political innovations in this region.[30]

Mycenaean weapons and ceramics were imported to the Povardarie region of the upper Vardar River, or their imitations were produced in Lower Macedonia during the Late Bronze Age. The earliest finds include a rapier sword from Tetovo in North Macedonia. Similar swords have been unearthed in Dodona, in

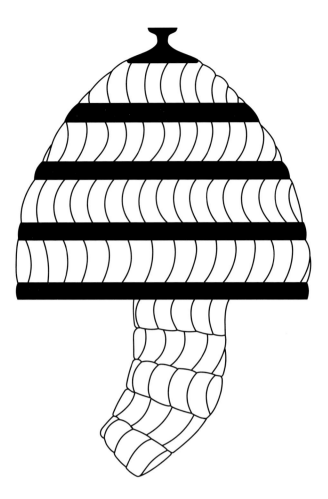

Figure 2.14. Reconstruction of a helmet
made with wild boar tusks, Klučka-Hipodrom, North
Macedonia. Late Bronze Age, 1300–1200 BC.
Modified from Petrova 1999:Figure 49.3 by J. Seagard.

Epirus as well as in Mediterranean Greece. The
Tetovo specimen dates to the Late Helladic IIIA
period, and may be interpreted as a Mycenaean import
to some local, high-ranking military leader. Among
other Mycenaean products, wild boar tusks recovered
from an urn at Klučka-Hipodrom in North Macedonia is noteworthy. The tusks were used in a manner
well known from the descriptions of weapons of
Achaian heroes in *The Iliad*—they formed a helmet
(Figure 2.14). Analogous helmets were a part of Mycenaean weaponry in the thirteenth century BC, during
the Late Helladic IIIB period. The Klučka-Hipodrom
find represents the northernmost Mycenaean helmet
used by a tribal leader or ruler.[31]

The Kingdoms of the Iron Age

In the territory of Macedonia, during the Iron Age,
and especially in the Iron Age II phase, characteristic bronze votive or cult finds were produced that
archaeologists call 'Macedonian,' or more precisely
'Paeonian,' bronzes. These objects were related to a
solar cult among the Paeonians and were associated
with priests who belonged to the ruling class of the
Paeonian society. The tomb in the vicinity of Marvinci
testifies to the economic and cultural development
of the Paeonians. About four hundred objects linked
to the solar cult were deposited in this female burial,
including needles in the shape of spectacles, *phalerae*,
bird-shaped pendants, and amber beads or buttons. At
another site in North Macedonia, Milci, a high-ranked
woman was unearthed alongside prestigious bronze
grave goods, such as a wand, pendants, disks, and
bracelets (Figure 2.15).[32]

Along the lower Vardar River, numerous finds represent the Iron Age, including weapons from Lisičin
Dol in North Macedonia.[33] The spears in that burial
were not used by a member of the military aristocracy,
but rather by an individual at the lower level in the
hierarchy, indicating that several military classes existed in Paeonian society between the eighth and sixth
centuries BC.

During the transition from the Iron Age II phase
to the Archaic period in Macedonia, the necropolis of
Sindos in Greece was used sometime between 560 and
430 BC. Both in terms of chronology and the repertoire of grave goods, the Sindos cemetery is similar
to the necropolis at Trebenište in North Macedonia.
The lavish burials at Trebenište represent members of
the local aristocracy or the rulers themselves (see also
Chapter 9, this volume). The exquisite finds from this
cemetery include gold masks and bracelets and sandal-
shaped gold sheets (Figure 2.16), as well as vessels
made of silver and bronze, imported from Greece (for
examples, see Figures 9.20 and 9.23, this volume). In
addition to the gold, silver, and bronze jewelry and
masks, bronze defensive weapons, such as helmets,
greaves, and shields, and iron offensive weapons were
also deposited in the burials at Trebenište. In the Lake
Ohrid region, such finds were found as well at Gorna
Porta (Figures 2.17 and 2.18), and also in Pelagonia, in
the Petilep tumulus at Beranci.[34]

In Serbia, two large tumuli with cremated individ-
uals were excavated at Atenica. In the central grave of
Mound I, jewelry, large amounts of amber, glass beads,
and many other finds were found (for an example, see
Figure 9.21, this volume). The central burial of Mound
II contained rivets and coating from iron knives,

Figure 2.15. Reconstruction of a female burial with 'Macedonian' bronzes, Grave 111, Milci, North Macedonia. Early Iron Age, 700–650 BC. *Reconstruction by B. Husenovski, illustration by D. Gusev.*

Figure 2.16. Sandal-shaped gold sheet, Trebenište, North Macedonia. Early Iron Age, 550–450 BC. National Museum of Serbia, Belgrade. *Photo: National Museum of Serbia.*

numerous amber beads, and many bronze pendants. Based on the size of the mounds and the grave goods, it is assumed that a princess and her son were buried in Mound I, and a prince was interred in Mound II. In Novi Pazar, also in Serbia, a large tumulus with a central wooden construction was discovered. Imported objects, such as Attic pottery, metal vessels, amber, gold, and silver jewelry, were found in this tomb (for examples, see Figures 1.21 and 9.20, this volume). Someone positioned very high in the social hierarchy appears to have been buried in this grave during the first quarter of the fifth century BC (for additional details about Atenica and Novi Pazar, see Chapter 9, this volume). In addition to Novi Pazar and Atenica, there are a few more princely graves in the region that can be dated to the end of the sixth and the beginning of the fifth century BC. These include Pećka Banja near Prizren in Kosovo and Petrova Crkva near Novi

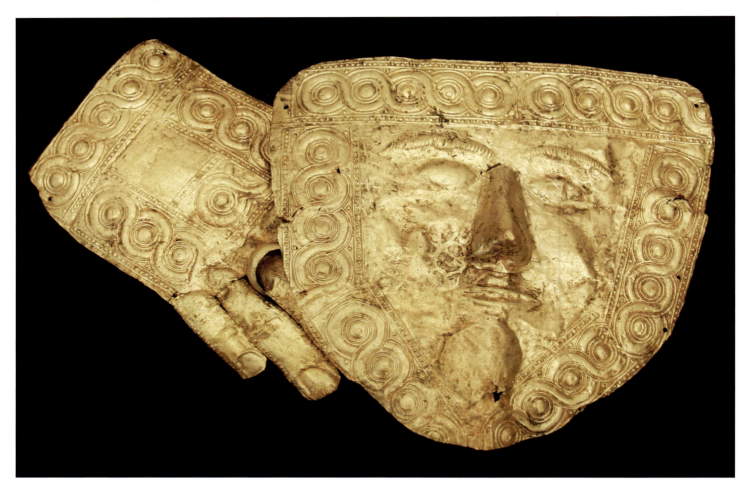

Figure 2.17. Gold mask and glove with a ring, Gorna Porta, North Macedonia. Early Iron Age, 550–450 BC. Institute for Protection of Cultural Heritage and Museum–Ohrid. *Photo by B. Taneski.*

Pazar in Serbia, where many imported luxury goods were buried with the members of the local tribal aristocracy.[35]

In the region of Thrace, the Odrysian kingdom emerged during the fifth century BC, representing the union of more than forty Thracian tribes and twenty-two previously autonomous kingdoms. During the reign of kings Teres and Sitalces, the kingdom was at its zenith and extended over a great part of the eastern Balkans. The Odrysian military strength was based on a strong tribal aristocracy, and the wealth of the kingdom is evident in rich grave constructions with enormous quantities of precious metal finds. Gold and gilded silver phialae, amphorae, and rhytons were found in the treasures of Panagyurishte, Rogozen, Borovo, and many others (see also Chapter 10, this volume).

In Albania, the long period of continual burials in the tumuli at Barç, Kuçi i Zi I, and Kuçi i Zi II indicates a lasting ancestor cult. These burials are chronologically synchronous with those in the tumuli in Visoi, Saraj, and Brod in the Pelagonia region of North Macedonia.[36]

At the end of the sixth century and the beginning of the fifth century BC, the regions of Albania, Macedonia, and Thrace began to be influenced by the Greek Archaic period and this continued during the Classical period, into the fourth century BC. Over the course of this era, one of the most significant manifestations of a centralized, bureaucratic society occurred—the minting of coins. Coinage enabled the Paeonian tribal organizations to grow into kingdoms because the economic, political, and cultural benefits from this activity became an entrance ticket into the world of Hellenic culture. The silver mines and the close proximity to the developed Greek colonies and the coast enabled the Paeonian tribal polities of the Derrones, Edones, Byzaltes, and others to increase monetary production as early as the sixth century BC.

Although they were distributed over a wider geographic area, most of the Derrones probably lived between the central and upper parts of the Vardar and Struma rivers. Their coins were minted in silver after the Euboean standard in denominations of octo- and decadrachms, weighing between 34 and 41 grams, as well as tetrobols. They are designated with the legends ΔΕΡΡΟΝΙΚΟΣ, ΔΕΡΡΟΝΙΚΟΝ, ΔΕΡΡΟΝΙ, and ΔΕΡΡΟ, indicating the tribal affiliation, as shown by the names of the rulers ΕΥΕΡΓΕΤΕ(Σ), ΕΧ..., ΕΓΚΟ(ΝΟΥ), even in the sixth century BC. This suggests that the Derrones were organized into a complex tribal polity or a tribal kingdom (for a discussion of Iron Age sociopolitical organizations, see Chapter 8, this volume). Another interesting find of a tetrobol

Figure 2.18. Bronze helmet, Gorna Porta, North Macedonia. Early Iron Age, 550–450 BC. Institute for Protection of Cultural Heritage and Museum–Ohrid. *Photo by B. Taneski.*

with the name of King Doki(mos?) can be linked to the Derrones. This tetrobol was minted according to the same regional standard in the vicinity of the town of Štip in North Macedonia, located in the presumed Derronian territory.[37]

The reorganization of Paeonian tribes into a new societal form, similar to those of the Classical kingdoms in the broader region, persisted into the fifth and fourth centuries BC. This is demonstrated by the coins minted in silver by the presumed Paeonian rulers Teutaos, Bastareus, Nikarchus, and Symon, until the emergence of Lycceus, a Paeonian ruler who was considered to have been the founder of the Paeonian dynasty (Figure 2.19). His son and grandson are mentioned in Greek historical sources, and their names appear on coins as being kings. Lycceus minted coins after the reduced Phoenician standard—tetradrachms, drachms, and tetrobols in silver—and an inscription mentions him together with Thracian and Illyrian kings—Cetriporis and Grabus—related to an agreement made against the Macedonian king Philip II.[38]

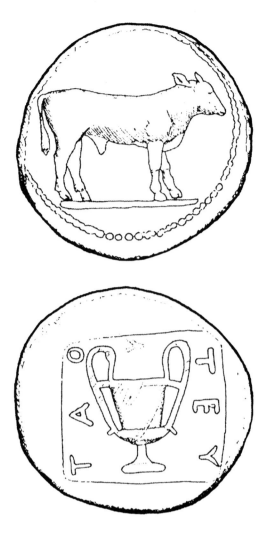

Figure 2.19. Silver coin of the
Paeonian king of Teutaos (450–425 BC),
Demir Kapija, North Macedonia.
*Modified from Lilčić 1995:49
by J. Seagard.*

There is no information in the historical sources
about Lycceus's successor, Patraus, but an inscription
from 289/88 BC notes that he was the father of the
Paeonian king Audoleon. Audoleon was the first king
from this region who used the title of ΒΑΣΙΛΕΟΣ on
his coinage, about the same time generals of Alexander
the Great also gave themselves the title after his death
in 323 BC. They were known as the Diadochi kings
and fought for the control over the empire in 306–305
BC.[39] The title of *basileos* for Audoleon also occurs in

both inscriptions and written sources. The fact that
he belonged to the Hellenistic community and the
civilized world was of importance for the Paeonian
society. His grandson, Dropion, dedicated a statue
for Audoleon in Delphi, and he is also mentioned on
another statue from Olympia as a king and founder
of the Paeonian *koinon*, the term for a federation or
commonwealth in the ancient Greek world. This king
marked the end of the Paeonian dynasty which later
became a part of the great Macedonian state.[40]

Proximity to the Greek colonies on the Mediterranean shore, cultural influences from the Greek world,
the rich mines, and the development of urban life all
contributed to the emergence of tribal kingdoms in
the regions of Macedonia and Paeonia, and to the survival of this significant historical process in the written
sources and in the archaeological record.

Conclusions

This chapter has provided a general overview of major
social changes in the central and southern Balkans
from the Neolithic to the Iron Age. Over time, the
accumulation of goods and the control of key resources
initiated vital transformations in prehistoric farming
societies that led to the establishment of various
competing social groups. These groups gradually transformed into elites, and were promoted as such within
their own communities as well as at regional scales.

This process started in the Neolithic with the
increased reliance upon farming and animal husbandry when smaller groups or entire communities were
in charge of food storage or distribution. With the
adoption of metals as a novel part of material culture,
these processes of social differentiation intensified
during the Chalcolithic. Access to and distribution of
specific resources (particularly ore and salt) were tightly controlled, leading to more frequent conflicts and
promoting the important roles of emerging leaders.
This can be seen not only in the spatial organization
of settlements but also in the burials of emergent
elites. Villages adopted a more defensive character,
with the centralization of buildings and the construction of ditches and palisades that protected them.
Higher-ranked individuals were buried with gold and
copper goods. These processes coincided with sociopolitical dynamics based on power that continued
into the Bronze Age when social stratification and the
prominence of elites were distinctively manifested. In
this period, settlements became larger and were often
built at higher elevations in the hills, while weapons
made of metal became more prominent. In the final

phases of this era, elites were buried under mounds, foreshadowing a tradition practiced more commonly over the course of the Iron Age.

The Iron Age was the last stage of the long process toward social stratification, which started in the Neolithic and led to the first tribal kingdoms in the Balkans during the first millennium BC. The establishment of these first kingdoms was also the final step in the crystallization of ethnic identities in the Balkans that contributed to the transformation of prehistoric tribes into proto-urban populations, such as the Paeonians, Macedonians, Thracians, Illyrians, and Dardanians, among others. During this dynamic era, these early kingdoms absorbed influences from the Greeks, Egyptians, and Persians into their culture, religion, and economy, which were reflected in the mortuary customs and beliefs. The princely graves of this period testify to the importance of the elites in the world of the living as well as in the world of the dead. This was the final stage of a process that unfolded over millennia—a momentum that closed the doors of prehistory and opened the gates into history with the development of kingdoms, states, and the urban centers of Antiquity.

Notes

1   Ivanova et al. 2018.
2   Naumov 2013.
3   Nikolov 1989; Prendi and Aliu 1971.
4   Kitanoski et al. 1990; Mitkoski 2005.
5   Garašanin and Bilbija 1988.
6   Naumov et al. 2018a; Naumov et al. 2021.
7   Naumov et al. 2018b.
8   Harding et al. 2006.
9   Schulting and Fibiger 2012.
10 Naumov 2015a.
11 Naumov 2011; Šemrov and Turk 2009.
12 Chausidis 2010; Naumov 2013; Sanev 2006.
13 Chapman and Gaydarska 2015; Dimitrijević et al. 2010; Dimitrijević et al. 2021.
14 Naumov 2014.
15 Bacvarov 2008; Borić and Stefanović 2004; Naumov 2013; Nemeskéri and Lengyel 1976.
16 Kostov 2007; Mitovski 2018; Radivojević and Rehren 2016; Šljivar 2006.
17 Antonović 2009; Gale et al. 2003; Mitovski 2018; Radivojević et al. 2010; Simoska and Sanev 1976.
18 Bailey 2000.
19 Nikolov and Bacvarov 2012.
20 Nikolov 2010.
21 Bailey 2000; Harding et al. 2006; Naumov et al. 2021; Nikolov and Bacvarov 2012.
22 Nikolov 1991; Nikolov 2010.
23 Bailey 2005; Kolištrkoska Nasteva 2005; Naumov 2014; Prendi 2018.
24 Anthony et al. 2006; Dergachev and Sorokin 1986; Gheorghiu 1994; Simoska and Sanev 1976.
25 Petrova 1996:3–21.
26 Hammond 1967; Hammond 1976.
27 Hammond 1972; Heurtley 1939.
28 Garašanin 1983.
29 Garašanin 1983; Mikulčić 1966; Petrova 1999.
30 Mitrevski 1997; Petrova 1999.
31 Mitrevski 1995; Petrova 1999.
32 Chausidis 2017; Husenovski 2018; Mitrevski 1999; Petrova 1999.
33 Videski 1999.
34 Kuzman 2018; Lahtov and Kastelic 1957; Mikulčić 1966; Petrova 1999; Vokotopoulou 1985.
35 Vasić 1987b.
36 Andrea 1976; Petrova 1996; Petrova 1999.
37 Petrova 1999.
38 Tod 1968.
39 Dittenberger 1924.
40 Bousquet 1952:136–40; Pouilloux 1950:22–33.

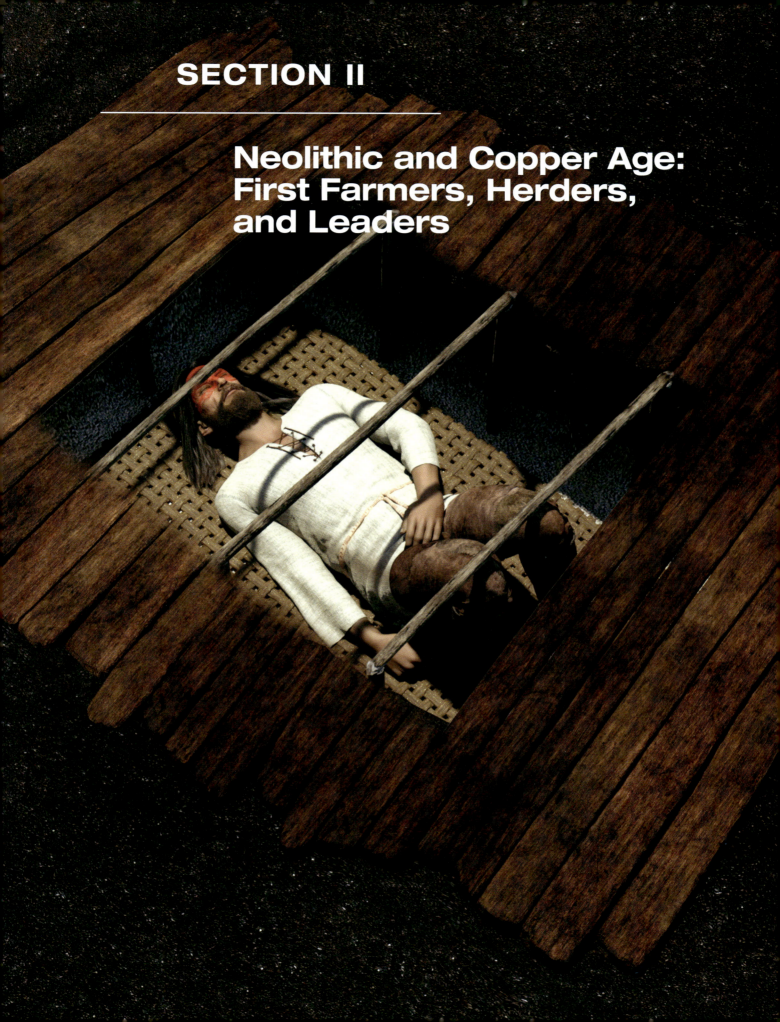

SECTION II

Neolithic and Copper Age: First Farmers, Herders, and Leaders

CHAPTER 3

Communities and Monuments in the Making

Neolithic Tells on the Great Hungarian Plain

Attila Gyucha, William A. Parkinson, András Füzesi, and Pál Raczky

ARCHAEOLOGISTS IN EUROPE use the Arabic word *tell* to refer to a specific kind of archaeological site that grows up vertically over time.[1] From northern Africa through southwestern Asia and into southeastern Europe, tell sites were created at many different times throughout prehistory and in historic times.[2] Tell sites are created when people live on the same piece of land for hundreds or thousands of years—for example, a large section of the modern city of Tel Aviv is a tell site that has been occupied for millennia.

Archaeologically, tell sites tend to be associated with sedentary farming populations that built houses made of mud brick or wattle-and-daub, a kind of adobe technique. Because the walls of these houses are made of mud, they are relatively short-lived and need to be renewed or reconstructed regularly. Sometimes they are deconstructed or burned and rebuilt on the same spot. Other times, they are abandoned and rebuilt somewhere else on the settlement. When built on the same spot, prior to reconstruction, a new settlement layer is laid down by leveling the old house

remains, and the settlement begins to build up over time, eventually forming a mound (Figures 3.1, 3.2, and 3.3). This is what the word means in Arabic—a mound or hill. Some tell sites in the Near East reached heights of over thirty meters, but tell sites in southeastern Europe usually are much more modest, with most less than five meters in height (Figure 3.4).

In the southern Balkans—in central and northern Greece, Bulgaria, North Macedonia, and the European part of Turkey—many tells were formed right at the beginning of the Neolithic, during the seventh millennium BC, as the first farmers moved into Europe. Farther north, in the central and northern Balkans and the Carpathian Basin, tell sites were only established several hundred years after the first agricultural populations had migrated into the region, at the turn of the sixth and fifth millennia BC (Figure 3.5).[3]

In this chapter, we discuss these later tells, which, in many cases, were the first large, permanent farming settlements in their regions. As a result, these centers would have triggered unprecedented social and political developments by providing ideal venues for ambitious groups and individuals to introduce new forms and mechanisms of control and power. We focus here on the Late Neolithic period of the Great Hungarian Plain and present three examples to demonstrate the different ways in which these sites were formed, and how their communities developed their own social and political organizations (Figure 3.6).

Figure 3.1. Prehistoric tell site with the reconstructed ruins of a Medieval monastery, Vésztő-Mágor, Hungary. *Photo by A. Gyucha.*

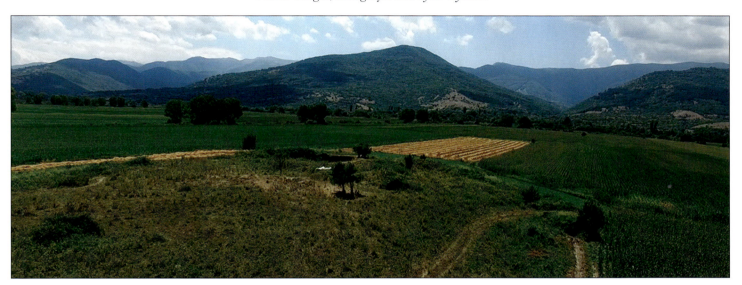

Figure 3.2. Neolithic tell site, Veluška Tumba, North Macedonia. *Adapted from Naumov et al. 2020:Figure 1.*

Figure 3.3. Neolithic tell site, Bapska, Croatia. *Photo by M. Burić.*

Figure 3.4. Tell stratigraphy, Vésztő-Mágor, Hungary.
Photo by A. Gyucha.

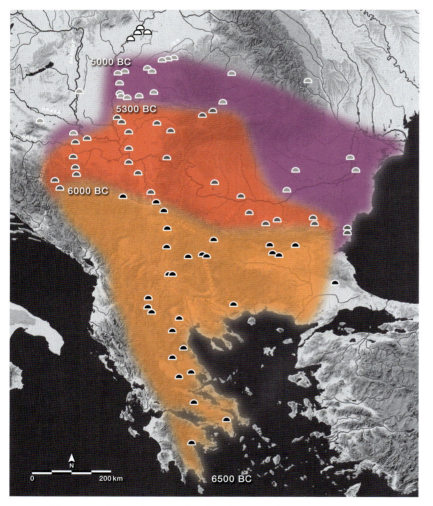

Figure 3.5. Map showing the distribution of Neolithic tell sites over time in southeastern Europe. *Modified from Raczky 2015:Figure 1 by D. Lonhardt and E. Rodriguez.*

The Neolithic Revolution

Of the various watershed moments in human prehistory, few were as dramatic or had as many far-ranging consequences as the transition from a mobile lifestyle based on hunting and gathering to one based on agriculture, animal husbandry, and sedentary settlements. This transition—known as the 'Neolithic Revolution'—occurred in different parts of the world at different points in time since the beginning of the Holocene, over 10,000 years ago.[4]

Although diffusion and adaptation of ideas might have played a major role in the spread of the Neolithic way of life in some parts of Europe, an array of recent studies have confirmed that in southeastern Europe Neolithization unfolded primarily through migration from the Near East.[5] In areas such as the Great Hungarian Plain or the Thessalian Plain in Greece, large, uninhabited tracts of land were suddenly colonized by new people who brought with them the entire 'Neolithic package,' which included domesticated plants and animals as well as other traditions associated with a sedentary, agricultural lifestyle. These other traditions included domestic crafts, such as manufacturing pottery and making polished stone axes to cut down trees (Figure 3.7). In those areas that clearly were colonized by Neolithic farmers, all these traditions and objects showed up at the same time. In other areas, such as in the Iron Gates region of the Danube River, there already were a large number of specialized, sedentary foragers, and the different aspects of the 'Neolithic package' were adopted piecemeal, and more gradually, over hundreds of years.[6]

The Regional Importance of Tells

Tells in the Neolithic of southeastern Europe commonly were focal sites in their respective regions and attracted the permanent aggregation of regional populations. The questions of why some specific spots on the landscape were occupied for much longer than others and why they became important are difficult to answer. Excavations typically have exposed only small areas and have revealed the upper sections of tells—the lower layers that represent the earliest history of these sites have remained largely unexposed. Additionally, systematic research in the immediate and broader surroundings of tells has only recently been initiated in southeastern Europe, making it difficult to understand how tell sites functioned within their regional contexts.

Some scholars have argued that tell sites evolved on specific spots in the landscape and became more

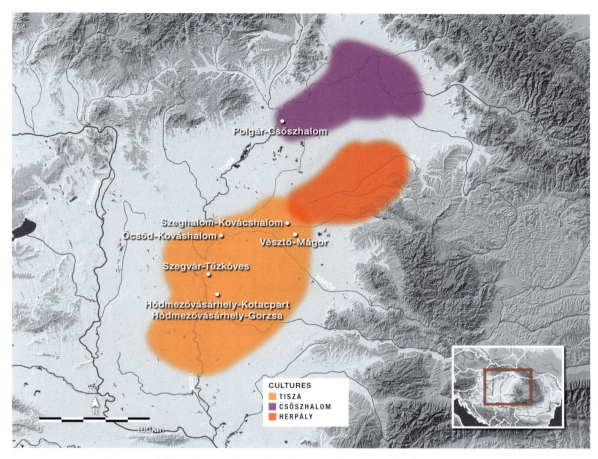

Figure 3.6. Map showing the cultural units and sites in the Carpathian Basin mentioned in the text. *Illustration by A. Gyucha, F. Paár, and E. Rodriguez.*

attractive than others because of their high degree of connectivity and the specific histories of these locales. Many have pointed out that the early layers in tell sites indicate that those communities were successful in long-distance trading activities and were able to acquire distant materials and goods. Raw materials of stone tools recovered from tells on the Great Hungarian Plain frequently made their way to these sites from hundreds of kilometers away (Figure 3.8).[7] Other exotic materials from these sites in the Carpathian Basin, such as *Spondylus* shells from the Adriatic or Aegean Sea, also suggest that these sites were plugged into extensive trade networks.[8]

Tell sites also likely had significant histories that made them special places for rituals and other activities.[9] In other regions,[10] certain places on the landscape gained prestige and value because they were the historical locations for specific ceremonies that themselves encouraged the aggregation of groups from numerous different, far-flung communities.

Recent research across southeastern Europe indicates that when new groups were attracted to tell sites, they frequently settled in areas outside the confines

Figure 3.7. Ceramic vessel with animal relief, Hódmezővásárhely-Kotacpart, Hungary. Early Neolithic, 6000–5500 BC. Hungarian National Museum, Budapest. *Photo by Á. Vágó.*

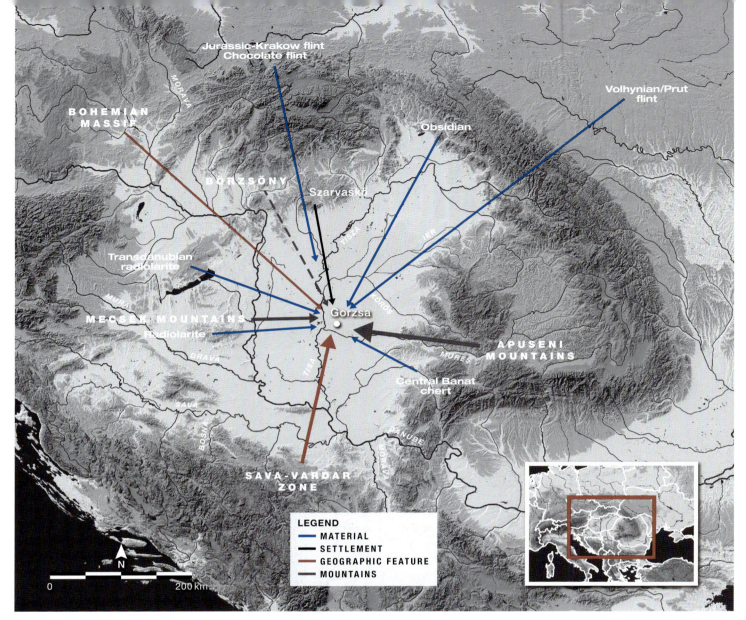

Figure 3.8. Sources of polished and chipped stone tool raw materials at the
Neolithic tell of Hódmezővásárhely-Gorzsa, Hungary.
Modified from Szakmány et al. 2009:Figure 6 by E. Rodriguez.

of the tells. Some of these tell-centered settlement complexes were inhabited by many hundreds or even thousands of people.

These aggregated communities had a strong connection to the past through their ancestral links, and the tell sites themselves represented this deep history. Neolithic people likely understood the relationship between the height of the tells and the time required for the founder communities to create them through continual habitation and rebuilding.[11] Some have argued that the re-construction of houses and the settlement over time by the inhabitants was the "physical and social expression of continuity with

the ancestors, who once lived in the same place."[12] Through the long history embedded in their physical features, tells may have been perceived as habitation monuments,[13] and the evolution of these anchors for community identity likely became central themes in ritual narratives and related ceremonies.

The symbolic importance of tells is also signaled by large-scale communal projects, such as the construction of massive enclosures and moats around them. These works required the close and enduring cooperation of large numbers of people, and, as with historical narratives and ceremonies relating to the history of the tells, promoted group solidarity and identity formation in these settlements.[14] These enclosures and moats might have symbolically separated the tells from the surrounding settlements, but might also have had defensive functions at the times of external violent

Figure 3.9. Ceramic anthropomorphic figurine, Bardhosh-Prishtina, Kosovo. Middle or Late Neolithic, 5200–4600 BC. National Museum of Kosovo, Prishtina. *Photo by Á. Vágó.*

Figure 3.10. Ceramic seated anthropomorphic figurine, Szegvár-Tűzköves, Hungary. Late Neolithic, 5000–4500 BC. Koszta József Museum, Szentes. *Photo by Á. Vágó.*

conflicts. These defensive functions further reinforced the focal role of tells for the villagers—in those contexts, as the essential sources of security.

Tells and Social Differentiation

Although archaeologists traditionally describe Neolithic societies as 'egalitarian,' Neolithic people clearly understood the concept of hierarchy. Ceramic anthropomorphic figurines and face pots that evoke supernatural forces, such as deities or powerful ancestor spirits, frequently are recovered from Neolithic sites throughout southeastern Europe (Figures 3.9, 3.10, and 3.11).[15] These finds reflect cosmologies and belief systems where the mundane lives of humans were subordinated to higher powers. But the Neolithic

people also perceived hierarchical relationships between different individuals and social groups, such as families, households, and lineages. Within this context, the nucleated social environment of tell sites would have had a significant impact on social dynamics, especially with regards to the potential for social differentiation.

Neolithic societies commonly are portrayed as achievement-based, where each person was considered equal at birth, and prestige and status was not inherited but earned over one's lifetime, based on one's gender and personal merit, experience, skills, and charisma.[16] Evidence for organized planning on some Neolithic tells, in addition to monumental building

Figure 3.11. Ceramic face pot, Biatorbágy-Tyúkberek, Hungary. Middle Neolithic, 5200–5000 BC. Budapest History Museum. *Photo by Á. Vágó.*

Tells as Social Arenas for Differentiation and Hierarchy

We cannot overestimate the social impacts that the emergence of large, complex, nucleated settlements would have had on the trajectory of early village life. In many different historical contexts, the development of large sites also coincided with the emergence of marked social differentiation. For Neolithic communities across the Great Hungarian Plain who had lived in small, dispersed villages and hamlets for a thousand years, the aggregation to specific places about 7,000 years ago would have required new ideas concerning social rules, conventions, and community organization. And size mattered a lot. The co-residence of a few dozen, or even a hundred, people would have demanded radically different organizational and leadership mechanisms than that of several hundreds, or thousands, of people trying to sort out how to live together (see also Foreword, this volume).[19] Thus these mechanisms and structures would have differed profoundly at small tells with relatively small numbers of people and at settlement complexes where large populations aggregated onto and around the tells.

Ethnographic and ethnohistoric analogies suggest that the social organization of large Neolithic communities in the Carpathian Basin would have been structured according to ancestor-based descent groups, such as households and lineages, as well as along other corporate social units that cross-cut them, such as clans, moieties, and sodalities. These nucleated sites with hundreds or thousands of inhabitants would have created an ideal venue for competition among these groups, and each of them would have claimed ancestral histories in relation to these settlements that would be evoked during ceremonies and other performances. Ethnographically, the groups that founded the settlements regularly possessed privileged statuses that afforded their members important roles in decision-making and governance.[20] The leading clans and lineages frequently were challenged by latecomer groups through disputes about rights and narratives associated with seniority, and thus superiority in status, in the villages. These negotiations routinely gave rise to conflicts, many times brought about revisions in cosmology to justify new group privileges, and sometimes led to fundamental modifications in community and leadership structures.[21] The claim of access to the tells as ancestral monuments likely would have been a focus of negotiations between rival groups at Neolithic settlement complexes on the Great Hungarian Plain.

It remains unclear whether systems of durable hereditary inequality emerged during the Neolithic. In egalitarian societies, leaders regularly do not exercise

projects, which would have required a large amount of coordination and communal labor, have encouraged some researchers to speculate on the existence of more formalized hierarchical political systems during the Neolithic.[17] The archaeological record also suggests that there was some differential treatment of the dead at funerals and differential access to wealth in different households during the Neolithic.[18] Nucleated tell settlements, which had larger, more diverse, and dense populations, provided social contexts that would have permitted, if not encouraged, social differentiation and incipient forms of hereditary hierarchy to emerge.

actual authority over other community members; however, the complex organizational requirements to sustain extensive, dense, socially heterogeneous settlements, rife with their own social and political challenges, may have laid the groundwork for the establishment of fundamentally different leadership structures. When the equilibrium between status and equality was disrupted by the emergence of these new, dynamic social settings, institutionalized, hereditary leadership positions and formal ranks inherited at birth could have emerged. In those instances, political and ritual authority could have been consolidated and legitimized by claims to a specific ancestor or group associated with the founding of the tell itself.

Ethnographic and ethnohistoric examples of different village societies include an impressive diversity of political structures, from collective forms of governance through institutions such as village councils, to truly autocratic forms of leadership.[22] Sometimes markedly different leadership models occurred even in contemporaneous, neighboring communities.[23] In some cases, periodic cycling between egalitarian and hierarchical systems occurred within the same communities.[24] There is no reason to assume that the later Neolithic aggregated communities of southeastern Europe lacked a similarly broad scale of variation in their political structures. Larger communities, like the Neolithic tell-centered settlement complexes on the Great Hungarian Plain, likely varied tremendously in this respect.

Below, we present three case studies to illustrate variation in the developments of Late Neolithic settlement complexes on the Great Hungarian Plain. We focus particularly on how social differentiation manifested itself in the archaeological record at these sites.

Polgár-Csőszhalom

Polgár-Csőszhalom, located in the upper Tisza River valley, represents the northernmost periphery of tells in southeastern Europe (see Figure 3.6). It was introduced into Neolithic scholarship in 1929, when V. Gordon Childe and Ferenc Tompa discussed the remarkable polychrome pottery from the site.[25] Excavations in 1957 demonstrated that the 3–3.5 m high mound was a tell, and based on the findings, the Csőszhalom Culture was distinguished as a Late Neolithic unit of the northern Great Hungarian Plain.[26]

A multi-disciplinary research project began across the 91 km²-large Polgár Island in the early 1990s. Surface surveys throughout the microregion concluded that, in addition to Polgár-Csőszhalom, two

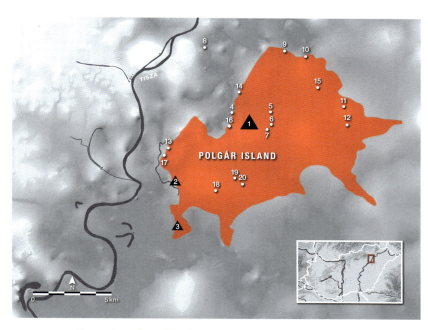

Figure 3.12. Late Neolithic settlement network on the Polgár Island microregion. Triangles indicate tell sites, dots represent hamlets and small villages. *Modified from Mesterházy et al. 2019:Figure 1 by A. Füzesi and E. Rodriguez.*

additional tells and seventeen hamlets and small villages comprised the Late Neolithic settlement network (Figure 3.12). At the local scale, a series of geophysical surveys and excavations were performed, bringing about substantial outcomes regarding settlement and social organization. The most important contributions of the geophysical surveys were the identification of a complex ditch system encircling the mound as well as the discovery of a habitation area extending over 67.5 ha around the tell (Figure 3.13).[27]

The excavations revealed that the encircling ditches were expanded as the tell grew both horizontally and vertically. In the central part of the mound, thirteen to sixteen radially aligned houses were constructed that were deliberately burnt and replaced by new ones several times. A two-story building was erected in the very center of the tell at the beginning of the site's occupation, between 4920 and 4785 BC. The construction of this building may have created a collective reference point for the long-term maintenance and reproduction of the local social system. However, in the wake of the horizontal expansion of the tell and the enclosure, the central cohesive force seems to have been lost. Buildings were no longer erected in the middle of the mound and small, symbolic buildings, imitating the larger structures, were constructed,

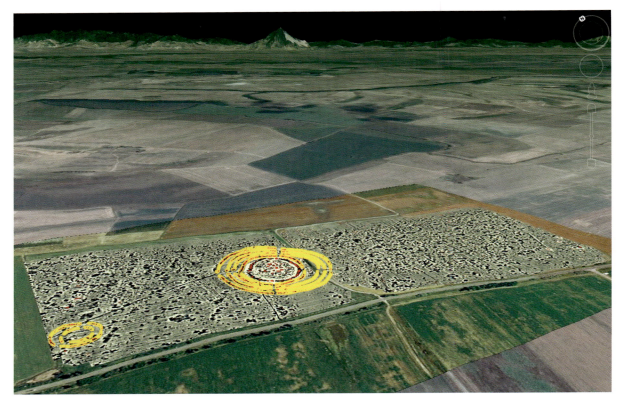

Figure 3.13. Results of magnetometric prospection at the Late Neolithic settlement complex of Polgár-Csőszhalom, Hungary. The central tell enclosed by multiple concentric ditches and a smaller circular enclosure to the southwest are highlighted. *Modified from Mesterházy et al. 2019:Figure 2 by L. Rupnik.*

encircling an empty central area. In the final phase, the ditches of the enclosure were backfilled during the course of a single event, bringing an end to community activities on the settlement mound. One visible outcome of this disintegration process was the creation of a smaller enclosure southwest of the tell (see Figure 3.13).[28]

Prior to a motorway construction, rescue excavations exposed 4 ha of the external settlement east of the Polgár-Csőszhalom tell between 1995 and 2006. In addition to hundreds of settlement features, including 73 residential buildings, 124 burials were uncovered in the vicinity of the houses. The comparative analysis of these graves and the twenty-one burials uncovered on the mound revealed a distinctive pattern. The tell area was dominated by male and child burials, while female burials were more prevalent in the external settlement. In addition to the practice of an unusually strict dichotomy in the placement of the dead in the context of the Late Neolithic Great Hungarian Plain (that is, females were placed on

their left, males on their right side), variation in grave goods also reflected sex-based differentiation.[29] It would appear that the introduction of these conventions was associated with the creation of a new identity at Polgár-Csőszhalom.

In addition to differences in burial treatment, the outstanding role of the tell for the Polgár-Csőszhalom community is signaled by other distinctive practices as well.[30] Copper artifacts were found exclusively in this area of the settlement complex. Thus they appeared only in a symbolic context as defined by the community. Moreover, recurring communal events, including feasting, also occurred on the tell. The scale and nature of these events are best illustrated by the fact that the abundance of animal bones is over two hundred times higher on the tell than in household contexts on the external settlement.[31]

It seems a reasonable assumption that fundamentally egalitarian social relations survived in the community of the Polgár-Csőszhalom settlement complex owing to institutionalized community regulations, such as the restricted location of use of specific materials and events, including regular feastings. However, over time, the importance of the tell as the focal point for the community appears to have decreased.

This process coincided with increasing richness of grave goods in the burials of the external settlement. A good example is a female burial with a large number of exotic *Spondylus* objects (Figures 3.14 and 3.15). This assemblage may indicate the emergence of a tendency for "privatization" of surplus at the site to express individual prestige and status.

Szeghalom-Kovácshalom

Like many settlement mounds across southeastern Europe, the Szeghalom-Kovácshalom tell in the eastern section of the Great Hungarian Plain attracted enthusiastic amateur archaeologists as early as the dawn of the twentieth century (see Figure 3.6). The first professional excavations at the site, however, occurred only in the late 1960s.[32] A century after the initial works on the tell, the Körös Regional Archaeological Project launched new, state-of-the-art investigations in 2010. Surface surveys were carried out, geophysical, geomorphological, and geochemical investigations were performed, and targeted excavations were conducted to explore the evolution of the tell in its local and broader contexts (Figure 3.16).[33]

The Szeghalom-Kovácshalom tell started as a small village around 5200 BC, in the later phase of the Middle Neolithic. A sequence of superimposing house remains characterizes this initial period. The 'organic' tell development through subsequent building and rebuilding activities over generations also continued into the Late Neolithic, which started about 5000 BC.

The site started to grow sometime around 4900 BC. Surface and geophysical surveys identified a massive settlement that developed around the tell. By 4700 BC, this settlement covered about 90 ha and it probably was home to well over one thousand people at its peak (Figure 3.17). The major demographic source of this growth was populations from the surrounding microregion where dozens of small villages and hamlets, very similar to the initial Szeghalom-Kovácshalom site, had been occupied in the previous period. The inhabitants of Szeghalom-Kovácshalom likely belonged to numerous clans and lineages, and these groups formed spatially distinct neighborhoods when they moved into the large village.

The population expansion coincided with dramatic changes in settlement development. Residential activities terminated on the tell about 4900 BC, and profoundly different depositional activities accounted for site formation: using sediments from the immediate landscape, the mound was deliberately elevated by about 2.5 m in height. During this process, another earthwork, a moat, was also constructed to encircle the tell. Approximately 20,000 m³ of sediments

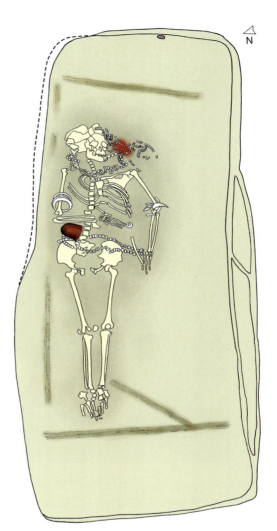

Figure 3.14. Female burial with jewelry, a vessel at the hip, and ocher near the head, Feature 836, Polgár-Csőszhalom, Hungary. *Modified from Raczky and Anders 2017:Figure 6.5.1 by K. Sebők.*

Figure 3.15. *Spondylus* bracelets and a ring from a female burial, Feature 836, Polgár-Csőszhalom, Hungary. Late Neolithic, 4900–4600 BC. Déri Museum, Debrecen. *Photo by Á. Vágó.*

Figure 3.16. Collection of radiocarbon samples, Szeghalom-Kovácshalom, Hungary. Note the complex stratigraphy in the lower sections with superimposing building remains. *Photo by A. Gyucha.*

were moved over the course of these large-scale construction works, which would have required the coordination and cooperation of the entire local population. At this time, the enclosed mound became a venue for regular communal gatherings, during which sacrificial rituals were performed and, as at Polgár-Csőszhalom, large amounts of wild game were consumed.

These alterations in tell formation and use may have been triggered by a radical sociopolitical shift in the growing village from the dominance of a single group to a more distributed power structure. The privileges of tell dwellers, the descendants of the founding community and possibly powerful leaders, may have been successfully challenged by latecomer groups. This is indicated by the termination of residential use and the introduction of more collective activities on the tell. The symbolic importance of the mound as identity anchor for the entire Szeghalom-Kovácshalom community was demonstrated, as well

as enhanced, by the increase in its height and its separation from residential sectors with the moat, as well as through gatherings and performances in which the representatives of various co-residential groups and factions would have participated.

After 4800 BC, another major shift occurred: the communal, inclusive ceremonies discontinued and a cemetery was founded on the tell. The small number of burials relative to the large population of Szeghalom-Kovácshalom—presumably only forty to seventy-five people were interred on the tell—implies that the graveyard was the resting place of select people with prominent social positions (Figure 3.18). Most likely, one or more kin groups at the large village earned privileged status, and were capable of monopolizing access to the mound to bury their dead. Currently, no information is available regarding the question of whether these statuses translated into actual authority over others in the village. However, if that occurred, resistance to social inequality and institutionalized power could have been one of the factors that led to the abandonment of the Szeghalom-Kovácshalom settlement complex, sometime after 4600 BC.

Figure 3.17. LiDAR image overlaid with the results of magnetometric prospection at the Late Neolithic settlement complex of Szeghalom-Kovácshalom, Hungary. Lighter colors mark higher and darker colors mark lower elevations. The dark grey and black linear features in the landscape are ancient paleochannels. The magnetic features in yellow indicate houses that surrounded the central tell. *Illustration by A. Gyucha and P. R. Duffy.*

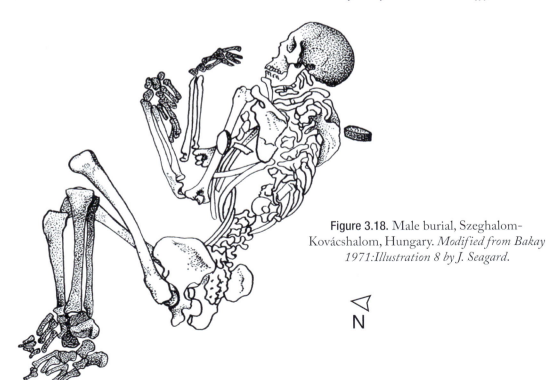

Figure 3.18. Male burial, Szeghalom-Kovácshalom, Hungary. *Modified from Bakay 1971:Illustration 8 by J. Seagard.*

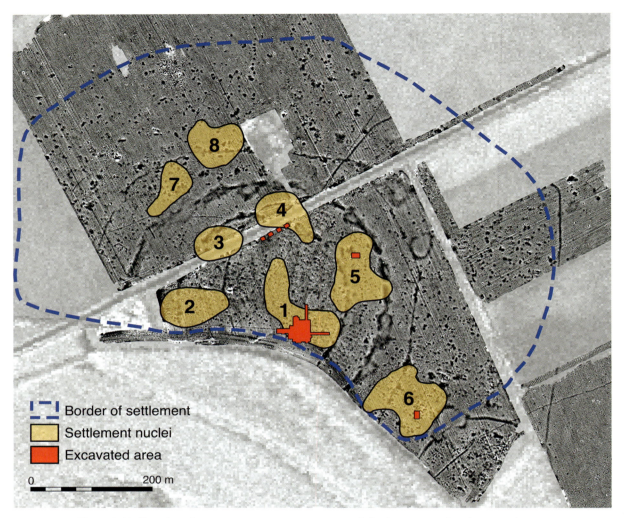

Figure 3.19. Results of magnetometric prospection and the locations of settlement clusters and excavation units at the Late Neolithic settlement complex of Öcsöd-Kováshalom, Hungary. Note the multiple, concentric ditches indicated by dark lines in the image. *Modified from Füzesi et al. 2020:Figure 10.4.1 by A. Füzesi and J. Seagard.*

Öcsöd-Kováshalom

The Late Neolithic village at Öcsöd-Kováshalom was the largest, central site of a cluster of eleven contemporaneous settlements that lined up along the confines of the floodplain of the Tisza and the Körös rivers (see Figure 3.6). The site has been explored since the early 1980s, using an array of archaeological field techniques, including stratigraphic coring, surface survey, excavation, and most recently, geophysical survey.[34]

At Öcsöd-Kováshalom, a tell-like mound was surrounded by seven additional clusters of houses separated by uninhabited areas. The entire site extended over an area of approximately 45.5 ha,[35] representing the permanent aggregation of small-scale, previously autonomous, dispersed village communities (Figure 3.19). Radiocarbon dates from the 130–160 cm thick stratigraphy of the central, tell-like mound indicate that the site was formed over the course of about two centuries, between 5200 and 4980 BC, during the transitional period from the Middle to the Late Neolithic on the Great Hungarian Plain.

A recent, large-scale magnetometer survey revealed a complex enclosure system of three large, concentric ditches surrounding the central mound.[36] The diameter of the outermost ditch exceeded 500 m. Some other features of this enclosure that are unusual at large Neolithic sites on the Great Hungarian Plain include regularly spaced gaps that interrupted the continuity of the ditch system as well as a series of small, round structures attached to the outer ditch.

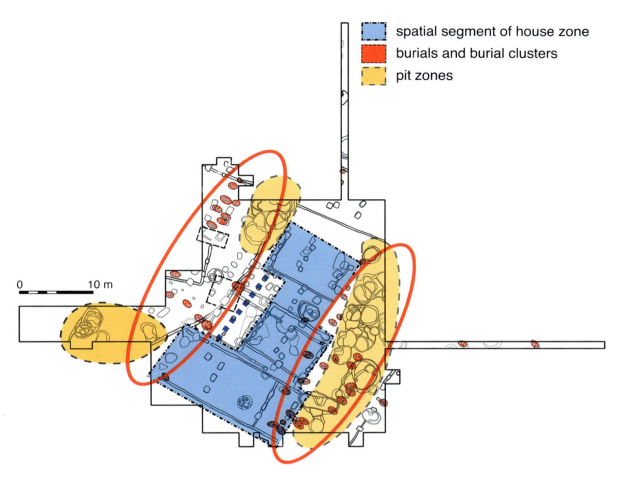

Figure 3.20. Map of the main excavated area at Öcsöd-Kováshalom showing the spatial segments of the house zone (blue), the pit zones (yellow), and the burial clusters (red). *Modified from Raczky et al. 2018:Figure 6 by A. Füzesi and J. Seagard.*

This enclosure can be classified as one of the so-called "pseudo-ditches" that are known from central and western Europe. These features were created through consecutive digging and backfilling of particular ditch sections. Thus the Öcsöd-Kováshalom enclosure represents major periodic labor investments that may have unfolded through the collective action of people, the number of which likely exceeded the number of inhabitants that lived in the aggregated village. It is possible that a significant proportion of the microregional population participated voluntarily in these earthworks to create, and recreate, a community monument in the context of the focal site of Öcsöd-Kováshalom.

Regarding the central tell-like mound at the Öcsöd-Kováshalom settlement complex, the excavated archaeological features indicate concentric activity zones. Pits and burials tethered to specific residential structures constituted spatial segments within the site (Figure 3.20). This suggests the co-occurrence of mundane and symbolic activities at the local scale that were performed within kin-based, extended household

units, and thus represent a site-specific intermeshed task-scape configuration.[37] Differences in wealth and social status cannot be identified among the household units on the central, tell-like mound.

The excavations on this mound brought to light the remains of four timber-framed houses with bedding trenches, dating to the earlier occupation period. During the later phase, a new settlement unit of six houses was established at the site. This major spatial reorganization would have required the cooperation of the several households that occupied the mound.

Burials, characterized by highly diverse symbolic treatments, were not physically separated from the domestic sphere at Öcsöd-Kováshalom. However, a unique trait of the tell-like mound's spatiality was that the majority of the forty-nine recovered burials were not directly related to individual buildings.

Instead, these graves were located in the northwestern and southeastern sections of the mound and were spatially associated with the larger-scale unit of residential structures (see Figure 3.20). This organization indicates that the deceased were considered as a kind of community of their own. The large number of human bones uncovered from refuse pits across the site suggests that the manipulation of the community of the dead was regularly practiced by the community of the living, including the selective replacement of the burials of specific individuals interred earlier and their replacement by other privileged individuals. Consequently, although information is unavailable regarding marked social inequalities among the occupants of the large Öcsöd-Kováshalom village, differences in status and prestige were expressed by the locational placement of the dead at the settlement complex.

Conclusions

Archaeological evidence for formalized social stratification and durable, institutionalized hereditary inequality is lacking from the Late Neolithic Great Hungarian Plain.[38] There are no exquisite burials and lavish tombs of chiefs, kings, or queens. The settlements have not provided evidence for class-based neighborhoods, and other structures associated with power and authority, such as palaces, granaries, and walled temples, also did not exist in the Neolithic.

However, the archaeological record clearly demonstrates a significant degree of variation in sociopolitical organization at Neolithic tell-centered settlement complexes. Thus the Late Neolithic aggregated communities did not follow one single model with respect to organizational principles and leadership structures. Deviations from egalitarian principles—including the emergence of hereditary rank—may have taken place. Nevertheless, the archaeological data indicate that if hereditary ranks were adopted within some communities, they did not last for many generations.

Within the context of these Neolithic farming societies, tells provided important social arenas where various groups and individuals could negotiate and demonstrate their differences and express their inequalities. Resistance to these emerging social inequalities may have been one of the reasons why almost all the nucleated tell sites on the Great Hungarian Plain were abandoned after several hundreds of years of occupation during the middle of the fifth millennium BC. The establishment, and particularly the long-lasting maintenance, of institutionalized social inequalities and formal hierarchies is a difficult process,[39] and the archaeological, historical, and ethnographic record from all around the world testifies to the application of an array of measures to prevent them from developing—fissioning is one of these measures.[40]

Despite the fact that the tell mounds offered ideal locations for habitation in the flat and frequently inundated landscapes on the Great Hungarian Plain, most of them remained unoccupied for thousands of years after they were abandoned at the end of the Neolithic period. The fact that the majority of these prominent sites were actively avoided throughout the Copper Age suggests that their symbolic importance persisted for many generations to come. Some tell sites eventually were used for burials. The cemeteries that sometimes were established on top of tells in subsequent periods indicate that some groups may have used these symbolically charged sites to claim a higher social status.[41] About two thousand years later, when tells once again were (re-)established on top of the abandoned Neolithic tells, these meanings had been forgotten as the sites assumed important new roles in the more hierarchical communities of the Bronze Age. Interestingly, several of these tell sites once again regained their symbolic significance as community landmarks, when monasteries and cemeteries commonly were established on them in historic times (see Figure 3.1).[42]

Notes

1   Instead of *tell*, the terms *magoula* and *toumba* are commonly used in Greece. For general discussion of tell development and function, see Chapman 1989; Horváth 2009; Kotsakis 1999.

2   Blanco-González and Kienlin 2020; Kienlin 2012; Kienlin 2015a; Rosenstock 2009.

3   Gogâltan 2003; Raczky 2015.

4   Cole 1970.

5   Hofmánová et al. 2016; Mathieson et al. 2018.

6   Tringham 2000.

7   Faragó 2017; Starnini et al. 2015.

8   Tálas and Raczky 1987.

9   Chapman 2012.

10 For example, Fernández-Götz 2018; Kelly and Brown 2014.

11 Nanoglou 2001.

12 Chapman 1989:39.

13 Brami et al. 2016; Raczky and Sebők 2014.

14 Borić 2015.

15 Bailey 2005; Hansen 2007.

16 Bailey 2000; Chapman 1991; Whittle 1996.

17 Drașovean 2007.

18 Arponen et al. 2016; Borić 1996; Horváth 1987; Müller 2012; Raczky and Anders 2008.

19 Feinman 2011; Johnson 1982; Müller 2015.

20 For examples, see Flannery and Marcus 2012.

21 A well-documented example is the Oraibi Split in Arizona at the beginning of the twentieth century: Whiteley 1988.

22 Colson and Gluckman 1951; Fox and Sather 2006; Longacre 1970.

23 Knauft 1993; Suttles 1990.

24 Fürer-Haimendorf 1969; Leach 1954.

25 For the early history of research at the site, see Raczky et al. 2007.

26 Bánffy and Bognár-Kutzián 2007.

27 For a detailed discussion about research at Polgár-Csőszhalom, see Mesterházy et al. 2019; Raczky and Anders 2008.

28 Raczky 2018; Raczky and Sebők 2014.

29 Anders and Nagy 2007.

30 Raczky and Anders 2010.

31 Raczky et al. 2011.

32 For a detailed summary of early research at Szeghalom-Kovácshalom, see Gyucha et al. 2019.

33 For details, see Gyucha et al. 2015; Gyucha et al. 2019; Parkinson et al. 2018.

34 For a summary of previous research at Öcsöd-Kováshalom, see Raczky and Füzesi 2016.

35 Füzesi et al. 2020.

36 For a detailed discussion, see Füzesi et al. 2020.

37 Raczky et al. 2018.

38 Porčić 2012; Porčić 2019; Siklósi 2013.

39 Earle 1997; Flannery and Marcus 2012.

40 Clastres 1987; Hansen and Müller 2017; Paynter and McGuire 1991; Sastre 2008.

41 Gyucha 2015.

42 The Late Neolithic Tell Project associated with investigations at Öcsöd-Kováshalom was funded by the National Cultural Fund of Hungary (NKA Grant K-135073). Funding for the research at Szeghalom-Kovácshalom came from the National Science Foundation (BCS-0911336, BCS-1012374, OISE-1030436, BCS-1122468, BCS-1325112) and the Wenner-Gren Foundation for Anthropological Research (ICRG).

CHAPTER 4

The Emergence of a New Elite in Southeast Europe

People and Ideas from the Steppe Region at the Turn of the Copper and Bronze Ages

János Dani, Bianca Preda-Bălănică, and János Angi

THE IDENTIFICATION AND recognition of the social elite within a past society has been a long-standing subject of debate in archaeology, especially regarding the early stages of prehistory.[1] This is impacted by the lack and limitation of archaeological and historical sources, such as the survival and the degree of fragmentation of the archaeological record and contexts, the scarcity of information about symbolic structures, social institutions, and cultural traditions, or the incomplete knowledge about other "contextualized meanings,"[2] and of course, the absence of written sources. However, the opinion of Anthony Harding, according to which "we can be reasonably sure that certain individuals, buried in elaborate tombs with numerous high-quality grave goods, were special enough to be called elite,"[3] seems entirely acceptable.

There can be several causes for the emergence of a social "elite:" ideological/religious, economic, or strategic/military (violence or 'naked force').[4] The first undeniable signs of social inequality are linked to the discovery and first widespread use of metals (that is, copper and gold) around the middle of the fifth millennium BC in east-central and southeastern Europe. At this time, richly furnished burials were in many cases parts of Copper Age communal cemeteries, and these graveyards expressed the importance of social cohesion and unity. This is the period, around 4300–4200 BC, when the first evidence for East European connections with steppe cultures and migrations can be identified in the Carpathian Basin (Figure 4.1).[5] At the same time, during this era, which is known as the time of the scepter-bearers (*Zepterträger*), symbolizing the growing power and high social status of exceptional individuals, some male burials were equipped with stone maces, zoomorphic scepters (Figure 4.2), and even swords, such as the composite one made from wood, bone, and flint from Giurgiuleşti in Moldova.[6]

In contrast to the Copper Age community-centered traditions, at the very end of the fourth millennium BC, a significant change can be observed with the widespread appearance of a new burial rite: burial mounds (tumuli or kurgans) expressing the individuality and, in certain cases, the greatness and power of the deceased (Figure 4.3).[7] The extensive distribution of these mounds in southeastern Europe is closely related to the westward movement of Yamnaya populations from the steppe region around 3100 BC (Figure 4.4).

Figure 4.1. Map showing the sites mentioned in the text. *Illustration by F. Paár and E. Rodriguez.*

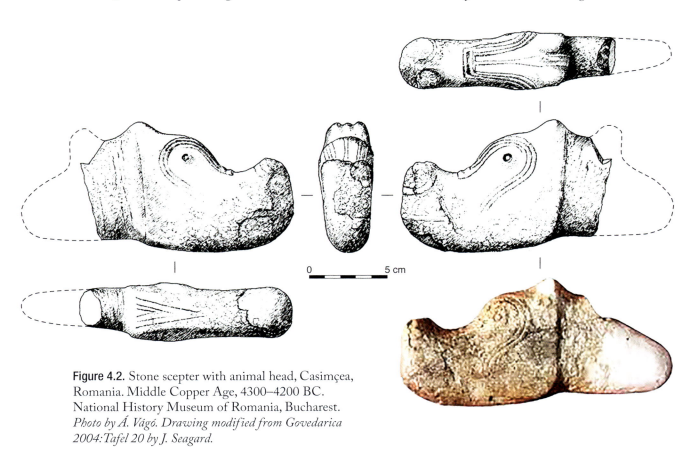

Figure 4.2. Stone scepter with animal head, Casimçea, Romania. Middle Copper Age, 4300–4200 BC. National History Museum of Romania, Bucharest. *Photo by Á. Vágó. Drawing modified from Govedarica 2004:Tafel 20 by J. Seagard.*

Figure 4.3. Prehistoric kurgan, Hajdúnánás-Fürj-halom, Hungary.
Photo by J. Dani.

The Migration of Prehistoric Mobile Pastoralist Populations into Central and Southeastern Europe

The power of migration and mobility as major triggers of cultural change is one of the most controversial and yet unsettled issues in prehistoric archaeology. The concept was either fully embraced earlier within the culture-historical paradigm or completely rejected later by the school of New Archaeology. On the one hand, in the culture-historical approach, archaeological cultures were equated with homogeneous groups of people sharing a circumscribed territory and specific material culture, and therefore change was seen as caused by influences from outside, through either the migration of people or the diffusion of ideas. On the other hand, proponents of the New Archaeology, or processual archaeology, focused more on internal dynamics of societies, hence indigenous developments were emphasized as the main cause of cultural change.[8] Due to methodological difficulties in identifying clear evidence for migration in the archaeological record, migration as an explanatory model for sociocultural transformations had been completely rejected for decades.[9] However, the migration of peoples from the east into the Carpathian Basin is a well-known and—through ancient and historical written sources—well-documented, recurrent process from at least the time of the Scythians (seventh to sixth centuries BC) to the time of the Cumans and Mongols (thirteenth century AD). Therefore migration as a major potential driver for sociocultural changes cannot be ignored.

During the past few decades, several scholars have engaged with migration as a social process and have tried to build a theoretical foundation for its study. In many cases, the "push" factors, or root causes, of large-scale migrations were perceived to have been related to some negative effects of climate change. This especially holds true when decrease in annual precipitation occurred, which would have influenced the quality and quantity of the pastures, and thus the amount of the livestock that was central to the subsistence strategy of pastoral societies. Other mechanisms that would have pushed communities to migrate include collapse in the local political system at the area of origin,[10] or a combination of both political collapse and climatic deterioration.

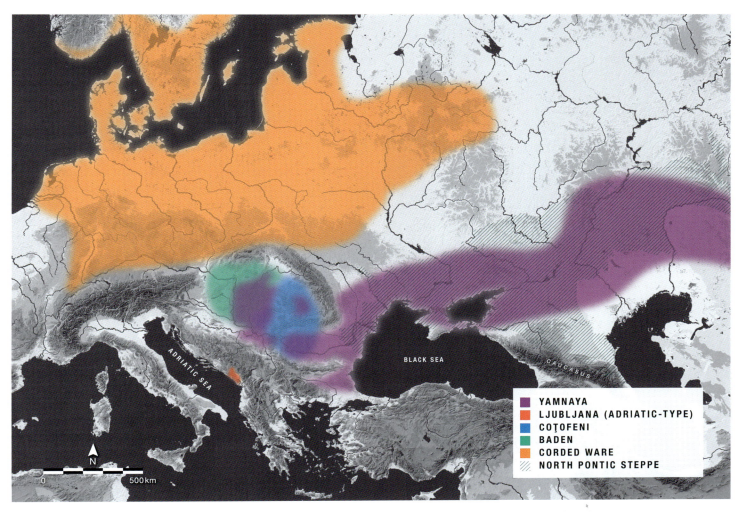

Figure 4.4. Map showing the distribution of Yamnaya around 3000 BC and other cultural units mentioned in the text. *Modified from Heyd 2013:Figure 30 by J. Dani and E. Rodriguez.*

Developments in the natural sciences have brought migration back into focus as one of the key factors that shaped prehistoric Europe, with consequences reaching as far as the genetic make-up of modern Europeans. Ancient DNA studies have identified a significant influx of steppe ancestry into central Europe during the first half of the third millennium BC, related to populations of steppe origins.[11] Furthermore, advances in stable isotope analyses have enabled researchers to investigate the lives of particular individuals, and these studies have revealed more complex patterns of mobility than previously thought.[12] Some researchers recently have focused on the role played by this migration in the transmission of pathogens, like *Yersinia pestis*, that could have caused a plague pandemic; however, this is a matter of ongoing debate.[13]

This overall picture becomes even more complicated when the movement of Yamnaya populations is connected not only with changes in material culture, economy, or ideology but also with the spread of new languages, namely Indo-European languages, which are widely spoken throughout present-day Europe. However, the connection between the Yamnaya migration and the spread of Indo-European languages is highly debated, and some scholars consider it a hypothesis that still needs to be substantiated.[14] Thus one of the most challenging endeavors of current research is disentangling the different long-term and deep processes through which material culture, genetic ancestry, and languages spread.[15] Conversely, so is identifying evidence of their possible conjunction during the first half of the third millennium BC, especially given what is at stake—a better understanding of the identity of modern Europeans.[16] This is perhaps the reason why so far professional discourse has been dominated by grand narratives of events with continental-scale impacts, which, in turn, gave rise to criticisms by scholars who stress the danger of simplistic scenarios and argue for more bottom-up approaches.[17]

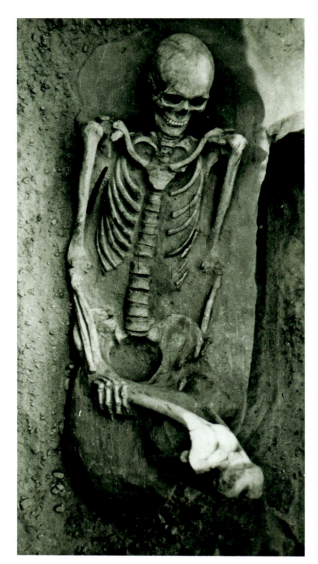

Figure 4.5. Burial, Grave 1, Csongrád-Kettőshalom, Hungary. Middle Copper Age, 4300–4200 BC.
Photo by K.B. Nagy. Courtesy of Gy. Pálfi.

Individuality is the New Way: The Man, The Warrior, The Herder, and The Other

The Man

Over the course of the migration of the Yamnaya populations, individuals with steppe origins reached the Carpathian Basin. However, this was not the first time such an event had occurred. Archaeological and bioarchaeological information suggests there was an earlier movement of people from the east, during the second half of the fifth millennium BC.[18] The best example is an individual recovered from Csongrád-Kettőshalom in Hungary (Figure 4.5). The man's body was sprinkled with red ocher, and grave goods included an obsidian blade as well as limestone, copper, and *Spondylus* shell beads. Zsuzsanna K. Zoffmann and Antónia Marcsik analyzed the osteological remains of this individual as well as those found in Yamnaya burials (Figure 4.6), and they described their significance as newcomers in the Carpathian Basin, also delineating skeletal morphological dissimilarities from the local, autochthonous population.[19] These results have been reinforced by the most recent aDNA studies.[20] However, extensive bioarchaeological studies of the Yamnaya burials have not been conducted in their westernmost distribution area, and thus important aspects, such as similarities and differences in the mortuary treatment of men and women in kurgans, cannot be discussed.

A common view about Yamnaya populations is that the funerary arena was dominated by men and that they were the main beneficiaries of these rituals, while

Figure 4.6. The first photo-documented kurgan excavation in southeastern Europe in 1910, Sárrétudvari-Balázshalom, Hungary. *Photo: Déri Museum, Debrecen.*

Figure 4.7. Kurgan excavation, Medisova humka, Žabalj, Serbia. *Photo by P. Włodarczak. Courtesy of P. Włodarczak and the "Danubian Route of Yamnaya Culture" project funded by the National Science Center, Poland.*

the presence of women in burial mounds was only secondary. This hypothesis is not sufficiently supported, and data from across southeastern Europe provide interesting patterns. In Bulgaria, the sex ratio seems to be quite balanced.[21] In Romania, however, the published literature suggests that male burials were more frequent.[22] This also seems to have been the case in the kurgans of Serbia, even though the sample there is quite small (Figures 4.7 and 4.8).[23] More precise information comes again from Hungary, where Zsuzsanna K. Zoffmann collected information from forty-three individuals from the Carpathian Basin;[24] here, the ratio of males to females among the graves is 19:9. Thus it appears that men were buried under kurgans more than twice as frequently as women, at least in the Carpathian Basin. For the moment, information about the genetic relationship of the Yamnaya population with one particular region or microregion is missing. At the same time, the male dominance and patrilocality of the descendant Corded Ware societies from northwestern Europe is not only suggested by new aDNA results[25] but is also supported by the computer-aided analyses of burial practices and grave goods.[26] Based on these results, it is not unreasonable to assume patrilineal descent and a male-focused worldview in the westernmost Yamnaya communities.

As mentioned earlier, the introduction of the new eastern European burial rite, the construction of burial mounds, placed the focus on individuality, as opposed to the cemetery-based traditions of the preceding period, which emphasized the importance of community. Between about 3100 and 2600 BC, not just the core area of the Yamnaya Culture, the northern Pontic–Caspian steppe region, but also its westernmost

Figure 4.8. Central burial, Medisova humka, Žabalj, Serbia. Early Bronze Age, 2800–2600 BC. *Photo by P. Włodarczak. Courtesy of P. Włodarczak and the "Danubian Route of Yamnaya Culture" project funded by the National Science Center, Poland.*

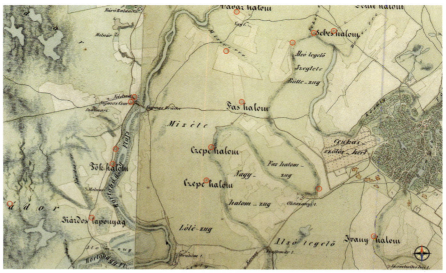

Figure 4.9. Map from the nineteenth century with rows of kurgans ('halom') along paleochannels, vicinity of Nádudvar, Hungary. *Illustration by J. Dani.*

Figure 4.10. Graphical reconstruction of the central kurgan burial, Medisova humka, Žabalj, Serbia. *Illustration by M. Podsiadło. Courtesy of P. Włodarczak and the "Danubian Route of Yamnaya Culture" project funded by the National Science Center, Poland.*

distribution, the Great Hungarian Plain, were dotted with thousands of mounds (Figure 4.9). The large kurgans served not only as burial places but also as monuments of power and remembrance. In addition, they were also a new type of sacrificial or sacred places. It is not by chance that kurgans were built, in many cases, in special, previously used or respected, places, creating in this way a complex social landscape.

In kurgans, the first grave was dug into the ancient ground surface, then the mound was built on top of it. Over time, additional graves often were placed into the mound, and sometimes these later interments were followed by adding another soil layer on top of the kurgan to enlarge it. It is common to find traces of fire or small hearths either on the ancient surface or between the different layers of the mound—these are indicators of ritual activities performed during these different stages. The dead were placed in rectangular or sometimes oval pits, usually on their backs and with their knees flexed, more rarely crouched on the side, oriented with the head toward the west (Figure 4.10). The arrangement of the funerary structure was complex, and it consisted of internal steps leading to the burial chamber that was covered with wooden beams and textile mats. The bottom and the walls of the pit were given special attention, and probably were covered with mats, hides or furs, cushions, and even pillows.[27] Ocher was sprinkled on the pit bottom, on the deceased, especially around the head, or small lumps were placed near the body.[28] The number of grave goods is low, and this seems to be another general characteristic of the burial rite. When artifacts are present, they typically consist of ornaments made of precious metals, or bone and pottery. However, some outstanding burials suggest the emergence of a new elite strongly linked to interregional networks.

Figure 4.11. Copper hammer-axe and dagger, Sárrétudvari-Őrhalom, Hungary. Early Bronze Age, 2800–2500 BC. Déri Museum, Debrecen. *Photo by I. Czinegéné Kiss.*

The Warrior

Prior to the Yamnaya expansion, during the Late Copper Age Baden period, wealth and prestige was reflected by animal (mainly cattle) depositions and sacrifices in burials.[29] The rise of a new elite was indicated not only by alterations in previous social traditions (such as new burial rites, changes in the belief system) but also by the introduction of new prestige goods. New types of jewelry and weapons as well as the monumental burial architecture of kurgans, sometimes with stone sculptures (stelae), became the new media of prestige. All these ideas arrived in the late fourth millennium BC, and became predominant with the Yamnaya people, then spread quickly throughout Europe, fostering the emergence of elites participating in interregional interactions. Accidental finds and the richest male burials illustrate that new personal weaponry, including willow-leaf-shaped daggers, shaft-hole axes, and hammer-axes made of precious metals or copper, served as symbols of power and warriorhood (Figure 4.11). At the same time, unique grave assemblages—maybe the most sophisticated example comes from Gruda Boljevića in Montenegro—furnished with similar hammer-axes but made of stone also appeared (Figure 4.12). Some locally manufactured, carefully crafted stone axes—for example, axes from Dad in Hungary and from Băleni in Romania (Figure 4.13)—signify that the elite of indigenous communities sometimes adopted the status symbols of the Yamnaya herders. These artifacts are close in shape to the battle-axes recovered from male Corded Ware burials in northern Europe, which are stone axes crafted with a hole for hafting and have been interpreted as designed specifically for combat purposes. This points to the extent of emerging interregional networks through which objects and ideas were distributed and transformed across the continent during this period.

Besides weapons, individuals were also buried with special ornaments. Some might have been spectacular necklaces made from the teeth of wild animals, such as the one made from wild boar tusks and teeth in the burial of the Gabrova tumulus near Kamen in Bulgaria (Figure 4.14). Hair rings were also an important artifact class. The spiral type of hair rings has a longer history; they had already reached the Lower Danube during the last third of the fourth millennium BC as an innovation brought along by earlier, pre-Yamnaya, steppe interactions. At that point, they were simple items made of silver wire and were placed in both

Figure 4.12. Polished stone axe with gold shaft-hole cap, Gruda Boljevića, Montenegro. Early Bronze Age, 3100–3000 BC. Museums and Galleries of Podgorica. *Photo by Á. Vágó.*

Figure 4.13. Polished stone battle-axe, Băleni, Romania. Early Bronze Age, 3000–2600 BC. "The Royal Court" National Museum Complex, Târgoviște. *Modified from Ilie et al. 2010:Plate 6 by J. Seagard.*

0   5 cm

Figure 4.14. Necklace made from boar teeth and tusks, Gabrova, Kamen, Bulgaria. Early Bronze Age, 3200–3000 BC. National Archaeological Institute with Museum, Sofia. *Photo by K. Georgiev. Courtesy of St. Alexandrov.*

male and female burials.[30] During the first half of the third millennium BC, these spiral hair rings occurred in various regions of Europe, and became associated especially with male burials. More massive items were also manufactured from gold or silver (Figure 4.15). In this period, new ring types were also produced. They include the Leukas type, with a rhomboid cross-section, drop-shaped form, and pointed ends, the Mala Gruda hair rings, similar in shape but with only one pointed end and the other one conical, found in

lavishly furnished graves,[31] and the crescent Zimnicea hair rings, with an oval cross-section, recovered from both flat cemeteries and kurgans. Their occurrence in elite burials over broad areas, as is the case of the Leukas type, suggests actively maintained interregional networks through which ideas, knowledge, and exotic items were circulated, and values were shared among the elites of various areas, including the Aegean, the Balkans, and the Carpathian Basin.[32] The slightly different ways in which these rings were used, either as parts of sophisticated hair ornaments or as earrings, may have been adapted to conform to local norms and fashion rules.[33] Massive hair rings, along with

Figure 4.15. Silver necklace and gold spiral hair rings, Grave 5, Chernyova, Troyanovo, Bulgaria. Early Bronze Age, 2700–2500 BC. National Archaeological Institute with Museum, Sofia. *Photo by K. Georgiev. Courtesy of St. Alexandrov.*

hemispherical discs made of precious metals that likely served as dress ornaments (for example, at the Dusnok-Garáb mound in Hungary[34]), commonly are found in association with prestige weapons in the graves, symbolizing the warrior's prestige and beauty in both life and death.[35] This may be the starting point of the "new understanding of personhood—specifically male self-identity—rooted in both social practices and cultural representations" that Paul Treherne noted in his analysis of the "warrior's beauty."[36]

The Herder

The Yamnaya populations are known only from their burials, as their settlements are invisible in the archaeological record. Not a single Yamnaya settlement site has been identified in the western area of Yamnaya distribution, and only a handful are known from the area of their origin, such as the third horizon of the multi-layered settlement from Mikhaylovka in Russia.[37] Most researchers presume that they pursued a mobile way of life, wandering deep into the steppes, searching for rich pastures and setting up mobile wagon camps that left no archaeological traces. This high degree of mobility was related to key innovations in transportation, in particular the wheel and the wagon, that were already present in the late fourth millennium BC.[38] Evidence for their use is quite solid in the

North Pontic region, where Yamnaya burials containing wooden wheels and other wagon parts have been found.[39] In the western distribution area, similar data are much more scarce, but the findings from Plachidol in Bulgaria give us some insight about the significance and importance of wheeled transportation in this region as well (Figure 4.16).[40]

The relationship between Yamnaya mobility, migration, and horse domestication is a matter of ongoing debate. Although recent research results on the ancient horse genome, as well as on the origins and spread of domesticated horses generally, question the role of horses in Yamnaya mobility, other analyses suggest that they may have played an important role in the expansion of nomadic communities from the steppe.[41]

Comparing the environmental conditions of the Great Hungarian Plain, which is the westernmost part of the vast Eurasian steppe belt, with the North Pontic steppe zone, the former is more diverse and has many mosaic-like, varied habitats. It is important to distinguish the various territories of the Great Hungarian Plain: many areas were not suitable for permanent settlements and agricultural activity but could have been

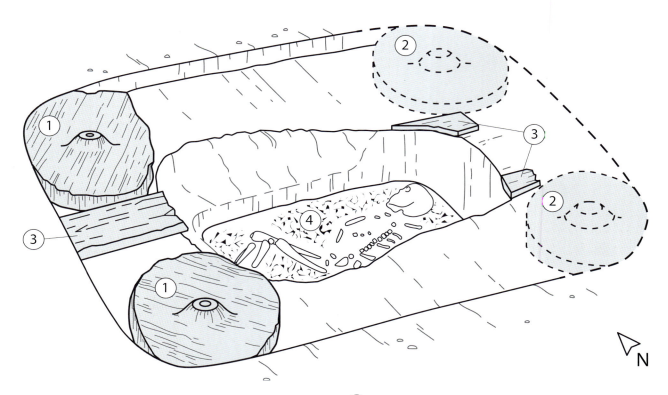

Figure 4.16. Reconstruction of a kurgan burial with wooden wheels of a wagon, Plachidol, Bulgaria. Early Bronze Age, 2900–2600 BC. *Modified from Panayotov 1989: Figure 64 by J. Seagard.*

1. wooden wheels found
2. wooden wheels conjectured
3. planks covering the burial pit
4. remains of organic material (felt?) covering the body

used for nomadic, or semi-nomadic, stock-raising. This is the case today, for example, in the Hortobágy region in eastern Hungary. Climatic and ecological conditions in the steppe region were arid enough to provide an ideal environment for the mobile pre-Yamnaya and Yamnaya herders, but they would not have been favorable for more sedentary, agricultural communities. Kurgans in the Carpathian Basin are located in at least three different geographical zones suitable for three or more subsistence strategies: 1) river valleys and lowlands, which were wet in certain periods of the year; 2) highlands, which were surrounded by mountains, for example the inner territory of Transylvania;[42] and 3) the foothill zones. With regard to the Pontic, Caspian, and Kazakhian steppe regions, the management of livestock itself could have resulted in various, extensive or intensive, economic trajectories.

In addition, the mobile communities also had other ways to supplement their subsistence, including, in some cases, different forms of plant gathering.[43]

As a result of stable isotope and phytolith studies in the Pontic–Caspian steppe region, we now are able to describe the paleodiet of the Yamnaya populations as diverse with high adaptive potential. Their diet was adapted to the local climate (degree of aridity and yearly precipitation), the local paleoenvironment (exploitation of local food resources, such as wild animals and plants), and most typically the local economy (domesticated animals). The data indicate that the Yamnaya people consumed a mixed, protein-rich diet, consisting of the milk and meat of herbivores, local plants, and a certain amount of aquatic resources in territories close to rivers.[44]

The Other

Even though low grasslands were most likely the areas targeted by these populations, they could have been attracted to different areas for specific reasons as well. Recent studies highlighted this trend for present-day

Slovakia, where copper, gold, and silver sources are located in the central Slovakian Carpathian Mountains.[45] The Yamnaya presence in this area is supported by steppe elements in the local Baden cultural milieu, as indicated by the pottery found in Košice-Barca that shows cord decoration and has good analogies in the northwestern Pontic region.[46] The spread of Yamnaya populations into the Slovakian mountains has been validated by recent lead-isotope analysis of the copper weapons unearthed from Sárrétudvari-Őrhalom in eastern Hungary: the raw material for these items came from the territory of modern Slovakia (see Figure 4.11).[47] This also suggests the development of a new interregional network system that differed from that of the previous period.

Nevertheless, the precise nature of the relationships between the steppic newcomers and the indigenous communities remains poorly understood. Firstly, the cultural impact and the human impact should not be perceived as the same thing, meaning that burial customs and prestige objects might have spread among local communities through other processes, such as diffusion, and not necessarily through the arrival of large groups of people.[48] This is well illustrated by the pre-Yamnaya chronological horizon when burial practices and prestige objects of steppe origins occurred north and south of the Lower Danube; however, they were unrelated to significant population movements.[49] Secondly, when it comes to the actual forms of interactions, different scenarios have been proposed, ranging from neutrality to exchange or assimilation and even violence.[50] The latter image of violent groups of young men wandering through Europe and decimating local populations gained popularity in recent years, as seen in several scholarly papers[51] and sensational titles in popular science publications. For example, in March 2019, *New Scientist* published the following headline: "Story of the most murderous people of all time revealed in ancient DNA."[52] However, no bioarchaeological studies published so far testify to a particularly violent lifestyle for the Yamnaya. The mechanisms of five hundred years of interaction need to be assessed in their full demographic, chronological, and geographical complexity. For instance, an interesting region in this respect is southern Bulgaria, where Yamnaya tumuli take a particular form in terms of burial ritual and grave goods as a consequence of interactions with local communities.[53] Bottom-up studies from various areas could provide very different pictures of the Yamnaya social organization and interactions with the autochthonous populations.

Changes in Material Culture: Forging New Identities with Clay, Metal, and Stone

The profound changes that took place at the beginning of the third millennium BC become even more apparent when looking at how pottery, metal, or stone objects occurred in different archaeological contexts, how they were adopted, and how their meanings were transformed as they were used to fulfill different functions.

Among the sparse finds from Yamnaya burials, ceramic materials are one of the most underrepresented artifact types in the Carpathian Basin. As opposed to the elaborate and rich ceramic assemblages of the preceding Late Copper Age Baden and Coțofeni cultures, only a few 'local' ceramic forms are known from Yamnaya contexts. On the one hand, many kurgans in Hungary, Romania, Serbia, and Bulgaria were built over earlier Late Copper Age sites, including settlements and cemeteries. Other burial mounds incorporated sherds of Late Copper Age cultures. Finally, in some cases, Late Copper Age pottery came to light from Yamnaya graves, which can suggest synchronism and special kinds of relationships, possibly including co-residence, between autochthonous and incoming populations.[54]

The decorated pedestalled bowls, ornamented inside and/or outside with cord impressions or incised motifs, such as the one from Grivița, Romania (Figure 4.17), are some of the most interesting finds of the Yamnaya and the succeeding Catacomb cultures. These ceramics are called 'censers' (referring to their function) in the North Pontic–Caspian Yamnaya territories, and they were distributed in the North Caucasus as well.[55] Beyond the censers of steppic pastoralist tribes, these decorated pedestalled bowls are frequent artifacts in the Southeast European Late Copper Age and Early Bronze Age.[56] Some of them are richly decorated with incised and incrusted geometric motifs and served as grave deposits in lavishly furnished tumulus burials, attesting to their ritual functions. At first glance, it seems obvious to link the Southeast European and the steppe pedestalled bowls, but beyond their formal similarity, the exact relationship between the two artifact groups has not yet been fully clarified.[57] In addition to pedestalled bowls, cord-decorated beakers were relatively common in the ceramic inventories of the Yamnaya kurgan burials.[58]

Figure 4.17. Ceramic vessel, Grivița, Romania. Early Bronze Age, 2700–2500 BC. Paul Păltănea History Museum, Galați. *Courtesy of A. Frînculeasa. Modified by J. Seagard.*

Biconical or bellied amphorae with suspension handles also are found occasionally in the kurgans of the Carpathian Basin, such as in Graves 4 and 7 at Sárrétudvari-Őrhalom, indicating direct contacts to the east, with Transcarpathia and the Budzhak region in Moldova and Ukraine.[59] In addition, sets of unique vessels from the Adriatic tumuli, such as funnels, highly decorated plates and jars, reflect individual needs and the status of the local ruling elite, of which Gruda Boljević a is only one example (Figure 4.18).[60] These extremely rich 'princely burials' with outstanding grave goods from Montenegro are classified—mainly on the ground of the types of and the special ornamentation technique applied on burial vessels—as a local variant: the (South) Adriatic type of the Ljubljana Culture.[61]

In contrast, when looking at the metal items of the era, an opposite trend can be noticed. Whereas only a few metal objects have been recovered from Baden sites,[62] the arrival of the East European Yamnaya coincided with a significant intensification in metallurgical activities in the Carpathian Basin. The newcomers brought not just new types of metal objects, such as weapons and jewelry, but in addition to gold and copper, other metals (such as electrum, silver, and sometimes exotic gold-silver-copper alloys) were also introduced.[63]

A spectacular development also occurred in metallurgical technology: craft specialists began to use multi-part molds for casting shaft-hole axes (Figure 4.19). Although, in the beginning, the raw material was pure copper, later the craftsmen used arsenic copper and other alloys to produce tools and weapons of higher quality.[64] The emergence of new weapon types, including daggers, shaft-hole axes, and slender hammer-axes, was not only the result of a new ideological background but also a consequence of individual needs required by a mobile way of life (for example, the protection of livestock, multi-functionality, ease of use). In the case of axes, the formal design and the selection of raw materials were determined by functional considerations. For example, shaft-hole axes made of precious metals serving as symbols of power, as 'royal scepters' (like a silver shaft-hole axe from Mala Gruda in Montenegro), were not only much smaller and slimmer but were also much more sophisticated than an average axe manufactured for everyday activities or combat. Differences in the contexts in which these axes are found also support this notion. Massive copper shaft-hole axes are absent from kurgans, and usually occur in hoards or as single depositions.[65] One of the most important hoards of the period was recovered at Vâlcele/Bányabükk in Romania, containing dozens of shaft-hole axes (Figure 4.20).[66]

The importance of metal objects and the artisans producing them is also illustrated by the appearance of a new category of burials that contain grave goods designed for specific activities, such as tools, raw materials, and semi-finished or finished products. These objects are interpreted as the expression of the role of the deceased as craftsmen, metalworkers (metal founders and smiths) in particular, during their life.[67] Some of the earliest examples of these burials have been recovered from Yamnaya kurgans, and they became more common during the subsequent

Figure 4.18. Burial assemblage, Gruda Boljevića, Montenegro. Early Bronze Age, 3100–3000 BC. Museums and Galleries of Podgorica. *Photo by Á. Vágó.*

Figure 4.19. Ceramic casting molds for shaft-hole axes and flat chisels, Üllő, Hungary. Early Bronze Age, 2400–2200 BC. Ferenczy Museum Center, Szentendre. *Photo by L. Szászváry. Courtesy of R. Patay.*

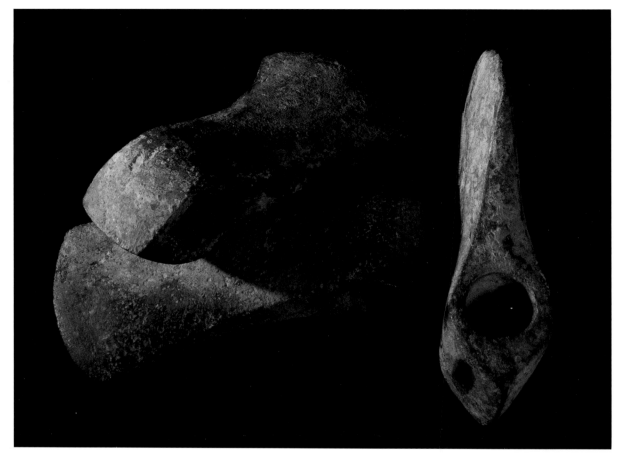

Figure 4.20. Copper shaft-hole axes, Vâlcele/Bányabükk, Romania. Transition from the Late Copper Age to the Early Bronze Age, 3000–2600 BC. Márton Roska Collection, University of Debrecen. *Photo by I. Czinegéné Kiss. Courtesy of P. Forisek.*

Catacomb period.[68] Even though this tradition has not been identified in the westernmost distribution area of the Yamnaya burials, the transmission of the idea is signified by some later graves in central and western Europe dating to the third millennium BC.[69] A possible interpretation of these burials suggests itinerant metalworkers in the beginning and permanent metallurgical workshops established later.[70]

In addition to new weapon types, Yamnaya people also used metal and bone discs, hair rings of various types, and, albeit rarely, necklaces consisting of biconical or tubular beads made of precious metals, like gold, electrum, and silver.[71] One of the best examples for the unique combinations of different jewelry types was found in the Chernyova tumulus at Troyanovo in Bulgaria (see Figure 4.15). Some of the new personal adornments appeared as a result of the development of new local production centers that employed advanced, innovative techniques.[72] Excavations of several Yamnaya burials in Chernyova yielded multiple massive hair rings crafted in two different ways: solid pieces made by casting or by plating a copper wire with a silver sheet or, in exceptional cases, by plating a silver wire with a gold sheet.[73] New types with subtle differences were also introduced, as mentioned above, and their differential geographic distributions probably were related to distinct regional production centers.[74]

Anthropomorphic stone stelae were also produced during this period. Their occurrence in southeastern Europe is related to the arrival of the Yamnaya populations, as many of them are similar to those found in Ukraine and Moldova. The two major types include aniconic stelae, which are less subtle and considered earlier, and anthropomorphic stelae, which are more elaborate and considered later.[75] Aniconic objects have been unearthed in Hungary and Slovakia, and in many cases, they marked Late Copper Age Baden cemeteries.[76] The anthropomorphic ones display body parts, clothing, and accessories, as well as sometimes tools and weapons, such as axes and daggers. In the

Figure 4.21. Stone stele with a warrior in full attire and shaft-hole axes,
Baia Hamangia, Romania. Transition from the Late Copper Age to the Early Bronze Age,
3000–2600 BC. Histria Museum Complex. *Photo by S. Ailincăi.*

eastern European steppe, stone stelae have usually
been found in association with kurgans. North of
the Lower Danube, an anthropomorphic stone stele
was found in secondary context near a burial mound
at Baia Hamangia in Dobruja (Figure 4.21). Other
examples from Transylvania, however, typically are
stray finds.[77] A similar pattern can be recognized south
of the Danube, in the northeastern part of Bulgaria,
where several stone stelae have been recovered. Five
stelae were found in kurgans at the above-mentioned
Plachidol cemetery, however not in spatial association
with specific burials.[78] An additional four stelae were
discovered in Ezerovo as chance finds, and another
one from Nevsha was placed near a cemetery dating to
the Bronze Age.[79]

Epilogue

The Yamnaya migration had a significant impact on
the development of European prehistory between
3100 and 2600 BC. The preceding, continuous development from the dawn of the Neolithic to the Copper
Age/Eneolithic period changed radically,[80] bringing
fundamental alterations in the genetic and cultural
make-up of the continent. The result, as we can see
in the next chapters, was the emergence of a colorful
world during the Bronze Age, from the Caucasus to
Iberia and from Scandinavia to Italy.

Notes

1   B. Preda-Bălănică wrote her contribution to this paper with the support of the ERC Advanced Project 788616, entitled The Yamnaya Impact on Prehistoric Europe (YMPACT).

2   Kristiansen 2001.

3   Harding 2015:117–18.

4   Earle 1997.

5   Gogâltan 2011; Govedarica 2004.

6   Govedarica 2016a; Govedarica and Kaiser 1996; Harțuche 2005.

7   However, it is important to note that the construction of large earthen tumuli began in the Middle Eneolithic period (Lower Mykhailivka, Kvitiana, Post-Stog cultural traditions), from the first half of the fourth millennium BC (Rassamakin 2011).

8   Burmeister 2017; Hakenbeck 2008.

9   For a more detailed analysis regarding the changing and challenging history of migration versus autochthonous development in archaeological theory, see Anthony 1990.

10   Anthony 1990; Kaiser 2016; Prien 2005.

11   Allentoft et al. 2015; Haak et al. 2015.

12   Gerling et al. 2012.

13   Rascovan et al. 2019; Rasmussen et al. 2015.

14   Klejn 2017.

15   Anthony 2020.

16   This can be seen in the worldwide interest in this topic. For example, in August 2019, *National Geographic* published an article entitled "Who were the first Europeans?" addressing in part the Yamnaya migration.

17   Furholt 2019.

18   Marcsik 1974; Zoffmann 2000.

19   Marcsik 1979; Zoffmann 1978; Zoffmann 2006; Zoffmann 2011.

20   Allentoft et al. 2015; Haak et al. 2015; Olalde et al. 2018.

21   Kaiser and Winger 2015:125.

22   Frînculeasa et al. 2017:231–32.

23   Koledin et al. 2020.

24   Zoffmann 2011:Tab. 3.

25   Goldberg et al. 2017.

26   Bourgeois and Kroon 2017.

27   Heyd 2011.

28   Frînculeasa et al. 2015:83; Kaiser and Winger 2015:117.

29   György 2013; Horváth 2019.

30   Frînculeasa et al. 2015.

31   Vasileva 2017.

32   Vasileva 2017.

33   Vasileva 2017.

34   Dani et al. forthcoming.

35   Treherne 1995:120–30.

36   Treherne 1995:106.

37   Anthony 2007:320.

38   Horváth 2015.

39   Kaiser and Winger 2015:118, 134–35.

40   Frînculeasa et al. 2015:53.

41   Fages et al. 2019; Gaunitz et al. 2018; Librado et al. 2021; Wilkin et al. 2021.

42   Ferenczy 1997.

43   Kaiser 2010; Kaiser 2016; Kaiser 2017; Shishlina 2008; Shishlina 2013; Shishlina et al. 2009; Shishlina et al. 2012.

44   Shishlina 2008; Shishlina et al. 2009; Shishlina et al. 2012.

45   Bátora 2016.

46   Bátora 2016.

47   Dani et al. forthcoming.

48   Burmeister 2016:42.

49   Frînculeasa et al. 2015.

50   Bátora 2016; Heyd 2011:545; Kaiser and Winger 2015:133.

51   Kristiansen et al. 2017.

52   Barras 2019.

53   Kaiser and Winger 2015.

54   Frînculeasa et al. 2015:75–78, Fig. 11; Kaiser and Winger 2015:132–34, 136.

55   Kaiser 2019:245–53, Abb. 135.

56   Kaiser 2019:253–57; Kulcsár 2009:121–41, 308–19.

57   Kaiser 2019:255–57.

58   Frînculeasa et al. 2015:67, Fig. 13.

59   Ivanova 2013.

60   Govedarica 2018.

61 Baković and Govedarica 2010.

62 Bondár 2019.

63 Dani et al. forthcoming.

64 Dani 2013.

65 Hansen 2011:143.

66 Roska 1933; Roska 1959.

67 Bátora 2002.

68 Bátora 2002; Dani 2013.

69 Bátora 2002; Dani 2013.

70 Dani 2013.

71 Dani and Szeverényi 2021.

72 Dani 2013.

73 Frînculeasa et al. 2015.

74 Vasileva 2017.

75 Telegin and Mallory 1994.

76 Endrődi 1995; György 2014:152, 195–97; Horváth 2006:97.

77 Rişcuţa 2001:141.

78 Kaiser and Winger 2015:135.

79 Kaiser and Winger 2015:135.

80 Anthony and Chi 2010.

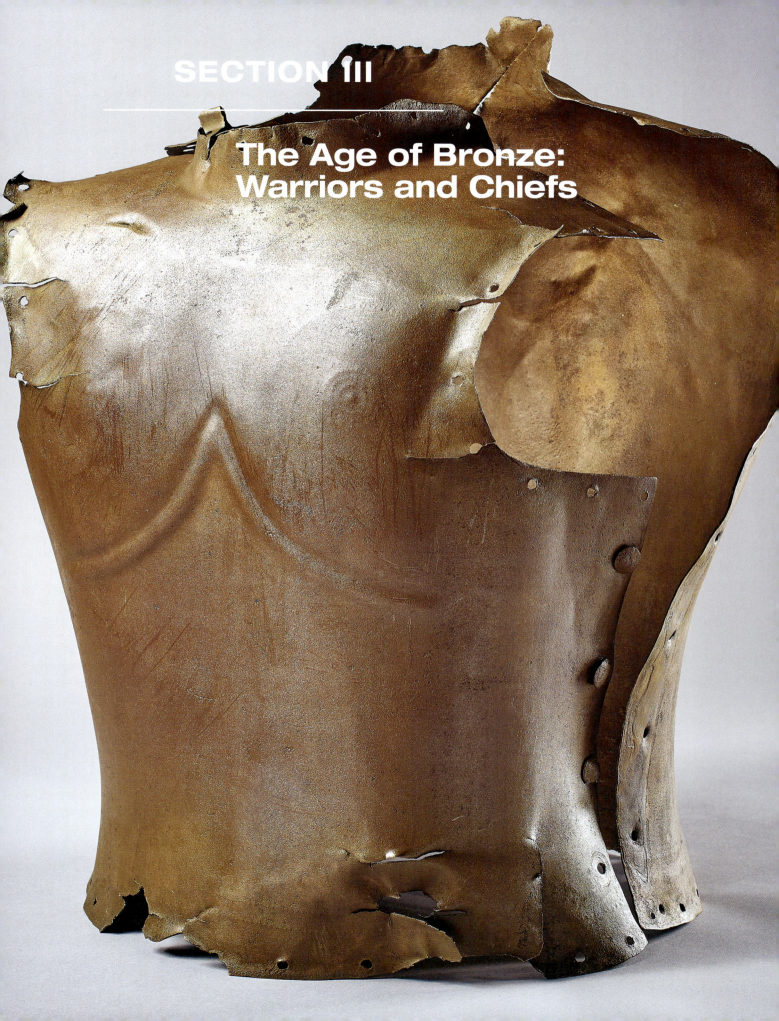

The Age of Bronze:
Warriors and Chiefs

CHAPTER 5

Treasures of the Warlords, Bronze Smiths, and Farmers of the Late Bronze Age

Hoard Deposition in Hungary and Transylvania

Gábor V. Szabó and Botond Rezi

ONE OF THE MOST typical assemblage types of the European Bronze Age is represented by hoards containing a rich, diverse array of bronze and gold artifacts that were deposited and concealed in the ground, in the dark caverns of caves, in the depths of bogs, cast into the waters of rivers and lakes, or carefully hidden in settlements. At least twelve thousand metal hoards of this type are known from the vast territory extending from the British Isles to the Caucasus, and countless more still lie hidden in the ground in numbers we cannot even hope to estimate.

Compared to other regions of Europe, an outstandingly high number of bronze hoards dating from the 400-year-long period of the Late Bronze Age, from the fourteenth to the tenth centuries BC, have come to light in the Carpathian Basin—over five hundred such assemblages are known from Hungary,[1] while some three hundred are from Transylvania.[2]

Even though the mode of deposition of this enormous number of assemblages varies, as does their composition, archaeological scholarship realized by the mid-twentieth century that most Bronze Age hoards had been assembled according to specific patterns and norms. In some cases, the function of the deposited objects, their ornamentation, or their biographies played a role in their selection. In others, the emphasis was on their weight and amount. The carefully chosen objects often were subject to specific treatments—they were folded or tucked into each other, or hacked or broken into smaller pieces (Figure 5.1). The intentional damage to these objects also follows certain patterns: in some cases, the artifacts were broken into pieces of roughly similar size or weight, in others, the jewelry items, weapons, and bronze vessels were ruthlessly smashed or torn apart to render them unfit for use.[3]

The norms and customs reflected in deposition patterns governed not only the composition of the assemblages but also the position of individual artifacts within a hoard.[4] Another intriguing feature of the deposition patterns is that certain object types were only placed in particular environments. For example, most finds of intact defensive arms, such as cuirasses, have been recovered from bogs and rivers, and a similar regularity can be noted in the case of swords—of the several hundred Late Bronze Age swords known from Hungary, the intact examples were almost without exception buried far from settlements or cast

Figure 5.1. Bronze hoard of broken objects, Zsáka-Dávid tanya, Hungary. Late Bronze Age, 1150–1050 BC. Déri Museum, Debrecen. *Modified from Szabó 2019a:Figure 82 by J. Seagard.*

into rivers.[5] It is at least as striking that in contrast to swords, assemblages with deliberately fragmented and broken bronze objects have been predominantly brought to light in Bronze Age settlements in Hungary. Sickles were also treated in a particular manner: although they were never deposited in burials between the thirteenth and ninth centuries BC, several thousand are known from hoards.[6] Another apparent custom was that artifact types of particular importance, such as bronze vessels and swords, were arranged in certain ways as part of the deposition ceremony.[7]

Some of the patterns that can be distinguished regarding the composition, treatment, and arrangement of the items selected for deposition reflect pan-European norms that are also attested in Hungary. Regional deposition practices often remained unchanged for long centuries. In eastern Hungary, for example, the frequency of emblematic hoards containing intact jewelry and weapons alongside occasional superb bronze vessels is strikingly high from the sixteenth to the tenth centuries BC (Figure 5.2). Assemblages of this type are lacking in Transdanubia, where these objects were either placed in burials or were broken up and intentionally damaged before their concealment.[8] Regional differences are apparent in the number and condition of artifacts selected for deposition. In some regions, hoards composed of several thousand items and weighing as much as 100 kg are not infrequent, while in others, assemblages made up of ten to fifteen objects and weighing 1–2 kg are regarded as outstanding finds. Regional differences also can be noted in how and to what extent the artifacts chosen for deposition were damaged.

Why Were Hoards Concealed?

The deposition of metalwork, a widespread practice in the European Bronze Age, is a singular, unique phenomenon that has no obvious ethnographic or historical parallels.[9] The possible rationale(s) for the deposition and concealment of these valuable items, and of bronze as raw material, have been hotly debated issues in European archaeological scholarship since the nineteenth century. Two main approaches have been developed among specialists concerning the interpretation of how hoards were assembled and the ultimate reason for their deposition—some researchers have argued for the ritual nature of the practice, while others have made a case for more quotidian motivations.[10]

Some believe that hoards were concealed for profane reasons based on the rationale underlying

their deposition. Most leading scholars working in the countries of the Carpathian Basin during the twentieth century interpreted the bronze hoards as representing the concealment of valuables in times of trouble and unrest. Others argued that they can be regarded as founders' hoards, or stocks of raw material that were buried by metalsmiths, so they could be recycled and recast in the future. Hoards containing broken and miscast artifacts, as well as ingots and bronze cakes, were assigned to this deposition type. An explanation for the intentional fragmentation of the artifacts was that it would make their transportation easier, or that it reflected the practice of apportioning metal to conform to standard weight units. Hoards made up of large series of apparently unused, more or less identical object types were understood as representing merchants' stock-in-trade and were assigned to this deposition type too. Hoards with items that were lost or accidentally dropped in water were also sometimes classified into this category.

The profane interpretation of hoards was challenged from the very beginning—the proponents of an alternative explanation argued that most hoards had been buried for ritual reasons. According to this line of thought, the deliberately concealed gold and bronze items had been offerings and votive gifts to various deities and supernatural beings. Assemblages that could be associated with burials, but had been buried independently of graves, were also relegated to this type. The main argument for the ritual nature of hoards was their 'selectivity.' This perspective assumed that the contents of hoards were selected in accordance with specific cultural criteria, the deposited items were carefully arranged (Figure 5.3), and, even though the composition of hoards differed from one region to the next and from one period to the other, certain patterns could be discerned. This made a strong case for interpreting the acts of hoard deposition as having been regulated by rituals.[11]

It has been suggested that a special category among ritual hoards was represented by assemblages that had been "withdrawn" from the profane world because they contained 'dangerous' or ritually impure artifacts, such as jewelry or tools, that had been cursed or weapons tainted by blood taken from an enemy as part of military booty.[12]

It has been repeatedly pointed out by scholars favoring a ritual perspective that the lavish array of valuables chosen for the sacrifice was not merely a display for the supernatural or otherworldly powers. In this scenario, underlying the sacredness of the act, rational economic and social interests were also present. The individual or community performing the deposition simultaneously flaunted its economic

Figure 5.2. Bronze vessel assemblage, Hoard 2, Hajdúsámson, Hungary. Late Bronze Age, 1050–950 BC. Déri Museum, Debrecen. *Photo by Á. Vágó.*

power and largesse through the abundance of the sacrificed commodities withdrawn from daily use and circulation. Viewed from this perspective, Bronze Age depositions are akin to what is termed competitive exchange or conspicuous consumption in ethnographic studies—the greater the wealth an individual or community is capable of destroying, the higher the prestige and social status that can be acquired.[13]

From the early 2000s, studies of deposition acts were enriched by a new and more sophisticated approach that looked beyond the binary separation of the sacred from the profane.[14] The basic tenet of this approach is that the act of deposition was a ritualized social practice that also affected different aspects of quotidian life. From this perspective, hoards are conceptualized as sacrificial or votive deposits that were strongly intertwined with the social relations that characterized the world of chiefdoms and with

Figure 5.3. Carefully arranged bronze objects in a hoard, Parád-Várhegy, Hungary.
Late Bronze Age, 950–850 BC. Dobó István Museum, Eger.
Modified from Szabó 2019a:Figure 122 by J. Seagard.

the chains of gift exchanges that were essential to the functioning of the economy and the circulation of specific commodities.

The study of the cultural biographies of the deposited artifacts—including how they were used, their function, and their treatment during the deposition—plays an important role in this approach for it can shed light on the new meanings they acquired during their use-life, during the different life-cycles of their owners, and on the occasion of their deposition. A symbolic meaning may be associated with a deposited item—such as a miniature cuirass,[15] a larger than average piece of jewelry,[16] or a socketed axe that was sacrificed to memorialize a completed communal work. Other objects represented themselves and were deposited in the course of a transition ritual, such as weapons associated with a man who had passed weapon-bearing age, or jewelry that could no longer be worn by a girl

or a woman. Important additional shades of meaning could be associated with votive deposits, including the sacrifice of a gift, such as an exotic bronze vessel crafted in a distant land and received from a prominent person (Figure 5.4).

In more recent studies of deposition practices, particular attention has been paid to the relationship between hoards and the ancient landscape. It has been convincingly demonstrated that this relationship was governed by strict rules similar to those applied in the selection of a hoard's artifacts and their arrangement. It has been argued that the landscape was ritualized for Bronze Age communities, and that the location of hoards coincided with major hubs in this 'mentalscape.'[17] The deposition of multiple hoards in a well-defined area marked sacred precincts, boundaries, or processional ways.[18] In other instances, the deposition of a hoard would imbue a location with cosmological or ritual meaning, even though this same location appeared to be neutral or profane to the modern eye.

New studies have pointed out that deposition acts most likely played a key role in the construction and maintenance of cultural memory. Acts of deposition infused a place in the landscape with a specific identity, the ritual act sacralized the selected location, while the ceremony and the assemblage of special or highly-prized items created emotional and social memories. In this sense, hoards were critical building blocks of collective memory and generated a sense of cohesion for a particular community.[19]

Ten Dimensions of Deposition: Case Studies from Recent Research

The rich diversity exhibited in the composition of the hoards and the many different kinds of contexts where they have been found suggest that there is no one-size-fits-all interpretation for the deposition of metal hoards. These assemblages reflect a wide range of rationales and rituals that led to the concealment of one or another hoard during the Late Bronze Age, and

the various arguments making a case for a profane or ritual explanation often complement each other.

In the following, we illustrate the colorful world of Late Bronze Age hoards and deposition customs through ten case studies from Hungary and Transylvania in Romania (Figure 5.5). The examples shed light on how the deposition itself was part of an elaborate ritual (Ecseg), or how the artifacts selected for concealment as part of a hoard reveal fascinating details about the life-cycle and identity of the owners of the assemblages (Pázmándfalu, Tállya-Várhegy), while an extraordinary gold artifact demonstrates how exceptional items were vested with a symbolic meaning pointing beyond the object itself (Szeged). Some hoards offer an idea of how long it took to amass them and have much to reveal about the connections and economic power of the communities that accumulated the assemblages (Bandul de Câmpie/Mezőbánd). Other hoards provide insights into the possible

Figure 5.4. Bronze situla, Hajdúböszörmény, Hungary. Late Bronze Age, 1050–950 BC. Déri Museum, Debrecen. *Adapted from Szabó 2019a:Figure 19.*

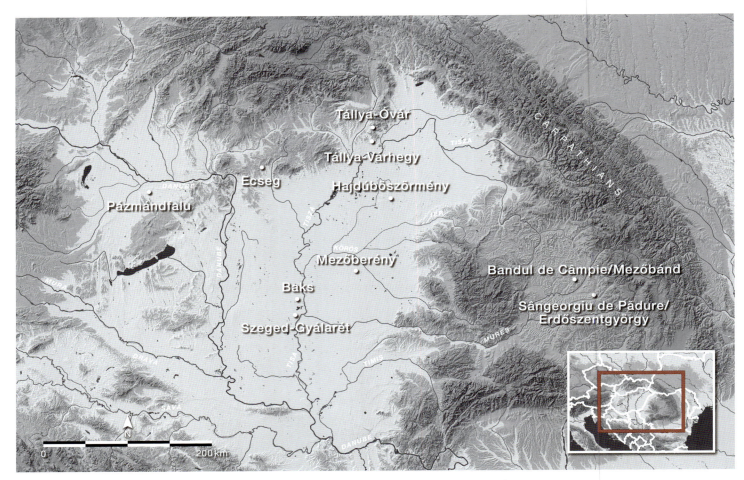

Figure 5.5. Map showing the sites discussed in detail in the text.
Illustration by F. Paár and E. Rodriguez.

reasons underlying the deposition of various artifacts (Baks, Tállya) or exemplify what the material wealth of a chiefly household looked like (Tolcsva). Finally, other hoards demonstrate how the act of deposition forged a link between collective memory and the ancestral ritual landscape (Sângeorgiu de Pădure/Erdőszentgyörgy, Mezőberény).

1. A Sophisticated Ritual: Ecseg-Bogdány-dűlő

The Ecseg hoard offers an excellent illustration of how the deposition of countless Late Bronze Age hoards was part of an elaborate, performance-like ceremony. Each and every artifact selected for the hoard and the ceremony of deposition itself no doubt had a specific meaning for the participants attending the event that followed strict ritual rules.

Discovered in 2016, the hoard of 106 artifacts weighed an impressive 8.5 kg (Figure 5.6). It seems

likely that the person or community selecting the objects of the hoard followed the same rules as with other similar assemblages from the period. The composition of the hoard and its artifact types correlate well with the so-called Kurd-type hoards of the thirteenth to twelfth centuries BC.[20] The period's diverse deposition practices, which varied from one region to the next, are reflected in hoard compositions, ranging from assemblages made up of unique jewelry or weapons to small assemblages comprising mainly tools and implements, and to hoards containing objects that together weighed as much as 25 to 50 kg. The Ecseg hoard represents the latter type, often composed of several hundred objects, including offensive and defensive weapons, tools and implements, as well as jewelry, such as brooches and bracelets.[21]

In the case of the Ecseg hoard, however, a specific deposition practice is indicated not only by its composition but also by the mode of burial. A glance at what we know about the interment of the assemblage strongly points toward a purposeful, carefully orchestrated sequence of actions,[22] in which the location selected for the deposition was also of

Figure 5.6. Bronze hoard concealed in a cauldron, Ecseg-Bogdány-dűlő, Hungary. Late Bronze Age, 1250–1150 BC. Dornyay Béla Museum, Salgótarján. *Modified from Szabó 2019a:Figure 22 by J. Seagard.*

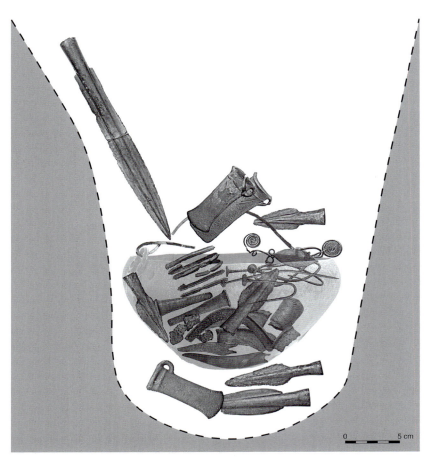

Figure 5.7. Reconstruction of the original context
of the Ecseg-Bogdány-dűlő hoard.
Modified from Szabó 2019a:Figure 28 by J. Seagard.

prime significance. The hoard was concealed at some distance from a contemporaneous settlement, in a spot which lay beyond the sphere of daily life. A pit roughly 50 cm deep was dug for the hoard, then a socketed axe and two spearheads were laid on the pit's floor, onto which the worn bronze cauldron filled to the brim with bronze artifacts was placed. No matter how worn, the cauldron probably held some special meaning for the community. The objects placed in the cauldron were carefully arranged—two knives, pieces of a saw blade and broken sickles at the bottom, onto which the less spectacular, large lumps of bronze were heaped, followed by plate fragments, sickles, and socketed axes. The fragments of a hacked bracelet, a bundle of

bronze pins, two brooches, and a large spiral bracelet were carefully set on the very top. Another large spiral bracelet was laid atop the filled cauldron, after which some earth was thrown over it, and the assemblage was closed with two socketed axes and a spearhead. Finally, a long spear was thrust into the pit, which then was backfilled with earth (Figure 5.7).

The composition of Hoard F from the hillfort on Bullenheimer Berg in Germany furnishes convincing proof that depositions were on occasion accompanied by spectacular performances.[23] In this hoard, the bronze axe plunged into the body of an amphora filled with various bronze items is an eloquent demonstration that the act of deposition was part of an elaborate sequence of actions. A sophisticated ritual is suggested by the large amounts of poppy seeds as well as mushroom, blackberry, red sorrel, dead-nettle, violet, birch leaf, and bark remains found at the bottom of the amphora. It would appear that the participants had drunk a narcotic potion prepared from these plants before the deposition of the hoard.[24]

2. A Funerary Ritual: Pázmándfalu

Made up of the typical artifacts of the warrior aristocracy of the thirteenth and twelfth centuries BC, the three hoards found on the outskirts of Pázmándfalu in western Hungary had been buried on a small floodplain islet (Figures 5.8 and 5.9).[25] Hoards 1 and 2 lay some 3 m apart and contained the full bronze weaponry and personal belongings of a single individual, most likely an outstanding military leader (Figure 5.8). Hoard 1 comprised battle-axes, a dagger, a helmet broken into smaller pieces, a drinking cup, and costume adornments, alongside horse harness and wagon fittings. Hoard 2 was made up of carefully arranged bronze objects—a folded sword, four large spearheads, a pair of knives with ornamented blades, a socketed chisel, a short sword, and two larger cuirass fragments (Figure 5.9). Hoard 3 was an independent, smaller assemblage, probably deposited at a later date, with the weapons and personal articles of a less prominent warrior.

The composition of the three hoards from Pázmándfalu and the deliberate destruction of their objects share numerous similarities with the funerary assemblages of prominent warriors in the thirteenth and twelfth centuries BC.[26] Were we unaware of the find context of the Pázmándfalu hoards, in light of their objects, we would be highly inclined to regard the assemblages as the grave goods of a wealthy warrior. It therefore seems likely that their depositions can

Figure 5.8. Bronze weapon assemblages, Hoards 1 and 2, Pázmándfalu, Hungary.
Late Bronze Age, 1250–1150 BC. Rómer Flóris Museum, Győr.
Modified from Szabó 2019a:Figure 34 by J. Seagard.

Figure 5.9. The original context of
the second hoard at Pázmándfalu, Hungary.
Adapted from Szabó 2019a:Figure 33.

be related to death and funerary rites, during which the artifacts expressing the deceased's identities were interred separately from the bodies.

The sets of objects in the Pázmándfalu hoards are linked by many strands to an emblematic assemblage of the period's elite uncovered in Grave 2 of the burial mound at Čaka in western Slovakia.[27] In addition to vessels used during the funerary feast, the burial chamber constructed over the remains of the funerary pyre contained the burnt fragments of a cuirass broken into tiny pieces, a set of weapons, various personal articles, and the adornments of a wagon and its harnessing equipment.[28]

The deposition of Hoards 1 and 2 at Pázmándfalu and the intricate burials with similar sets of objects may be regarded as reflections of the efforts by some families at the peak of the warrior hierarchy to establish a firm foundation of their ambitions for power through the creation of a hero's cult. An ostentatious ritual, during which the objects embodying the deceased's identity were dramatically sacrificed, bolstered the respect for the deceased, which indirectly benefited his descendants and family. The elevation of warriors to heroes and the myths woven around them no doubt played an important role in the cohesion of the warrior clans and military retinues emerging at this time. Therefore, it is likely that the Pázmándfalu hoards testify to the existence of a hero cult in the Carpathian Basin during the Late Bronze Age. This interpretation is also supported by the deposition of Hoard 3 at Pázmándfalu,[29] concealed at a later date. In this case, it is possible that the funerary set of another prominent member of the community was deposited near the virtual monument of a distinguished warrior from the past.

3. The Bronzesmith's Treasure: Tállya-Várhegy

The Tállya-Várhegy hoard was buried on a mountain towering over the surrounding landscape on the western fringes of the Zemplén Mountains in northern Hungary, at a barely accessible location on a steep mountain slope, far from any contemporaneous settlements.[30] The choice of location for the deposition act was perhaps motivated by the sweeping panorama, a view which in all likelihood included the territory of the community that had concealed the assemblage (Figure 5.10).

The hoard of seventy-two bronze objects was made up of costume adornments, jewelry, a bundle of sickles, a spearhead, and a dagger, as well as a bronzesmith's set of tools, including small anvils, punches,

Figure 5.10. The findspot of the Tállya-Várhegy hoard, Hungary.
Adapted from Szabó 2019a:Figure 55.

and a socketed chisel (Figure 5.11). Given its composition, the hoard fits in nicely with a chronologically and regionally well-defined group of hoards from northeastern Hungary. Assemblages of this type were common on the eastern fringes of the Bükk Mountains and the northern Great Hungarian Plain during the fourteenth and thirteenth centuries BC.

The hoard's artifacts can be divided into several distinct groups, suggesting that they had been carefully selected according to a specific cultural code, and that these groups reflect the many layers that constituted the identity of one particular person. Viewed from this perspective, the Tállya-Várhegy hoard evokes the figure of a remarkable man whose costume and weapons signify his local roots and traditions, while European analogies to his metalworking tools add a supra-regional dimension to his persona. His bronze- and goldsmithing skills, indicated by the metalworking

tools, were perhaps his most distinctive and most respected capabilities. Lavish costume adornments, including an unusual pin with an ornate head for fastening garments and decorative mounts that were sewn onto the garment, signal the individual's membership in the community's elite, while the weapons, a spearhead and a dagger, indicate his links with the world of warriors. The hoard's sickles could be symbols of his connection to arable lands, but they equally may have been included among the deposited objects as part of the period's ritual paraphernalia, a sort of sacral currency. The bracelets may have played a similar role, although we cannot exclude the possibility that they were a reference to female relatives—perhaps wives or children—of the man personified by the hoard. In this

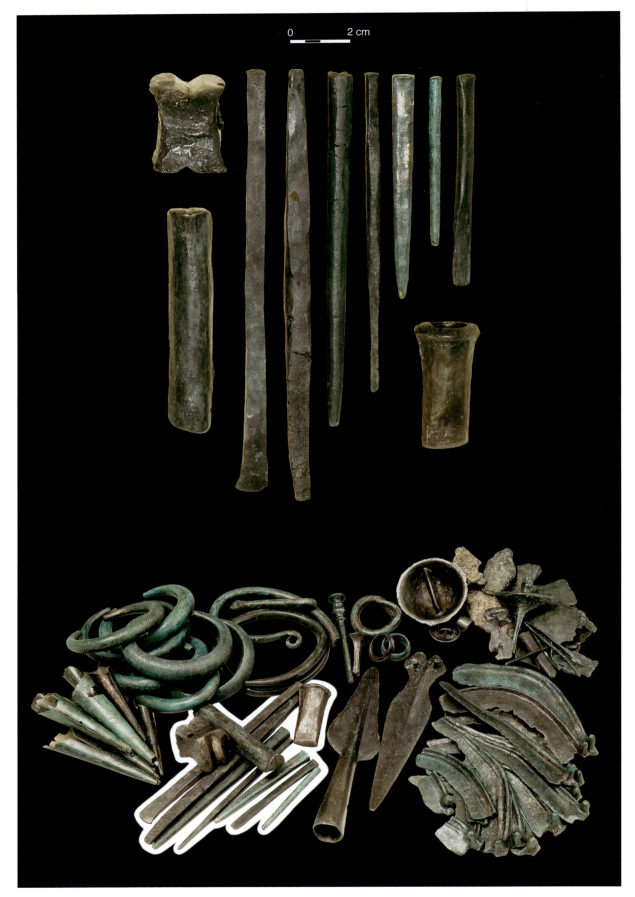

Figure 5.11. Bronze hoard, Tállya-Várhegy, Hungary. Late Bronze Age, 1350–1250 BC. Items representing the smith's toolkit are highlighted. Herman Ottó Museum, Miskolc. *Modified from Szabó 2019a:Figures 52 and 53 by J. Seagard.*

	Bandul de Câmpie	Uioara de Sus	Șpălnaca II	Aiud	Gușterița II	Dipșa	Bicaz I	Bicaz II
Bronze lumps	1669	2299	973	1027	60	264	406	476
Saws	517	384	483	18	57	16	1	6
Sickles	261	1244	421	197	165	138	24	91
Other	148	561	569	27	153	57	22	34
Bronze belts	109	42	111	66	27	5	1	6
Small ornaments	91	628	206	10	122	44	1	15
Axes	22	1244	299	136	101	51	21	77
Weapons	21	354	128	62	56	27	19	31
Total weight in kg	229.19	1133	1200	732	784	92.42	221.101	156.891
Total number of artifacts	2838	5812	2751	1595	749	611	495	736

Figure 5.12. Numeric composition of the eight largest Transylvanian Late Bronze Age hoards. *Table by G.V. Szabó.*

interpretation, the deposition of the hoard was part of a more comprehensive ritual, perhaps mortuary in nature, during which some personal belongings of the community's highly-esteemed and respected smith were deposited in an area that had strong association with his life-cycle and identity.

This interpretation is supported by the so-called 'smith-and-warrior' type hoards known from other regions, such as the Génelard hoard from France, which contained an array of smithing tools and personal weapons, and Hoard 2 from the Loučka hillfort in the Czech Republic, made up of battle-axes, anvils, and hammers.[31]

4. A Three-Thousand-Year-Old World Record: Tons of Treasures from Transylvania

The thirteenth and twelfth centuries BC saw the onset of an unprecedented upswing in the deposition of hoards in Transylvania, unparalleled elsewhere in Europe. Several hundred bronze assemblages were buried during a relatively short, 100–150-year period, during which the nature and composition of the concealed hoards also underwent striking changes. The hoards of the preceding period, made up of finer jewelry and weapons often crafted to individual preferences, were supplanted by assemblages containing thousands of bronze cakes and lumps, alongside tools and implements, such as socketed axes, sickles, and saw blades, produced in large series. One unique trait of the period's hoards is that over two-thirds of the items selected for deposition were deliberately damaged, reflecting a practice possibly regulated by ritual norms.

One of the most dazzling features of the new deposition practice was the incredible growth in the number and overall weight of the artifacts in the hoards, perhaps best illustrated by the fact that the period's eight largest hoards from Transylvania contained more than fifteen thousand objects, which added up to almost five tons of bronze (Figure 5.12).[32] The composition of these hoards and their sheer number would suggest that the main purpose of their accumulation was not their presentation as a votive sacrifice; instead, these assemblages of immense value appear to have been amassed for some other reason. Given the long period of hoarding acts and the diversity of artifacts, it is possible that these hoards comprise multiple votive assemblages deposited subsequently over a longer period of time at ancient cult places.

With its weight of 230 kg and number of 2,838 artifacts, the Bandul de Câmpie/Mezőbánd hoard is the second-largest bronze assemblage of the European Bronze Age, and eclipses by far even the largest Transylvanian hoard (Figure 5.13).[33] The hoard was discovered in 1959 in a shallow pit at the edge of a stream valley, remote from the known contemporaneous centers. This monumental bronze assemblage was made up of lumps, saw blades, sickles, and bronze belts, alongside twenty-one weapons, including swords, spearheads, and daggers, as well as twenty-two socketed axes. The overwhelming majority of the deposited objects had been deliberately broken. The composition of the hoard and the traces of manipulation on the artifacts provide clear evidence that the

Figure 5.13. Selected objects from a bronze hoard, Bandul de Câmpie/Mezőbánd, Romania.
Late Bronze Age, 1250–1150 BC. Mureş County Museum, Târgu Mureş.
Photo by B. Rezi.

hoard had been assembled purposefully, probably according to the period's ritual norms and regulations. The assemblage also includes more poorly-made tools and jewelry, as well as items that had been broken into pieces of more or less identical size. Semi-finished products and ingot fragments intended for processing also are present in this hoard.

The artifact types in the Bandul de Câmpie/Mezőbánd hoard suggest that the assemblage had been amassed over a longer period of time, and that it contains the accumulated wealth of at least four Bronze Age generations. The objects were crafted at the turn of the thirteenth and twelfth centuries BC. The cultural and trade contacts of the community assembling the hoard extended across all of Transylvania,

as shown by the flanged sickle types and some distinctively East European sickles. In addition to local bronzes, the assemblage also contains West European types, such as Rixheim swords, a type with a distinctive hilt distributed west of the Alps, Sieding–Szeged-type belt mounts fashioned from sheet bronze bearing fanciful geometric designs, crescentic pendants, and pins with perforated heads that are uncommon finds in Transylvania.

5. Weapons of the Divine Heroes: Szeged-Gyálarét

An enigmatic gold object came to light at Gyálarét on the outskirts of Szeged in May 2017, on a hillock that had once risen above the surrounding floodplain of the Tisza River. Its size, form, and ornamentation resembled the bronze greaves of the Late Bronze Age.

Five conical pendants and three domed mounts were also recovered during the survey of the findspot of the crumpled greave (Figure 5.14).[34] The greave is a delicate gold sheet hammered into an oval form with two pairs of perforations on each side, indicating that it had been secured to a backing of organic material.

Among the defensive arms of Late Bronze Age warriors, bronze greaves were imbued with a special meaning of their own.[35] They were rarely placed in burials, while the exemplars deposited as parts of hoards often were damaged intentionally. The significance of the greave from Szeged-Gyálarét is that it is the first Bronze Age greave crafted from precious metal found in Europe. The uniqueness of the golden greave suggests that this piece not only embodied the social status of its owner but that it had been vested with spiritual power and accorded special treatment.

However, it is equally feasible that the object had not been the possession of a living individual but had been attached to a cult statue before its deposition. The existence of a special cult associated with greaves is underpinned by an extraordinary assemblage from northern Italy. A pit uncovered in the Late Bronze Age–Early Iron Age cemetery of Desmontà di Veronella contained two bronze greaves which lay one above the other and once had been secured to a piece of wood, perhaps part of a cult statue. The location of the greaves had probably been marked by a wooden stele or column because at a later time humans were buried around this pit.[36] Similar costume elements vested with a symbolic role that had been worn over the course of rituals or ceremonies are known from other sites dating to the same period. One of the most curious is an enormous arm spiral from Abaújdevecser in Hungary that originally had been deposited in a bog.[37] With its weight of 12 kg, this bronze spiral had been made for a veritable giant because the usual weight of these jewelry items was rarely over half a kilogram (Figure 5.15).

The potential range of meanings ascribed to the Gyálarét greave can best be likened to the gold head ornaments of western Europe.[38] These unusual objects resembling caps probably played a similar role as the Gyálarét artifact: they were part of the cult paraphernalia and insignia of rank, and as such, they highlighted the power of a particular individual or a group, or possibly of a transcendent being.

6. A Hoard in the Home: Baks-Temetőpart

Some Late Bronze Age hoards were not closed assemblages that had been buried as votive sacrifices. The find contexts of these hoards suggest that they had not been intended as sacrificial deposits, but instead represented the wealth of a household that had been

Figure 5.14. Golden greave and its reconstruction, Szeged-Gyálarét, Hungary. Late Bronze Age, 1250–1150 BC. Móra Ferenc Museum, Szeged. *Modified from Szabó 2019a:Figures 62 and 63 by J. Seagard.*

Figure 5.15. Bronze oversized arm spiral, Abaújdevecser, Hungary. Middle Bronze Age, 1900–1700 BC. Herman Ottó Museum, Miskolc. *Modified from Szabó 2019a:Figure 68 by J. Seagard.*

accumulated for practical or ritual reasons, and were reserves from which objects could be withdrawn if the need arose. Conversely, new items also could be added to these hoards.

Several hoards of this type were recovered from the settlement of Baks-Temetőpart located on an islet-like mound rising above the marshland of the Tisza River

Figure 5.16. Three bronze hoards from a settlement, Baks-Temetőpart, Hungary. Late Bronze Age, 1050–950 BC. Móra Ferenc Museum, Szeged. *Modified from Szabó 2019a:Figures 70–72 by J. Seagard.*

(Figure 5.16). Two bronze hoards and a gold hoard, as well as roughly three thousand additional bronze artifacts collected during a metal detector survey across the site, attest to the wealth of the occupants of the Late Bronze Age village (Figure 5.17).[39] Life in the village, one of the major centers in the southern Great Hungarian Plain that was home to several hundred people, ceased around 900 BC, for reasons unbeknownst to us. The extent and unexpectedness of the calamity and catastrophe that befell the settlement is reflected by human bones scattered over the site and the mass of valuable bronze objects among the ruins of the houses. The hoards from Baks constitute a new category of hoard—a domestic hoard.

All three hoards at the site were found in the settlement's central part, within an area of about 50 m in diameter; this area was densely built up with houses and various auxiliary buildings. It seems likely that the hoards from Baks-Temetőpart signify the habitation area of one of the community's leading families or clans. The reserves of broken and intact artifacts were part of the occupants' wealth that had been hoarded or hidden in their homes. The composition of objects in the two bronze hoards is similar, suggesting that they were accumulated for a similar reason—a votive gift, a funerary sacrifice, or perhaps a dowry.

Figure 5.17. Metal stray finds from the settlement of Baks-Temetőpart, Hungary. Late Bronze Age, 1050–950 BC. Móra Ferenc Museum, Szeged. *Modified from Szabó 2019a:Figure 75 by J. Seagard.*

The three hoards and the immense number of bronze artifacts recovered from the remains of the abandoned village offer a fairly good idea of the amount of metal objects that were circulated in Late Bronze Age settlements. These objects included tools and implements for daily use as well as various sets of other artifacts that were stored in containers; these likely were hoarded for practical reasons. One advantage of bronze, a commodity whose acquisition was no easy task, was that it could be recycled. Therefore even broken bronze objects were valuable, which explains why special care was taken to collect and preserve them. Intact objects as well as broken or damaged pieces, casting waste, and bronze cakes were tangible parts of a household's wealth. The hoarded bronze functioned as a reserve that could be used at any time—as weapons, as working tools, or as currency in practical or ritual transactions. The metal objects and raw material safeguarded in homes signified their owner's power and wealth. The accumulated valuables were most often stored in dwellings, although sometimes they were kept in a central location for boastful display. In other cases, they were carefully hidden within buildings and only rarely removed from the place of concealment.

7. A Peek into a Treasury: Tállya-Óvár

The hoard discovered at Tállya-Óvár was deposited under the floor of a building constructed of timber logs, daubed with clay, and located in the settlement's central area (Figure 5.18).[40] The bronze weapons, tools, implements, and jewelry in the hoard, as well as the ornate clay vessels and food remains found among the building debris, would suggest that the house once had been occupied by one of the hillfort's leading families that headed a large household. The finds offer a glimpse into the world of a powerful Bronze Age clan with wide-ranging connections.

The value of a hoard for a Bronze Age community, such as the one found at Tállya-Óvár, lay not only in the amount of bronze raw material it contained but also in the utilitarian and symbolic importance of certain pieces. The twenty-two socketed axes and the

Figure 5.18. Find circumstances of a bronze hoard, Tállya-Óvár, Hungary.
Illustration by G.V. Szabó and J. Seagard.

four sickles could have been sufficient for meeting the needs of an extensive chiefly household. The large and heavy winged axe was a formidable weapon, a token of high rank, whose owner was a member of the warriors' world. The sword hilt and the oval ring, a rare type, perhaps part of a ceremonial harness set, also probably were associated with high-status individuals (Figure 5.19).

The Tállya-Óvár hoard can be interpreted as a family reserve accumulated in a prominent household that could have been mobilized in times of need. It seems likely that the accumulation of metalwork reserves was

a general practice in wealthier households during the Late Bronze Age. The size and value of these hoards varied to a great extent. Some smaller assemblages of a few items represented the riches of a family. Other hoards comprising a broad array of artifacts, weighing as much as 30 to 40 kg, can likely be linked to individuals with a higher social status. Finally, there were chiefly hoards, with valuable, prestigious bronze and gold objects that reflect the most preeminent ranks within Bronze Age social hierarchies.

The Homeric epics, which memorialize Greek traditions that were practiced in the Late Bronze Age and Early Iron Age, often mention family treasures similar to that of Tállya-Óvár.[41] Homer used the word *keimelia* to denote treasures of this type, which comes

Figure 5.19. Bronze hoard, Tállya-Óvár, Hungary.
Late Bronze Age, 950–900 BC. Herman Ottó Museum, Miskolc.
Modified from Szabó 2019a:Figure 95 by J. Seagard.

from the Greek word 'to lie,' and can be translated as 'treasures lying heaped.'[42] In his study of the world of the Homeric epics, Moses I. Finley made the following point about treasures stored in households: "Such objects had some direct use value and they could provide aesthetic satisfaction, too, [. . .] but neither function was of real moment compared to their value as symbolic wealth or prestige wealth. The twin uses of treasure were in possessing it and in giving it away, paradoxical as that may appear. Until the appropriate occasion for a gift presented itself, most treasure was kept hidden under lock and key. It was not 'used' in the narrow sense of that word."[43]

In some ancient European societies, including the era of the Late Bronze Age, reciprocal gift giving and gift exchanges might have been one of the principal socioeconomic driving forces.[44] By accepting a gift, the recipient had committed himself, for he was expected to give something in return: political support, military

aid, or an important raw material or commodity. The gift givers often catered to genuine needs by presenting their dependents with tools and weapons. Sometimes, services were paid for in this manner and alliances were often sealed with gift exchanges.

Chieftains enhanced their prestige through extravagant (and seemingly wasteful) gift-giving and the spectacular sacrifice of their valuables, whereby they demonstrated that they were in possession of the necessary power and support of the spirits to be able to amass a similar amount of wealth in the future.

The Bronze Age hoards discussed above fit well into the overall picture of archaic gift economies.[45] These assemblages, whether deposited for sacrificial purposes or representing the wealth of a family carefully guarded at home, can be regarded as treasures collected over successive generations that also had

Figure 5.20. Bronze hoard, Hajdúböszörmény, Hungary.
Late Bronze Age, 1050–950 BC. Hungarian National Museum, Budapest.
Adapted from Szabó 2017:Figure 9.

been enriched with items acquired through gift exchanges. Each object in these hoards had a story to tell, a narrative of how it had been acquired—weapons acquired as booty evoked heroic deeds, an astonishing bronze vessel preserved the memory of a guest-friendship, while other pieces preserved the memory of the donor. These narratives also added to the value of the gift when it was passed on.

8. Feasting Sets and Armories: Lavish Hoards from Eastern Hungary

Dozens of bronze hoards containing superbly crafted weapons, magnificent jewelry, and vessel sets used during feasts were concealed on the Great Hungarian Plain in the eleventh and tenth centuries BC. The increasing number of exceptionally lavish hoards attests to the transformation of deposition practices and possibly to a change in the social status of the individuals concealing these hoards—they are perhaps an indication that the local clans ruling their world in previous eras had been supplanted by a smaller group of elite individuals with more concentrated power.

The best-known assemblage of this type from eastern Hungary was uncovered on the outskirts of Hajdúböszörmény in 1858. The hoard contains swords, helmets, and vessels all made of bronze, and was discovered when two day-laborers dug a shallow pit for a hearth. Two helmets lay on top, underneath were found two lavishly ornamented bronze situlae (that is, magnificent, bucket-shaped vessels crafted from sheet bronze and used as containers for wine or other beverages), two cauldrons, a large strainer vessel, and two cups, all of which had been placed over thirty carefully arranged swords. Originally made up of some forty items, the hoard is an emblematic assemblage of the European Late Bronze Age (Figure 5.20).[46]

One of the most remarkable assemblages among the sumptuous Late Bronze Age hoards was found during illicit metal detecting on a Late Bronze Age hillfort in northeastern Hungary.[47] The rich and well-preserved bronze assemblage, outstanding even by European hoard standards, was made up of a situla decorated with a sun-disc and bird figures, four large arm spirals of sheet metal, three cups of sheet metal, two intact cauldrons, a twisted neck ring, and the ear guards of a helmet. The situla was said to have been deposited upside-down and the cauldrons were also placed inside it with their mouth downward. The small bronze cups stacked on top of each other, the

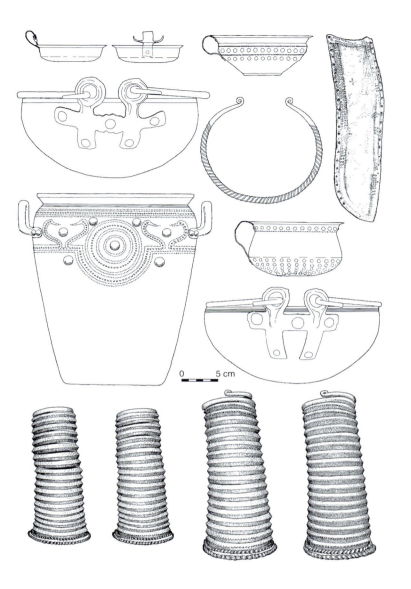

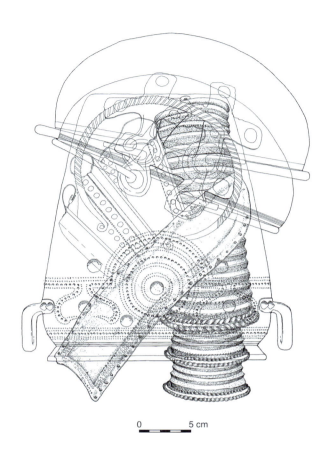

Figure 5.21. The probable find circumstances of a bronze hoard found during an illegal metal detector survey at a fortified settlement in northeastern Hungary. Late Bronze Age, 1050–950 BC. *Adapted from Szabó 2013:Figure 6.*

torque, the arm spirals, and the ear guards were also inside the situla (Figure 5.21). This magnificent find probably was smuggled out of Hungary and eventually made its way into a private collection. Although known only from photographs, this unique assemblage is one of the most dazzling representatives of bronze hoards found in Hungary—its individual pieces and the assemblage as a whole embody the absolute peak of Late Bronze Age metalwork in the Carpathian Basin during the eleventh and tenth centuries BC.

9. The Inscribed Landscape: Sângeorgiu de Pădure/Erdőszentgyörgy

Prehistoric communities often infused various elements of the landscape with symbolic meaning. In some cases, it was the act of deposition that inscribed a particular landscape element with a special significance and incorporated the act of the votive sacrifice into a community's collective memory.

In 1904, a bronze hoard of horse gear fittings, twenty-three socketed axes, arm rings, six remarkable drinking vessels, and an exceptionally well-preserved, ornate cauldron came to light on the outskirts of Sângeorgiu de Pădure/Erdőszentgyörgy, a village in the valley of the Kis-Küküllő River in Transylvania. Two other, lavishly ornamented cauldrons were discovered at this site in 1928, and a metal detecting survey of the area in 2009 yielded yet another cauldron that had been deposited upside-down (Figures 5.22 and 5.23).[48]

It remains unclear whether the two assemblages and the solitary cauldron had been parts of the same

Figure 5.22. The findspot of a bronze cauldron recovered in 2009, Sângeorgiu de Pădure/Erdőszentgyörgy, Romania. *Photo by G.V. Szabó.*

presumably were used for serving alcoholic beverages during various ceremonies, suggested also by the cups and scooping vessels found in association with them.

The repeated deposition acts at Sângeorgiu de Pădure/Erdőszentgyörgy indicate that this location had a special meaning in the landscape for local Late Bronze Age communities that was recognized through recurring rituals. This interpretation is supported by other bronze finds from the site, which predate the period when the cauldrons were buried by two to three hundred years. Although a contemporaneous settlement is not known from the immediate vicinity of the hoards, there were two Late Bronze Age hillforts nearby, on the left bank of the Kis-Küküllő River, the broader areas of which did not yield any bronze finds.[50]

It would appear that the collective memory of Late Bronze Age communities settling in this region incorporated a structured mentalscape that can be broadly reconstructed. The Kis-Küküllő Valley undoubtedly played a prominent role in this mentalscape, probably marking an imaginary boundary between two landscape elements with different meanings. The river's left bank was the setting of daily life and its activities, while the bronze hoards deposited on the hills rising above the right bank testify to the area's special ritual significance. The location where the hoards were deposited offers a splendid view of the two hillforts that dominated the opposite side of the river, surrounded by fertile fields and pasturelands.

10. Sword Sacrifices on the Grassy Plain: Mezőberény-Telek-dűlő

A pair of swords buried at Mezőberény on the grassland of the southern Great Hungarian Plain in the tenth or ninth century BC illustrate how an act of deposition can infuse a seemingly neutral location of a landscape with a new meaning.[51]

The fragments of two cup-hilted swords were found within 5 m at the site. It seems likely that the swords had been deposited next to one another, and that they were only recently dislodged from their original positions due to agricultural activities (Figure 5.24).

Swords intended as votive offerings were usually deposited in special locations in the Carpathian Basin. In Hungary, they were often cast into rivers and lakes—over forty intact Bronze Age swords have been recovered from the Danube and Tisza rivers, mostly in the proximity of ancient crossing places and fords.[52] Several swords were concealed, either alone or in groups, in caves or rock-shelters, as for example at Vyšný Sliač in Slovakia, where six swords and a few personal jewelry items were deposited in a limestone

hoard or if they had been buried separately in the course of three, unrelated deposition acts. Whichever the case, the three hoards are more or less contemporaneous and were buried in the tenth century BC. The objects fit in neatly with other hoards composed of the period's typical feasting paraphernalia and various personal artifacts, such as the Fizeșu Gherlii II/Ördöngösfüzes II hoard.[49]

The most remarkable pieces found at Sângeorgiu de Pădure/Erdőszentgyörgy are the bronze cauldrons with twisted hangers looped through cross-shaped handles attached to the vessel body, which were produced in Transylvanian workshops. These cauldrons

Figure 5.23. Two hoards discovered in 1904 and 1929 at Sângeorgiu de Pădure/Erdőszentgyörgy, Romania. Late Bronze Age, 950–900 BC. Mureș County Museum, Târgu Mureș and National Museum of Transylvanian History, Cluj-Napoca. *Photo by B. Rezi.*

chimney,[53] and at Recsk in northeastern Hungary, where a hoard of nine swords were hidden under a large piece of rock.[54]

Another distinctive trait of sword hoards is that, in contrast to other hoard types, they were always interred far from settlements. The objects from Mezőberény eloquently illustrate this point—the find-spot lay in the center of what was a flat, uninhabited grassland during the Bronze Age. The nearest contemporaneous settlements were some 3–4 km away. Several similar sword depositions are known from this area: a single sword came to light at Hódmezővásárhely-Batida, while two finely-made bronze swords, buried alongside two socketed axes, were found at

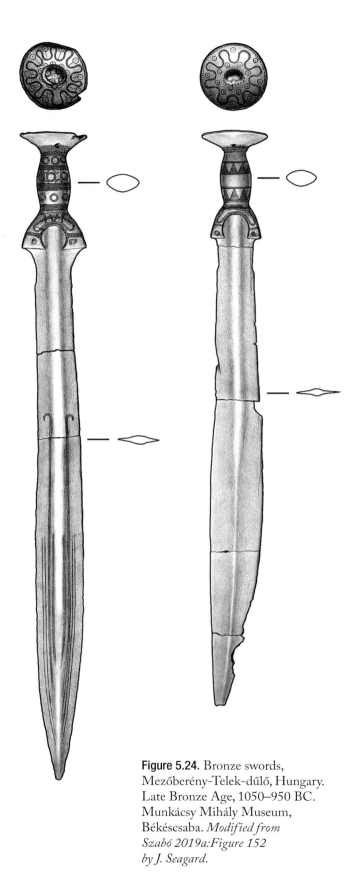

Figure 5.24. Bronze swords, Mezőberény-Telek-dűlő, Hungary. Late Bronze Age, 1050–950 BC. Munkácsy Mihály Museum, Békéscsaba. *Modified from Szabó 2019a:Figure 152 by J. Seagard.*

Hódmezővásárhely-Kútvölgy. The closest parallel to the deposition mode of the Mezőberény swords is from Orosháza-Gyopáros, where two strongly worn, but nevertheless good-quality, swords were found on the shore of a small lake (Figure 5.25).[55]

In light of the above, it seems more than likely that the Mezőberény swords and similar depositions located far from contemporaneous settlements in the southern Great Hungarian Plain were buried by communities that colonized a formerly uninhabited region. Owing to growing cattle herds, a major source of prestige during this era, areas suitable for animal husbandry became more valuable. Simultaneously, the proper demarcation of boundaries was an important concern. The leading families of the communities settling in these grasslands claimed the possession of particular lands through deposition rituals at those locations that had a special meaning for both their own community and their neighbors.

Another feasible interpretation of the interment of the Mezőberény swords is that the two weapons carried the memory of some martial action. In this case, the breaking of the swords perhaps symbolized the defeat of their owner.[56] However, their differing proportions and decorations may indicate that two different individuals owned these objects. An additional important clue for the interpretation of this hoard is that other deposition acts were not performed in the area either earlier or subsequently, and thus the burial of the swords perhaps marked one particular event and its location as well as infused the local landscape with a new meaning.

Conclusions

The practice of burying hoards of bronze metalwork flourished in the period spanning the centuries from 1300 to 900 BC, designated as the Late Bronze Age in European archaeological scholarship. During these four hundred years, the continent, including the Carpathian Basin, underwent profound and spectacular transformations—this era witnessed dynamic population growth, the colonization of previously uninhabited regions, major changes in farming techniques, a manifold increase in the number of cultivated plant species, the spread of a new eating and drinking culture, an increasing connectivity between regions lying far from each other, and the appearance of new, previously unencountered social organizations and ideologies.

Late Bronze Age chiefdoms took many different forms and their political complexity and size varied even within a particular region. Under certain

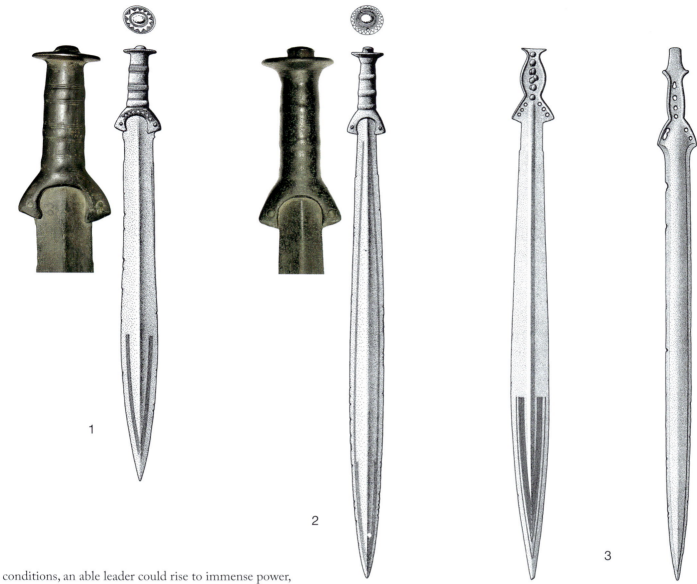

conditions, an able leader could rise to immense power, and muster and command a relatively large military retinue. Aside from organizing raids to seize the resources of neighboring groups, these war chiefs would have had the means to forge extensive alliance systems and to launch more ambitious campaigns, leading to the emergence of distinctive social formations, as spectacularly illustrated by the cemetery uncovered at Neckarsulm in southern Germany, dating to the twelfth century BC. The finds suggest that this site was the burial ground of a warrior fraternity recalling the 'male band' (*Männerbund*) known from the ethnographic record, an early form of the military retinues described in ancient sources.[57]

Another major pillar of Late Bronze Age social organization was the patriarchal household that was integrated into the chiefdom system and organized

Figure 5.25. Bronze swords from the broader region of the Mezőberény hoard:
1) Hódmezővásárhely-Kútvölgy;
2) Hódmezővásárhely-Batida;
3) Orosháza-Gyopáros. All in Hungary. Late Bronze Age, 1250–950 BC. Tornyai János Museum, Hódmezővásárhely and Szántó Kovács János Museum, Orosháza. *Modified from Szabó 2019a:Figure 156 by J. Seagard.*

around powerful, respected males of leading families. These households incorporated family members, other families, slaves, and voluntarily joined free men who, in exchange for their work, were offered protection and a secure livelihood by their leaders. These leading households were dominated by 'sword-bearing' men, whose territories were organized around larger farmsteads or smaller hillforts located 5–10 km apart from one another.[58]

As indicated by weapons in the hoards discussed above, one salient feature of the region's Bronze Age chiefdoms was constant rivalry and internecine aggression and competition. A class of warriors emerged around the leaders, who periodically launched raids and more ambitious campaigns for booty against neighboring or more distant adversaries. The appearance of defensive armor, such as shields, helmets, and cuirasses, as well as the widespread use of swords, attest to a professional weapon-bearing social stratum of warriors whose life was essentially determined by raids, warfare, and violence.[59]

The might and power of the competing elite households was based in large part on how well they organized the procurement and steady supply of metals. Sickles and socketed axes played a prominent role in farming and in woodland clearance for gaining new farmland, and thus were of strategic importance in the period's food production boom. Yet the concealment of hoards indicates that there were also non-utilitarian dimensions to bronze objects—their possession, their extravagant sacrifice, and their generous distribution as gifts played a crucial role in the display and maintenance of the elite's prominent position within society.

Notes

1   Kemenczei 1996:Abb. 36.

2   Ciugudean et al. 2008:47–52; Kemenczei 1996:Abb. 36; Rusu 1963:205–10.

3   Bradley 2005:151–64; Hansen 2016a; Rezi 2011.

4   Fontijn 2002:259–72.

5   Kemenczei 1988; Kemenczei 1991; Szathmári 2005.

6   Fejér 2017.

7   Soroceanu 1995:37–45; Soroceanu 2005; Soroceanu 2011b.

8   Hansen 2005; Vachta 2008.

9   Fontijn 2002:20; Hansen 2002; Hansen 2013b; von Brunn 1968:238–39.

10 For overviews of the various interpretations of deposition practices, see Ballmer 2015:2–6; Fontijn 2002:13–35; Huth 1997:4–62.

11 Hänsel 1997; Hansen 1994:381–96; von Brunn 1968.

12 Kristiansen 2002; Randsborg 2002.

13 Bradley 1990:39; Hansen 1994:374; Taylor 1993:18–22, 33–42; Vachta 2008:116–17.

14 See Ballmer 2015; Fontijn 2002; Hansen 2005:211–12; Hansen 2013b; Neumann 2014; Vachta 2016.

15 Windholz-Konrad 2012:Abb. 19.

16 Hellebrandt 2011.

17 Ballmer 2010; Hansen 2008.

18 A good example of the latter is the ancient mountain route along the Traun River in Austria: thirty-six hoards were buried along an 18-km-long section of this watercourse: Windholz-Konrad 2012.

19 For example, Fontijn 2002; Hansen 2016b; Neumann 2014; Szabó 2019a:32–34, 168–69, 177–90.

20 Hansen 2005:215, 218, 221; Mozsolics 1985; Váczi 2014:275–82.

21 Szabó 2019a:25–34.

22 For a discussion of the predetermined order and arrangement of the artifacts according to specific patterns, see Soroceanu 1995:37–45.

23 Hagl 2008; Hagl 2009.

24 Hagl 2008; Hagl 2009.

25 Szabó 2019a:35–45.

26 Clausing 2005; Sperber 1999.

27 Točík and Paulík 1960.

28 Točík and Paulík 1960.

29 Szabó 2019a:Fig. 35.

30 Szabó 2019a:59–68.

31 Génelard: Thevenot 1998; Loučka: Čižmář-Salaš and Salaš 2009:74, Abb. 4–5.

32 Rusu 1981:377–80, Table 1; Soroceanu et al. 2017:69–71.

33 Soroceanu et al. 2017.

34 Szabó and Czukor 2017.

35 Clausing 2002; Mödlinger 2017:217–64.

36 Mödlinger 2017:225; Salzani 1986.

37 Hellebrandt 2011.

38 Gerloff 2003; Schauer 1986; Sperber 2003.

39 Szabó 2019a:76–88.

40 Szabó 2019a:99–108.

41 Hom. Il. 6.54–58; Hom. Od. 4.690.

42 Fekete 2013; Finley 1977:61; Fischer 1973.

43 Finley 1977:61.

44 Hansen 2016b:212–21; Neumann 2014:42–43; Vachta 2016:173–74.

45 Mauss 1990.

46 Mozsolics 1984; Szabó and Bálint 2016.

47 Szabó 2013:798–801, Figs 3–7.

48 Rezi 2017.

49 Petrescu-Dîmbovița 1978:Taf. 257:11–13, 15–16; Soroceanu 2008:92–106.

50 Rezi 2017:41–43, Figs 8, 19–21.

51 Szabó 2019a:163–66.

52 Szathmári 2005.

53 Uhlár 1959.

54 Mozsolics 1985:180, Taf. 141–42.

55 Hódmezővásárhely-Batida: Kemenczei 1988:355, Taf. 39; Hódmezővásárhely-Kútvölgy: Kemenczei 1988:394, Taf. 45; Orosháza-Gyopáros: Kemenczei 1991:102, Taf. 23, 143, Taf. 35; Tarbay 2016.

56 Čivilyté 2009:145.

57 Knöpke 2010.

58 Sperber 1999:629–37.

59 Harding 2007:149–69.

CHAPTER 6

Peace and War in the Bronze Age on the Eastern Frontier of the Carpathian Basin

The Evolution and Manifestation of Social Stratification

Florin Gogâltan and Corina Borș

"We can begin with simple social categories,
such as *personal items, prestige goods and trade goods*."

(Kristiansen and Larsson 2005:35)

THE EXPRESSION "eastern frontier of the Carpathian Basin" is used here in order to designate five historic regions in Romania, which were given the names of Banat, Crișana, Sătmar, Maramureș, and Transylvania after World War I (Figure 6.1). In part, they cover political-historical entities from the time of the Hungarian Kingdom (AD 1000–1538) and later of the Principality of Transylvania (AD 1541–1711).

Transylvania, thanks to its natural resources of salt, gold, silver, copper, and iron, was one of the richest regions in prehistoric Europe, at least in terms of raw materials. The diversity of the environment, with generous and balanced spaces for practicing agriculture and animal breeding, helped ensure the economic success of its inhabitants. To these were added the many natural routes of communication that facilitated access to distant sources of raw materials from which exotic prestige goods were made (for example, tin, amber, *Columbella*, *Cardium*, and *Dentalium* shells). All these marked the time and manner of the development of Bronze Age communities in the eastern Carpathian Basin.

But how were these communities socially structured? Anthropological studies offer various models that have been accepted or criticized by archaeologists, depending on their scientific training, professional experience, attachment to a mentor, or even political positions.[1] It is not our intention to propose a theoretical discussion on this subject, but only to review the most relevant archaeological discoveries, especially the more recent ones, that provide information about the evolution and manifestation of social stratification for the period between about 2700 and 900 BC. Similar to studies of other periods in the prehistory of the Carpathian Basin,[2] we will follow the traces of social inequality in material culture, settlements, and mortuary practices over the course of the Bronze Age.

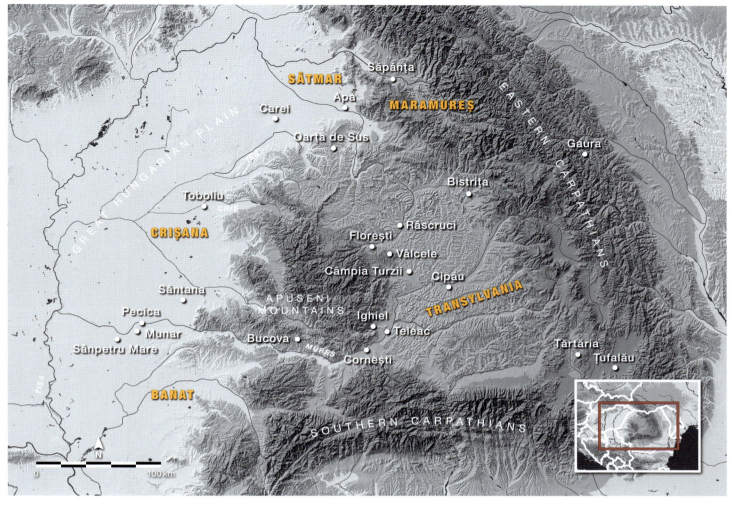

Figure 6.1. Map showing the regions and sites mentioned in the text.
Illustration by F. Paár and E. Rodriguez.

Indigenous and Migrant Populations during the Transition from the Copper to the Bronze Age

Starting in the third millennium BC, some significant changes are evident in Copper Age social organization. The settlements in the plains of western Romania, including the regions of Banat, Crișana, and Sătmar, remained small and dispersed. Like most of the villages in the fourth millennium BC in the Carpathian Basin, these sites also lacked fortifications. During the third millennium BC, hundreds of burial mounds, or kurgans, were constructed that changed the regional landscape to this day (for an extensive summary, see Chapter 4, this volume). These earthen mounds have impressive dimensions, with diameters up to 70 m and heights up to 6 m (Figure 6.2), and archaeological investigations have led to the discovery of wooden burial structures beneath them.[3] The deceased was placed in a characteristic crouching position and was usually associated with organic deposits, such as textiles, as well as ocher; an outstanding example has recently been excavated at Bucova near the village of Dudeștii Vechi.[4] Such findings have been attributed to the

so-called 'Yamnaya package,'[5] contributing to arguments for the immigration of an intrusive population from the North Pontic steppe to the plain between the Tisa River and the Apuseni Mountains.

In Transylvania and Maramureș, the gradual warming of the climate beginning in the Subboreal (approximately 3800 BC to 800 BC) allowed areas of higher altitude to be inhabited. The Late Copper Age communities of the Coțofeni Culture adapted to the mountain landscapes by pursuing specific economic activities in those areas. Their high degree of mobility, due to the continuous search for the most suitable places for breeding their animals, resulted in short-term, seasonal settlements without fortifications. Caves became a constant refuge for these shepherds and their animals.[6] Regarding the funerary practices of the Coțofeni communities, their burial mounds in western Transylvania were small and located on high grounds, between 400 and 1,000 m in altitude, providing good visibility. These tumuli commonly have a stone mantle

Figure 6.2. Prehistoric burial mound, Sânpetru Mare, Romania.
Adapted from Diaconescu et al. 2017:75.

and the documented funerary rites are different from those of the immigrant Yamnaya people. Burial inventories are poor, with the sparse occurrence of metal objects, such as golden hair rings or *Brillenspirale* copper pendants.[7]

The burial mounds of the Yamnaya population are distributed in the valleys of major rivers in western and central Transylvania and are characterized by the use of red ocher and wooden constructions, such as those at Câmpia Turzii, Cipău, and Răscruci. Analogies in the North Pontic region suggest that sometimes anthropomorphic stone stelae were placed on top of

these kurgans (Figure 6.3). A total of eight such stelae are known from Transylvania.[8] Their monumentality and anthropomorphic features, to which is added the depiction of some weapons, indicate that they manifested the privileged, perhaps heroic, position of the deceased within their communities.[9] Massive copper shaft-hole axes served as status symbols for the Yamnaya people, and a great number of them have been recovered from settlements, caves, and hoards, or as isolated deposits.[10] The most representative hoard in Transylvania was recovered at Vâlcele/Bányabükk—in 1928, at least fifty-five shaft-hole axes were found

Figure 6.3. Reconstruction of a prehistoric burial mound, Florești, Romania.
Modified from Rotea 2009:Figure 4 by J. Seagard.

Figure 6.4. Selection from a hoard of copper shaft-hole axes, Vâlcele/Bányabükk, Romania. Transition from the Late Copper Age to the Early Bronze Age, 3000–2600 BC. National Museum of History of Transylvania, Cluj-Napoca. *Modified from Soroceanu 2012:Plate 37 by J. Seagard.*

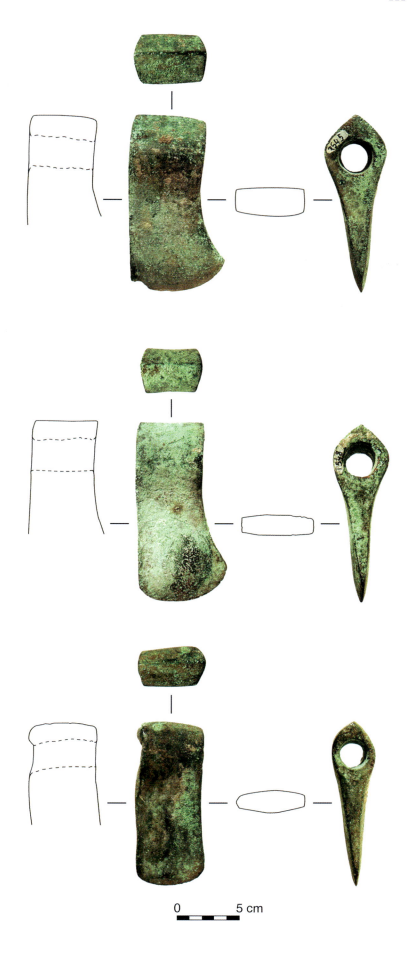

accidentally, which makes this assemblage one of the largest hoards of its era (Figure 6.4).[11] The presence of clay molds in settlement contexts demonstrates the local production of these and other types of axes, providing links between the North Pontic steppe zone and Central Europe.[12]

The exploitation of copper, gold, and silver ores in Transylvania, as well as the richest salt sources in the Carpathian Basin, brought about profound social shifts already in the Copper Age. An emerging elite likely would have controlled access to these resources and the distribution of finished products, and the commoners would have provided the required food and labor force for metal exploitation and production. Some scholars argue that the migrating Yamnaya communities brought a series of technological innovations (such as wheels, wagons, new weaponry), a new subsistence economy based on specialized breeding and cattle herding, the use of secondary products (like milk), as well as a new ideology to Central and Southeast Europe, including the Carpathian Basin.[13] Toward the end of the first half of the third millennium BC, the new weapons and personal adornments, along with funerary furniture and anthropomorphic stone stelae, became the visual representations of elevated social status in a transregional context. This trend persisted into the following centuries and reached full force during the peak of the Bronze Age.

Tells and Social Differentiation in the Early and Middle Bronze Age

During the Bronze Age, radical changes in settlement strategies allow us to identify periods of social stability and tension. Through long-term habitation and successive building and rebuilding episodes, some villages developed into artificial settlement mounds, so-called *tells* (Figure 6.5; for a discussion of tell developments

0   5 cm

Figure 6.5. Middle Bronze Age tell settlement, Toboliu, Romania.
Photo by F. Gogâltan.

in the Neolithic, see Chapter 3, this volume). These sites started as regular, flat settlements, but over time, they developed into mounds and thus differed visibly from other contemporaneous residential sites in terms of both architectural patterns and thickness of occupation layers.

Tells were focal elements in the Bronze Age settlement system of the Carpathian Basin, and their development covers a period of approximately one thousand years, from about 2500 to 1500 BC. Based on the thickness of stratigraphic sequence and the number of habitation layers, it is useful to distinguish tells proper from tell-like settlements. Tells have more than 1 m of stratigraphy and three or more habitation layers, whereas tell-like sites have a stratigraphy less than 1 m and at least two habitation layers. In addition, we call mound-like settlements those sites that have similar general physical and material characteristics to those of tells and tell-like sites, but where archaeological excavations have not been carried out, and thus their stratigraphy is unknown.

In the Carpathian Basin, a total of 188 Bronze Age tells, tell-like sites, and mound-like settlements have been identified,[14] out of which forty-six are located in Romania's current territory. These sites occur exclusively in western Romania, and they have not been documented in Transylvania and Maramureș.[15]

Tells evolved as a consequence of favorable environmental conditions in the Carpathian Basin. Although other processes, including deliberate sediment and garbage depositions, also accounted for

their evolution, they formed primarily through the successive accumulation of debris from houses made of wood and plastered with clay (Figure 6.6; see also Chapter 3, this volume). Therefore the construction practices employed by the inhabitants directly influenced the formation of tells. The layout of these sites followed 'Hippodamian principles' (that is, a certain ordering of houses and streets) that remained the same throughout the development of these settlements. Enclosing elements, such as ditches and palisades, also contributed to the evolution of mounds.[16]

In order to address pathways to social stratification in the Bronze Age societies of the eastern Carpathian Basin, we summarize here the results of recent research into the demographic and sociopolitical centers of the era—the tell sites.

In western Romania, recent archaeological investigations have been concentrated on the tell settlements of Pecica[17] and Carei.[18] Similarly important are the non-invasive explorations carried out at various sites in the Ier Valley, the Carei Plain, and the Someș Valley in northwestern Romania.[19] These are added to the results yielded by the project entitled "Living in the Bronze Age Tell Settlements: A Study of Settlement Archaeology at the Eastern Frontier of the Carpathian Basin" endorsed by the Romanian Ministry of National Education and conducted between 2013 and 2016.[20]

The initial goal of this project was to recover formerly unpublished archaeological information from museums in Romania, to collect relevant samples for radiocarbon analyses, and to perform a series of non-invasive studies. The latter included the collection of locational data, new topographic measurements,

Figure 6.6. Stratigraphic sequence of a Middle Bronze Age tell settlement, Toboliu, Romania.
Adapted from Lie et al. 2019:Figure 11.

aerial photographing, and geophysical surveys.[21] Due to time constraints, however, these studies were limited to the Mureş Valley and the tributaries of the Criş rivers. Thirty-six out of the forty-six known multi-layered settlements are located in these areas.

Remarkable results were obtained by geophysical surveys at these sites. At Munar, in the Banat region, geomagnetic prospection was conducted in an area of about 8.7 ha, covering about 60 percent of the Middle Bronze Age multi-layered settlement.[22] On the edge of a terrace, two circular ditches, approximately 3–4 m in width, were identified. The inner ditch surrounds an area of about 70 by 40 m (0.28 ha), while the outer ditch encloses about 110 by 60 m (0.66 ha). A gap of 5 m in both ditches suggests a possible entrance. Most magnetic anomalies, as well as Middle Bronze Age pottery fragments, are located outside the enclosure. Of great importance is another ditch that seems to enclose the archaeological features documented out-side the Middle Bronze Age ditches; it was possibly cut by another rampart dating to the Late Bronze Age (Figure 6.7).

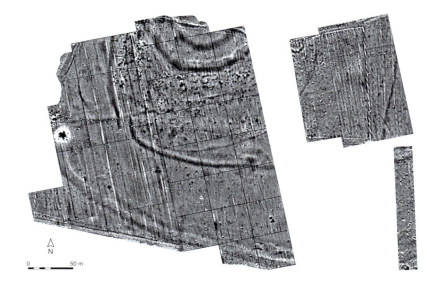

Figure 6.7. Results of magnetometric prospection at the Middle Bronze Age tell of Munar, Romania.
Modified from Gogâltan 2016b:Figure 5 by J. Seagard.

Figure 6.8. Results of magnetometric prospection at the Middle Bronze Age tell of Toboliu, Romania. *Modified from Gogâltan et al. 2020:Figure 6.8 by J. Seagard.*

Magnetometric surveys indicated extensive ditch systems at other tells as well. At Toboliu in the Crişana region, geophysical prospection covered 2.56 ha and revealed two concentric ditches, approximately 20 m apart and 10–15 m in width, that fully enclosed the tell. The outer ditch surrounds an area of about 1.8 ha. There may have been two, diametrically opposed, 10–13 m wide entrances across the outer ditch (Figure 6.8). Following the interior of the smaller ditch, a possible palisade was identified in the eastern part of the mound. Moreover, fairly well-preserved, burnt houses were detected between and beyond the two ditches.[23]

The geophysical survey also revealed several pit anomalies located both within and outside the fortified area. The pit and house anomalies outside of the mound indicate an external settlement in the immediate vicinity of the tell at Toboliu. The intensive surface survey also supported this conclusion. Ceramic sherds securely assigned to the Middle Bronze Age and dispersed fragments of burnt daub were found across an area of about 158 ha. This makes the external settlement at Toboliu the largest one surrounding a Bronze Age tell in the Carpathian Basin documented so far.[24]

Apart from non-invasive explorations, our research design also incorporated targeted excavations. In order to collect samples for radiocarbon dating and obtain data about domestic structures, two neighboring tell settlements, located approximately 7 km away from each other, were chosen for excavation: Sântion and Toboliu. After several excavation campaigns, it became clear that both sites followed the general process of Bronze Age tell formation (that is, several phases of construction and reconstruction of surface dwellings made of wood and plaster), however, each showed unique developmental characteristics as well.

The most interesting results came from the site of Toboliu. Excavations there demonstrated that the thickness of Bronze Age deposits on the northeastern margin of the mound was about 3.2 m, while in the center it was 4 m (see Figure 6.6). Five construction phases, each corresponding to a distinctive residential structure, were identified. The buildings had a rectangular floor plan oriented to east–west, and were made of wattle and daub on a light framework of upright posts. An exceptional finding was a well-preserved floor made of wooden planks (Figure 6.9). Besides typical household assemblages, bronze items were also found on the tell, and metal casting was attested on the mound by two clay tuyères and a stone casting mold. These artifacts illustrate that the Toboliu tell community participated in long-distance exchange

Figure 6.9. Remains of a wooden house floor from the Middle Bronze Age, Toboliu, Romania.
Adapted from Lie et al. 2019:Figure 8.

networks; an interpretation reinforced by saltwater *Dentalium* sea shell beads recovered from the site.[25]

This research provided new information concerning social practices at Bronze Age tells and tell-like settlements in the eastern Carpathian Basin. The non-invasive geophysical investigations helped us understand the relationship of the sites to their local environment, suggesting how the landscape was exploited for the needs of a particular community, and the excavations allowed us to reconstruct tell formation processes in the specific climate conditions of the Carpathian Basin. Our results also signified that tells were not always occupied simultaneously in a particular microregion, and confirmed the hypothesis that the evolution of multi-layered settlements varied by microregions in the Carpathian Basin during the Bronze Age.[26] Furthermore, evidence for settlement activities beyond the fortified tells indicates that these multi-layered sites were often just one part of a more complex settlement system, the social dynamics and development of which have yet to be adequately explored.

A recent, excellent synthesis on bronze metallurgy at Bronze Age tells from the Carpathian Basin expands our knowledge about the social position of the inhabitants at these sites.[27] Let us just take the example of the Pecica tell on the Mureş River in the Banat region. From older excavations at this site, nineteen bronze objects, one item made of gold, and fifty-five artifacts related to metal processing—mainly molds for the casting of axes—are known. One can also add numerous fragments of slag, small crucibles, and small bronze objects unearthed during the recent campaigns from 2005 to 2015.[28] The production and presence of weapons, such as disc-butted axes and halberds, as well as gold objects attest to the wealth and elevated status of groups living on Bronze Age tells.

Tells had complex architectural plans, with buildings organized alongside one another within a fortification system (see Figures 6.7, 6.8, and 6.9). The diversity and high quality of the archaeological material recovered demonstrate that the people who lived at these sites participated in broad, intensive intercultural trade networks. Some specialists describe the multi-layered sites of the Bronze Age in the Carpathian Basin as proto-towns, or as semi- or proto-urban centers. In some microregions, their function as central places is confirmed by the existence of secondary settlements, or by the fact that no other contemporaneous tells developed in their close proximity.[29] However, some researchers do not share these views, arguing that there were no major social or political differences between Neolithic and Bronze Age tell sites of the Carpathian Basin,[30] and that stable urban centers emerged only in the first millennium BC.[31]

The warrior identity of some leaders in these Bronze Age tell societies is demonstrated by several hoards that include weapons, such as axes with symbolic ornaments (see Chapter 5, this volume), as well as by daggers, spearheads, and axes that have been uncovered from burial contexts. Interestingly enough, the circulation of Baltic amber in the Carpathian Basin and the contexts in which such artifacts were found clearly show that the popularity of amber evolved at the tell settlements. The value and symbolic meaning attached to amber is indicated by the regular occurrence of these finds in the contexts of burials and hoards, where they are usually associated with gold artifacts. Therefore a certain degree of social differentiation was a feature of Bronze Age societies during the first half of the second millennium BC.[32]

As mentioned above, there are no multi-layered settlements encircled by fortifications in Transylvania and Maramureș. The archaeological record indicates that the settlements in these regions were relatively modest in terms of size and structural complexity.[33] Also, even though hundreds of graves have been excavated across these territories, they do not indicate significant degrees of social differentiation.[34] This situation, however, contrasts sharply with the large number of bronze, gold, and silver objects. Reflecting the warrior identity, bronze hoards from sites in Maramureș and Transylvania, such as Gaura (modern Valea Chioarului), Ighiel, Săpânța, and the former Turda County, contain beautiful collections of battle-axes symbolically decorated with solar ornaments.[35]

In the Middle Bronze Age, some time after 1700 BC, bronze swords appeared as the first weapons intended for professional military personnel.[36] One of the most important findings to understand the profound transformations leading to armament is the bronze hoard found at Apa, in northwestern Romania, in 1939. The assemblage consists of six bronze objects: two swords, three battle-axes of different types, and one spiral armguard (Figure 6.10).[37] Similar swords were traded over long distances as prestige items.[38]

In Transylvania, many gold objects dating to the Middle Bronze Age have been uncovered. The most spectacular ones include gold axes from Țufalău,[39] various types of ornaments from the open-air sanctuary at Oarța de Sus,[40] and the golden vessel from Bistrița (Figure 6.11).[41] These finds demonstrate the ability of Transylvanian metallurgical centers to produce objects of exceptional value. All in all, the gold artifacts and the appearance of the first bronze swords, spears, and battle-axes are undeniable evidence for an increasingly stratified society in Transylvania over the course of the Bronze Age.

Mega-Forts and Warlike Societies in the Late Bronze Age

The apogee of Bronze Age social dynamics is marked by its latest phase, from about 1500 to 800 BC. During the Late Bronze Age, the largest fortified settlements of prehistoric Europe were built in the southwestern part of modern Romania, in the lower Mureș Basin. Some of these 'mega-forts,' as they have been called by Anthony Harding,[42] have been systematically excavated at Corneşti, Sântana, and Munar over the last ten years. The results of these excavations provide vivid images about peace and war in the Bronze Age societies of the eastern frontier of the Carpathian Basin. In addition to profane or ritual depositions of weaponry in hoards at these sites, the massive fortification systems, which covered hundreds—or even thousands—of hectares, are indirect evidence for intergroup conflicts. Direct evidence for conflicts during the Late Bronze Age includes burnt and violently destroyed hillforts, weapons showing traces of use, and even warriors wounded or killed on battlefields.[43]

The largest mega-fort is Corneşti, distinguished by four ring-shaped, earth-and-wood ramparts as well as ditches. The innermost ring encircles an area of 71 ha, the second 214 ha, the third 507 ha, and the outermost 1,765 ha.[44] Also noteworthy is the complex gate system that provided access, or prevented easy entry, to this mega-fort.[45] The beginning of the Corneşti settlement dates to the transition from the sixteenth to the fifteenth century BC, and it was abandoned in the tenth or the ninth century BC.[46]

At Sântana, recent archaeological investigations have revealed three enclosures, designated as I, II, and III (Figures 6.12 and 6.13). Enclosure I has an approximately rectangular shape with rounded corners, enclosing almost 20 ha. Its defensive architecture consists of a ditch and a palisade. The largest enclosure, Enclosure III, covers an area of approximately 82 ha and has an oval shape with its northern side almost

Figure 6.10. Bronze hoard, Apa, Romania. Middle Bronze Age, 1700–1500 BC. National History Museum of Romania, Bucharest. *Photo: National History Museum of Romania.*

Figure 6.11. Gold vessel, Bistrița, Romania. Middle Bronze Age, 1900–1700 BC. Bistrița-Năsăud Museum Complex, Bistrița. *Photo by Á. Vágó.*

Figure 6.12. Aerial photograph of the Late Bronze Age settlement of Sântana, Romania. *Adapted from Gogâltan et al. 2019:Figure 4.*

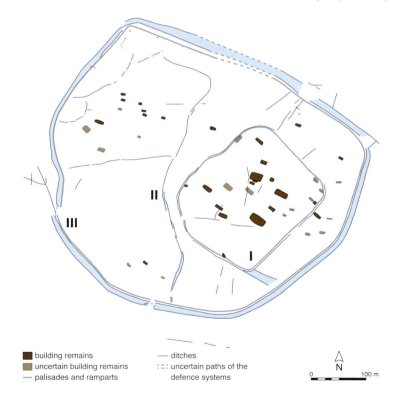

■ building remains   — ditches
■ uncertain building remains   ⋮⋮⋮ uncertain paths of the
— palisades and ramparts   defence systems

0   100 m

Figure 6.13. Interpretation of magnetometric prospection at the Late Bronze Age settlement of Sântana, Romania. Roman numbers indicate the enclosures. *Modified from Gogâltan et al. 2019:Figure 7 by J. Seagard.*

straight. The defensive elements of Enclosure III include a large earthen rampart, a palisade wall on the edge of the rampart, and two ditches that ran along most of the enclosure's length. The magnetometric surveys at Sântana also offer an initial insight into the settlement layout within the fortification system. Most structures measured 10–20 m in length; however, some were truly impressive in size, with lengths exceeding 50 m (Figure 6.13).[47] At present, it seems the fortification system of Enclosure III was in use throughout the fourteenth century BC.[48]

The third mega-fort, Munar, represents an exceptional case in the Carpathian Basin. In contrast to other tell sites, the Munar tell was not abandoned at the end of the Middle Bronze Age, but instead habitation continued into the Late Bronze Age. In this later period, a large fortification system was constructed, with the outermost enclosure consisting of a rampart and a ditch and enclosing about 15 ha. As in the case of other contemporaneous fortifications in the lower Mureș Basin, the dirt from the ditch was used to build the rampart. The rampart measures 1.5 m in height and 15 m in width (see Figure 6.7).[49]

The excavations and systematic surveys testify to the burning of strongholds at Corneşti, Sântana, and Munar. The palisade of the innermost ring at Corneşti was set on fire; however, it cannot be determined

Figure 6.14. Fired clay sling projectiles in burnt debris, Sântana, Romania. Late Bronze Age, 1400–1300 BC. Arad Museum Complex, Arad. *Adapted from Gogâltan and Sava 2018:Figure 5.*

whether this was the result of a direct attack or whether it was destroyed in the aftermath of a siege.[50] At Sântana, our research confirmed that the fortified area was besieged. We found in situ evidence that the clay wall and its timber structure, as well as the palisade, were attacked with fired clay sling projectiles and bronze arrows, and ultimately, the wall was torched (Figure 6.14). The area where the attack occurred is approximately 400–500 m in length, and is located in the northern segment of Enclosure III. The considerable number of projectiles, coupled with the extremely violent attack of a large sector of the Enclosure III defensive system, suggest a siege performed by an expeditionary force at Sântana, rather significant in numbers and very well trained (Figure 6.15).[51]

Only charismatic leaders had the political power to enforce and manage the construction of large earthen strongholds, such as those at Corneşti, Sântana, and Munar. These leaders were the products of a social system based upon economic, religious, and implicitly hierarchical criteria. We can only imagine the huge amount of effort that was invested into the construction of these fortifications. Moreover, recurrent repairs of the clay walls, as noticed at Sântana, or the cleaning of the defensive ditches were additional tasks that needed to be carried out regularly. The day-and-night defense of these sites would have involved a large number of warriors that the settlement communities, or even entire hinterlands, could not sustain. Thus the defensive organization must have had a broader demographic base, involving the participation of certain allies. The extreme size and simplified fortification elements of the third and fourth enclosures at Corneşti raise the possibility that these constructions could have had a symbolic meaning or a special function, such as marking the designated space of the community or protecting the settlement against savage animals or predators. The defensive capacity of these extensive enclosures may have been limited when large-scale military conflicts occurred.

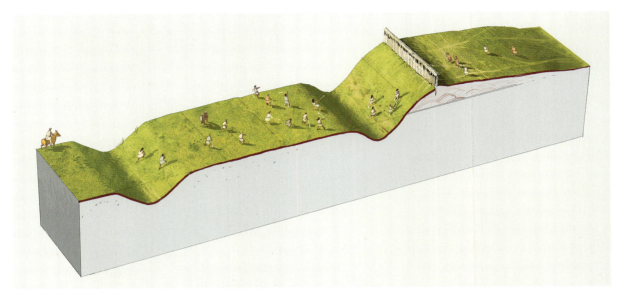

Figure 6.15. Reconstruction of the siege at the Late Bronze Age settlement of Sântana, Romania.
Adapted from Gogâltan et al. 2019:Figure 27.

Figure 6.16. Aerial photograph of the Late Bronze Age settlement of Teleac, Romania.
Adapted from Uhnér et al. 2019:Figure 17.

In Transylvania and Maramureș, the first fortified settlements occurred centuries later than in the lower Mureș Basin. Although there are hundreds of bronze hoards dating between 1450 and 1200 BC, with a fair number and great diversity of offensive and defensive weapons,[52] fortified settlements in these regions were not established before 1200 BC. These sites are attributed to the Late Bronze Age Gáva Culture.[53] The most representative fortified settlement of this period in Transylvania is Teleac, located in the southwestern part of the region, along the Mureș Valley (Figure 6.16). At this site, an 800-m-long wooden framed box-rampart filled with earth and two outer ditches protected an area of 30 ha.[54] Recent investigations suggest that the settlement was densely inhabited, with an estimated population of about 1,200 people. Around the fort, fifteen contemporaneous, open settlements were documented.[55] The excavations and geophysical explorations indicate that the entire fortification

Figure 6.17. Bronze torques, Tărtăria, Romania. Early Iron Age, 900–800 BC. National History Museum of Romania, Bucharest. *Photo by Á. Vágó.*

system was destroyed by fire sometime in the late tenth century BC. As at Sântana, fired clay slingshots provide the evidence for a siege.[56]

In addition to the rich settlement record, hoards also indicate an increased degree of violence and the presence of a warrior elite during the Late Bronze Age. These hoards date to about 1300 to 900/800 BC and contain various swords,[57] or in other cases, objects related to "male panoply and metal stock."[58] Such weapons, deposited in ritual contexts (such as in rivers and lakes, on mountain peaks, or in caves), represent direct negotiations between the dedicators and their divinities for success and good luck in battle, or expressed gratitude for the social status that the owners of the hoards achieved (for examples and interpretations of Late Bronze Age hoards in the Carpathian Basin, see also Chapter 5, this volume).[59]

The first iron objects of the eastern Carpathian Basin, which were manufactured in the tenth century BC, were weapons, including swords, daggers, and axes.[60] They suggest strong links with Greece's

contemporaneous warrior elites.[61] The transition from bronze to iron weapons was gradual, as the rich iron deposits of Transylvania began to be exploited and blacksmiths adapted to the new technology.

The beginning of the Iron Age is marked by the movement of some communities from the south that were responsible for the burning of the largest fortification in Transylvania, Teleac. They are the ones who founded a new center of power in the Mureş Valley at Tărtăria (Figure 6.17). The possible fortification and numerous iron spears and axes discovered at Tărtăria indicate the continued persistence of a warrior ideology into this new era.[62]

Concluding Remarks

The portrayal of the Bronze Age elite as "warrior aristocracies . . . buried in richly furnished graves, often in a barrow with sets of weapons, which could also be deposited in hoards"[63] has been severely criticized by some authors.[64] However, this impassioned debate makes archaeological research beautiful and challenging. New scientific research and major discoveries on the eastern border of the Carpathian Basin—including the Early Bronze Age burial mounds, the multi-layered settlements of the Middle Bronze Age, the Late Bronze Age mega-forts, and an Early Iron Age center—permit us to paint a more nuanced picture of a world of peace and war. Following Early and Middle Bronze Age sociopolitical developments, the Late Bronze Age saw the rise of powerful hierarchical leaders who commanded the construction and regular maintenance of massive earthen fortifications and many times ordered formal armies with professional soldiers supplied with specialized weaponry to perform large-scale sieges.

Notes

1   For examples, see Kienlin and Zimmerman 2012.

2   Parkinson 2006; Pawn 2012; Siklósi 2013; Zalai-Gaál 2010.

3   Diaconescu et al. 2017.

4   Krauß et al. 2016.

5   Harrison and Heyd 2007:193–203, Fig. 45.

6   Popa 2016.

7   Ciugudean 2011:23–27.

8   Gogâltan 2016a:430–34.

9   Hansen 2013b.

10   Dani 2013.

11   Soroceanu 2012:109–14, Pl. 37–43; Szeverényi 2013:662–63, Fig. 1.

12   Chernykh et al. 2002.

13   Frînculeasa et al. 2015:84–86.

14   Gogâltan 2017:30, Map 1.

15   Gogâltan 2014:15, Fig. 1.

16   Gogâltan 2008; Jaeger 2016.

17   O'Shea and Nicodemus 2019:68–76.

18   Molnár and Ciută 2017.

19   Kienlin et al. 2017:107–17.

20   Gogâltan et al. 2020.

21   Gogâltan 2016b:88.

22   Sava and Gogâltan 2017.

23   Gogâltan et al. 2020:80, Fig. 6.8.

24   Fazecaș and Lie 2018:31, Fig. 3.

25   Lie et al. 2019.

26   Kienlin et al. 2018.

27   Găvan 2015.

28   Găvan 2015:209–12.

29   Gogâltan 2010:39–40.

30   Kienlin 2015a:56–57.

31   Harding 2018:331–34.

32   Gogâltan 2016b:103.

33   Boroffka 1994; Gogâltan 2019.

34   Bălan et al. 2018.

35   Soroceanu 2012.

36   Molloy and Horn 2020:123.

37   Soroceanu 2012:17–20, Figs 1–5.

38   Ling et al. 2019:19–21; Pernicka et al. 2016:82.

39   Puskás 2018:244–45, Fig. 34.

40   Kacsó 2004:Fig. 39.

41   Gogâltan and Marinescu 2018.

42   Harding 2017.

43   Vandkilde 2011.

44   Krause et al. 2019:136.

45   Heeb et al. 2014:86, Fig. 19; Szentmiklosi et al. 2011:830, Fig. 12:a–c.

46   Lehmphul et al. 2019:274, 276.

47   Gogâltan et al. 2019:Figs 8–9.

48   Sava et al. 2019:174.

49   Sava and Gogâltan 2017.

50   Szentmiklosi et al. 2011:827, Fig. 7.

51   Gogâltan and Sava 2018.

52   Soroceanu 2011a:Figs 2–4.

53   Bălan 2013:Fig. 1.

54   Uhnér et al. 2019.

55   Uhnér et al. 2018:389.

56   Uhnér et al. 2019:188, Fig. 12.

57   Bader 1991.

58   Pare 2019:Table 1.

59   Soroceanu 2011b.

60   Pare 2017:65–69.

61   Hansen 2019:214–19.

62   Borș et al. 2017.

63   Kristiansen and Larsson 2005:218.

64   Brück and Fontijn 2013; Kienlin 2015b.

CHAPTER 7

Weapons and Warriors in the Late Bronze Age of the Northern and Central Balkans

János Gábor Tarbay and Jovan D. Mitrović

TOWARD THE LATE BRONZE AGE, sometime between the fifteenth and twelfth centuries BC, fortified mega-settlements ruled over the landscapes of Transylvania (see Chapter 6, this volume),[1] the Serbian Banat,[2] and the southern part of the Great Hungarian Plain.[3] The fortifications of these sites are so colossal that they are clearly visible on satellite images and their extent rivals that of modern settlements today. Orosháza-Nagytatársánc, in southern Hungary, is one of these mega-settlements. It covers 113 ha, and it was surrounded by a double enclosure of ramparts and ditches, with at least two gates (Figure 7.1).[4] During the construction of these monumental structures, fundamental social and cultural shifts occurred in southeastern Europe, including social stratification, major metallurgical innovations, the emergence of novel crafts, and the formation of new social groups. As discussed extensively in the previous chapter, scholars have argued that some of these shifts were facilitated by the appearance of more aggressive elite groups and 'warrior' specialists,[5] whose bellicose activities literally left marks on the besieged settlements and on hundreds of weapons recovered from Late Bronze Age sites.

Through the exploration of weaponry and its development, technology, and use, this chapter focuses on violence in the Late Bronze Age as it related to broader sociopolitical developments. This era in the northern and central parts of the Balkans began around 1500 BC and terminated around 900 BC, with some regional differences. During this long period of time, due to intensive interactions between these regions, the material culture of modern-day Serbia, Bosnia and Herzegovina, Croatia, and southern Hungary showed many similarities, especially with regard to bronze weaponry. By discussing the archaeological evidence, this chapter provides an overview of the weaponry and the warrior identities that emerged in the northern and central Balkans in the final phase of the Bronze Age (Figure 7.2).

The Technology of Prestige and Death

The warrior equipment of the Late Bronze Age is the product of a long development of bronze technology, the roots of which extend far before this period. The Balkan Peninsula is abundant in various ores and minerals, and the earliest metal production likely occurred in the central Balkans.[6] The local copper sources provided an ideal setting for the development of bronze metallurgy, including mining, the processing of raw materials, and the production of advanced metal goods.

Figure 7.1. Satellite image of a Late Bronze Age mega-fort, Orosháza-Nagytatársánc, Hungary. *Google Earth image.*

Bronze played a leading role in aesthetic expression throughout the Bronze Age. By improving metallurgical techniques, bronze jewelry, weapons, and tools became more complex and gradually richer in their decoration, which led to the emergence of diverse weaponry at the end of the Middle Bronze Age and the beginning of the Late Bronze Age. In the northern and central Balkans, iron metallurgy intensified only after the ninth century BC; however, the offensive weapons were still imitating their bronze predecessors. Excellent examples include bimetal swords, which resemble their Bronze Age forerunners, but which were manufactured with a blade made from a new material: iron.[7]

Over the course of the Late Bronze Age, melee weapons were the most common. However, the use of leather shields and weapons like clubs in combat is also highly likely, but unlike their bronze variants (such as spears, swords, daggers, and axes), these organic materials were not preserved due to environmental conditions.[8] Ranged weapons were also present in the Balkans in the form of javelin-like spearheads and arrows.

The invention of alloying allowed metalsmiths to make more resilient weapons (Figure 7.3). This technology reached its peak during the Late Bronze Age, resulting in the development of various metalworking tools and specialized manufacturing techniques, some of which are still used in modern bronze and iron foundry practices. The basis of Late Bronze Age weapon production was metal casting, usually performed using bivalve ceramic or stone molds. Such finds, which were used to cast swords or spearheads, are known from settlements in the northern Balkans.[9] Some swords, like a specimen from Benkovac in Croatia with a pseudo-openwork hilt, were made by the lost-wax casting technique.[10]

A potential crafting center might have been located in northwestern Serbia. Anthony Harding suggested that flange-hilted swords may have been manufactured in southern Pannonia or in the central Balkans, and that the 'Balkan Route' was used for their distribution toward the south.[11] Spearheads also reflect advanced technologies of the time. In bivalve molds, a casting core was inserted with the aid of a rod, which allowed precise casting with thin walls, competing with modern objects in the appearance of the products.[12] Notably, some of the larger arrowheads found in Serbia could have been made in the same way.[13] In the socket of some spearheads, like the one from Kikinda in Serbia, even the tip of the wooden shaft was preserved. Judging from the results of neutron

Figure 7.2. Map showing the sites in the central and northern Balkans and the Carpathian Basin mentioned in the text and the major Balkan trade routes during the Bronze Age. *Reconstruction of trade routes is based on Filipović 2018:Figure 1. Illustration by F. Paár and E. Rodriguez.*

tomography analysis, these shafts were shaped out of a larger log or a branch, similarly to their West European counterparts (Figure 7.4).[14]

Based on casting molds recovered from the Balkans,[15] the tool/weapon socketed axes were made in a manner similar to spearheads. Exceptions include large winged axes, which were cast without a core. As as-casts,[16] winged axes were unsuitable for hafting, and thus were formed by phases of cold hammering and/or annealing. Traces of similar post-casting treatment, particularly cold hammering by metal or stone hammers, also can be observed on other weapons, such as swords and spearheads.[17] According to the metallographic analyses of Late Bronze Age

Figure 7.3. Reconstruction of a Late Bronze Age metal workshop.
Modified from David-Elbiali 2006:Figure 212 by J. Seagard.

swords and spearheads from Serbia, the treatments
of spearheads were variable, while swords received a
considerable amount of post-casting treatment by cold
working of the edges and annealing.[18] The hardened,
razor-sharp cutting edges imply that these weapons
were indeed capable of causing harm in combat. In
Transdanubia and southeastern Hungary, where
swords and spearheads comparable to the ones from
the northern Balkans have been recovered, there are
numerous cases of weapons with traces of use. These
include swords with extremely worn hilts, and in many
cases, their cutting edges show micro-notches and
damage caused by blade-on-blade contact (Figure
7.5).[19] From the northern Balkans, extensive use-wear
data are unavailable; however, Barry Molloy's recent
results on Serbian Late Bronze Age materials suggest
a similar trend regarding the usage of weapons in
that region.[20]

Defensive weapons and armor, including metal
shields, cuirasses, helmets, and greaves, represent
another aspect of weapon technology, closely related to
the technology used to produce gold and bronze ban-
quet vessels. The manufacture of armor started with
the casting of a semi-finished product, which was then
formed by cycles of cold hammering and annealing
until it gained its desired shape.[21] Much of the armor

Figure 7.4. Bronze
spearhead with wooden
shaft remains, Kikinda,
Serbia. Late Bronze
Age, 1300–1100 BC.
Hungarian National
Museum, Budapest.
*Neutron tomography image
by Z. Kis (Centre for
Energy Research, Nuclear
Analysis and Radiography
Department), photo by
J.G. Tarbay, modified by J.
Seagard.*

0   2 cm

Figure 7.5. Bronze swords with traces of use: a) hammered blade with a U-shaped notch; b) sharpening traces; c) V-shaped notch caused by blade-on-blade contact; d) asymmetrical dent caused by fighting. a: Bela Crkva, Serbia. Late Bronze Age, 1400–1300 BC; b–d: Veliki Gaj, Serbia. Late Bronze Age, 1200–1000 BC. Hungarian National Museum, Budapest. *Microscope-camera images by J.G. Tarbay, modified by J. Seagard.*

Figure 7.6. Bronze, decorated sword, Veliki Gaj, Serbia. Late Bronze Age, 1200–1000 BC. Hungarian National Museum, Budapest. *Photo and microscope-camera images by J.G. Tarbay, modified by J. Seagard.*

was equipped with practical elements like folded rims, making it more resilient against blade impacts, or with perforations that helped assemble the metal parts with their organic base.[22] Fine examples include richly decorated helmets, which were most likely fastened onto leather or wool bases by rivets.[23] Advanced metal techniques, such as the cast-on method,[24] were applied to cast the knobs of these helmets onto their metal sheet body.[25] As with offensive weapons, the metal sheet armor and defensive weapons were functional objects, but the small number of known examples suggests that they were utilized mainly by the elite members of Late Bronze Age societies.

The Late Bronze Age was most likely the first era when weapons with 'identities' were created.[26] Both defensive and offensive weapons were sumptuously decorated using different techniques (such as chasing or embossing) and were often adorned with celestial and other symbolic motifs, like solar barges, spirals, and mythical birds. The artistic design of these weapons implies that the objects played a key role in warriors' self-representation. It is possible that the motifs also served to empower the weapons and their owners with supernatural skills and capabilities, or to provide symbolic protection during combat (Figure 7.6).

On Protection in Combat

Brave Thrasymedes provided the son of
Tydeus with a sword and a shield (for he had
left his own at his ship) and on his head he set
a helmet of bull's hide without either peak or
crest; it is called a skull-cap and is a common
headgear. Meriones found a bow and quiver
for Ulysses, and on his head he set a leathern
helmet that was lined with a strong plaiting of
leathern thongs, while on the outside it was
thickly studded with boar's teeth, well and
skillfully set into it; next the head there was
an inner lining of felt.

—Book X, Homer's *Iliad*

The need for protection of the most vulnerable
parts of the human body led to the development of
armor (helmets, cuirasses, greaves) and defensive
weapons (shields).[27] The earliest helmets were probably made of leather or other organic materials. It is
presumed that the first bronze helmets in southeastern
Europe, which had a conical shape and a cast knob,
were derived from Aegean boar tusk helmets. Excellent examples to illustrate this transition include a
helmet from an unknown location imitating boar tusk
motifs as well as the bronze helmet from Knossos-
Venizeleio in Greece dating from the fifteenth century
BC (Figure 7.7). In the central and northern Carpathian Basin, similar helmets appeared around the
thirteenth century BC.[28] In the northern Balkans,
however, decorated cap helmets are the most common.
These masterfully made specimens were equipped
with long, cast-on knobs and cheek pieces and were
covered with parallel ribs and star-shaped ornaments
(Figure 7.8).[29] These helmets were found as deliberately broken objects in several large, ritual hoards in
northern Croatia and Serbia.[30] An exception is the
helmet from Bajmok in Serbia, which was found
intact, similar to some other specimens from the
Danube River in Hungary.[31]

Now when the son of Lycaon saw him
(Diomedes) scouring the plain and driving
the Trojans pell-mell before him, he aimed
an arrow and hit the front part of his cuirass
near the shoulder: the arrow went right
through the metal and pierced the flesh, so
that the cuirass was covered with blood.

—Book V, Homer's *Iliad*

Figure 7.7. Bronze, conical-shaped helmet, Tomb 5,
Knossos-Venizeleio, Greece. Late Bronze Age, 1500–1400
BC. Heraklion Archaeological Museum. *Photo: Heraklion
Archaeological Museum, Hellenic Ministry of Culture &
Sports, Archaeological Receipts Fund.*

Figure 7.8. Bronze cap helmet with star-shaped
ornaments, unknown provenance. Late Bronze Age,
1200–1100 BC. Hungarian National Museum,
Budapest. *Photo by Á. Vágó.*

Figure 7.9. Bronze cuirass, Pilismarót-Danube River, Hungary. Late Bronze Age, 1200–1100 BC. Szent István Király Museum, Székesfehérvár. *Photo by Á. Vágó.*

Bronze cuirasses had breast and back plates, covering the torso of the warrior. This armor is one of the rarest finds in continental Europe,[32] therefore it is highly likely that only warriors with elevated social status would have owned them, and that leather specimens were much more common. Evidence for composite cuirasses is known both from the Aegean and southeastern Europe. Such armor consisted of bronze discs, bosses, and metal sheet parts sewn on leather plates.[33] The full metal armor appeared about 1500 BC in the Aegean.[34] Emblematic is the panoply from a burial at Dendra, which consisted of fifteen separate pieces, protecting its owner's neck, shoulders, and a part of his legs.[35] Simple cuirasses without additional protecting elements have been recovered from eastern Europe as well; however, so far no such finds have been found in the northern Balkans. In the Carpathian Basin, the cuirass from Pilismarót-Danube River in Hungary is the best preserved (Figure 7.9). This marvelous find was made of two thick bronze sheets, with a decoration that imitates the naked body of a male warrior. Riveted parts along its edges suggest that it was worn on a leather or organic base.[36]

Weapons for Combat

In addition to cuirasses, greaves were also essential parts of the Late Bronze Age warrior's armor, as they served to protect the lower parts of legs. Bronze greaves with perforated edges, which were riveted onto organic materials, imply that the first greaves were crafted out of leather.[37] A stunning greave made of gold and deposited in a folded state from Szeged-Gyálarét in southeastern Hungary also belongs to this group (see Figure 5.14, this volume).[38] This find is particularly important, as it is the only gold defensive armor from the entire territory of central Europe, and it is also a clear sign that the wearing of greaves had a special role in the self-representation of elite warriors. Greaves were probably invented in the Aegean; a fine example was uncovered in one of the previously mentioned Dendra burials in Greece, dating to the late fifteenth or early fourteenth century BC. Bronze greaves were introduced in the Carpathian Basin and the northern Balkans between 1200 and 1100 BC, and their use continued into the eighth and seventh centuries BC of the Early Iron Age.[39] In these regions, various greave designs appeared. Some exhibited clear western Carpathian or Italian connections,[40] while others, decorated with large, embossed patterns, giving a harmonic appearance to these masterpieces, were related to western Europe.[41]

Shields are suitable for providing passive protection for any part of the warrior's body from trauma- and ranged-weapons. At the same time, they can also be used for active blocks during close combat situations. Shields can be divided into larger versions, such as battle shields and light shields, and smaller variants, like bucklers. They were generally made of organic materials (leather, wood, twisted plants) throughout prehistory and, as well-preserved Irish examples suggest, even during the Bronze Age.[42] From the Carpathian Basin and the northern Balkans, only so-called Lommelev–Nyírtura-type metal shields are known, dating between 1300 and 1100 BC. Their reconstruction is possible only with the aid of the northernmost example from the Lommelev marshlands in Denmark because all southeastern European finds, such as ones from Otok-Privlaka in Croatia, were deposited as ritually broken objects in hoards.[43] The shield from Lommelev had a diameter of 69 cm and weighed 2 kg. It was equipped with a large boss and a metal handle, and with a rolled-over rim that served to deflect impacts of bladed weapons. It was also adorned with embossed dots arranged in an elegant shape of a sun beam.[44] Some argue for the influence of the Lommelev–Nyírtura-type on a bronze shield found in Delphi, Greece.[45]

The group of offensive weapons that were used to attack, inflict injuries, or take life includes several different types. In the Late Bronze Age northern and central Balkans, these can be broadly divided into melee/close combat (such as daggers, swords, axes, lances) and ranged weapons (such as javelins, bows, and arrows).[46]

Daggers are double-edged, close-combat weapons about 10–30 cm in length, used for stabbing and thrusting.[47] In Early Bronze Age southeastern Europe, small, triangle-shaped types were common and these eventually developed into elongated variants at the beginning of the Middle Bronze Age.[48] In the central Balkans, daggers exhibiting Aegean influences were also found.[49] As a result of the widespread adoption of swords and knives, daggers lost their importance, and during the Late Bronze Age, only smaller, individual forms were utilized in the northern Balkans. Most notable are the so-called Peschiera-style daggers, with a characteristic leaf-shaped blade. Several of these daggers and their local variants were found in intentionally fragmented conditions in hoards, like Boljanić in Bosnia and Herzegovina and Privina Glava in Serbia, along with fragments of other weapons (Figure 7.10).[50] Daggers with similar designs were present in many territories at that time between western and southeastern Europe, including Italy, the Carpathian Basin, and even Greece where they were hafted onto ivory handles.[51]

Swords are the most emblematic weapons for close combat from the Late Bronze Age. These weapons have a double-edged blade that was longer than that of the daggers (more than 30 cm). The outlines of their edges can be leaf-shaped, narrow, or wide, depending on different combat techniques. Their ergonomic, metal or organic handles fit into their users' hands perfectly, allowing precise thrusting and striking motions.[52] The predecessors of these swords occurred for the first time in the Aegean around the third millennium BC, in the guise of elongated daggers with central ribs.[53] In eastern Central Europe, the first swords were manufactured during the Middle Bronze Age, and gained their classic shape as early as 1600 BC. These are the so-called Hajdúsámson–Apa-type swords, which are masterfully crafted and decorated with rich patterns on their handles and blades (Figure 7.11). At the same time, long swords in the Aegean were decorated with gold, and their hilts were crafted in amber, ivory, and even lapis lazuli.[54] During the

Figure 7.10. Bronze hoard, Privina Glava, Serbia. Late Bronze Age, 1300–1100 BC.
National Museum of Serbia, Belgrade. *Photo: National Museum of Serbia.*

Late Bronze Age of the northern Balkans, swords were placed in burials and hoards alike. Most are flange-hilted with parallel-edged blades, following standard Central European styles and supplemented with organic hilt plates. In the case of the metal-hilted specimens with leaf-shaped blades, strong Carpathian relations, in addition to western ones, can be observed in the northern Balkans (Figures 7.12 and 7.13).[55] At the end of the Late Bronze Age and beginning of the Early Iron Age, alongside long swords, short variants were also produced, such as the so-called Tešanj-type swords, which were characteristic objects in a small area between the Una and Bosna rivers. This weapon is about 40 cm long, and has a strong mid-rib and a relatively straight blade that is perfectly suitable for stabbing movements (Figure 7.14).[56]

Spearheads were one of the most common offensive weapons during the Late Bronze Age. The different spearheads used in this era also have predecessors that can be traced back at least to the Early Bronze Age.[57] Depending on their shape and length,

spears could have had several functions. The larger pieces with widened blades may have been lances for thrusting (Figure 7.15), while the ones with narrow and long blades could also have been hafted as slashing spears or used as halberd-like weapons. It is likely that the shorter versions were utilized as javelins.[58] Most spearhead types from the northern Balkans are closely related to Carpathian forms.[59]

Pisander then seized the bronze battle-axe, with its long and polished handle of olive wood that hung by his side under his shield, and the two made at one another. Pisander struck the peak of Menelaus's crested helmet just under the crest itself, and Menelaus hit Pisander as he was coming towards him, on the forehead, just at the rise of his nose; the bones cracked and his two gore-bedrabbled eyes fell by his feet in the dust.

—Book XIII, Homer's *Iliad*

Axes are multi-functional objects that, in ancient times, served as both tools and weapons. As heavy (approximately 0.4–0.5 kg) weapons with elaborately

Figure 7.11. Bronze, richly decorated sword, Apa, Romania. Middle Bronze Age, 1700–1500 BC. National History Museum of Romania, Bucharest. *Photo by Á. Vágó.*

Figure 7.12. Bronze, metal-hilted sword, Kastav, Croatia. Late Bronze Age, 1100–900 BC. Archaeological Museum in Zagreb. *Photo by Á. Vágó.*

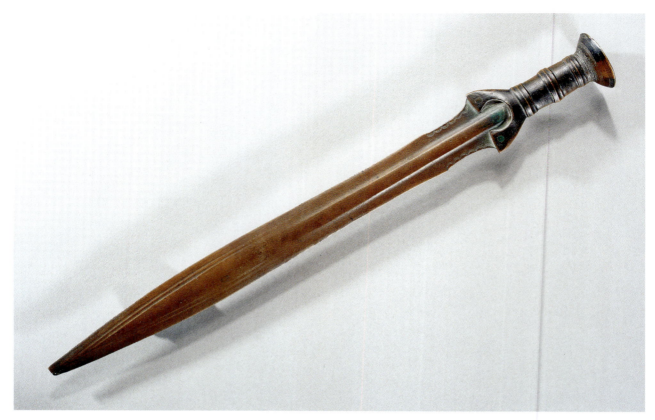

Figure 7.13. Bronze, metal-hilted sword, Grižane, Croatia. Late Bronze Age, 1000–900 BC. Archaeological Museum in Zagreb. *Photo by Á. Vágó.*

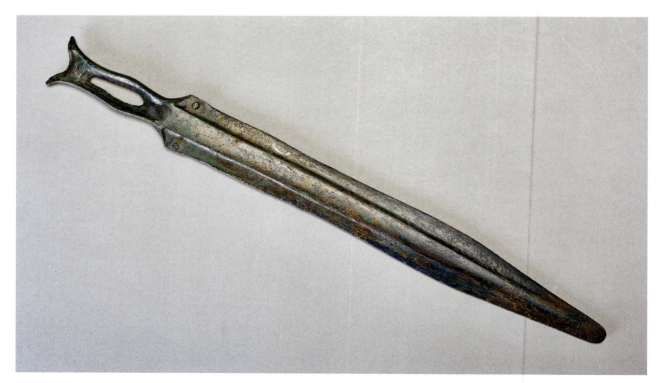

Figure 7.14. Bronze, Tešanj-type sword, Matijevići, Croatia. Transition from the Late Bronze Age to the Early Iron Age, 850–750/700 BC. Archaeological Museum in Zagreb. *Photo by Á. Vágó.*

Figure 7.15. Bronze spearheads, Tenja, Croatia. Late Bronze Age, 1300–1100 BC. Archaeological Museum in Zagreb. *Photo by Á. Vágó.*

manufactured blades and razor-sharp edges, they were particularly suitable for penetrating armor or causing serious injuries in close combat. The development of Bronze Age axes started with shaft-hole axes at the end of the Copper Age and the beginning of the Bronze Age (for examples, see Chapter 4, this volume).[60] Several forms with various functions developed prior to the Late Bronze Age. The shaft-hole axes, disc-butted axes, two-arm battle-axes, large winged axes, and socketed axes could also have been used as weapons. The disc-butted specimens are notably heavy shaft-hole axes, with one edge and a somewhat simpler design compared to their predecessors. These objects are particularly characteristic of the northeastern Carpathians, and occur only rarely in the Balkans.[61] Their use became less common toward the end of the Late Bronze Age, when several locally developed socketed axes and heavy winged axes became prevalent (Figure 7.16).[62]

Finds related to archery are surprisingly rare across eastern Europe, and especially in the central Balkans, where only thirty-five arrowheads dating to

the Late Bronze Age have been found.[63] These bronze arrowheads are the result of a long development, starting from stone and organic materials, such as antler and bone, to versions made of bronze with tangs or sockets.[64]

Weapons in Context

In terms of archaeological contexts, Bronze Age weapons come primarily from hoards or have been found as stray finds. This critically hinders our ability to study 'warrior identities.' Unlike some parts of western Europe (for example, in the Alps, where numerous examples of lavish burials with weapons are known),[65] in the Carpathian Basin and the northern Balkans, such assemblages are rare. The general lack of 'warrior' graves is well illustrated by the mere sixteen Late Bronze Age burials containing swords that have been recovered from the 38,000-km² region

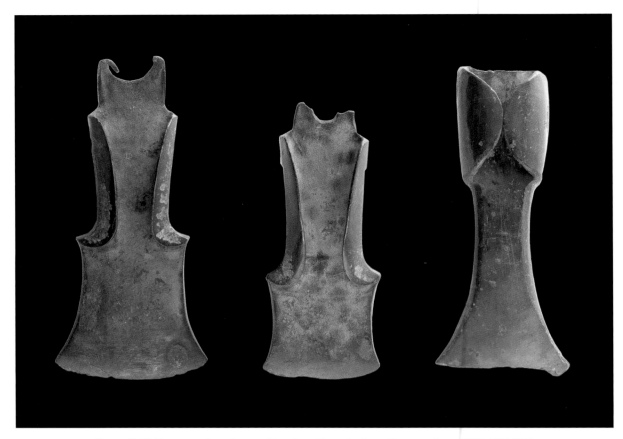

Figure 7.16. Bronze winged axes, Kapelna, Croatia. Late Bronze Age, 1000–900 BC. Archaeological Museum, Osijek. *Photo by B. Jobst, modified by J. Seagard.*

of Transdanubia in the Carpathian Basin.[66] In the northern Balkans, burials with swords and spears from this period are also quite scarce.[67]

Regarding grave assemblages with weapons, it is also questionable whether they belonged to professional warriors—that is, a certain elite group. Weapons could have been deposited with a person who never took arms but was buried as a warrior. They could also, however, have been placed beside an individual who had a well-trained physique and healed combat injuries—an actual professional warrior. There are also cases where skeletal traumas indicate that the deceased died during combat, but no weapons were put in their graves.[68] A fine example for a probable fallen or executed warrior was found at the end of the nineteenth century at Keszthely Mound 1 in Hungary, where a Late Bronze Age inhumation burial of a male with a richly decorated sword was recovered from a chamber tomb (Figure 7.17). Early reports noted that a part of his skull, the occiput, was cut off.[69] From the northern Balkans, an important instance of a Late Bronze Age burial with weapons is known from Velika Gorica in Croatia. Because the individual was cremated, by means of osteological indicators, it cannot be determined whether the deceased was a warrior during his life, but the grave goods were clearly

intended to give that impression. The burial contained a sword and a spearhead with a spear butt, both ostentatiously decorated. The identical motifs on these weapons suggest that they may have been parts of a single, personal set. Two large knives and a unique socketed axe were also placed in this grave. Among the rest of the finds from the same context, pins and a razor are notable because they may have symbolized the concept of 'warrior beauty' discussed by Paul Treherne.[70] The sword and the spearhead are partially melted, and were intentionally bent and broken into pieces. Such weapons can be symbols of authority or valor, which would be bent or broken and never used again due to their close connection with the deceased.[71] The treatment of the weapons in the Velika Gorica grave resembles the treatment of the deceased, who was also transformed and fragmented by fire during the cremation ritual.[72] The highly personal objects unearthed in this burial may have been substitutions for the deceased's warrior identity, which was destroyed or transformed symbolically as a part of the funerary ceremony.[73]

The accumulation of weapons is more pronounced in hoards because weapons may have been separated from warriors at a certain stage of their life for various ritual reasons (for examples, see Chapter 5, this volume). During the Late Bronze Age in the Carpathian Basin, several swords, and even some defensive weapons, were ritually deposited in rivers. In a handful of cases, the deposition of swords also occurred in the northern Balkans, in the Danube, Morava, Drina, and Sava rivers. This practice also has counterparts in western Europe, and it was one way to 'surrender' weapons during the Late Bronze Age. Hoards of weapons in wetlands are traditionally interpreted as votive offerings to deities, whereas more recent approaches relate them to life-cycle rituals of warriors.[74] Dryland hoards are the best examples of the manifestation of warrior identities. The content and treatment of these assemblages reflect a coherent concept and an intentional selection of objects. Among the numerous examples from the northern Balkans, two Serbian assemblages are worth mentioning here: Topolnica and Markovac-Grunjac. The Topolnica hoard consists of twenty-one artifacts, including four pairs of leg spirals, three arm rings, two pins, two socketed axes, and six swords (Figure 7.18).[75] This is clearly a weapon set that would have belonged to multiple warriors, probably a 'band of brothers.' The composition of this assemblage is similar to that of several contemporaneous hoards in the northeastern Carpathian Basin. An important example is the Zalkod hoard from northern Hungary found accidentally within a prehistoric settlement during a major flood episode. This stunning assemblage resembles in many ways the Topolnica hoard—it originally contained eight swords along with personal ornaments, including five arm spirals, four leg spirals, and a pin, as well as some other, small bronze objects, which since have been lost (Figure 7.19).[76] The Zalkod hoard also likely represents of a group of warriors. The similarities between these two contemporaneous assemblages raise the possibility that the deposition of the Topolnica hoard may have been carried out by people who had come from the northeastern Carpathian Basin, or who were familiar with the ritual traditions practiced there. These individuals may have been a 'foreign military escort' for a local warlord, or perhaps they were local mercenaries returning with their exotic goods.[77] For these multiple sword depositions, the interpretation presented by Katherine Harrel with respect to the shaft graves at Mycenae, which date to a hundred years earlier, should be taken into account. She explained the co-occurrence of multiple swords in the same contexts there as the indication of a ritual practice, during which swordsmen gave back their swords to their deceased leader.[78] A similar interpretation has been proposed for the deposition of Late Bronze Age swords in northeastern Hungary.[79]

The Markovac-Grunjac assemblage, mentioned previously, is a large scrap hoard from northeastern Serbia that includes finds with links to Moravia,

1a ÁBRA.

1b ÁBRA.

Figure 7.17. Chamber tomb with a male burial, Keszthely, Hungary. Late Bronze Age, 1400–1300 BC. *Adapted from Lipp 1885:Figure 1.*

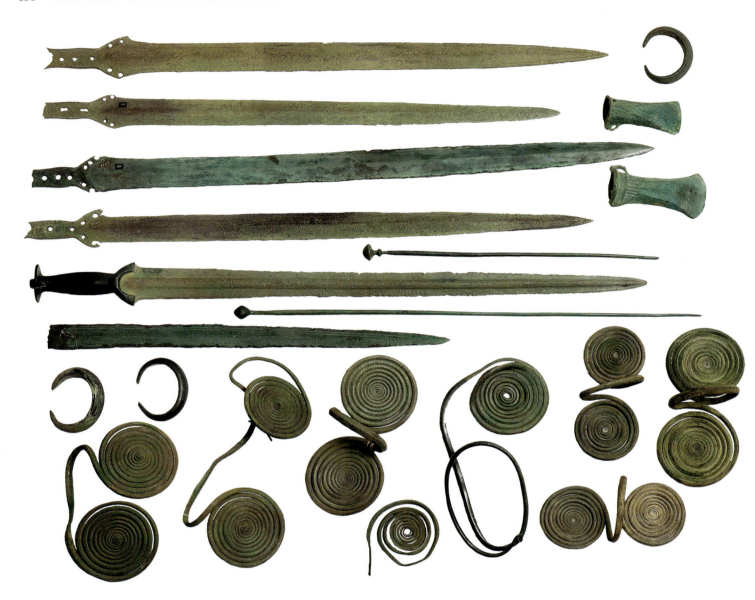

Figure 7.18. Bronze hoard, Topolnica, Serbia. Late Bronze Age, 1300–1200 BC.
The Krajina Museum, Negotin. *Photo: The Krajina Museum.*

Transdanubia, and the northern Balkans. This assemblage contains several weapons: twenty-two spearheads, eight daggers, fourteen swords, one helmet, and one greave. Based on the macroscopic observations of the shortened spearhead tips and narrow dagger blades, some of these weapons appear to have been used. However, the most remarkable aspect of this hoard is the conditions of the objects—without exception, the weapons are fragmentary or broken into small pieces, while some items were intentionally bent or damaged along the edges.[80] Thus the Markovac-Grunjac assemblage reflects a hoarding tradition of weapons that amplifies the ritual message through quantity and treatment. According to Kate Anderson, the large-scale deposition and destruction of weapons may have been a part of post-conflict cleansing ceremonies, which provided a formal framework for warriors to distance themselves from traumatic experiences before they returned to society.[81]

Weapons and Connections

During prehistory, the northern and central parts of the Balkan Peninsula had major routes that linked Central Europe with the eastern Mediterranean and Asia (see Figure 7.2).[82] The location of these routes across the central Balkans is a frequent subject of debates. The northern and central Balkans are connected to the Carpathian Basin by several major rivers. The most important route into the northern Balkans from the north would have been the Danube River, which starts in modern-day Germany, crosses the

Figure 7.19. Bronze hoard, Zalkod, Hungary. Late Bronze Age, 1300–1200 BC.
Jósa András Museum, Nyíregyháza. *Photo by Á. Vágó.*

Carpathians, and eventually empties into the Black Sea. Trade between the Balkans and the eastern Mediterranean likely occurred via the Black Sea. Other rivers in the region, like the Drava and Sava, were also important routes in a western network, while the Tisza River provided access to the heartland of the eastern Carpathian Basin. In addition, the interactions of central Balkan communities with the south occurred exclusively via specific routes, most notably the valleys of the Morava, Vardar, Nišava, Isker, and Marica rivers.

During the first half of the Late Bronze Age, from 1400 to 1200 BC, there was apparently little or no direct interaction between the southeastern part of the Balkans (that is, the northern Aegean) and the northern and central Balkans. On the other hand, it seems that contacts with the Aegean world, both by land and sea, took place primarily on the western shores of Greece. Interregional connections during this time are best represented by certain sword types, like the Sauerbrunn–Boiu–Keszthely and the Riegsee types. The former type appeared sporadically, and examples of this type from the Balkans are clearly related to the Carpathian–North Italian sphere.[83] The few Riegsee swords found in the northern Balkans have loose connections with Central Europe.[84]

Interactions between the northern Balkans and the Carpathian Basin, as well as with the western and northern regions of Europe, intensified between 1200 and 1100 BC. This process is well illustrated by the presence of defensive weapons (such as helmets, greaves, and shields) of Carpathian Basin origins at sites in the northern Balkans, as well as the deposition of flange-hilted swords that followed Central European design trends. This is also the time when spearheads from the eastern Carpathian Basin appeared in the northern Balkans. Fine examples include those with profiled mid-ribs or stepped blades from Serbia.[85] On the other hand, the long, Alpine-type specimens indicate contacts with western Europe.[86] Unlike the previous period, when Mycenaean weapons arrived exclusively through trading activities or down-the-line exchange, in this era, these weapons, and likely their bearers, reached the central Balkans directly. Apparently, population movements typically unfolded via the valley of the Morava River.

Interestingly, there may have been highly specialized craft centers for the manufacturing of weapons and warfare equipment. A center situated near the iron ore seam in eastern Serbia stands out the most, represented by a large amount of identical weapons.[87] Connections impacting weapon craftmanship between the central Balkans and the Carpathian Basin persisted into the following period, between 1100 and 850 BC. During this era, the decrease in the number of weapons in the northern and central Balkans coincided with a dramatic decrease in metal hoarding.[88] In parallel with the emergence of a new pottery style in the northeastern Carpathians (Gáva style pottery), swords with cup-shaped pommels characteristic of that territory became prevalent across many regions (see Figures 7.12 and 7.13).[89]

Arms trafficking, at least in the modern sense, did not exist during the Bronze Age, but the geographic distribution of Late Bronze Age weapons may have been influenced by several other factors. In particular parts of the northern Balkans, like northern Croatia around the thirteenth and twelfth centuries BC, the metal objects' stylistic designs and the patterns of object selection and treatment in depositions were so similar to those of Transdanubia that we can assume they were products of communities that shared the same metallurgical and ritual traditions.[90] Toward the central Balkans, local designs were developed in combination with foreign stylistic elements and objects from the southern, northern, and western parts of Central Europe. In addition to direct exchange, we cannot exclude the possibility that local metalworkers borrowed certain attractive foreign styles. The weapons from the northern and central Balkans fit this trend. Most helmets and greaves found in the interfluve of the Drava and Sava rivers are identical to those in Transdanubia and its adjacent areas. There is evidence for the development of autonomous sword designs and, at the same time, for the emergence of regional variants of larger European sword types, supporting the possibility of style adaptation and/or imitation.[91]

As noted previously, the ritualized exchange of weapons across regions is also plausible, especially when the possession of a particular object corresponded to great prestige. It is likely that the rare appearance of greaves with rich, embossed geometric patterns, and mostly western European parallels, can also be explained in this way.[92]

The advanced weapon technology and the diverse, specialized types of weapons are strong indicators for the existence of professional warriors in the northern Balkans during the Late Bronze Age (Figure 7.20).[93] Mobility has been an essential part of a warrior's life in all historical periods. Late Bronze Age warriors likely crossed vast areas, carrying their own equipment and looting goods, slaves, and prestigious foreign artifacts and trophies. Weaponry and exotic goods recovered from the northern Balkans but typical for northeastern Hungary, Italy, and western Europe may have been associated with the activities of these specialists, who participated in war campaigns of their own or served as mercenaries or military escorts of local chiefs, as seems to have been the case with the Topolnica hoard.[94]

Conclusions

In the Late Bronze Age of the northern and central Balkans, weaponry, funeral customs, votive offerings, and hoards all represent important sources for exploring the ideological framework of warrior identities. In addition to the introduction of new technologies, there was also a fundamental ideological transformation, including a shift in focus from collective to individual values.

The development of a masculine ethos was a fundamental part of this process,[95] including the acceptance of intentional boasting as a part of life.[96] More precisely, this new ideology was marked by an increasing emphasis on social and gender-related categorizations and was expressed through conspicuous funerary rites, such as burial mounds, prestigious votive gifts placed in rivers, and the wasteful deposition of weaponry as a part of a life-cycle ritual. This ideological background is also noticeable on the

weapons, which, in many cases, were produced to high technological and aesthetic standards. The local Late Bronze Age craftsmen were no less innovative than in the rest of Europe. They developed various types of techniques, technologies, and a diverse range of specialized weaponry. Their products were highly functional objects that were able to cause or deflect serious damage during combat.

Concerning the distribution of Late Bronze Age weaponry, the presence of foreign, or even exotic, styles signals strongly interconnected regions.[97] Among the

Figure 7.20. Idealized reconstruction of an elite warrior from southeastern Europe. *Illustration by A.M. Tarbay and J. Seagard.*

several possible scenarios for this high degree of inter-connectedness, different kinds of mobility associated with a warrior class, such as war campaigns or the movement of military escorts, likely best explain this phenomenon.

Late Bronze Age battlefields, like Tollense in Germany,[98] have not been identified in the northern and central Balkans. The potential number of warriors participating in battles and the nature and intensity of warfare were discussed by Anthony Harding.[99] He reasoned that the number of warriors in each party could not have exceeded several thousands, and that conflicts were more likely resolved via individual combats between heroes who represented their respective communities and not through battles of standing armies opposing each other.[100] However, based on the construction of large fortifications and traces of sieges in Transylvania, some argued that large-scale conflicts were more frequent than heroic combats in that region, including perhaps even clashes between armies or sizeable warrior bands (see Chapter 6, this volume).[101] The complexity of weapon technology and use-wear patterns on weapons also support this idea.

There is still much research to be conducted in the future to understand more precisely the various aspects of warfare and warriors in the Late Bronze Age northern and central Balkans. The current archaeological evidence suggests that this may have been an era of professional warriors and intensified violence between warrior bands, smaller communities, and ambitious leaders. It was during this period when a world of conflicts similar to those described in the Homeric epic poems emerged. The only difference is that the deeds of Balkan warriors were not sung by poets and eventually written down—their deeds only can be revealed from the archaeological record left behind by the warriors themselves.

Notes

1   Gogâltan et al. 2019; Szentmiklosi et al. 2011.

2   Molloy et al. 2020.

3   Czukor et al. 2017.

4   Banner 1939; Czukor et al. 2017:218–20, Fig. 5.1; Lichtenstein and Rózsa 2008:49, Figs 11.9, 12.9, 14.

5   Molloy 2018:218–19; Otto et al. 2006; Parker Pearson 2005.

6   Jovanović 1980:152; Jovanović and Ottaway 1976. For recent research, see Antonović 2009; Kienlin 2013; Radivojević et al. 2010.

7   Harding 1995:84, Pl. 35.262.

8   Jantzen et al. 2011:422–24, Fig. 5; Kontny 2015; Mödlinger 2011:56–58; Needham et al. 2012:486; Osgood 1998:37–40; Uckelmann 2012:68–73.

9   Harding 1995:77, Pl. 31.243; Karavanić 2009:Fig. 46.2; Vasić 2015:61, Pl. 16.212.

10   Armbruster 2000:78–85; Harding 1995:Pl. 35.264; Wirth 2003:114–28.

11   Filipović 2015a:397; Harding 1984:164; Mason et al. 2016.

12   Gavranović 2011:31, Fig. 33; Trommer and Bader 2013.

13   Vasić 2015:75–76, Pl. 18.371–76.

14   Falkenstein et al. 2017; Tarbay et al. 2018; Urbon 1991.

15   For example, Gavranović 2011:Fig. 97.9–11; Karavanić 2009:Pl. 41.6–7, 42.1–5, 12–13, 44.1; Žeravica 1993:Pl. 22.284–87, 289, 292, 23.303, 32.435, 37.504.

16   Žeravica 1993:73, Pl. 20.249.

17   Mödlinger 2011:35–41; Siedlaczek 2011:116.

18   Molloy 2018:209–13, 220, Fig. 10.7.

19   Kristiansen 2002:330, Figs 3–4, 7; Tarbay 2015:31–33, Fig. 2; Tarbay 2016:Figs 3–6; Tarbay 2019:142, Figs 11, 14.1–2. Metalwork wear-analysis of the Bela Crkva and Veliki Gaj swords were carried out in the framework of Project No. 134910, which has been implemented with the support provided by the National Research, Development, and Innovation Fund of Hungary, financed under the PD-20 funding scheme.

20   Molloy 2018:214–16, Fig. 10.9.

21   Mödlinger 2017:148–49, 257–61; Needham et al. 2012:484; Uckelmann 2012:108–16.

22   Mödlinger 2017:195–202; Molloy 2009:1059–60, Fig. 5.

23   Bartík 2009:Fig. 2; Szabó 2013:806.

24   Armbruster 2000:85–88; Ersfeld 1990:40.

25   Mödlinger 2017:158–67, Fig. 2.49; Szabó 1994.

26   Kristiansen 2002:329–30; Pearce 2013:64.

27   Thorpe 2013.

28   Borchhardt 1972:18–23, Pl. 37.11I; Hencken 1971:17–39; Mödlinger 2013:395, Fig. 5; Mödlinger 2017:23–24, 31–42, Figs 2.2, 2.8; Snodgrass 1982:25–26, Pl. 7.

29   Clausing 2001:207–17; Hencken 1971:146–47; Mödlinger 2017:42–53, Pl. 3, 21.

30   Jovanović 2010:Pl. 59.497; Mödlinger 2017:47–53, 77; Vinski-Gasparini 1973:Pl. 44.2, 48.31, 66.37.

31   Szabó 2013:806–807, Fig. 11.

32   Mödlinger 2017:181–88.

33   Douzougli and Papadopoulos 2010:25, 31–32, Figs 5, 8; Kytlicová 1988; Mödlinger 2017:172–74; Schauer 1982a.

34   Mödlinger 2017:171.

35   Snodgrass 1982:21; Verdelis 1967:8–18, Fig. 2, Suppl. 1–17.

36   Petres and Jankovits 2014:43–47, Figs 2–3, 6–11.

37   Krahe 1980:Fig. 58; Snodgrass 1982:24–25.

38   Szabó and Czukor 2017:Fig. 3.

39 Clausing 2002; Mödlinger 2017:219, 224, 229, 234–35, 249; Schauer 1982b:132–55; Snodgrass 1982:53.

40 Mödlinger 2017:222–33.

41 Mödlinger 2017:233–37.

42 Needham et al. 2012:486; Osgood 1998:37–40; Uckelmann 2012:68–73.

43 Patay 1968; Uckelmann 2012:14–21, Pl. 5.6.

44 Uckelmann 2012:Pl. 2–3.

45 Molloy 2018:208–209.

46 Thorpe 2013.

47 Harding 2000:277.

48 Filipović and Milojević 2015:20–23, Fig. 4; Kovács 1973:160–64; Papadopoulos 1998; Schwenzer 2004.

49 Filipović and Milojević 2015:20–23.

50 Garašanin 1975:Pl. 64.10–12, 66.4; König 2004:Pl. 14–15, 17.

51 Gavranović 2011:120; König 2004:28–29; Milojčić 1955:158; Mozsolics 1973:64–66; Papadopoulos 1998:29–30, Pl. 22.136; Peroni 1956:72–73.

52 Harding 2000:277; Keeley 1996:50; Mercer 2006; Molloy 2010:404; Papadopoulos 1998:3.

53 Kilian-Dirlmeier 1993:9–11, Pl. 1.1–5; Sandars 1961:17.

54 Bader 1991:37–51; Filipović 2015a:69; Harding 1995:70–71, Pl. 28.230; Kemenczei 1991:8–10; Novotná 2014:19–23; Snodgrass 1982:14–15, 93–94.

55 Harding 1995:7–97; Molloy 2018:205.

56 Harding 1995:59–60.

57 Leshtakov 2015:256–58.

58 Leshtakov 2015:252–53; Schauer 1979:69–70; Tarot 2000:40–49; Vasić 2015:10–11, 52, 60, Pl. 10.136, 15.211.

59 Bader 2015; Leshtakov 2015:260–67.

60 Antonović 2014:88–98.

61 Mozsolics 1973:14–22.

62 Harding 2007:78–79; Snodgrass 1964:166–67; Žeravica 1993:74–106.

63 Filipović 2015b:260–63.

64 Filipović 2015b; Vasić 2015:70–76.

65 Clausing 2005.

66 Tarbay 2020:50–54, Fig. 12, List 2.

67 Harding 1995:23–80; Molloy 2018:221; Vasić 2015:11, 15–16.

68 Georganas 2018; Lloyd 2015:14–16; Whitley 2002:219–23, 227.

69 Lipp 1885:370–73.

70 Harding 1995:62–64; Karavanić 2009:57–58, 61, Pl. 60–62; Stare 1957:Y5–Y6; Treherne 1995.

71 Grinsell 1961:477.

72 Brück 2006.

73 Anderson 2018:224.

74 Fontijn 2002:211–31; Harding 1995:28, 41–42, 50, 66, 71, 75, 78; Szathmári 2005.

75 Jovanović 1972; Jovanović 1975.

76 Mozsolics 1985:11–17, 216, Pl. 7–10.

77 Kristiansen 2018b:24–27, 41.

78 Harrel 2014:10–15.

79 Mozsolics 1984:90–91.

80 Jovanović 2010:Pl. 30.244, 31–37, 38.288, 59.497.

81 Anderson 2018:220, 223.

82 Filipović 2015a:393–401; Parović-Pešikan 1986; Parović-Pešikan 1995.

83 Harding 1995:23, Pl. 5.26; Neumann 2009:106–108, Figs 4, 7.

84 Harding 1995:71–72.

85 Vasić 2015:Pl. 7.83–87, 8, 9.112–22, 11.147–58, 12–14.

86 Vasić 2015:Pl. 15.

87 Vasić 2001:97.

88 Vasić 1982:268, Fig. 1.

89 Harding 1995:78–79.

90 Karavanić 2009:88–134; Turk 1996; Váczi 2014.

91 Harding 1995:15–20, 23–24, 35–44, 49–52, 71–78; Neumann 2009; Pabst 2013:Figs 1–3.

92 Mödlinger 2017:233–37.

93 Molloy 2018.

94 Kristiansen 2018b:24–27, 41; Molloy 2018:218.

95 Weiss and Taruskin 1984:1–3.

96 Sherratt 1987; Sherratt 1994.

97 Molloy 2018.

98 Jantzen et al. 2011.

99 Harding 2007.

100 Filipović 2015a:395–98; Harding 2007:33.

101 Molloy 2018:218–20.

The Age of Iron:
Traders and Aristocrats

CHAPTER 8

Tribal States or Stately Tribes?

The Origins of the 'Barbarian' Kingdoms of the Southern Balkans

Michael L. Galaty and Rudenc Ruka

I N ORDER TO ADDRESS the origins of southern Balkan Iron Age societies—the Illyrians, Paeonians, Dardanians, Thracians, and Macedonians (Figure 8.1)—and the extent of their hierarchical organization, we must first address the nature and evolution of their political systems. How were they organized? How was power shared or exercised among and between individuals? Was one's power and standing based on military prowess, religion, control of trade, all of these, or none?

We can learn something about ancient Balkan peoples from historical sources, written by Greeks and Romans, beginning in the mid-fourth century BC. The people who lived in this region were, by all accounts, forces to be reckoned with, "formidable in outward bulk" but possessing "no regular order," of "dubious loyalty and unstable character," who, if they united and chose to rebel, "would be impossible to check."[1] But is this true? Were the societies of the southern Balkans truly disordered and chaotic, or is this just propaganda? The implication is that they lacked formal leaders. If so, how did these societies function, and is it correct to refer to Balkan 'kings,' whether prehistoric or otherwise?

The Greeks who colonized the eastern Adriatic shore during the Archaic period (beginning in the seventh century BC) at places like Apollonia and Epidamnus, in modern-day Albania, referred to the societies they encountered there as an *ethnos* (sing.), here translated as a 'people:' "After the Liburni there come the Illyrian people. The Illyrii dwell by the sea as far as Chaonia, which lies opposite Corcyra, the island of Alcinous."[2] Use of the term 'ethnos' in this context (versus the plural, *ethne*) is interesting. It implies some degree of cohesion over a large distance, from Liburnia in the north to Chaonia in the south. The Romans, for their part, referred to Balkan peoples as *gentes* (pl.): "Those are *gentiles* of one another . . . who have the same name," that is, an extended family.[3] Thus, if historical sources are to be believed, ancient Balkan societies were not nations in the modern sense of the word. Nor were they states. Rather, they seem to have been 'tribal' in anthropological terms: fluid, segmentary sociopolitical systems, composed of various lineages or clans and, ultimately, families, not unlike native North American tribes.[4] That being the case, is it, in fact, appropriate to refer to Balkan 'kingdoms,' whether in the Iron Age or earlier?

Archaeologist Nicholas Hammond has suggested that when Greeks used the word 'ethnos' to describe barbarian peoples, they were not highlighting only,

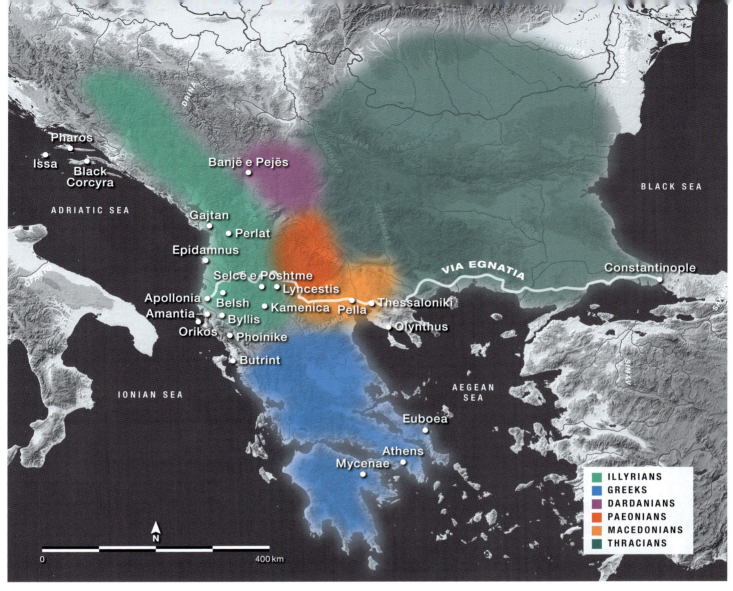

Figure 8.1. Map showing the locations of the main Balkan ethne, the Via Egnatia, select Greek colonies, select *poleis*, and other place names mentioned in the text. *Illustration by J. Klausmeyer, F. Paár, and E. Rodriguez.*

or primarily, cultural or linguistic differences; rather, the emphasis was on sociopolitical dissimilarities.[5] The Illyrians, and those like them, lacked state-level political systems, which in Greece supported city-states, the so-called Greek *poleis*. Whereas the Greeks (the Dorians, in particular) had once depended on a tribal system, that of the *phylai*,[6] which Cleisthenes resurrected in 508 BC, it had long since been replaced. Likewise, when the Romans described Balkan gentes, they acknowledged parallels between their own political system, which, particularly early on, recognized the primary importance of Roman family structures, and that of the Balkan tribes.

To sum up, then, Late Iron Age Balkan societies were not like those of contemporary Greeks and Romans. They were noticeably different and were perhaps tribal.[7] Contrary to the propagandists, they did have identifiable leaders. We know many of their names: Bardylis, Cleitus, Pyrrhus, Monunius, Agron,

Teuta, Gentius, and, depending on who you ask, Alexander. The degree to which these leaders were kings—or in the case of Teuta, a queen—is open to debate. The scant historical references to Bardylis and his son, Cleitus, and their contemporaries, all of which were written well after their deaths, suggest they behaved more like chiefs than kings and led small polities based out of villages and accompanying hilltop forts. Alexander the Great, of course, ruled an empire. The question of just how Balkan chiefs were transformed into emperors bears directly on world history—did that transformation require a hierarchical re-ordering of societies that were generally egalitarian? Or can we trace such transformations to earlier periods, during which the Mediterranean stage was set for the rise of Greece and Macedon, to the detriment of upstarts, like the Illyrians and Dardanians?

Figure 8.2. Plan of Gajtan hill fort, near Shkodër, Albania. Gajtan's walls were likely constructed sometime after 800 BC, but the site was first occupied much earlier, in the Late or Final Neolithic, ca. 4500 BC. *Adapted from Wilkes 1992:Figure 12 by J. Klausmeyer and J. Seagard.*

Prehistory

It is not an exaggeration to say that the origins of the barbarian kingdoms of the southern Balkans are shrouded in mystery. We know little about them and what we do know is based solely on archaeology, not history. As described in Chapters 6 and 7 in this volume, the Balkan Bronze Age was a period of dynamic change, during which small, relatively long-lived, non-hierarchical farming villages were replaced by larger, more complex settlements, often built on high ground. This process may have been the result of settlement agglomeration, thus an internal development, or the arrival of new peoples, or both. Novel settlement patterns were accompanied by new forms of burial in so-called tumuli, or burial mounds. The course and timing of this process seems to have

varied by region, but in most places, it was complete by the Early Bronze Age (about 3000 BC). The most common interpretation is that largely egalitarian social systems were replaced by systems of ranking, in which one lineage is thought to have dominated all others. The leaders of top-ranked lineages, who, in anthropological terms, may have been 'big men' or chiefs, operated out of newly constructed hillforts and were buried at the centers of tumuli, sometimes surrounded by retainers and members of their families. The sources of a Bronze Age chief's power were many, but he almost certainly depended first and foremost on support from his kinsmen, those both closely related and more distant. As a result, his position was precarious—he could be replaced at any time and his lineage might be demoted. Balkan Bronze Age chiefs were typically buried with weapons. These were sometimes imported, in some cases, from as far away as Mycenaean Greece.[8] Control of foreign trade may have been an additional source of power, or at least elevated status, along with administration of economy,

Figure 8.3. Burial mound, Kamenicë, Korcë, Albania. Late Bronze Age and Early Iron Age, 1300–600 BC. The tumulus was used and expanded in several phases. *Courtesy of L. Bejko.*

in general. That said, we have little evidence from Bronze Age settlements anywhere in the Balkans for specialized craft production. Control of the economy may have been limited to control of foodstuffs, like livestock, which in addition to being raised, could have been acquired through raids.

What is striking, then, about the Balkan Early Iron Age, which began about 1000 BC, is how little changed as compared to the Bronze Age. Iron Age peoples continued to live in relatively large settlements, often hillforts (Figure 8.2), and bury their dead in mounds (Figures 8.3 and 8.4). External trade contacts remained limited. In some regions, such as southern Illyria, traders shifted their focus from weapons to pottery. Economic systems were, as yet, non-specialized. When change did come, it came from the outside in the form of migrations, for example, by Celts, and colonization by various Classical Greek city-states. In the absence of migrations and colonization, the later, so-called 'developed' Iron Age may have looked much like the Early Iron Age.

Migration and Colonization

Contrary to expectations, intensifying colonial interactions with Greece, beginning as early as the eighth century BC, did not stimulate massive social changes in the southern Balkans, at least not immediately. These interactions did not lead directly to transformations in social organization and increased hierarchy,

Figure 8.4. Burial structure in the Kamenicë tumulus, Korcë, Albania. Late Bronze Age, 1225–1175 BC. *Courtesy of L. Bejko.*

overturning thousands of years of trans-egalitarian sociopolitical behaviors; rather, these changes challenged ancient egalitarian social structures, but never managed to replace them completely. Likewise, migrations, primarily from the north, including the well-documented Celtic migrations but also

Figure 8.5. Mosaic ("The Beauty of Durrës"), Epidamnus (Durrës), Albania.
Late Iron Age, 350–300 BC. *Photo: National Historical Museum of Albania.*

movements of people from the east, had the primary effect of forcing Balkan peoples out of their homes, and to the south. These pressures did not stimulate political change, such as the creation of formalized systems of leadership or standing armies. If anything, they seem to have inhibited social evolution, at least in the short term.

The Greeks built colonies at various points along the eastern Adriatic (see Figure 8.1). The first of these was sponsored by Corinth and placed, in the 630s BC, by Corcyreans at Epidamnus, later known as Dyrrachium, now Durrës in modern-day Albania (Figure 8.5). The city was purportedly located there at the invitation of the local Albanian tribe, the Taulantii. Another colony was constructed, again by Corinthians, joined later by Corcyreans, to the south of Epidamnus, on a bend of the Vjosa River, about 10 km from the

sea (Figures 8.6 and 8.7). According to tradition, it was built on high ground, alongside an existing Illyrian trading post, in 588 BC,[9] and, eventually, named Apollonia (Figure 8.8). No other colonies were founded on the mainland north of Epidamnus, but three were established on islands in Dalmatia—Black Corcyra (on Korčula), Issa (Vis), and Pharos (Hvar, founded in 385 BC). Of the three, Black Corcyra appears to have failed. According to later, mostly Roman, historians, the colonists at both Issa and Pharos experienced conflict with local Illyrians but managed to survive.

With colonies at Corfu, Epidamnus, and Apollonia, and later in Dalmatia, the Greeks were well positioned to control Adriatic trade.[10] Apollonia and Epidamnus became primary access points to the Balkan interior and, eventually, terminals for the Via Egnatia, which was built in the second century BC by the Romans, following existing roadways, crossing the entire peninsula, and arriving at Constantinople via Thessaloniki (Figure 8.9; see also Figure 8.1). During the sixth and

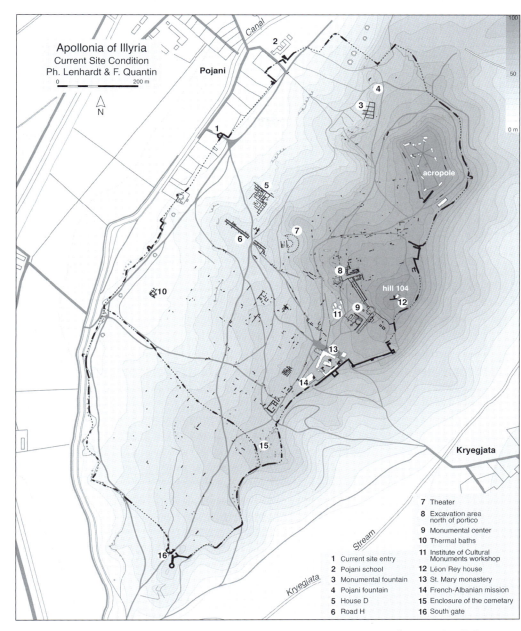

Figure 8.6. Map of Apollonia, Albania. Founded in the Late Iron Age, ca. 588 BC.
Modified from Dimo et al. 2007:Figure 66 by J. Seagard.

Apollonia of Illyria
Current Site Condition
Ph. Lenhardt & F. Quantin

1	Current site entry
2	Pojani school
3	Monumental fountain
4	Pojani fountain
5	House D
6	Road H
7	Theater
8	Excavation area north of portico
9	Monumental center
10	Thermal baths
11	Institute of Cultural Monuments workshop
12	Léon Rey house
13	St. Mary monastery
14	French-Albanian mission
15	Enclosure of the cemetary
16	South gate

Figure 8.7. Aerial photo of Apollonia, Albania.
Adapted from Dimo et al. 2007:frontispiece.

Figure 8.8. Stele depicting Phalakra and Neagenes, two colonists, Apollonia, Albania. Hellenistic Period, 250–150 BC. National Historical Museum of Albania, Tirana.
Photo: National Historical Museum of Albania.

Figure 8.9. An extant segment of the Via Egnatia, Spathar, Librazhd, Albania. Roman Period, 200–100 BC. *Courtesy of L. Bejko.*

fifth centuries BC, Greek pottery, including amphorae, which presumably held wine, and prestige goods, such as jewelry, were imported in large numbers to Illyria and Dardania (Figure 8.10). These items were clearly of value to aspiring chiefs, and are found in their tombs, sometimes referred to as 'princely graves' (Figure 8.11).[11] It is unclear what was offered to the Greeks in return, but ores (particularly silver), salt, grain, cured meat, and dairy products, honey, bitumen (from the mines at Selenicë in Albania), slaves, and mercenary services are all good possibilities.

Similar Greek trade goods made their way into Paeonia, via Macedonia, and Thrace from numerous Greek colonies in the northern Aegean, many founded by Euboea beginning in the late eighth century BC, some of which are found up the valleys of the Vardar and Strymon rivers. None of these colonies grew into large cities like Epidamnus and Apollonia; many of them stayed small, or were eventually consolidated, as at Olynthus.[12] Nevertheless, during this period, incredible wealth was poured into Thracian tumuli, including fine Greek pottery and fabulous metalwork (for images, see Chapter 10, this volume). Thracian

tribes could also access various Greek colonies along the Black Sea coast, many of which were built beside existing Thracian towns by Megarans and Milesians beginning in the seventh century BC.

Contact between the Balkan tribes and Greek city-states and colonies waxed and waned throughout the course of the eighth to fourth centuries BC, depending, in part, on the situation in Greece. For example, the Peloponnesian War (431–404 BC) appears to have caused major disruptions. What evidence there is for sociopolitical change is to be found along the Greek frontiers—with Illyria, Macedonia, and Thrace, and to a lesser degree, at the colonies themselves.

The frontier zone separating northwestern Greece and southern Illyria is demarcated by decreasing numbers of *poleis* as one heads north. Of the 1,035 *poleis* listed in *An Inventory of Archaic and Classical Poleis*,[13] only twenty-six are Epirote. An additional eleven are "Adriatic," and all of these were colonies, including Apollonia and Epidamnus. Of the Epirote *poleis*, a handful are located in the border zone between Greece and Illyria: Amantia, Bouthroton (Butrint), Byllis, Orikos, and Phoinike. All are south of the Shkumbin River, and none is considered to be a *polis* in the political sense of the word. Two had

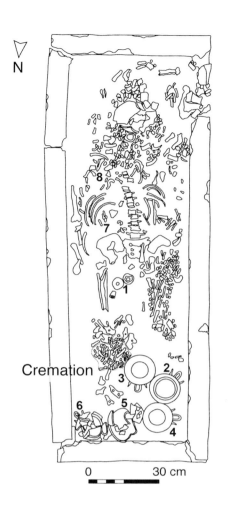

Figure 8.10. A burial with sarcophagus and imported Greek grave goods, Grave 55, Tumulus 9, Apollonia, Albania. Late Iron Age, 550–500 BC. *Courtesy of L. Bejko, modified by J. Seagard.*

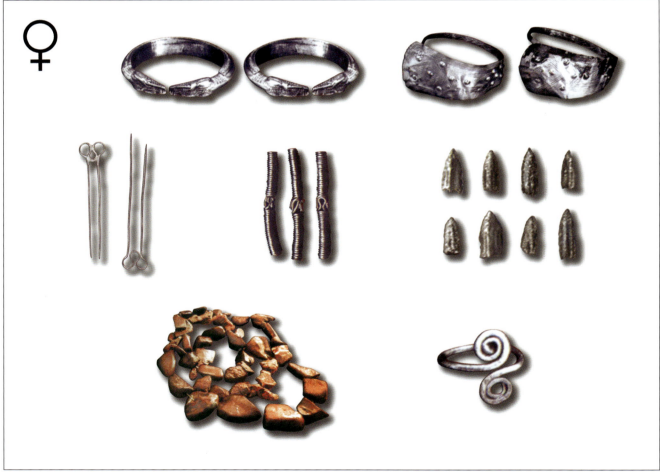

Figure 8.11. Princely (and princessly) bronze, silver, and amber grave goods,
Banjë e Pejës, Kosovo. Late Iron Age, 600–400 BC. National Museum of Kosovo, Prishtina.
Modified from Mehmetaj 2019:Figures 16–17 by J. Klausmeyer and J. Seagard.

Figure 8.12. Architectural element, Amantia, Albania.
Roman Period, 200 BC–AD 400. National Historical Museum of Albania, Tirana.
Photo: National Historical Museum of Albania.

adopted some of the architectural characteristics of Greek cities—a temple and stadium at Amantia (Figure 8.12) and a theater and stoa at Bouthroton— but civic–administrative buildings are conspicuously absent at all five. As such, the southern Illyrian '*poleis*' were not the capitals of developing city-states with regional systems of administration. They were tribal centers, led by chiefs, whose ability to speak Greek did not define them as Greek. Instead, the tribal nature of their political systems marked them as barbarians.

The situation in Macedonia and Thrace was rather different. As compared to the Adriatic, there were many more colonies along the north Aegean littoral, and correspondingly more *poleis*. All of these were Greek-speaking, many were urbanized, and several supported state-level political systems. The majority of the Thracian poleis in the *Inventory*, including those of the Chalcideans (numbering sixty-seven), are defined politically. Likewise, of the seventeen Macedonian *poleis*, six, including Pella, are political. Two possessed constitutions. However, whereas the Greeks in Thrace appear to have been confined to the coast, allowing limited contact with Thracians, those in Lower Macedonia penetrated the interior, or Upper Macedonia, via the Axios (Vardar) River, making regular contact with Illyrians, Paeonians, and Dardanians. This produced a frontier zone and hybridized cultures, not unlike those of southern

Illyria but largely absent from highland Thrace. Importantly, unlike southern Illyria, there were no aspiring *poleis* in the tribal zones bordering Macedonia. Thus, by the mid-fourth century BC, Macedonia had emerged as a precocious, evolving proto-state. Members of the Argead Dynasty (founded by Perdiccas I in 700 BC) spoke Greek, emulated Greek political systems, were in regular contact with southern Greek city-states, having easy access via the Aegean, and could tap an interior zone rich in resources, with no serious competitors among their neighbors. In Thrace, under the guidance of the Odrysian 'king' Teres, the Thracians formed a tribal confederation in 480 BC, drawing together upwards of sixty tribal groups (see Chapter 10, this volume). The Illyrian tribes remained divided against themselves, independent, and capable of unity in times of war only. Thus it was the Macedonians who experienced social transformation, resulting in hierarchies that approximated those of the southern Greek city-states. The Illyrians and Thracians, along with the Paeonians and Dardanians, remained trans-egalitarian—when hierarchy did emerge, it was fleeting, anarchic, and did not foster formalized, reproducible, state-level political or economic systems.

Figure 8.13. Bronze Illyrian helmet, Perlat, Mirditë, Albania. Late Iron Age, 500–400 BC. National Historical Museum of Albania, Tirana. *Photo: National Historical Museum of Albania.*

Figure 8.14. Bronze Illyrian greaves, Belsh, Albania. Late Iron Age, 400–300 BC. National Historical Museum of Albania, Tirana. *Photo: National Historical Museum of Albania.*

The Rise of Macedonia

The single dominant factor affecting Late Iron Age Balkan political systems and driving changes in social organization was the rapid rise of the Macedonian state. For many generations, the Argead Dynasty ruled Macedonia proper only. Their territory did not expand beyond their own ethnos. This changed, however, during the reign of Perdiccas II (ruled 448–413 BC), who sought to subdue the Lyncestae, an independent Greek tribe, allied to the Mollosians, situated in Upper Macedonia. The Lyncestae, it seems, were unwilling or unable to prevent Illyrian raids across their territory into Lower Macedonia. This conflict came to a head in 423 BC at the Battle of Lyncestis, at which the Macedonians and their Spartan allies were defeated by a combined force of the Lyncestae and Illyrians (Figure 8.13). The ultimate effect of this battle was to draw the Macedonians into the Peloponnesian War on the side of the Spartans, which further stimulated Macedonian state formation.

The period following the reigns of Perdiccas and his son, Archelaus, was marked by discord and disunity. Stability was eventually restored to the Macedonian state by Amyntas III (393–370/369 BC), father of Philip II (359–336 BC). According to historical accounts, Amyntas was expelled from Macedonia by Illyrians in 393/392 BC, only to regain his throne with the help of the Thessalians. This first Illyrian incursion marks the beginning of a phase, lasting some two centuries, during which Illyrian, and sometimes Dardanian and Paeonian, tribes appeared frequently on the world stage, always as raiders or pirates (Figure 8.14). Thus Philip II's first official act as king was to attack the Illyrians and retake Upper Macedonia, which he did against Bardylis (a charcoal-burner, who is said to have fought on horseback against Philip at the age of 90),[14] in 358 BC. However, Philip's actions against Bardylis, and later, his son Cleitus, who was allied with or had married into a Dardanian tribe, had the unexpected effect of forcing the Illyrians to ally with the Thracians and Paeonians against Macedon. He is said to have defeated this coalition in 356 BC on the day his son, Alexander III, was born.[15]

During the rest of his reign, Philip continued to fight barbarians, suffering many wounds. Historians describe their tribal affiliations with more and more accuracy through time: for example, the Dardani in 346 BC, the Triballi in 339 BC, and the Autariatae in 336/335 BC. Wilkes suggests these were calculated forays meant to secure Macedon's rear in advance of an invasion of Persia.[16] It was, of course, Alexander, not Philip, who eventually launched the invasion. Before departing, though, he also fought Illyrians, including Cleitus, son of Bardylis, his father's old nemesis. Alexander the Great died in 323 BC, and was succeeded in Macedonia by Cassander (ruled 305–297 BC), who founded the Antipatrid Dynasty. One of Cassander's main military goals was to take Epirus, ruled at the time by Glaucias. In 317 BC, Glaucias offered asylum to an exiled Mollosian prince, Pyrrhus, who was raised in exile by the Taulantii, in the vicinity of Epidamnus. Pyrrhus was restored to the Epirote throne in 303/302 BC at the tender age of twelve. Notably, he was the first Illyrian to come into conflict with the rising power of Rome, against whom he fought several 'pyrrhic' victories. It was Pyrrhus (d. 272

Figure 8.15. Silver stater of Monunius from a hoard, Kreshpani, Albania. Hellenistic Period, 280 BC. Numismatic Cabinet, Institute of Archaeology, Tirana. *Photo by A. Meta.*

BC) who first succeeded in transforming Epirus into a state-like polity, which, predictably, influenced the Illyrians. In 280 BC, for the first time ever, an Illyrian 'king,' Monunius of Dardania, issued a coin, a silver stater (Figure 8.15). His monumental tomb may have been one of ten discovered at Selcë e Poshtme in Albania, built in imitation of those at Vergina in Macedonia (Figures 8.16 and 8.17).

Figure 8.16. Monumental tomb, No. 3, Selcë e Poshtme, Albania. Hellenistic Period, 270–230 BC. *Photo by J. Buzo.*

Figure 8.17. Iron and silver scabbard, Selcë e Poshtme, Albania.
Hellenistic Period, 300–200 BC. National Historical Museum of Albania, Tirana.
Photo: National Historical Museum of Albania.

Illyria north of the Shkumbin River remained relatively quiet during the period leading up to the Illyrian Wars, which began in 229 BC. The Dardanians under Longarus attacked the Macedonian state in 240 BC, but for the most part, the northern Illyrian tribes remained disengaged from the wider Mediterranean world. Their chiefs continued to receive Greek trade goods and occupied the numerous forts that dot the western Balkan landscape. Things began to change in the 230s BC, when Agron, an Ardiaean, and his men, who were based in northern Albania near Shkodër, first took to the seas in *lembi*, small, fast boats used to attack Greek and Roman merchant ships. Upon Agron's death in 231 BC, command of the Ardiaean forces passed to his widow, Teuta, who raided south along the Adriatic coast as far as Messenia. These raids, and the corresponding threat to Mediterranean trade, soon drew the attention of the Romans. They launched a series of three wars against the Illyrians, which began in 229 and ended in 167 BC, with the defeat of Gentius.

Roman Conquest

By the time of the Illyrian Wars, the Balkan ethne had experienced some five hundred years of contact with Greece. By that time, all Balkan peoples had been exposed to hierarchical social systems. In some places, like Macedonia and Epirus, these contacts transformed local political systems, leading to the creation of territorial states. In other places, like southern Illyria, state-like systems emerged based on the development of Hellenized urban centers. The more common response, however, was not secondary-state formation, but rather resistance.[17] Balkan tribes resisted conquest by outside powers and power-grabs by their own chiefs. Ironically, those regions that were the least politically complex—those situated along the eastern Adriatic coast and inland—were the first to be attacked by the Romans and the least able, or likely, to assimilate. As a result, by the time of Christ, Paul might visit Illyricum,[18] and preach in the Latinized coastal cities, but the names of the various independent tribes of Illyrians, Dardanians, Paeonians, and Thracians were surely unknown to him, having largely passed from memory.

Having won the wars with the Ardiaeans, the Romans set about incorporating the conquered territories. Their wars with Macedonia, which began in 214 BC, devastated the southern Illyrian countryside, such that it seems to have been largely abandoned during the last two centuries BC. Nevertheless, several later Roman emperors, including Diocletian (born AD 244), hailed from Illyria. Thus, until they were forcibly drawn into the Roman Empire, the vast majority of Balkan peoples lived a tribal existence. Their leaders exercised power through force, but force has limits. They never managed to create systems of administration,[19] economic specialization, and taxation necessary to fund state enterprises. They were 'kings' in name only, if anything, because they lacked kingdoms. With the exception of Macedonia, true tribal states never formed in the Balkans. Rather, stately tribes ruled the day. When threatened, they melted into the mountains, such that one thousand years after the Roman conquest, Anna Comnena, a Byzantine princess, could write of the "Arbanites," who were, presumably, ancestors of the modern Albanians.[20]

Notes

1   Justin, *Epitome*, 11.1, 6; Thucydides, *History*, 4, 126.

2   Pseudo-Scylax, *Periplus*, 22, quoted by Wilkes 1992:95.

3   Cicero, *Topica*, quoting Scaevola, 6, 29.

4   Galaty 2002.

5   Hammond 2000. See also Hall 2007:49–53, who describes, based on the historical references, the different kinds of ethne in operation in various parts of Classical Greece. He makes an important distinction, for example, between "consolidated" (regionally large, multiple centers) and "dispersed" (diasporic, *poleis*-based) ethne (Hall 2007:51). In our estimation, and combining the terminology of both Hall and Hammond, the Illyrian ethne were consolidated, tribal ethne, based out of multiple, loosely interacting, non- or pseudo-*polis* centers.

6   Hall 2007:52.

7   "[E]thnos and polis should not be juxtaposed, since they do not represent alternative modes but rather different levels of social organization" (Archibald 2000:214), as quoted in Hall (2007:50). Furthermore, according to Hall (2007:51), "it is not so much that polis and ethnos occupy different organizational levels as that they belong to entirely different categories."

8   See examples in the recently published *Hesperos* volume, Vlachopoulos et al. 2017.

9   But see Stocker and Davis 2006, who argue for an earlier foundation date, sometime in the very late seventh century BC.

10   Cabanes 2008.

11   Babić 2002.

12   Tiverios 2008.

13   Hansen and Nielsen 2004.

14   Wilkes 1992:120.

15   Wilkes 1992:121.

16   Wilkes 1992:122.

17   Resistance was a common, logical response to incorporation the world over; see Scott 2010. In this respect, the Balkan situation was not unique.

18   Rom. 15:18–19.

19   See Hall 2007:49, with discussion of what functional characteristics separated the Classical *poleis* from earlier Greek systems of administration, and from other, contemporary systems of sociopolitical organization (e.g., the ethne), both Greek and non-Greek.

20   Anna Comnena, *Alexiad, IV.*

CHAPTER 9

Kings of Crossroads

Warriors and Traders of the Hallstatt World of Central Europe and the Iron Age Balkans

Hrvoje Potrebica and Andrijana Pravidur

I N THE FIRST MILLENNIUM BC, Europe was divided into two parts that were geographically separate, but mutually intertwined. Greece and the Mediterranean saw the emergence of a new, high culture and the beginning of European civilization, while the Etruscans also began their development in the central part of the Apennine Peninsula. The new spirit and ideas penetrated into the European mainland as a result of trade contacts. At the same time, in the remaining part of continental Europe, the world of fortified hilltop settlements, or hillforts, of the Early Iron Age evolved on the foundations of the extensive, fairly uniform Urnfield Culture of the Late Bronze Age. This was a time when iron became widely used, trade contacts grew stronger across the continent, and new elites emerged as a class of influential and wealthy people who held leading roles in their societies (see Chapters 5, 6, and 7, this volume).

While the Late Iron Age of Central Europe, from the fourth century BC to the Roman conquest, is characterized by the La Tène Culture, usually associated with the Celts, the Early Iron Age of this region, dating from the eighth to the fifth centuries BC, is called the Hallstatt period after the eponymous Austrian site with a large necropolis and salt mines. In the territory of the so-called Hallstatt Cultural Complex, stretching from eastern France to western Hungary, the beginning of the Iron Age saw the appearance of fortified settlements in prominent, elevated locations. These hillforts were the centers of the social, economic, and cultural life for large communities, and therefore it is likely that they were seats of chieftains who ruled over surrounding areas, controlled the exploitation of local resources, and oversaw the specialized production and exchange of goods (such as glass, metal, and pottery production). Encounters with members of other communities also took place at these hillforts, providing opportunities for the flow of materials and the circulation of technologies and ideas that linked European societies together into a strong communication network. The cemeteries of these settlements were one or multiple groups of burial mounds, tumuli, of varying size. The tumuli of the leading members of communities stand out, sometimes with their monumentality and always with the rich repertoire of grave goods.

The eastern part of this large cultural complex, the Eastern Hallstatt Circle, stretches to the Carpathian Basin, and is enclosed by the Danube River (Figure 9.1). A characteristic feature of this area is the appearance of an ideology of eastern, steppe origin during the transition between the Late Bronze Age and Early Iron Age, reflected primarily by the spread of some technological innovations, especially those pertaining to horse equipment. This extensive region

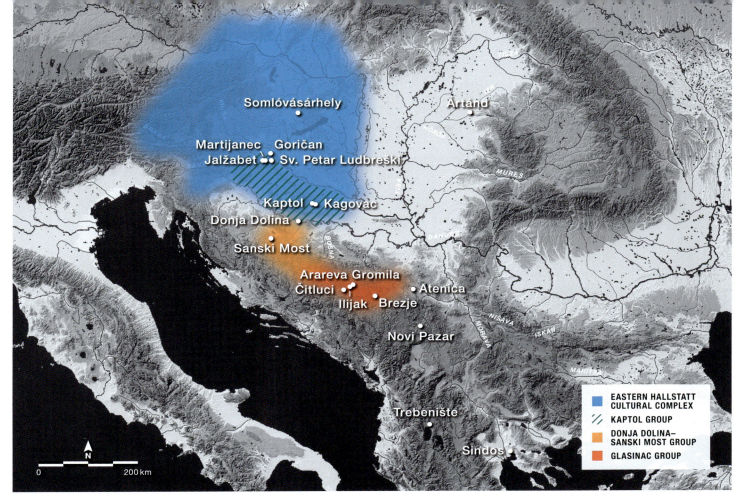

Figure 9.1. Map showing the cultural units and sites mentioned in the text.
Illustration by H. Potrebica, A. Pravidur, F. Paár, and E. Rodriguez.

was inhabited by several cultural groups that shared similar material culture, from pottery shapes and ornaments to attire, personal ornaments, weapons, and horse gear.

Farther south, the Iron Age groups living across the Balkans were rather different from the Central European Hallstatt Cultural Complex in terms of their material culture and developmental trajectories. However, it was precisely the regular interactions between these two large cultural spheres in the area of the southern Carpathian Basin that became a key driving force in the Iron Age communication network that linked Europe from the Baltic Sea to the Mediterranean, and from the Atlantic Ocean to the steppes north of the Black Sea.

Cultural Landscapes: Iron Age Cultural Groups and Elite Interactions

The Kaptol Group

The Hallstatt Cultural Complex is a patchwork of a number of more or less homogeneous cultural units, with the Kaptol Group situated in the southeastern part of its extensive territory.

The Kaptol Group occupied the Požega Valley, in central and western Slavonia, and northwestern Croatia, along with some neighboring regions in the Mura and Drava river basins (see Figure 9.1). Communities living in this region engaged in various economic activities, from tilling and herding to exploiting natural resources, such as mining graphite deposits in the hills of Slavonia.[1] Although some lowland settlements must have existed, especially in river valleys, due to recent, intensive agricultural activities only a few such sites are known. One of them is located at Sv. Petar Ludbreški.[2] A hoard of molds for casting bronze objects discovered in this settlement is indicative of the existence of metallurgical centers that operated from the Late Bronze Age to the beginning of the Iron Age.

The fortified settlements on prominent hilltops are much more visible and better known, and one such example is the Kaptol hillfort. Surrounding these hillforts, there were barrow cemeteries with tumuli that differed greatly in size—from monumental mounds of more than 50 m in diameter, such as the one at Jalžabet, to some barely visible ones. The

Figure 9.2. Central chamber with *dromos* (ritual corridor), Tumulus III, Kaptol-Čemernica, Croatia. Early Iron Age, 650–600 BC. *Photo by H. Potrebica.*

deceased were cremated in full attire, with offerings, and their remains were then buried in wooden chambers, along with an array of grave goods. In some cases, the wooden chambers were reinforced with drystone walls from the outside and then the central structures were covered with earthen mounds of various dimensions (Figure 9.2).

Trade must have been an important economic factor and the communities in this region controlled important trade routes leading from the Alps to the Danube River. They also managed contacts between Central Europe and the Iron Age groups in the Balkans as well as farther afield, with the highly developed Mediterranean communities of Greece and Italy. Such contacts are demonstrated particularly by the burials of the ruling elite of the Kaptol Group, with graves containing rare, imported, precious items from all over Iron Age Europe. A group of sites in northwestern Croatia consists primarily of mound cemeteries, such as Goričan, Jalžabet, and Martijanec, which include several monumental mounds. Of these tumuli, Gomila in Jalžabet is the largest one in Croatia and one of the largest across Central Europe. Another

cluster of sites is located in the Požega Valley. This closed valley is encircled by five ranges of hills that reach heights of nearly 1,000 m on the northern side, with a single natural passage to the south. This microregion was of importance throughout prehistory, resulting in significant archaeological sites, particularly those dating to the Iron Age.

Kaptol is undoubtedly the central and best known site in the Požega Valley, located on the Papuk Hill and incorporating a fortified settlement and two cemeteries from the Iron Age. In the southern cemetery of Kaptol-Čemernica, fourteen tumuli have been excavated, but the actual extent of this necropolis is impossible to determine because most of it has probably been destroyed by recent, intensive agricultural activities. Two burials that contained Greek imports of defensive weaponry are considered to have been princely graves. In addition to a Greco-Illyrian helmet, the warrior buried under Tumulus IV also had a pair of Greek-type greaves (Figure 9.3). On the other hand, the offensive weapons from this burial, including two spears and a shafted axe, as well as horse gear, represent the Pannonian, Hallstatt world to the north. The same can be said about a pair of multi-headed pins, which, in the Hallstatt Culture, were the insignia of powerful warriors. The third, local component is illustrated by the central pieces of a feasting set—three ceramic vessels decorated with bull-head protomes.[3]

Figure 9.3. Selection of objects from a princely grave, Tumulus IV, Kaptol-Čemernica, Croatia. Early Iron Age, 650–600 BC. Archaeological Museum in Zagreb. *Photo by I. Krajcar.*

Thus the display of the power of the prince from Tumulus IV at Kaptol-Čemernica incorporated three distinctive components—local products as well as Hallstatt and Greek imports. On the other hand, all the power insignia interred with the prince from Tumulus X point to the south. The imported Greek defensive equipment is represented by a Corinthian helmet, with the closest analogies from the princely grave at Arareva Gromila at Glasinac in Bosnia and Herzegovina (see below). A decorated whetstone is another remarkable artifact from Tumulus X. Such objects occur in the majority of princely graves across the area of the Kaptol Group, and were the insignia of powerful warriors in the Glasinac Culture to the south.

The fact that the Greek imports recovered from Kaptol and the Požega Valley are by far the northern-most finds of their types clearly illustrates the outstanding role that the Kaptol Group had in the interaction network of the European Early Iron Age. The unique pottery types with beautiful decorations found at Kaptol, such as *kernoi*, *askoi*, tripods, and pots decorated with bull-heads or metal sheets (Figure 9.4), make it one of the most peculiar groups of this period in southeastern Europe. Most fine ceramic vessels are coated with graphite, providing them with a special, metallic shine. Among the major sources of wealth and power of the princes of Kaptol must have been graphite mining; a mine located in close proximity to the archaeological site was exploited even in the mid-twentieth century.

The northern necropolis of Kaptol, Gradca, is located on the slope of the Papuk Hill, near the

Figure 9.4. Ceramic pot with bull heads, Tumulus 10, Kaptol-Gradca, Croatia. Early Iron Age, 700–650 BC. Archaeological Museum in Zagreb. *Adapted from Potrebica 2016:Figure 9.*

Figure 9.5. Chamber of a tumulus with in situ objects, Tumulus 6, Kaptol-Gradca, Croatia. Early Iron Age, 800–600 BC. *Photo by D. Doračić.*

hillfort. It consists of some twenty-five tumuli, seventeen of which have been excavated. Tumulus 6 was the largest mound in this cemetery, incorporating the richest Iron Age princely burial in Croatia (Figure 9.5). While the central grave dates to the beginning of the eighth century BC, a secondary burial was interred into the tumulus during the second half of the sixth century BC. The lavish grave goods of the central burial include nearly thirty different pots, some of them exquisitely decorated, and a large set of weapons, such as two pairs of iron axes, five iron spearheads, two sets of horse gear with iron bits and bronze strap separators, one bronze and one iron sword, a belt with iron and bronze pieces, a Hallstatt-type whetstone, and a bronze situla. The situla contained a large quantity of burnt metal objects, the most important being wheel hubs of a two-wheel wagon, pieces of an eastern-type composite armor, and fragments of two bowl-shaped helmets (Figure 9.6). The weapons recovered from this grave can be classified into two almost identical sets (on the basis of their functions), indicating that the central burial of Tumulus 6 could have been a double princely grave, some kind of a

'brothers-in-arms' phenomenon, which is extremely rare in Iron Age Europe.[4] This burial is older than both princely graves in the southern necropolis at Kaptol-Čemernica (Tumuli IV and X), and its two swords were not actively used as weapons. The bronze sword was imported from the western Balkans, and is about two centuries older than the burial itself. Thus this is an excellent example of the so-called 'traditional' weapons—these objects likely had lost their functional value by the time of their deposition and served as the insignia of military power and the symbol of continuity with a valued heritage. In contrast to the princes in the Kaptol-Čemernica necropolis, who demonstrated their sociopolitical power through valuable imports from different regions, all grave goods in Tumulus 6 at Kaptol-Gradca, including the situla, the wagon, and the bowl helmets, were deeply embedded in the Hallstatt world.

The second largest burial mound on the Papuk Hill, Tumulus 12, covered the grave of a woman of the highest social status. Remains of her superb attire included hundreds of extremely small beads, bone ornaments, and a miniature horseman made of ivory (probably part of an Etruscan fibula). As a rule, all female graves at Kaptol contained at least one, and sometimes as many as ten, spindle whorls. These artifacts might have been gender indicators. Furthermore, the woman buried under Tumulus 12 had sixteen loom weights, which may have been related to some kind of hierarchy reflected by the functional value of textile production tools used as grave goods.

Although the excavation of the fortified settlement at Kaptol is still in an early phase, it has yielded unexpected results testifying to the intensity of life at the site, which continued for nearly two centuries after the last burial mounds were constructed in its vicinity. In fact, a geophysical survey suggests that the dense population and highly organized space at the settlement represents an almost urban setting—unique in this part of Europe.

Kaptol was not the only center in the Požega Valley during the Early Iron Age. At Kagovac, 6 km east of Kaptol, another Iron Age center is currently being investigated. This site also contains a fortified settlement with two cemeteries. The western cemetery consists of thirteen large tumuli, and the southern cemetery encompasses fifteen very small burial mounds. Five mounds have been excavated in the past three years (Figure 9.7). All these tumuli were built at the beginning of the Hallstatt period, in the late eighth and the beginning of the seventh century BC.[5] Although the largest two (Tumuli 1 and 2) had elaborate stone structures constructed around wooden chambers, similar to those at Kaptol, an extremely rich warrior burial was also found under the smallest Mound A, in the southern necropolis at Kagovac, without visible internal structure of any kind. The pottery from the necropolis is typical of the Hallstatt area, and so is the majority of metal finds, such as a set of seven bronze fibulae from a rich female burial (Tumulus 1). Two imported items, a decorated bronze winged axe and a curved iron sword, testify to the importance of the east–west route that connected the Danubian and Alpine regions along the Sava Valley.

The burials of mighty warrior princes from the Požega Valley signify not only their elite status, but also the exceptional importance of this area in interregional communication networks. The power of those rulers came from the control they exerted over significant resources, such as graphite, and over key communication routes that connected the eastern Alpine region with the central Danubian region to the east and with the Balkans to the south. The cultural development of Iron Age communities in the Balkans took place within the framework of local processes and dynamics, but at the same time, this development played an important role in the circulation of raw materials and goods across the wider region.

Figure 9.6. Bronze situla filled with various artifacts during excavation, Tumulus 6, Kaptol-Gradca, Croatia. Early Iron Age, 800–600 BC. *Photo by D. Doračić.*

Figure 9.7. Burial chamber under excavation, Tumulus 1, Kagovac, Croatia. Early Iron Age, 700–650 BC. *Photo by H. Potrebica.*

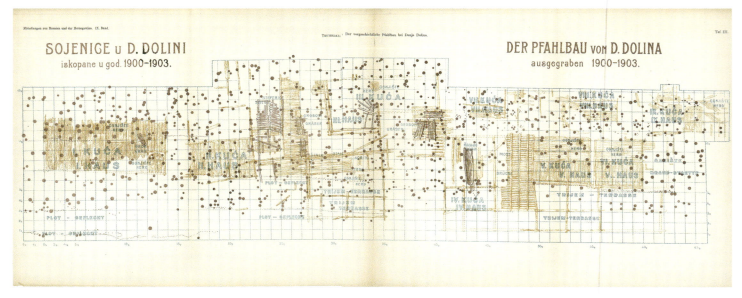

Figure 9.8. Plan map of a pile-dwelling settlement excavated at the beginning of the twentieth century, Donja Dolina, Bosnia and Herzegovina. Early Iron Age, 650–400 BC. The map shows well-preserved wooden structures, including nine dwellings, a bridge, a barn, stairs, and terraces as well as a wooden boat and six burials in wooden coffins. *Adapted from Truhelka 1904:Tafel III.*

The Donja Dolina–Sanski Most Group

The distribution of the Donja Dolina–Sanski Most Group,[6] the northernmost of the Iron Age cultural units in the Balkans, covers the Bosnian part of the Sava River basin between the Una and Vrbas rivers, and extends into the Sana Valley to the south (see Figure 9.1). The excavation of the prehistoric settlement and necropolis at Sanski Most at the end of the nineteenth century was the first significant archaeological investigation in this region.[7] However, the extensive excavations of Donja Dolina at the beginning of the twentieth century,[8] as well as a series of rescue and revision excavations in the following decades,[9] provided a large amount of new information and allowed the definition of this cultural group (Figure 9.8).

The area is abundant in iron ore and the Donja Dolina–Sanski Most Group developed an advanced metallurgical tradition. Even during the preceding Late Bronze Age, the settlement at Donja Dolina was an important workshop center, where bronze casting and the production of bronze objects using various techniques (casting, forging, embossing, engraving) occurred. This tradition continued intensively throughout the Iron Age.[10] The local production of iron objects, starting in the transition from the Bronze Age to the Iron Age, likely stimulated advancements in another important field of metal industry—mining, and the extraction, refining, and melting of iron ore. Extensive metallurgical activities were conducted at both Donja Dolina and Sanski Most as evidenced by numerous deposits of ore, molds, smelting vessels, and blacksmith tools at these sites.[11] Iron may also have been produced for export,[12] and the large amount and great variety of metallurgical finds from Donja Dolina suggest that this settlement was an extraordinarily important regional center where, alongside mining and metallurgy, trade developed as a substantial sector of the economy.[13]

The characteristic funerary customs of this cultural group are best known from the lavishly equipped female and male burials in the necropolis at Donja Dolina, where 179 graves have been excavated.[14] A quarter of these graves were cremation burials, predominantly from earlier periods, while the majority were flat graves with skeletal burials. The inception of the necropolis can be culturally linked to the Late Bronze Age, and it was used for interments until the end of the La Tène period in the first century BC. The grave goods in the Early Iron Age burials display similarities with the neighboring contemporaneous groups, such as the Glasinac Culture, but remarkable analogies that link this region to the Hallstatt groups in the north also occur. The commodities exchanged between these cultural areas are indicative of two-way communication, and the interaction networks of the Donja Dolina–Sanski Most Group extended as far as Greece.[15]

Figure 9.9. Double grave, Grave 3, Field of Stipo Čagrlja, Donja Dolina, Bosnia and Herzegovina. Early Iron Age, 650–600 BC. National Museum of Bosnia and Herzegovina, Sarajevo. *Photo by A. Pravidur.*

The archaeological record of the Donja Dolina–Sanski Most Group bears significant resemblances to that of the Požega Valley and the entire Kaptol Group. The relationship between these cultural centers and Greece is further emphasized by luxurious Greek imports and, in particular, by spectacular defensive weapons of Greek origin, such as helmets, greaves, and shield bosses, recovered from these centers.[16] These items were the prestige goods of the local elites, whose identity was deeply associated with a warrior ideology.

Certain elements of the indigenous material and spiritual culture reached distant regions, demonstrating the key position that Donja Dolina held in interregional distribution networks. In this respect, the connection between Donja Dolina, the Požega Valley, and the Glasinac Culture is perhaps best illustrated by multi-headed pins characteristic for Donja Dolina, which have been unearthed in elite burials at both Kaptol and Glasinac.[17] The geographic distribution of whetstones with bronze handles, a common status symbol in the Glasinac Culture,[18] shows the same pattern. During the seventh and sixth centuries BC, local Iron Age communities developed intensively, and this development coincided with major social changes, including an increasing degree of social differentiation and the emergence of elites.

Although princely graves, typical of the western and central Balkans, have not been found at Donja Dolina, the well-equipped male warrior graves in the necropolis might represent an Early Iron Age tribal aristocracy and ruling social class.[19] It is precisely these graves where numerous imported items were found, including particularly prominent defensive weapons. The finds include two Greco-Illyrian helmets,[20] for which the closest parallel is the helmet from Kaptol mentioned above. Greek shield bosses are particularly

common in Donja Dolina, with three bronze and five iron examples. Single finds of the same shield boss type have been discovered in some extremely rich graves of several other regional centers in the central Balkans and the Carpathian Basin, such as Čitluci at Glasinac in Bosnia and Herzegovina and Atenica in Serbia, and the Hungarian sites of Ártánd and Somlóvásárhely.[21] It appears that these shields played a significant role in the visual identity of the warrior elite at Donja Dolina, just as local types of swords and greaves, together with decorated whetstones, did in the Glasinac area. In addition to imported defensive weapons, the previously mentioned Donja Dolina-type pins, presumably a status symbol of lower rank, were also placed in male graves. Also, Greek bronze vessels have been recovered from a single burial at Donja Dolina, thus these artifact types occur much less frequently here than in the Glasinac area.

In addition to warriors, the Early Iron Age social structure in the region also included traders and various artisans who held prominent positions. Generally, the organization of these communities is defined on the basis of the interpretation of male graves, and their funerary goods indicate narrowly specialized social roles (Figure 9.9). We know very little if anything at all about the role of women in Early Iron Age communities. However, at Donja Dolina, the majority of female graves are richer than the male ones. If we do not consider grave goods solely as a reflection of material wealth but rather as an indicator of the social status of the deceased,[22] it is likely that these female burials reflect the special social position of women at Donja Dolina. This is also suggested by the large quantity of imported objects uncovered from these graves (nearly

Figure 9.10. Ritual bronze wagon with waterbirds, Glasinac, Bosnia and Herzegovina. Early Iron Age, 750–650 BC. Replica. National Museum of Bosnia and Herzegovina, Sarajevo. *Photo by A. Pravidur.*

The Glasinac Cultural Complex

The accidental discovery of the famous bronze wagon decorated with waterbirds during road construction in the Glasinac area by the Austro–Hungarian army in 1880 marked the beginning of systematic archaeological excavations in Bosnia and Herzegovina (Figure 9.10).[24] Subsequently, more than two thousand mounds have been registered and almost one thousand have been excavated in the Glasinac Plateau, covering about 1,000 km² in the eastern part of Bosnia and Herzegovina.[25] The mounds were organized into a complex network of necropolises that were used from the Early Bronze Age to the Late Iron Age.

Despite the extremely long span of their use and some variations in their arrangements, the general layout of these mounds remained almost the same: several burials from different periods were placed under a stone barrow and covered by a layer of earth. Although their dimensions vary, the majority of the mounds measure about 10 m in diameter. An additional regular feature of the Glasinac mounds is the presence of both cremated and skeletal burials in varying ratios throughout the duration of the Glasinac Culture (see Figure 9.1).

The material culture, and especially the evolution of specific local object types, suggests continuous cultural development. This is most apparent in the Late Bronze Age and Iron Age burials, which helped define the Glasinac Culture in terms of spatial extent, chronology, and artifact typologies.[26] The notion that a homogeneous material culture evolved in a specific area over a long period of time led to the association of the Glasinac Culture with the historical tribe of the Autariatae.[27] However, during the Iron Age, common traits in material culture in fact developed across a much larger area, stretching from eastern Bosnia, southwestern Serbia, Kosovo, and Montenegro, to northern Albania. This widespread distribution of a similar material culture is known as the Glasinac–Mati Cultural Complex.[28]

We can distinguish between at least two categories of grave goods that illustrate the social power of the Glasinac elite—products acquired through long-distance exchange and objects crafted locally. Similar to the Hallstatt Cultural Complex, the artifacts deriving from remote regions were either weapons or feasting sets. However, in the Glasinac Culture, feasting sets usually consist of carefully chosen bronze vessels—the products of Greek workshops.[29] On the other hand, local items that demonstrate the rising power of the emerging elites are mostly weapons, including whetstones with decorated bronze handles as well as Glasinac-type swords and bronze greaves.

as many as those in male graves). A diverse selection of imported fibulae illustrates this well—for example, a pair of wire fibulae with amber coating was manufactured in an Etruscan workshop in Italy.

The regular presence of textile production tools in female graves, especially spindle whorls, suggests a strong association between the textile production process (spinning and weaving) and women, both operationally and metaphorically. Given that a similar situation has been ascertained in the Hallstatt area,[23] it would appear that this concept extended across different regions. Additionally, a unique feature at the Donja Dolina cemetery—which has been identified during the current revision of the finds from the site and will be the focus of future research—is that female burials were equipped with weapons.

Its favorable geographic location, at the intersection of major roads, and its hinterland rich in various resources, iron in particular, made the Early Iron Age settlement at Donja Dolina one of the most prominent interaction hubs in this part of Europe. Its cultural connection with Pannonia and the Alpine region—that is, with the Hallstatt Cultural Complex—as well as with various cultural groups of the Balkans is reflected by the spatial distribution of numerous elements of the material culture.

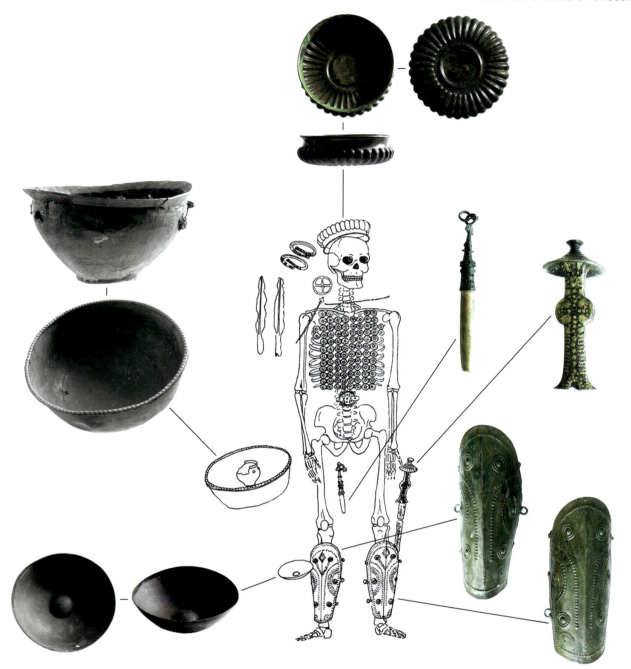

Figure 9.11. Princely grave, Grave 1, Tumulus II, Ilijak, Glasinac, Bosnia and Herzegovina. Early Iron Age, 700–650 BC. National Museum of Bosnia and Herzegovina, Sarajevo. *Modified from Benac and Čović 1957:Figure 6 and Jašarević 2014:Table 1 by J. Seagard. Photo by A. Jašarević and A. Pravidur.*

The substantial local component in the warrior equipment indicates a strong link between military and social statuses in Glasinac communities. This argument is best demonstrated by one of the richest Glasinac princely burials—Grave 1, discovered in the necropolis of Ilijak, under Tumulus II.[30] This burial dates to the seventh century BC, and contained, among other grave goods, a set of four imported bronze vessels, a Glasinac-type sword and greaves, and a sumptuously decorated whetstone (Figure 9.11).

Another princely grave in the same necropolis also had two Glasinac-type swords as well as a pair of Glasinac-type greaves (Grave 9 in Tumulus III).[31] However, in this burial, the clothing accessories are locally produced and much more modest, and a whetstone and imported bronze vessels are absent. Instead, two iron, Hallstatt-type battle-axes were interred with the deceased. This burial is one of the nine graves placed under Tumulus III, while Tumulus II contained only one grave. Thus the archaeological data suggest that the Glasinac military aristocracy rose from warrior clan leaders who became the leaders of larger communities over time.

Next in the chronological line of Glasinac princely graves is another single burial, Grave 2 under Tumulus XIII at Ilijak, which dates to the end of the seventh or the beginning of the sixth century BC. A Glasinac-type sword and greaves as well as a decorated whetstone and a bronze bowl were placed in this burial.[32] The princely Tumulus I in the necropolis of Brezje, which is somewhat later and dates to the first half of the sixth century BC, contained an eclectic set of grave goods, including an imported bronze bowl, a Glasinac-type sword, and two simple whetstones, but no defensive equipment, such as greaves, was found in the tumulus.[33]

Chronological studies indicate that the Glasinac-types of iron swords and greaves were deposited in princely graves over the course of a century and a half—a period that is much longer than that of their production and probable use. This suggests that a militaristic component played a strong role in the transfer of power over multiple generations for the Glasinac elite.

A decorated whetstone, similar to the example from Tumulus II at Ilijak, also appears in the next generation of princely graves, in Grave 1 in Tumulus II at Osovo, dating to the middle of the sixth century BC. Two imported bronze vessels were also recovered from the same grave,[34] one of which is identical to the bowl with an embossed rim excavated in Grave 1 under Tumulus II at Ilijak.

In the middle of the sixth century BC, Glasinac-type swords and greaves were no longer placed in burials, and horse equipment became a new element of power display. For example, horse gear was found in the extremely rich warrior burial of Grave 5 under Tumulus I at the necropolis of Čitluci, along with imported Greek objects, such as a bronze vessel, greaves, and a shield.[35]

The Iron Age on the Glasinac Plateau is distinguished by the regular occurrence of a strong element in the funerary tradition—the deposition of 'old' pieces of local warrior equipment in the burials. On the other hand, if one interprets grave inventories as displays of power, imported objects would illustrate the power of local elites derived from the control over long-distance interactions with the Greek world. Imports, such as Greek bronze vessels and defensive weapons,

indicate that the Donja Dolina–Sanski Most Group and the Kaptol Group, the latter as an exponent of the Hallstatt Cultural Complex, had fundamental roles in interregional networks. In addition to the circulation of Greek imports and the distribution of local prestige objects, such as ornamented whetstones, these communities were also receivers of foreign influences in regard to both material culture and ideology of power.

Their prominent geographic position, in combination with their military power, made it possible for the Iron Age Glasinac communities to extend their control over large areas in the central Balkans. Thus these communities became powerful stakeholders and centers of power in the communication network that linked the Mediterranean centers of luxury goods production with the Balkans and Central Europe that were rich in ores and other natural resources.[36] However, all the information we have about the Glasinac Culture comes from burial contexts, while their settlements have remained almost completely unexplored. In order to gain a more complete picture of Iron Age developments in this region of extreme importance for European prehistory, settlements must be identified and investigated, and settlement and burial data must be jointly studied.

Network of Contacts and Nodes of Power from the Eighth to the Middle of the Sixth Century BC: Warriors and Feasts

Because the Iron Age is perceived as a particular stage within a long-term, continuous cultural development, the period was defined based on two basic criteria—the widespread use of iron objects and the presence of weapons in burials. Therefore the appearance of both defensive and offensive weapons, typically following local traditions, in graves dating from the eighth century BC marked the beginning of the Iron Age across Central Europe and the Balkans. Changes in social and political organizations between the end of the eighth and the end of the seventh centuries BC resulted in the emergence of an elite ideology, demonstrated by rich warrior burials often defined as princely graves.[37] In these burials, the members of an emerging group that held economic, political, military, and spiritual power were interred.

The exceptional power of the Iron Age elite relied on two basic factors: the control of local natural resources—such as iron, copper, graphite, salt, as well as wood, honey, and resin—and the control over communication and exchange routes and mechanisms. Members of this supreme, 'princely,' class clearly displayed their privileged status through external

Figure 9.12. Selection of objects from a princely grave, Tumulus X, Kaptol-Čemernica, Croatia. Early Iron Age, 600–550 BC. Archaeological Museum in Zagreb. *Adapted from Potrebica 2013:Figure 54.*

'splendor.' Prestigious objects made of metal, glass, and amber, as well as luxurious imported metal or pottery vessels, were parts of their visual identity within their respective communities, and reminded others of their elevated status during their burial.

In the Hallstatt area, elite burials were usually located in the central part of large earthen mounds, while in the Balkans, the funerary architecture ranged from simple burial pits to stone mounds that sometimes reached monumental dimensions. Female elite graves commonly contained ornaments and costume elements made of glass, amber, bronze, and precious metals. Male princely graves, by contrast, included various kinds of weapons and horse gear, in addition to rich personal adornments. As in other regions of Europe, feasting sets, with numerous ceramic pots and, occasionally, fine imported metal vessels, were regularly deposited in these elite burials. These assemblages testify to the importance Early Iron Age elites attached to ritual gathering, socializing, and drinking.

In the southern part of the Carpathian Basin, rich princely and warrior graves appeared already at the very beginning of the Iron Age, simultaneously with the emergence of a new, complex interaction network that connected distant parts of Europe. Control over this network is also reflected in a special class of prestigious objects that derived their extreme importance not only from the raw material from which they were made, but also from the very fact that they were exotic and difficult to acquire, usually coming from great distances. Given that their primary role was for display of power, such objects also had to be highly visible and recognizable in order to deliver the message. Defensive weaponry (such as helmets, greaves, and armor) was by definition worn on highly visible parts of the body, making the insignia of great warriors ideal items of display (Figure 9.12).

Figure 9.13. Bronze Greco-Illyrian helmets, Donja Dolina, Bosnia and Herzegovina. Early Iron Age, 650–600 BC. National Museum of Bosnia and Herzegovina, Sarajevo. *Adapted from Blečić Kavur and Pravidur 2012:Plate 1:1, 2.*

Many of the weapons were Greek products, indicating the strong southern contacts of the Central European and Balkan elite. Influences and materials flowing in the opposite direction are archaeologically less visible; however, some artifacts manufactured in Central Europe were recovered from tumuli in the Balkans, such as battle-axes and horse equipment, and a Glasinac-type sword made it all the way to Apollo's Sanctuary in Delphi.[38]

In addition to these imported objects, a class of locally produced prestige objects was also placed in the princely graves. Whetstones with frequently lavishly decorated bronze handles were symbols of the highest status in the Glasinac Plateau, and two of those peculiar objects have also been discovered in burials at Kaptol. Multi-headed, Donja Dolina-type pins were deposited not only in the elite graves of the Donja

Dolina site but also in several tumuli of the Glasinac area and in one Kaptol burial.

The geographic distribution of these two types of locally crafted prestige objects reveals that the three centers of power at Kaptol, Donja Dolina, and on the Glasinac Plateau were bound into the same interregional network. This suggests that Greek helmets and greaves (Figures 9.13 and 9.14), once they reached this area, were probably redistributed (either individually or as sets) among members of these three elite groups, through this strong interaction network. Prestige artifacts were not simply objects of trade—they were circulated through regular gift exchange in order to establish and reinforce diplomatic relationships between the elites of different groups. This was a fundamental prerogative for sustaining communication among these groups at all levels.

An ideal social context for gift exchange is feasting. The practice of feasting was particularly prominent in communities where the social structure was dominated by warriors and the mythological structure by

Figure 9.14. Bronze greaves of Greek origin, Grave 5, Tumulus I, Čitluci, Glasinac, Bosnia and Herzegovina. Early Iron Age, 650–600 BC. National Museum of Bosnia and Herzegovina, Sarajevo. *Photo by A. Pravidur.*

heroes. It is likely that, albeit in various forms, warrior feasting was the backbone of Iron Age social order across Europe.[39] The formal gatherings of warriors over feasts strengthened, if not created, elites in Iron Age societies, who used such occasions to demonstrate their exclusivity within their own community. In addition, regular contacts between different communities enabled cultural transfer as well as promoted the exchange of goods between the representatives of neighboring or remote areas. It is possible that participants in Iron Age feasts not only defined but also quantified exchange between their communities during negotiations.

Storytelling was yet another important aspect related to feasting. In the case of encounters of groups belonging to different communities, storytelling was a kind of gift exchange. For the local elites, it was a tool for acquiring exclusive and exotic insights, ideas, perhaps also technologies, from areas far beyond their physical reach. In this way, the participants of these gatherings and feasts would consolidate their elite status within their own community, just as they would by acquiring and displaying prestigious goods. By recounting these stories for their communities, they distributed the acquired intangible assets. Local traditions were revived and reinforced in the same way, and probably on the same occasions. In the absence of scripts, oral narratives, aided by visual stimuli, were the only way to create a solid tradition necessary for stable and lasting social relations. The system of power transfer between generations, which guaranteed the continuity of the leading role of an elite group, must also have been based on the preservation and transfer of this tradition. This is where we can find the driving mechanism for the Iron Age heroic tradition, probably rooted in ancestral worship and manifested over the course of feasts and funerals.[40]

Therefore the feasting sets of pottery and metal vessels excavated in the graves of Iron Age community rulers in the southern part of the Carpathian Basin were instrumental conveyors of a wide range of social messages. In the area of the Glasinac Culture, princely graves contained meticulously collected assemblages of imported Greek bronze vessels.[41] However, in the Kaptol Group, such sets are more embedded in the Central European Hallstatt Culture tradition. The basic drinking set included a pot for a beverage and a drinking cup, but it sometimes also incorporated other special pottery types, such as vessels decorated with bronze or tin sheets (Figure 9.15), pots with protrusions in the shape of bull heads (see Figure 9.4), *kernoi*, or *askoi* (Figure 9.16).[42]

Figure 9.15. Ceramic vessel decorated with tin sheets, Tumulus 6, Kaptol-Gradca, Croatia. Early Iron Age, 800–600 BC. Archaeological Museum in Zagreb. *Photo by D. Doračić.*

Figure 9.16. Ceramic askos, Tumulus XII, Kaptol-Čemernica, Croatia. Early Iron Age, 650–600 BC. Archaeological Museum in Zagreb. *Adapted from Potrebica 2013:Figure 78.*

Time of Changes and the Age of 'Queens': The Sixth and Fifth Centuries BC in the Northwest Balkans

Sometime around 550 BC, the Hallstatt Culture to the east of the Alps went through fundamental cultural changes. Tumulus burials were abruptly discontinued, and for a long time the general opinion was that this momentum marked the collapse of the Hallstatt Culture, often explained by Scythian raids from the east. Recent research, however, suggests that this transformation was far more complex and less uniform across the cultural unit.[43]

During this time, in the Glasinac area, the proportion of cremation burials increased and their degree of richness decreased. The single exception is the mound of Arareva Gromila, with the last princely burial of the Glasinac Culture, which represents the sole cremated leader from Glasinac.[44] This famous grave contained, among other finds, a bronze Corinthian helmet and a bronze astragal belt. Dating to the third quarter of the sixth century BC, the burial represents the last flare of the former glory of rulers in the region (Figure 9.17). In the succeeding era, the opulence of the Glasinac graves slowly diminished, up to the point when typical local elements disappeared or were blended with strong southern Hellenistic influences, with scarce traces of the La Tène Culture from the north.

In the sixth century BC, being abundant in various ores, especially iron, the region around Sanski Most became important in the northern Balkans. The links to Donja Dolina secured Sanski Most's position in the prominent regional network to the southern Carpathian Basin.[45] By contrast, contemporaneous graves at Donja Dolina reflected a new horizon of the Late Hallstatt Culture (Figure 9.18). A distinguishing feature of this new cultural horizon are rich, almost exclusively female, graves. The assemblages from these burials display the combination of some specific local objects, such as twisted silver wire ornaments, amphora-shaped glass beads, and local fibulae types, with imported materials, such as coral and amber beads as well as the earliest La Tène fibulae.[46] This seemingly eclectic attire became practically a general standard across a large area around the Danubian part of the Carpathian Basin.[47]

In some regions, such as at Donja Dolina, inhumation burials remained common, indicating cultural continuity; however, across the Hallstatt Culture, including the Kaptol Group, a change in burial customs from cremation to inhumation marked a clear break with previous mortuary traditions. Nevertheless, once again, Kaptol seems to have become a unique place. Here, tumulus construction ceased rather abruptly around the mid-sixth century BC. At the same time, the settlement was reorganized and/or rebuilt in such a way that it bore a strong resemblance to urban centers in the Mediterranean, for example, in Greece and Italy (Figure 9.19); it is an exceptional example of a complex settlement with an urban layout east of the Alps in such an early period. Preliminary investigations at this extraordinary site suggest that its chronological development was similar to other sites of the same horizon across a wide area. These sites were abandoned sometime around the last quarter of the fourth century BC, when the fully developed La Tène Culture spread across Central Europe.[48]

Figure 9.17. Bronze Corinthian helmet, Tumulus Arareva Gromila, Glasinac, Bosnia and Herzegovina. Early Iron Age, 530–500 BC. National Museum of Bosnia and Herzegovina, Sarajevo. *Photo by A. Pravidur.*

Figure 9.18. Double grave, Šokić Field, Donja Dolina, Bosnia and Herzegovina. Late Iron Age, 400–300 BC. National Museum of Bosnia and Herzegovina, Sarajevo. *Photo by M. Vuković.*

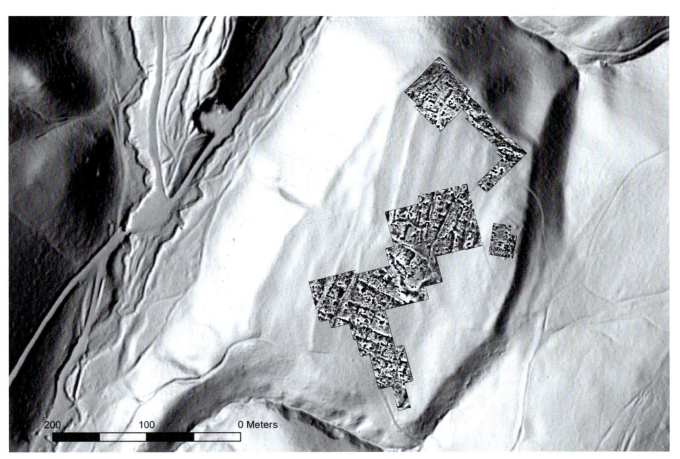

Figure 9.19. Results of magnetic prospection showing urban layout at the settlement of Kaptol-Gradca, Croatia. *Illustration by B. Mušič and J. Seagard.*

Figure 9.20. Bronze hydria, Novi Pazar, Serbia. Early Iron Age, 550–450 BC. National Museum of Serbia, Belgrade. *Photo: National Museum of Serbia.*

Figure 9.21. Gold pendant, Atenica, Serbia. Early Iron Age, 550–450 BC. National Museum in Čačak. *Photo: National Museum in Čačak.*

Kings of the Passage: Princely Graves of the Central Balkans in the Sixth and Fifth Centuries BC

In the central Balkans, southeast of the inner core of the Glasinac Culture, new princely graves emerged in the late sixth century BC. The best examples include the ones from Novi Pazar and Atenica in southwestern Serbia.

The princely grave at Novi Pazar has never been fully excavated because a medieval church and graveyard were built on top of the tumulus. The modern renovation of the church brought to light a wooden chest filled with a large number of gold and silver objects, bronze and silver vessels, glass beads of various kinds, an enormous number of amber artifacts, and Greek vessels made of silver and bronze as well as black-figure wares, such as an olpe decorated with a scene with Dionysus. Among the exquisite imported objects is a large bronze hydria (Figure 9.20). The burial dates to around 500 BC.[49]

Two monumental mounds excavated near the village of Atenica had splendid grave architecture and contained three rich cremation burials.[50] In addition to a warrior grave, the larger mound, Mound II, also incorporated a complex ritual structure, while two burials were recovered from Mound I—the central grave of an elite woman and a child burial, possibly male. Similar to the inventory of Novi Pazar, both mounds yielded ostentatious grave goods, including numerous carved and uncarved amber beads, gold and silver ornaments, and Greek bronze and ceramic vessels (Figure 9.21). A special class of objects from Atenica consists of horse gear and the remains of two wagons—a two-wheeled wagon was found in the female grave and a four-wheeled one in the male grave. In addition, the male burial also had weapons as well as ivory ornaments in a box. The date of the female grave corresponds to the Novi Pazar burial, around 500 BC, followed by the interment of the child somewhat later. The male warrior was buried between 530 and 500 BC.[51]

Fantastic burials with lavish golden masks and Greek imports from the Trebenište necropolis, located in North Macedonia, also belong to this late group of princely graves (Figure 9.22).[52] Although the graves at Trebenište were interred in a very short period of time, their splendor has remained unmatched across the Balkans. The wealth and power that they reflect is comparable to those of the Central European princely burials, such as Vix or Hochdorf, which appeared almost simultaneously and also contained objects from the Mediterranean. Some imported goods in the Trebenište necropolis, such as wagons, horse equipment,

Figure 9.22. A recently discovered old photograph of some unrestored finds from the Trebenište cemetery, North Macedonia.
Photo: Franciscan Monastery of St. Catherine, Kreševo.

and amber, indicate strong connections with regions to the north, probably with the Carpathian Basin. Additionally, Greek metal vessels testify to interactions with Greek colonies in Italy, and pottery and other luxurious items demonstrate regular contacts with southern Greece and the Mediterranean (Figure 9.23).[53]

Unlike most of the rich graves in the wider region, which were typically located near major settlements, a general feature of the central Balkan princely graves of the sixth and fifth centuries BC is that they were placed at crossroads or at significant points of prehistoric trans-regional interaction networks. This seems to indicate that control over long-distance trade routes was a crucial resource for these communities. An important route stretched from the Adriatic coast, where imports from Greek colonies in Italy arrived, to the interior of the Balkans.[54] On the other hand, similarities between the findings from the Trebenište and Gorna Porta cemeteries in present-day North Macedonia and the magnificent necropolis at Sindos in northern Greece,[55] in particular golden masks used in burial ritual (see Figure 2.17, this volume),[56] imply that there must have been strong connections between the elites of these two areas.[57]

Contacts to the north during the sixth and fifth centuries BC are much more elusive. Although the majority of researchers recognize the northern influence in the burial assemblages of the central Balkans, they rarely provide any further considerations.[58] An important point in this respect is that the significance of wagons present in the funerary ritual at Atenica links the region with the Carpathian Basin, which was a source of rare and prestigious commodities of other kinds, such as horses and amber.

The graves in Atenica, especially the treatment of the woman and child in Mound I mentioned previously, also indicate that kinship and/or affiliation with a particular lineage was a crucial component of status in the Iron Age communities of the central Balkans. In this scenario, monumental mounds may have been regarded as places where the physical landscape overlapped with the mythical landscape. At these places of outstanding importance, communities enacted funerary ceremonies that transformed the power of their rulers into a protective force for their ancestors.

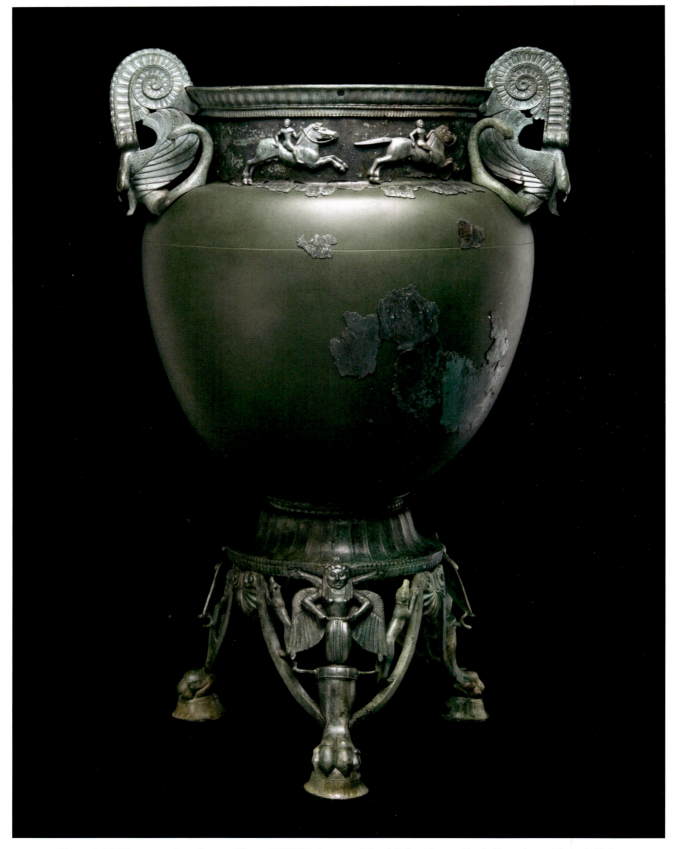

Figure 9.23. Bronze volute-krater, Grave VIII, Trebenište, North Macedonia. Early Iron Age, 550–450 BC. National Museum of Serbia, Belgrade. *Photo: National Museum of Serbia.*

Epilogue: The History and Globalization of Culture

At the end of the fifth century BC, the Early Iron Age cultural features diminished in the Carpathian Basin and blended into the widespread La Tène Culture. This was also a time when written history took the stage for the first time in this region with the Celts and Romans as the main protagonists. At roughly the same time, in the Balkans, Greek influence and then a Hellenistic cultural tide made powerful indigenous cultures less and less visible in the archaeological record, while in historical sources, various Illyrian tribes began to emerge (see Chapter 8, this volume). The first rulers of the intricate pan-European network of trade and exchange, facing the advent of history and impending 'globalization,' faded into myths, leaving only their monumental burials and lavish treasures to testify to their former glory.

Notes

1 Potrebica 2019:487–92.

2 Šimek 2004:88–102.

3 Potrebica and Rakvin 2019:34, 53–54, Table 8:1–3, cat. 42–44.

4 Potrebica 2012a:241–42.

5 Potrebica 2019:512–13.

6 Čović 1987a:232–86.

7 Čović 1987a:232; Fiala 1899a.

8 Blečić Kavur and Pravidur 2012:37, 39–45; Fiala 1899b; Truhelka 1904.

9 Čović 1961; Čović 1987a:232–86; Jašarević 2017:8–9; Marić 1964:5.

10 Čović 1987a:274–75.

11 Fiala 1899b:122–24, Figs 181–83; Truhelka 1904.

12 Marić 1964:37–38.

13 Čović 1987a:274–75; Potrebica 2003:217, 226.

14 Jašarević 2017; Marić 1964:6; Truhelka 1904.

15 Potrebica 1998:242; Potrebica 2003:223.

16 Potrebica 2003:223.

17 Majnarić-Pandžić 2002; Potrebica 2003:223; Potrebica 2013:88; Potrebica and Mavrović Mokos 2016:51–52.

18 Potrebica 2013:108.

19 Čović 1987a:280.

20 Blečić Kavur and Pravidur 2012:39–45, cat. 1–2, Fig. 2, Pl. 1:1–2.

21 Egg 1996:352; Horváth 1969:112; Kemenczei 2009:50.

22 Čović 1987a:280; Truhelka 1904:446–47, Taf. LVIII.

23 Potrebica and Fileš Kramberger 2021.

24 Ćurčić 1909; Govedarica 2017:39; Hochstetter 1881; Hoernes 1889.

25 Fiala 1893; Fiala 1895; Fiala 1896; Fiala 1897; Fiala 1899c; Fiala 1899d; Govedarica 1979:177; Govedarica 2017:40; Stratimirović 1893; Truhelka 1893.

26 Benac and Čović 1957; Čović 1987b; Gavranović 2011:32–38; Lucentini 1981; Teržan 1987.

27 Čović 1987b:642–43; Vasić 1991.

28 Čović 1987b:575; Vasić 1987a:572.

29 Čović 1983:147–51; Jašarević 2014.

30 Benac and Čović 1957:12, Pl. XVIII:1–4, Pl. XIX:1–3, Pl. XX:1–13; Fiala 1895:6–9, Figs 5–14, Taf. I:1, 1a.

31 Benac and Čović 1957:11, Pl. XV:12–14, Pl. XVI:1–4, Pl. XVII:1–6; Fiala 1895:11–12.

32 Čović 1987b:604–13; Fiala 1895:15–16, Figs 39–41, Taf. I:5.

33 Benac and Čović 1957:13–14, Pl. XXIII:1–7; Fiala 1897:13–14.

34 Benac and Čović 1957:14–15, Pl. XXVI:1–11, Pl. XXVII:1–14, Pl. XXVIII:1–4; Fiala 1899d:39–43, Figs 14–28, Taf. I:1–9.

35 Benac and Čović 1957:16, Pl. XXX:5–10, Pl. XXXI:1–20, Pl. XXXII:1–6; Fiala 1893:134–36, Figs 11–20.

36 Čović 1984.

37 Čović 1979; Čović 1987b:590–626; Palavestra 1984:98.

38 Kilian-Dirlmeier 1993:129–30, Nr. 449, Taf. 58.

39 Potrebica 2012b:19.

40 Potrebica 2013:126.

41 Jašarević 2014.

42 Potrebica 2010.

43 Potrebica 2008:210–12.

44 Benac and Čović 1957:20–21, Pl. XXXX:1–13, Pl. XXXXI:1–17.

45 Čović 1987a:281–86; Fiala 1899a.

46 Marić 1963; Popović 1996; Rustoiu 2012.

47 Dizdar 2015:54–56; Dizdar and Tonc 2018:58–59.

48 Potrebica 2019:498; Potrebica and Mavrović Mokos 2016:58–60.

49 Babić 2002; Mano-Zisi and Popović 1969.

50 Babić 2002; Đuknić and Jovanović 1966.

51 Đuknić and Jovanović 1965.

52 Krstić 2018.

53 Popov 2018.

54 Babić 2002:71; Babić and Palavestra 2018.

55 Despini 2016.

56 Kuzman and Ardjanliev 2018; Popović 1964.

57 Bouzek and Ondřejová 1988; Potrebica 2008; Vasić 1996.

58 Vasić 2003.

CHAPTER 10

Arrayed in Gold and Silver

The Lavish Kings of Ancient Thrace

Peter Delev

THE NAME 'THRACE' was given by the ancient Greeks to the barbarian country lying north of the Aegean Sea, the home of the North Wind—Boreus, a land of high mountains covered with snow, rich in grain and livestock, the land of the warlike, horse-breeding Thracians.[1] Ancient Thrace occupied the northeastern third of the Balkan Peninsula, north of the Aegean Sea, west of the Pontus Euxinus (Black Sea), and south of the Carpathian Mountains; the area corresponds to the territory of modern Bulgaria, southern Romania, northeastern Greece, and European Turkey. The valleys of the Axios (Vardar) and Morava rivers mark a rather indefinite dividing line between the lands of the Thracians to the east and those of the Illyrians, Macedonians, and Greeks in the western and southern parts of the Balkans. Some Thracians lived also in the northwestern corner of Asia Minor, to the east of the Bosporus and the Sea of Marmara (Figure 10.1).

Among the main geographical features of ancient Thrace, the ancient authors mention frequently the mountains Haimon (Haemus in Latin, nowadays the Stara Planina or Balkan Range) and Rhodope. The mighty stream of the Istros (Danube) River cuts its way across northern Thrace, accepting numerous tributaries on both sides. Southern Thrace was divided between high mountains and fertile river valleys, like those of the Strymon (Struma), Nestos (Mesta), Hebros (Maritsa), and Tonzos (Tundja).[2]

The Bronze Age and the Origin of the Thracians

The Bronze Age in the Balkans lasted over two thousand years, from the late fourth to the late second millennium BC. It was preceded, interrupted, and followed by repeated migratory movements, which may have been provoked by changes in climatic conditions and other factors. The amalgamation and settlement of various groups involved in this complex and multistage process, of which we have but very general and vague knowledge, resulted in the gradual consolidation of the ancient Balkan nations—the ancient Greeks in the southern parts of the peninsula, the Illyrians in the northwest toward the Adriatic Sea, and the Thracians in the northeast. Their languages—ancient Greek, Illyrian, and Thracian—belonged to the Indo-European family. It is usually assumed that in the course of the Bronze Age, the Indo-European peoples (whose related languages suggest a common origin) gradually wandered apart and resettled over an enormous

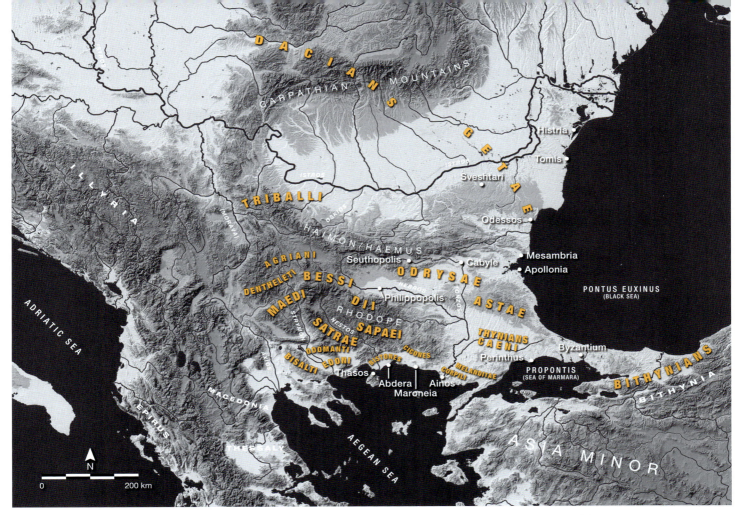

Figure 10.1. Map showing the main tribes, settlements, mountains, and rivers of ancient Thrace.
Illustration by P. Delev, F. Paár, and E. Rodriguez.

territory, mixing continuously with other populations on their way and in their respective final areas of settlement, which led to the progressive differentiation between their languages and cultures. The erection of burial mounds, or tumuli, which appeared for the first time in the Early Bronze Age, was among the cultural contributions of the newcomers (see Chapters 4 and 6, this volume). The use of tumuli later became a regular feature of Thracian burial customs.[3]

The Vulchitrun treasure stands out among the spectacular finds of the Bronze Age in Thrace. This extraordinary set of precious gold vessels was found in 1924 in the region of Pleven, and consists of one large, two-handled kantharos, one mysterious triple vessel, one large and three smaller one-handled cups, as well as two large and five small disks with bulbous grips in the middle—altogether over 12 kg of pure gold (Figure 10.2). The disks appear to be lids for other vessels, which have not been preserved, suggesting that what we know is but a fraction of the original set, an incredible treasure of enormous value, which poses many questions without ready answers.[4]

Thrace in the Early Iron Age

The transition to the Early Iron Age, from the eleventh to the sixth century BC, witnessed new migratory movements, affecting the whole of southeastern Europe and slowly settling down after a long and troubled period. As a part of these movements, the Phrygians passed from the Balkan Peninsula into Asia Minor. Together with them, or in a separate move, a group of Thracian tribes also crossed the Bosporus and settled in northwestern Asia Minor; they were known later as the Bithynians.[5]

A number of swords, spearheads, and battle-axes following Bronze Age prototypes are among the earliest iron objects found in Thrace. Regional varieties in iron weapons and ornaments are usually viewed as proofs for local-scale productions based on the rapid and universal introduction of iron metallurgy.[6] Among the other crafts of this era, ceramic manufacturing

Figure 10.2. Gold treasure, Vulchitrun, Bulgaria. Late Bronze Age, 1600–1100 BC.
National Archaeological Institute with Museum, Sofia. *Photo by N. Genov.*

Figure 10.3. Thracian dolmen, Hlyabovo, Bulgaria. Early Iron Age,
1100–700 BC. *Photo by N. Genov.*

is the best attested. The Early Iron Age pottery from Thrace is mainly hand-made and is regularly decorated with various incised or stamped geometric patterns.[7] Toward the end of the period, gray, undecorated, wheel-made pottery was gradually introduced.[8] The settlement system, which remains inadequately studied, seems to have comprised mainly small, unfortified villages and hilltop fortifications that served as places of refuge in times of danger.[9] Burial customs were varied, with inhumation and cremation both being practiced.[10] In a somewhat restricted area in the southeast, dolmens and rock-cut tombs were used in this period—the earliest stately tombs in Thrace and, at the same time, an unusually late manifestation of the megalithic tradition that had flourished in western Europe and the Mediterranean area in much earlier times (Figure 10.3).[11]

One of the most interesting archaeological finds from the Early Iron Age comes from Kazichene near Sofia and consists of three different vessels placed one inside the other: a hemispherical gold vessel, a large pottery bowl, and a still larger bronze cauldron. The assemblage is tentatively interpreted as a symbolic burial. A seventh century BC date is suggested by the cauldron, although the gold vessel is supposedly earlier.[12] Another outstanding find is the bronze figurine of a deer from Sevlievo, a masterpiece of geometric art (Figure 10.4).[13]

Thracian Tribes

In the fifth century BC, Herodotus mentioned many Thracian tribes, each with a particular ethnic name, but all with similar customs and traditions. He considered the Thracians one of the most numerous races in Europe.[14] Strabo affirmed later that, in his time, the number of Thracian tribes was twenty-two.[15] The gradual transformation of elective tribal chiefs into hereditary kings would have led to the establishment of primitive tribal states that were numerous and engaged in incessant wars among themselves. This created a fluidity of the political map—new tribes and reigning houses replacing the previous ones and sometimes successfully conquering their neighbors to create more or less stable political formations of a greater magnitude.[16]

The first tribal states seem to have appeared in ancient Thrace toward the end of the second and early in the first millennium BC. This process is reflected in the mythological figures of legendary kings, like Orpheus, Rhesos, Diomedes, Lycurgus, and Phineus, embodying the Greek perception of a monarchical system established at an early date throughout Thrace.[17]

An indefinite territory between the upper Hebros and the upper Strymon was occupied by the tribe of the Bessi (see Figure 10.1). They may also have inhabited parts of the Rhodope Mountains, where they held a famous oracular sanctuary of Dionysos.[18] Other tribes lived in the Rhodope as well, including the Satrae and the Dii.[19] The Sapaei, Bistones, and Cicones inhabited the southern slopes of the Rhodope and the Aegean coast.[20]

Of the tribes in the southwest, the Agriani, who were ruled by kings in the fourth century BC, lived along the upper reaches of the Strymon River, somewhere in the area of modern Pernik (see Figure 10.1). Their elite light infantry was highly esteemed by Alexander the Great.[21] Other Strymonian tribes were the Dentheleti, the warlike Maedi, and the Sinti,[22] while the area nearer the Aegean coast sheltered a considerable number of tribes, the most notorious being the Edoni, the Bisalti, and the Odomanti.[23] In the fifth century BC, a king of the Edoni minted heavy silver coins with his name and title: "Getas king of the Edonians."[24] Herodotus mentions the story of a king of the Bisalti who refused to join the Persian king Xerxes in his expedition against Greece and retired in the mountains. The king's six sons broke his interdiction and went with the Persians; he had them all blinded when they returned home.[25]

Figure 10.4. Bronze figurine of a deer buck, Sevlievo, Bulgaria. Early Iron Age, 800–600 BC. National Archaeological Institute with Museum, Sofia. *Photo by N. Genov.*

A number of tribal names are mentioned to the east of the Lower Hebros in the southeast (see Figure 10.1).[26] Herodotus and Xenophon placed here the Thynians, probably related to the Bithynians of Asia Minor, while in later times the Caeni and the Astae were predominant in the area.

The lands between the Haimon Mountains and Istros River in the northeast were inhabited by the Getae, who also spread to the north of the great river (see Figure 10.1). The Getae were horse-breeding people, and Thucydides mentions that they fought as mounted archers, like the Scythians.[27] At the end of the sixth century BC, they were defeated by the Persian king Darius, and in the fifth century BC, they had to accept the domination of the Odrysians, and were included in their kingdom. Later on, the Getae were mostly independent, usually divided into several tribes, each with its own king, but a couple of times uniting to form powerful political unions, notably under the great kings Dromichaetes, in the age of the successors of Alexander and Burebistas in the first century BC.[28] Many outstanding archaeological finds come from the lands of the Getae. In recent years, the discovery of a

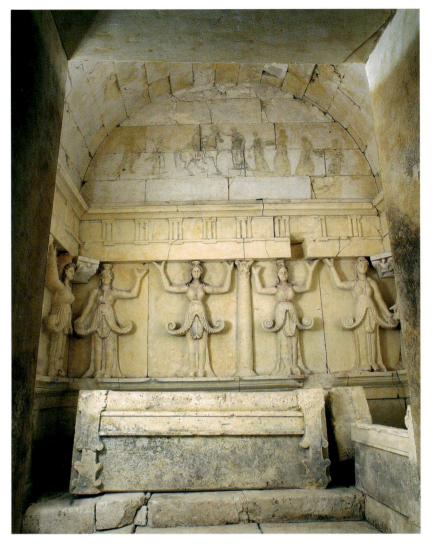

Figure 10.5. Tomb interior with relief caryatids and a wall-painting, Sveshtari, Bulgaria. Early Hellenistic Age, ca. 280–270 BC. *Photo by N. Genov.*

the rich burial finds from a tumulus in Vratsa should be mentioned in particular (Figure 10.6).[34]

Of the northern tribes beyond the Danube River, the Dacians in the southern Carpathian Mountains were the most important (see Figure 10.1). They bravely resisted the Romans under their king Decebalus, but were in the end conquered by the emperor Trajan.[35]

Greek Colonization and the Persian Invasion of Thrace

Between the eighth and sixth century BC, numerous Greek colonies came to be established along the Thracian littorals of the Aegean, the Propontis (Sea of Marmara) and the Pontus Euxinus (Black Sea).[36] These colonies became active commercial hubs that channeled an increasingly intensive and mutually profitable trade between the Greek *poleis* and the Thracians. From the beginning of the fifth century BC, Athens played a leading part in Thracian trade (Figure 10.7). Sometimes the Thracians would put the colonies under political pressure, forcing them to pay a tribute or ransom. There were cases, if rare, when individual cities were attacked, seized, sacked, and destroyed. But more often the prospect of mutual profit would prevail, so that the relations were mostly tolerant, and with time, many of the Greek coastal establishments became prosperous cities.

magnificent tomb at Sveshtari near Isperih provoked the excavations of an important fortified city from the time of Dromichaetes (Figure 10.5).[29]

The northwestern part of modern Bulgaria, to the west of the Oskios (Iskar) River, was inhabited by the Triballi (see Figure 10.1), another large tribal group headed in the fourth century BC by kings, some of whom we know by name.[30] In 376 BC, thirty thousand Triballi led by their king Hales invaded the Aegean coast in the south, laying waste the territory of Abdera.[31] In 339 BC, they inflicted a defeat on Philip II of Macedon at the height of his career,[32] and in 335 BC, withstood courageously the punitive expedition of his son Alexander, who finally came to terms with their king Syrmos.[33] Among many spectacular archaeological finds from the lands of the Triballi, the fourth century BC silver treasure from Rogozen and

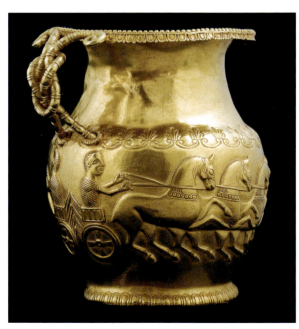

Figure 10.6. Gold jug, Vratsa, Bulgaria. Late Classical Age, 375–325 BC. Vratsa Regional Museum of History. *Photo by N. Genov.*

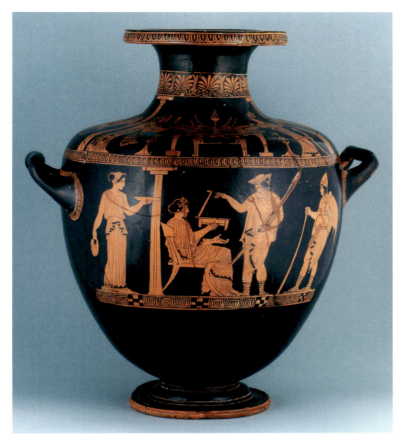

Figure 10.8. Gold ring with text presumably in Thracian, written in Greek letters, Ezerovo, Bulgaria. Classical Age, 500–400 BC. National Archaeological Institute with Museum, Sofia. *Photo by N. Genov.*

Figure 10.7. Red-figure Athenian ceramic hydria of the Painter of Cadmos, Bashova Mogila, Duvanli, Bulgaria. Classical Age, ca. 430–420 BC. Plovdiv Regional Archaeological Museum. *Photo by N. Genov.*

For a very long time, Greeks and Thracians lived in close contact and interacted through trade and exchange. This explains the existence of ample information on ancient Thrace and the Thracians in ancient Greek literature, a most fortunate occasion, for, with the exception of a few inscriptions, we do not possess any local written source from pre-Roman Thrace itself (Figure 10.8). In addition to the rich archaeological record, the information from ancient Greek (and, to a lesser degree, also Latin) authors permits us to reconstruct, if not always with the desired reliability and accuracy of detail, the history of the Thracians.[37]

For several decades in the late sixth and early fifth centuries BC, parts of Thrace fell temporarily under Persian domination (Figure 10.9).[38] The Scythian expedition of King Darius I led to the imposition of Persian rule over most of the Thracian littorals. It has been suggested that the prolific silver coinage of several tribes in the Lower Strymon area during this early age was developed in relation to the taxes imposed by the Persians.[39] Later on, both the general Mardonius and the son of Darius, King Xerxes, led great armies through southern Thrace during the Greek–Persian wars. The final victory of the Greeks brought the Persian domination in Thrace to an end in the early seventies of the fifth century BC.

The Odrysian Kingdom

The tribal state that played the most significant role in the history of ancient Thrace was that of the Odrysae.[40] Sometime after the Scythian expedition of Darius (or maybe, only after the invasion of Greece by his son, Xerxes in 480 BC), the Odrysian king Teres imposed his domination over an extensive territory in central and eastern Thrace. This could have been a lengthy process. He concluded a treaty with the contemporary Scythian king Ariapeithes, giving him a daughter in marriage. Teres was succeeded by his sons Sparadocus and Sitalces. The Greek historian Thucydides, who was a contemporary of Sitalces and his successor Seuthes, the son of Sparadocus, described the Odrysian kingdom as extending over the greater part of the Thracian lands, reaching the upper Strymon in the west, the Aegean coast in the south, and the Danube Delta in the northeast.[41]

Figure 10.9. Silver Achaemenid-type amphora, Kukova Mogila, Duvanli, Bulgaria. Classical Age, 500–450 BC. National Archaeological Institute with Museum, Sofia. *Photo by N. Genov.*

However, the tribes of the Rhodope region and those in the southwest, the Triballi in the northwest, and many other Thracians remained out of the sphere of Odrysian power. The Greek colonies along the coast also maintained their political independence, but were forced to pay for it with taxes and presents.[42] Thucydides asserts that the Odrysian kingdom was the wealthiest state in Europe in his time, the annual revenue of the kings surpassing 800 talents of gold and silver (over 20 metric tons).[43] He also recounts that in 429 BC, King Sitalces led a military operation with a huge army of 150,000 men that included not only those under his power but also volunteers from the independent Thracians.[44] A curious find

dating from this era, the end of the fifth century BC, was recovered in 2004 in a rich tumulus between the towns of Shipka and Kran in the Kazanlak Valley: a funerary mask of pure gold bearing the facial representation of a bearded man, presumably a portrait of the deceased (Figure 10.10).[45]

After a brief recession, the Odrysian kingdom lived through another period of prosperity under King Cotys I (383–360 BC). In his early reign, Cotys maintained good relations with Athens, and was awarded Athenian citizenship and a golden crown. It is recounted that learning of these distinctions, the Odrysian king proudly declared that he too would give the Athenians the rights of his tribe.[46] Later on, he fought against the Athenians, trying to displace them from the Thracian Chersonesos. He kept Greek mercenaries in his service and married their successive commanders, Iphicrates and Charidemos, to two of his daughters. Cotys minted silver and bronze coins with his name and effigy. His name also appears frequently on inscribed silverware.[47]

The Hellenistic Age

After the death of Cotys I in 360 BC, the Odrysian kingdom fell victim to dynastic strife, and was divided into three parts. The internal dissensions in Thrace helped the aggressive plans of the Macedonian king Philip II. In the early years of his reign, Philip successfully annexed the key region of Thrace around the Lower Strymon and Nestos, famous for its gold and silver mines. Later, he waged several wars against Cersobleptes, the son of Cotys, whom he eventually defeated in a great campaign between 342 and 340 BC; most Thracian lands south of the Haimon fell under Macedonian power. In 339 BC, Philip led a successful expedition against the Scythians who had crossed the Danube, but suffered a defeat from the Triballi on his way back—most of northern Thrace remained out of the sphere of direct Macedonian rule.[48]

During the time of Alexander the Great (336–323 BC), Thracian lands conquered by Philip were ruled by Macedonian governors.[49] After the death of Alexander, they were assigned to his former bodyguard Lysimachus, who proclaimed himself king in 305 BC. Lysimachus controlled the Thracian littorals with the Greek cities and coastal roads. However, independent Thracian kingdoms flourished in the interior, the two most powerful kings being Seuthes III in the south, possibly buried in the Golyamata Kosmatka tumulus (Figure 10.11), and Dromichaetes, the king of the Getae, in the north. The latter even succeeded in one of the many military conflicts in this era to capture Lysimachus with his whole army, but afterward graciously set him free.[50]

After the death of Lysimachus in 281 BC, Thrace was overrun by a massive invasion of Celtic tribes that also affected other areas of the Balkan Peninsula and Asia Minor (see also Chapter 8, this volume).[51] The Aegean littoral was disputed subsequently by major Hellenistic powers and finally ended in Roman hands in the second century BC, while the interior remained divided between local Thracian rulers. The archaeological record of this period is less brilliant and abundant in comparison to Classical and early Hellenistic times, which accords with the scanty historical evidence attesting political disintegration and incessant strife.[52]

Glimpses of Thracian Culture

Kings and Commoners

The Thracians were notorious for their bravery, bellicosity, and brutality. War had a permanent place in their way of life. Thracian armies were usually

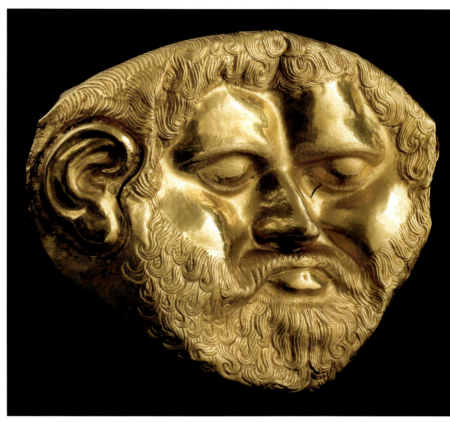

Figure 10.10. Gold funerary mask, Svetitsa Mogila, Shipka, Bulgaria. Classical Age, 450–400 BC. National Archaeological Institute with Museum, Sofia. *Photo by N. Genov.*

composed of light infantry and cavalry, reflecting the simple class structure of Thracian society. The mass of the peasants would fight as infantry, and in some areas (notably the Getae in the northeast), as mounted archers. The common weapons of the foot-soldier were a light, leather shield, often of crescent shape (called *pelta*), a couple of throwing spears, a short sword or dagger (a popular curved type was known as *machaira*), and a bow and quiver of arrows. The long 'Celtic' sword became widely popular in Hellenistic times as well as another fearful Thracian weapon, the so-called *romphaea*, a kind of spear with a very long, straight or slightly curved blade intended for cutting.

The aristocracy would fight on horseback, and the body of cavalry was the main striking force of Thracian armies. The usual equipment of the horseman consisted of a helmet, a cuirass, a pair of greaves, a light shield, a couple of throwing spears, a sword, and a bow and arrows (Figures 10.12 and 10.13). The horse trappings were frequently lavishly decorated with metal appliqués. The composition of the

Figure 10.11. Tomb interior, Golyamata Kosmatka Mogila, Shipka, Bulgaria. Early Hellenistic Age, ca. 300 BC. *Photo by D. Dimitrova.*

Figure 10.12. Bronze helmet, Satovcha, Bulgaria. Late Classical Age, 375–325 BC. National Museum of History, Sofia. *Photo by N. Genov.*

Figure 10.13. Bronze cuirass, Ruets, Bulgaria. Classical Age, 450–400 BC. National Archaeological Institute with Museum, Sofia. *Photo by N. Genov.*

Figure 10.14. Red-figure Athenian ceramic jug with Thracian warriors, Apollonia Pontica (Sozopol), Bulgaria. Classical Age, ca. 430–425 BC. Archaeological Museum, Sozopol. *Photo by N. Genov.*

Thracian army predetermined its usual tactics—they used swift and surprising attacks and retreats, all kinds of stratagems, ambushes, and the like (Figure 10.14).[53]

The Thracian warrior was the master in his home, while women were in principle deprived of rights and doomed to heavy labor both at home and in the fields. "The Thracians . . . use their women to till their land, to shepherd and raise their cattle and to serve them in every way like slaves," writes Plato.[54] It was usual for a man to have several wives, who were purchased from their parents. Marriage, childbirth, and burial were marked with celebrations, accompanied by food, drink, and various amusements. The Thracians had in general a great propensity for all kinds of feasts and festivities, the entertainment of guests, and the offering and receiving of gifts. They were intemperate in their food and drink, they dressed in colorful clothes, and wore ostentatious ornaments.[55]

The kings lived in fortified residences amid pomp and luxury. Herodotus says that the Thracian nobles despised manual labor and held that it was most honorable not to work, but to live on war and plunder.[56] Their common pastime was hunting, and they engaged routinely in incessant feasts and banquets. The most representative monuments of Thracian culture are connected with royalty and the aristocracy—magnificent tombs, ostentatious treasures, and expensive works of art.

Settlement Life and Urbanization

Throughout the first millennium BC, Thrace remained a predominantly rural country. The main part of the population lived in small, scattered villages, retreating in cases of danger to mountain or hilltop fortresses. The Greek maritime colonies were the first real cities in Thrace. Some settlements in the interior were gradually urbanized as seats of royal power or trading stations. Upon conquering southern Thrace, Philip II established new fortified cities in key locations; among these were Philippopolis (Plovdiv) on the Hebros River and Cabyle on the Tonzos River, near Yambol. The remains of a royal city have been excavated farther west in the Tonzos Valley, near Kazanluk—this urban center was called Seuthopolis after its founder, Seuthes III. A royal city of the Getae is being studied at Sveshtari in the north.[57]

Religion

The scattered information from Classical authors does not permit an exhaustive reconstruction of Thracian religious beliefs, mythological tradition, and cult practices (Figure 10.15). An obscure text by Herodotus lists among the gods worshipped by the Thracians Ares, Dionysus, and Artemis, the Greek deities of war, wine, and hunting, adding that the kings had a separate cult of Hermes.[58] Whatever the intended meaning of this controversial text was, the detachment of aristocratic cults seems a reasonable inference. Ancient authors also mention other Thracian deities, like Pleistor, Sabazius, and Bendis. An inscription found in the ruins of Seuthopolis notes city temples and altars.[59] The main Thracian sanctuaries, however, were situated in the open landscape, close to mountain tops, rocks, caves, springs, or other particular sites.[60]

The legends about mythological figures, like Orpheus, Zalmoxis, and Rhesos, transmit further

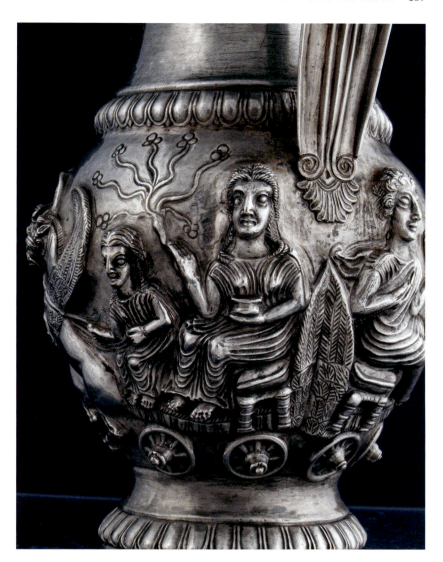

Figure 10.15. Silver jug with mythological figures in chariots drawn by winged horses, Rogozen, Bulgaria. Late Classical Age, 375–325 BC. Vratsa Regional Museum of History. *Photo by N. Genov.*

information on some important aspects of Thracian religion. On the border between the world of men and the world of gods, they carry notions pertaining to a heroic aristocratic doctrine, involving the practice of rites of initiation aimed at attaining immortality, eternal happiness, and association with the gods.[61]

Burial Customs

Beliefs in immortality are reflected in funerary practices, which are among the better attested manifestations of Thracian culture.[62] Some ancient authors mention the custom of mourning the dead, others suggest that Thracian funerals were rather occasions for joy and merriment because of the prevalent

Figure 10.16. Burial chamber, Shushmanets, Shipka, Bulgaria. Early Hellenistic Age, 300–250 BC. *Photo by D. Dimitrova.*

Figure 10.17. Tomb interior with frescoes, Kazanlak, Bulgaria. Early Hellenistic Age, ca. 280–260 BC. *Photo by N. Genov.*

notions that the deceased would enjoy a happy afterlife. In honor of the dead, the Thracians would sacrifice animals, feast, drink copious quantities of wine, and set up various games and competitions. The burial itself was either by cremation of the body on a pyre or by its inhumation in a grave or in a specially constructed tomb. An earthen tumulus was usually heaped over the burial; sometimes these burial mounds reached imposing dimensions.

Burials directly reflect social stratification in Thracian society. Exceptionally rich graves have been excavated at Duvanli, Vratsa, and many other sites with tumuli.[63] Between the fifth and third centuries BC, when ancient Thrace was living through an age of prosperity, it became usual to construct built tombs of varied and often exquisite architectural design for the burial of nobles (Figure 10.16).[64] A covered corridor

would lead to the burial chamber from the edge of the tumulus. Among the most impressive examples of Thracian funerary architecture are the imposing tombs at Mezek and Starosel.[65] The Kazanlak tomb, of smaller dimensions and built of brick, is famous for its superb frescos (Figure 10.17). The main scene depicts a Thracian nobleman wearing a diadem behind a table, holding the hand of a noble woman seated on a throne; on both sides of them is a procession of musicians, servants carrying food, wine, and different valuables, and grooms leading two riding horses, as well as a chariot with a team of four.[66] In a recently discovered tomb at Alexandrovo, the wall-paintings represent hunting scenes with hunters mounted and on foot, and dogs pursuing deer and boars.[67] The walls of the main burial chamber in the tomb at Sveshtari are decorated with relief figures of caryatids with raised hands supporting the vault, and a painted scene above shows a goddess offering a crown to a mounted Thracian prince (see Figure 10.5).[68]

Figure 10.18. Gold treasure, Panagyurishte, Bulgaria. Early
Hellenistic Age, 325–275 BC. Plovdiv Regional Archaeological Museum.
Photo by N. Genov.

Thracian Treasures

Burial goods placed with the dead in their tombs have
in most cases been looted long ago. The rare discoveries of ostentatious aristocratic burials preserved intact
offer us some insight into the fabulous wealth and
opulence of the Thracian aristocracy. Besides the finds
in graves and tombs, many sumptuous treasures have
been discovered buried in the ground, either because
they were hidden in times of danger and not retrieved
afterwards, or because they were intentionally deposited as ritual offerings. These treasures are among the
most impressive and admired heirlooms of Thracian
antiquity.[69]

The gold treasure from Panagyurishte, the best
known find in this group, was discovered fortuitously
in 1949, and consists of nine gold vessels of extraordinary splendor and craftsmanship—a two-handled
amphora, three jugs shaped like female heads, four

rhytons, of which two are shaped like deer heads,
one like a ram's head and the fourth like the forepart
of a goat, as well as a large, shallow dish with a central
knob, decorated with concentric rows of human heads,
acorns, and rosettes (Figure 10.18). The body of
the amphora and the upper parts of the rhytons are
decorated with multi-figure relief scenes, and the
handles are shaped like centaur, sphinx, or lion figures.
The magnificent quality of the vessels and their lavish
decoration suggest the hand of a great artist. The
treasure is dated to the late fourth or early third
century BC and has been attributed presumptively to
a goldsmith workshop in the Greek city of Lampsacus
in Asia Minor—it may have been a royal present from
an early Hellenistic king, possibly Antigonus the One-
Eyed or Lysimachus, to the contemporary Thracian
king Seuthes III.[70]

Figure 10.19. Silver appliqué from horse trappings representing a hunting horseman, Lukovit, Bulgaria. Late Classical Age, 400–350 BC. National Archaeological Institute with Museum, Sofia. *Photo by N. Genov.*

Several sumptuous silver treasures add their brilliance to the gold from Panagyurishte; those from Borovo and Rogozen feature exquisite drinking vessels, and the ones from Lukovit and Letnitsa include extraordinary horse-harness trappings (Figure 10.19).[71]

The Thracian Provinces of the Roman Empire

The Macedonian wars of Rome ended with the annihilation of the Antigonid kingdom and the establishment of the Roman province of Macedonia in 148 BC. Greece and Illyria also came effectively under Roman domination, and after 133 BC, the Pergamene kingdom became the province of Asia. The kingdom of the Thracians in Asia, Bithynia, lasted until 74 BC, when it also was turned into a Roman province.[72]

The Thracian interior remained for a long time aside from the main directions of Roman aggression in the east. While some Thracian kings, notably those of the Astae and the Dentheleti, were loyal Roman allies, other Thracians often made predatory incursions

into Roman-controlled territory, provoking retaliatory measures.[73] It would have been in one of these punitive expeditions that the Thracian Spartacus fell into Roman hands; in 73 BC, as an escaped gladiator he was to lead the greatest slave uprising in Italy.[74]

After his victory over Mark Antony, Emperor Augustus designed the plan of turning the Rhine and Danube rivers into a safe European frontier for the Roman Empire. In fulfilment of this, his general Marcus Licinius Crassus in 29/28 BC led a major expedition against the Thracian tribes along the southern bank of the Danube.[75] In the early years of Augustus's successor Tiberius, this territory was officially proclaimed a Roman province under the name of Moesia. Roman legions were permanently stationed along the new Danube frontier, while some 150,000 locals were resettled here from the territories across the river "with the kings and notables," probably in a move aimed at the demographic and economic stabilization of the new province.[76] Later, in AD 86, Moesia was divided into two provinces: the western part, comprising most of modern Serbia, was named Moesia Superior, and the eastern region, reaching as far as the Danube Delta and the Black Sea coast, became Moesia Inferior.[77]

A large Thracian kingdom ruled by a dynasty of Sapaean origin existed in the south as a Roman protectorate until the reign of Emperor Claudius, who established in its place a Roman province under the name of Thracia. The old Thracian aristocracy seems to have preserved its privileges under the Roman provincial government. The province was ruled by imperial *legati* sitting in Perinthus on the Propontis, while the most important urban center of the interior was the old city of Philippopolis, now called also Trimontium.

After the defeat of the Dacians by Emperor Trajan early in the second century AD, their territories across the Danube, including Transylvania, were also turned into a Roman province under the name of Dacia. The Roman victory over these northern Thracians was celebrated in a number of imposing monuments, including the column of Trajan in Rome.

The incorporation of the lands of the Thracians in the Roman Empire had a beneficial effect on their economic and cultural development in the following centuries. The integrated market of the enormous empire and the intensive internal commercial and cultural exchange, the lasting peace and political stability, and the gradual improvement of the status of the provinces and their indigenous population brought about an age of provincial prosperity. The extensive urbanization of the interior and the installation of a stable and efficient road system were among the most important positive outcomes of the establishment of Roman authority in Thrace. The cities shared in the cultural life of the empire, which gradually acquired a universal character. The direct influence of Roman traditions was more pronounced in Moesia and Dacia, while the Greek and Hellenistic legacy remained prevalent in Thrace.

The Thracian village was the social and cultural counterpart of the Roman cities. Thrace remained a predominantly agricultural territory, and the village population was the main producer of goods. Besides the free villages, there were large imperial domains and private estates where slave labor was exploited on a large scale. Many free peasants were enrolled in the army, and thus acquired Roman citizenship, a privilege obtained much more easily by city dwellers.

Culturally, the Thracian village was more conservative and preserved the old local traditions. In the ruins of hundreds of simple village sanctuaries, votive reliefs, statuettes, and dedications have been found bearing the image of the Thracian horseman—a specific local iconography embodying the idea of a protective divinity (Figure 10.20).[78]

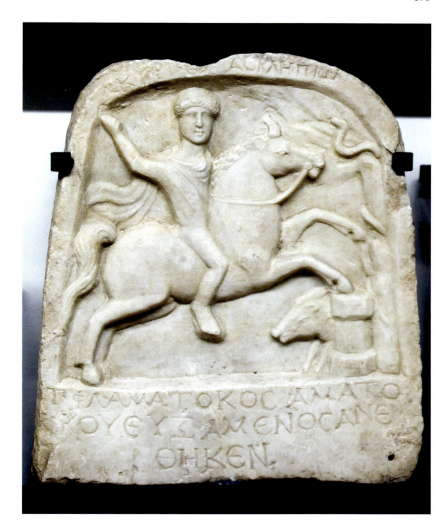

Figure 10.20. Votive relief with a horseman, Glava Panega, Bulgaria. Roman Period, AD 100–200. National Archaeological Institute with Museum, Sofia. *Photo by N. Genov.*

Conclusions

The history of the Thracians is one of gradual evolution from a comparatively primitive initial state—however, with signs of social differentiation and initial political organization already in the Late Bronze and Early Iron Ages—to a highly civilized and urbanized one in the centuries when they were incorporated into the Roman Empire. Passing through different stages along this protracted and uneven line of development, Thracian society saw the emergence of an opulent warrior aristocracy, leading to a condition of permanent internecine strife between the many warring tribes. This was only partially reduced with the appearance of larger, but rather unstable, territorial kingdoms with more or less centralized government; the Odrysian kingdom in the fifth and fourth centuries BC is the best example, while the northern Getae united their several tribes under one king only a couple of times and for short periods.

The impressive archaeological finds of lavish treasures and imposing tomb structures illustrate the affluence of the warrior aristocracy, topped by the enormous wealth and power of the kings even of smaller tribes, and especially by those of the greater, territorial kingdoms of ancient Thrace.

Notes

1   The origin of the names Thrace (in Greek Θράκη, Ion. Θρήκη) and Thracians (Θράκες, Θρῆκες) is unknown. Some mythographic versions make Thraike a daughter of Oceanus, a sister of Europa and a half-sister of Asia and Libya (Andron from Halicarnassus:fr. 7), others a nymph proficient in herbs and magic (Arr. Bithyn.:fr. 13 Roos/Wirth = fr. 61A FGrH). The country might have been called alternatively Perke or Aria in early times (Arr. Bithyn.:loc. cit.; Steph. Byz.:s.v. Θράκη), but the name Thrace is already firmly established in the Homeric poems. It is often suggested that the name sprang up as an exonym in Greek literary usage and originated from that of a local tribe somewhere in the Hellespontine area. See Fol 1997:142–43; Mihailov 1972:35–36; Popov 1999:56; Tomaschek 1893–94:1, 11–12.

2   On the territory and physical geography of ancient Thrace, see Bouzek and Graninger 2015; Casson 1926:3–101; Lenk 1936a; Mihailov 1972:35–46; Robson 1857:1176–80; Wiesner 1963:11–13, 24–32.

3   On the Bronze Age in Thrace, see Alexandrov et al. 2018 passim; Bonev 1988; Bonev 2003; Haag et al. 2017 passim; Katinčarov 1974; Katinčarov 1978; Mikov 1971; Leshtakov 2006; Panayotov 1995. On Thracian tumuli, see Kitov 1993; Mikov 1942; Mikov 1957; Škorpil 1898.

4   Bonev 1995; Chukalev and Dimitrova 2018; Matthäus 1989; Mikov 1958; Penkova and Mehofer 2018; Pernicka 2018; Sherratt and Taylor 1989; Venedikov 1987.

5   On the Early Iron Age in Thrace, see Chichikova 1974a; Gergova 1986; Hänsel 1976; Lásló 1997; Nekhrizov and Tzvetkova 2018; Shalganova and Gotzev 1995. On the migrations in the transition period, see Dimitrov 1971; Sandars 1974; Venedikov 1978. On the Bithynians, see Gabelko 2005; Vitucci 1953.

6   On the arms, see Bader 1991; Boroffka 1991; Buyukliev 1985; Kilian-Dirlmeier 1993; Stoia 1989; Vulpe 1990. On the ornaments, see Gergova 1980; Gergova 1987; Tonkova 2015.

7   Chichikova 1968; Gotzev 1994; Nekhrizov 2008; Nikov 2011; Nikov 2016.

8   Alexandrescu 1977; Bozkova 2017:73–87; Bozkova and Nikov 2009; Bozkova and Nikov 2019; Chichikova 1965; Chichikova 2004; Nikov 1999; Nikov 2012:146–49; Tsonchev 1959.

9   Chichikova 1974b; Gotzev 1997; Spiridonov 1979; Theodossiev 2011:15–17.

10   Gergova 1989; Kisyov 2009; Sîrbu 2003; Stoyanov 1992; Stoyanov 1997:111–63.

11   Delev 1984; Nekhrizov 2015; Özdogan 1998.

12   Fol 1975b; Stancheva 1973.

13   Venedikov and Gerassimov 1979:Fig. 9.

14   Hdt.:5.3.2.

15   Strabo:7 fr. 48; cp. Plin. N.H.:40–41.

16   Delev 2013; Delev 2014:12–14.

17   On legendary Thracian kings, see Delev 2014:55–59; Fol 1972:38–46.

18   Delev 2012a; Delev 2014:167–35.

19   Delev 2014:279–80, 431–35; Sarafov 1974.

20   Delev 1983; Delev 2014:210–14, 416–20.

21   Delev 2014:148–66; Fol 1975a:65–68; Gerov 1961:231–37; Petrova 1991; Petrova 1999; Sokolovska 1990.

22   Chichikova 1981; Delev 2014:228–37, 338–56, 439–45; Fol 1975a:69–71; Gerov 1961:159–76.

23   Delev 2007; Delev 2014:186–209, 286–303, 374–82.

24   Delev 2014:101, 300–301; Tacheva 1998.

25   Hdt.:8.116.

26   Delev 2010:96–103.

27   Thuc.:2.96.1.

28   Avram 2011; Crişan 1978; Delev 2000:392–96; Delev 2012; Fol 1975a:35–59; Pârvan 1926; Pârvan 1928; Pippidi and Berciu 1965; Vulpe 1938; Yordanov 2011.

29   On the excavations of the city, see Stoyanov 2015c; Stoyanov et al. 2006. For the tomb, see below.

30   Fol 1975a:9–25; Papazoglu 1978:9–86; Theodossiev 2000.

31   Diod.:15.36.1–4; cp. Aen. Tact.:15.8–9; Schol. in Aristid. Panath.:172.7.

32   Justin.:9.3.1–3.

33   Arr. Anab.:1.1.4–4.8; cp. Diod.:17.8.1; Strabo:7.3.8; Plut. Alex.:11.2; Curt.:9.6.20; Polyaen. Strat.:4.3.11.

34   On Rogozen, see Cook 1989; Fol et al. 1989; Marazov 1989. On Vratsa, see Torbov 2005.

35   Glodariu 2005; Grumeza 2009; Oltean 2007.

36   Blavatskaya 1952; Damyanov 2015; Danov 1947; Danov 1968:217–94; Grammenos and Petropoulos 2003; Grammenos and Petropoulos 2007; Hansen and Nielsen 2004:810–941; Isaac 1986; Pippidi 1971; Tiverios 2008.

37   For general reviews of Thracian history, see Cary 1752; Danov 1968; Danov 1979; Fol 1997; Hoddinott 1981; Kazarow 1926; Lenk 1936b; Popov 1999; Tacheva 1997; Valeva et al. 2015:33–105; Velkov et al. 1979; Wiesner 1963.

38 Balcer 1988; Fol and Hammond 1988; Vasilev 2015; Vassileva 2015.

39 Delev 2014:89–95, 99–109; Draganov 2000:27–62; Svoronos 1919; Youroukova 1992:9–33.

40 On the Odrysian kingdom, see Archibald 1998; Dobruski 1897:555–605; Fol 1972:115–54; Fol 1975a:93–195; Höck 1891; Kazarow 1933; Kazarow 1954; Lenk 1937; Todorov 1933:3–66; Tonev 1942.

41 Thuc.:2.96.1, 97.1–2.

42 See for example, Loukopoulou 2002; contra Veligianni-Terzi 2004, who denies any payments by the coastal cities toward the Odrysian kings.

43 Thuc.:2.97.3, 5.

44 Thuc.:2.96–101.

45 Kitov 2005. The unfounded suggestion of the excavator that the mask could have belonged to Teres, the founder of the Odrysian kingdom, amply reiterated by the media, is chronologically impossible.

46 Val. Max.:3.7.7.

47 Dobruski 1897:586–91; Fol 1975a:107–12, 141–66; Höck 1891:89–100; Peter 1997:112–24; Tacheva 2006:140–66; Todorov 1933:34–39.

48 Delev 1997; Delev 2015b; Yordanov 1998:11–97.

49 Delev 2004:106–22; Yordanov 1998:99–160.

50 Diod.:21, fr. 11, 12; Strabo:7.3.8, 3.14; Paus.:1.9.5–6; Polyaen. Strat.:7.25; Polyb.:fr. 102; Justin.:16.1.19; Plut. Demetr.:39, 52; Mor.:126 ef, 183 e, 555 de. On Lysimachus, see Delev 2004; Franco 1993; Landucci Gattinoni 1992; Lund 1992. On Seuthes and Seuthopolis, see Chichikova and Dimitrov 2016. On the Golyama Kosmatka tumulus, see Dimitrova 2015. On Dromichaetes, see Delev 2004:204–38; Pârvan 1926:55–65; Yordanov 1998:205–13.

51 Domaradzki 1984; Emilov 2015; Kazarow 1919.

52 Danov 1979:47–101; Delev 2003; Delev 2015a; Tacheva 1997:30–61.

53 On Thracian arms and warfare, see Best 1969; Kazarow 1916:71–85; Mihailov 1972:141–80; Stoyanov 2015d; Webber 2011.

54 Plato Leges:7, p. 805de.

55 On everyday life in Thrace, see Archibald 2015; Georgieva et al. 1999; Kazarow 1916; Kazarow 1930.

56 Hdt.:5.6.2.

57 On the settlement system and the urbanization in Thrace, see Nankov 2015; Popov 2002; Popov 2015.

58 Hdt.:5.7.

59 Mihailov 1964:No 1731; Mihailov 1997:No 5614.

60 Bayrakov 2016; Domaradzki 1994; Domaradzki 2003; Nekhrizov 2005; Sîrbu and Ştefănescu 2007. On a recent discussion about the so-called 'ritual pit-fields' in Thrace, see Bozkova 2016; Georgieva 2015.

61 On Thracian religion, see Fol 1986; Fol 1991; Fol 1994; Fol et al. 1976; Kazarow 1936; Mihailov 1972:213–56; Popov 1999:183–202, 213–56; Rabadjiev 2015.

62 On Thracian funerary rites and beliefs, see Georgieva 2004; Georgieva et al. 1999:216–41; Gergova 1989; Gergova 1996; Kazarow 1916:85–91; Kisyov 2009; Theodossiev 2011:19–35.

63 On Duvanli, see Filow and Welkow 1930; Filow et al. 1934. On Vratsa, see Torbov 2005.

64 On Thracian tombs, see Mikov 1955; Rousseva 2000; Rousseva 2002; Stoyanov 1990; Stoyanov and Stoyanova 2011; Stoyanov and Stoyanova 2016; Stoyanova 2015; Theodossiev 2007a; Theodossiev 2007b; Valeva 2015.

65 On Mezek, see Filow 1937. On Starosel, see Kitov 2003.

66 On Kazanlak, see Meyboom 2014; Mikov 1954; Vassiliev 1958; Zhivkova 1975.

67 On Alexandrovo, see Kitov 2004.

68 On Sveshtari, see Chichikova et al. 2012; Fol et al. 1986; Stoyanov 1998b.

69 Thracian treasures (alongside rich burial goods) have been displayed in a number of Bulgarian archaeological exhibitions in different countries. For some catalogs, see *Die Thraker…* 2004; Haag et al. 2017; *L'Or des cavaliers Thraces…* 1987; *L'Or des Thraces…* 2002; Marazov 1998; Martinez et al. 2015; *Traci…* 1989.

70 Simon 1960; Stoyanov 2004; Stoyanov 2015b; Venedikov 1961.

71 On Borovo, see Ivanov 1975; Stoyanov 1998a; Stoyanov 2015a. On Letnitsa, see Venedikov 1996.

72 On the Bithynian kingdom, see Gabelko 2005; Vitucci 1953.

73 Danov 1979:101–18; Delev 2018; Tacheva 1997:61–70; Walbank 1981.

74 From the abundant literature on Spartacus, see Bradley 1989:83–101; Strauss 2009.

75 Cass. Dio:51.23–27.

76 Strabo:7.3.10 (50,000, AD 4); Dessau 1887:No 3608 (100,000, AD 62–63).

77 Literature on the Thracian provinces of the Roman Empire (Moesia, Thracia, and Dacia) is enormous. See general overviews by Danov 1979:145–85; Dumanov 2015; Lozanov 2015; Tacheva 1997:150–235; Wilkes 1996; Wilkes 2000.

78 For a lucid overview on the various aspects and problems of the 'Thracian horseman,' see Venedikov 1976.

Bibliography

Ancient and Byzantine Authors

Aen. Tact.: Aeneas Tacticus. *Commentarius Poliorceticus.* In: *Aeneas Tacticus, Asclepiodotus, and Onasander*, translated by Illinois Greek Club, pp. 1–225. Harvard University Press, Cambridge, MA and W. Heinemann, London, 1928 (Loeb Classical Library 156).

Andron of Halicarnassus (fragments). In: *Die Fragmente der Griechischen Historiker, Teil 1: Genealogie und Mythographie*, edited by F. Jacoby. Weidmann, Berlin, 1923, No. 10.

An. Comn.: Anna Comnène, *Alexiade*, edited by B. Leib, 3 vols. Les Belles Lettres, Paris, 1937–45.

Arr. Anab.: Flavius Arrianus. *Anabasis Alexandri.*—Arrian. *Anabasis of Alexander and Indica*, in two volumes, with English translation by P.A. Brunt. Harvard University Press, Cambridge, MA and W. Heinemann, London, 1976–83 (Loeb Classical Library 236 and 269).

Arr. Bithyn.: Flavius Arrianus. *Bithynica* (fragments). In: *Die Fragmente der Griechischen Historiker, Teil 2: Zeitgeschichte*, edited by F. Jacoby. Weidmann, Berlin, 1926–30, No. 156. Also (with different numbering of fragments) in *Flavii Arriani quae extant omnia*, Volume II: *Scripta minora et fragmenta*, edited by A.G. Roos and G. Wirth, pp. 197–223. Teubner, Leipzig, 1968.

Cass. Dio: Cassius Dio. *Historia Romana.*—*Dio's Roman History*, in nine volumes, with English translation by E. Cary. Harvard University Press, Cambridge, MA and W. Heinemann, London, 1914–27 (Loeb Classical Library 32, 37, 53, 66, 82, 83, 175, 176, 177).

Cic. Top.: M. Tullius Cicero. *Topica.* In: Cicero. *On Invention. The Best Kind of Orator. Topics*, with English translation by H.M. Hubbel, pp. 377–459. Harvard University Press, Cambridge, MA and W. Heinemann, London, 1949 (Loeb Classical Library 386).

Curt.: Q. Curtius Rufus. *Historiae Alexandri Magni*—*Quintus Curtius*, in two volumes, with English translation by J.C. Rolfe. Harvard University Press, Cambridge, MA and W. Heinemann, London, 1946 (Loeb Classical Library 368–369).

Diod.: Diodorus Siculus. *Bibliotheca Historica.*—*Diodorus of Sicily*, in twelve volumes, with English translation by C.H. Oldfather (vol. 1–6), C.L. Sherman (vol. 7), C. Bradford Welles (vol. 8), R.M. Geer (vol. 9–10), and F.R. Walton (vol. 11–12). Harvard University Press, Cambridge, MA and W. Heinemann, London, 1933–67 (Loeb Classical Library 279, 303, 340, 375, 377, 384, 389, 390, 399, 409, 422, 423).

Hdt.: Herodotus. *Historiae.*—*Herodotus*, in four volumes, with English translation by A.D. Godley. Harvard University Press, Cambridge, MA and W. Heinemann, London, 1920–30 (Loeb Classical Library 117–20).

Hom. Il.: Homer. *The Iliad.* Translated by R. Fagles. Penguin, London, 1992.

Hom. Od.: Homer. *The Odyssey.* Translated by R. Fagles. Penguin, London, 1996.

Justin.: Marcus Iunianus Iustinus. *Liber historiarum Philippicarum.* O. Seel (ed.). *M. Iuniani Iustini Epitoma Historiarum Philippicarum Pompei Trogi. Accedunt prologi in Pompeium Trogum.* Teubner, Leipzig, 1972.

Paus.: Pausanias. *Descriptio Graeciae.* Pausanias. *Description of Greece*, in five volumes, with English translation by W.H.S. Jones. Harvard University Press, Cambridge, MA and W. Heinemann, London, 1918–35 (Loeb Classical Library 93, 188, 272, 297, 298).

Plato Leges.—Plato. *Laws*, in two volumes, with English translation by R.G. Bury. W. Heinemann, London and G. P. Putnam's Sons, New York, 1926 (Loeb Classical Library 187, 192).

Plin. N.H.: C. Plinius Secundus. *Naturalis Historia.*—Pliny. *Natural History*, with English translation by H. Rackham (vol. 1–5, 9), W.H.S. Jones (vol. 6–8), D.E. Eichholz (vol. 10). Harvard University Press, Cambridge, MA and W. Heinemann, London, 1938–62 (Loeb Classical Library 330, 352, 352, 370, 371, 392–94, 418, 419).

Plut. Alex.: Plutarchus. *Alexander.* In: Plutarch. *Lives*, in eleven volumes, with English translation by B. Perrin. Vol. 7: *Demosthenes and Cicero. Alexander and Caesar*, pp. 223–439. Harvard University Press, Cambridge, MA and W. Heinemann, London, 1919 (Loeb Classical Library 49).

Plut. Demetr.: Plutarchus. *Demetrius.* In: Plutarch. *Lives*, in eleven volumes, with English translation by B. Perrin. Vol. 9: *Demetrius and Antony. Pyrrhus and Gaius Marius*, pp. 1–135. Harvard

University Press, Cambridge, MA and W. Heinemann, London, 1920 (Loeb Classical Library 101).

Plut. Mor.: Plutarchus. *Moralia.*—*Plutarch's Moralia*, in fifteen volumes, with English translation by F.C. Babbit et al. Harvard University Press, Cambridge, MA and W. Heinemann, London, 1927–76 (Loeb Classical Library 197, 222, 245, 305, 306, 321, 337, 405, 406, 424–29, 470).

Polyaen. Strat.: Polyaenus. *Strategematon libri VIII*, edited by E. Woelfflin and L. Melber. Teubner, Stuttgart, 1970.

Polyb.: Polybius. *Historiae.*—Polybius. *The Histories*, in six volumes, with English translation by W.R. Paton. Harvard University Press, Cambridge, MA and W. Heinemann, London, 1922-1927 (Loeb Classical Library 128, 137, 138, 159–61).

Ps.-Scyl.: [Pesudo-]Scylax. *Periplus.*—*Pseudo-Skylax's Periplous. The Circumnavigation of the Inhabited World.* Text, translation, and commentary by G. Shipley. Second edition. Liverpool University Press, Liverpool, 2019.

Schol. in Aristid. Panath.: *Scholia in Aelium Aristidem, Panathenaicus.* In: *Aristides*, vol. 3, pp. 1–342, edited by W. Dindorf. G. Reimer, Leipzig, 1829 (repr. G. Olms, Hildesheim, 1964).

Steph. Byz.: Stephanus Byzantinus. *Ethnica.* M. Billerbeck et al. (eds.). *Stephani Byzantii Ethnica*, 1–5. De Gruyter, Berlin and New York/Boston, 2006–17 (Corpus Fontium Historiae Byzantinae 43/1–5).

Strabo: *Strabonis Geographica.*—*The Geography of Strabo*, in eight volumes, with English translation by H.L. Jones. Harvard University Press, Cambridge, MA and W. Heinemann, London, 1917–32 (Loeb Classical Library 49, 50, 182, 196, 211, 223, 241, 267).

Thuc.: Thucydides. *Historiae.*—Thucydides. *History of the Peloponnesian War*, in four volumes, with English translation by C.F. Smith. Harvard University Press, Cambridge, MA and W. Heinemann, London, 1919-1923 (*Loeb Classical Library* 108–10, 169).

Val. Max.: Valerius Maximus. *Facta et dicta memorabilia.*—Valerius Maximus. *Memorable Doings and Sayings*, in two volumes, with English translation by D.R. Shackleton Bailey. Harvard University Press, Cambridge, MA, 2000 (Loeb Classical Library 492–93).

References

Adler, M.A. 1989. Ritual Facilities and Social Integration in Nonranked Societies. In: *The Architecture of Social Integration in Prehistoric Pueblos*, edited by W.D. Lipe and M. Hegmon, pp. 35–52. Crow Canyon Archaeological Center, Cortez, CO.

Adler, M.A. and R.H. Wilshusen. 1990. Large-Scale Integrative Facilities in Tribal Societies: Cross-Cultural and Southwestern U.S. Examples. *World Archaeology* 22(2):133–46.

Ahlquist, J.S. and M. Levi. 2011. Leadership: What It Means, What It Does, and What We Want to Know About It. *Annual Review of Political Science* 14:1–24.

Alexandrescu, P. 1977. Les models grecs de la céramique thrace tournée. *Dacia* 21:113–37.

Alexandrov, S., Y. Dimitrova, H. Popov, B. Horejs, and K. Chukalev (eds.). 2018. *Gold and Bronze: Metals, Technologies and Interregional Contacts in the Eastern Balkans during the Bronze Age.* National Archaeological Institute with Museum, Sofia.

Allentoft, M.E., M. Sikora, K.-G. Sjögren, + 62 authors, and E. Willerslev. 2015. Population Genomics of Bronze Age Eurasia. *Nature* 522:167–72.

Anders, A. and E. Nagy. 2007. Late Neolithic Burial Rites at the Site of Polgár-Csőszhalom-dűlő. In: *The Lengyel, Polgár and Related Cultures in the Middle/Late Neolithic in Central Europe*, edited by J.K. Kozłowski and P. Raczky, pp. 83–96. Polska Akademia Umiejętności, Kraków.

Anderson, K. 2018. Becoming the Warrior: Constructed Identity or Functional Identity? In: *Warfare in Bronze Age Society*, edited by C. Horn and K. Kristiansen, pp. 213–28. Cambridge University Press, Cambridge.

Andrea, Z. 1976. Tumat e Kuçit të Zi. *Iliria* 6:165–233.

Anthony, D. 1990. Migration in Archaeology: The Baby and the Bathwater. *American Anthropologist* 92(4):895–914.

———. 2007. *The Horse, the Wheel, and Language: How Bronze Age Riders from the Eurasian Steppes Shaped the Modern World.* Princeton University Press, Princeton and Oxford.

———. 2020. Ancient DNA, Mating Networks, and the Anatolian Split. In: *Dispersals and Diversification: Linguistic and Archaeological Perspectives on the Early Stages of Indo-European*, edited by M. Serangeli and T. Olander, pp. 21–53. Brill's Studies in Indo-European Languages & Linguistics 19. Brill, Leiden and Boston.

Anthony, D.W., D.R. Brown, and C. George. 2006. Early Horseback Riding and Warfare: The Importance of the Magpie around the Neck. In: *Horses and Humans: The Evolution of Human–Equine Relationships*, edited by S.L. Olsen, S. Grant, and A.M. Choyke, pp. 137–56. BAR International Series 1560. Archaeopress, Oxford.

Anthony, D.W. and J. Chi (eds.). 2010. *The Lost World of Old Europe: The Danube Valley 5000–3000 BC.* Princeton University Press, Princeton.

Antonović, D. 2009. Prehistoric Copper Tools from the Territory of Serbia. *Journal of Mining and Metallurgy* 45(2):165–74.

———. 2014. *Kupferzeitliche Äxte und Beile in Serbien.* Prähistorische Bronzefunde IX/27. Franz Steiner, Wiesbaden.

Apicella, C.L., F.W. Marlowe, J.H. Fowler, and N.A. Christakis. 2012. Social Networks and Cooperation in Hunter–Gatherers. *Nature* 481(7382):497–501.

Archibald, Z. 1998. *The Odrysian Kingdom of Thrace: Orpheus Unmasked*. Clarendon Press, Oxford.

———. 2000. Space, Hierarchy, and Community in Archaic and Classical Macedonia, Thessaly, and Thrace. In: *Alternatives to Athens: Varieties of Political Organization and Community in Ancient Greece*, edited by R. Brock and S. Hodkinson, pp. 212–33. Oxford University Press, Oxford.

———. 2015. Social Life of Thrace. In: *A Companion to Ancient Thrace*, edited by J. Valeva, E. Nankov, and D. Graninger, pp. 385–98. Wiley Blackwell, Malden, MA.

Armbruster, B.R. 2000. *Goldschmiedekunst und Bronzetechnik: Studien zum Metallhandwerk der Atlantischen Bronzezeit auf der Iberischen Halbinsel*. Monographies Instrumentum 15. Mergoil, Montagnac.

Arponen, V.P.J., J. Müller, R. Hofmann, M. Furholt, A. Ribeiro, C. Horn, and M. Hinz. 2016. Using the Capability Approach to Conceptualise Inequality in Archaeology: The Case of the Late Neolithic Bosnian Site Okolište c. 5200–4600 BCE. *Journal of Archaeological Method and Theory* 23(2):541–60.

Avram, A. 2011. The Getae: Selected Questions. In: *The Black Sea, Greece, Anatolia and Europe in the First Millennium BC*, edited by G. Tsetskhladze, pp. 61–76. Peeters, Leuven.

Babić, S. 2001. Headgear of the Early Iron Age Tribal Chieftains: Social and Symbolic Aspects. *Zbornik Narodnog muzeja* 17:83–93.

———. 2002. 'Princely Graves' of the Central Balkans: A Critical History of Research. *European Journal of Archaeology* 5(1):70–88.

Babić, S. and A. Palavestra. 2018. Trebenishte and the Princely Graves of the European Early Iron Age. In: *100 Years of Trebenishte*, edited by P. Ardjanliev, K. Chukalev, T. Cvjetićanin, M. Damyanov, V. Krstić, A. Papazovska, and H. Popov, pp. 187–93. National Archaeological Institute with Museum and Bulgarian Academy of Sciences, Sofia.

Bacvarov, K. (ed.). 2008. *Babies Reborn: Infant/Child Burials in Pre- and Protohistory*. BAR International Series 1832. Archaeopress, Oxford.

Bader, T. 1991. *Die Schwerter in Rumänien*. Prähistorische Bronzefunde IV/8. Franz Steiner, Stuttgart.

———. 2015. Zur Chronologie der Lanzenspitzen im Karpaten-Donau Raum. In: *Bronze Age Chronology in the Carpathian Basin*, edited by B. Rezi and R.E. Németh, pp. 373–91. Mega, Târgu Mureș.

Bailey, D.W. 2000. *Balkan Prehistory: Exclusion, Incorporation and Identity*. Routledge, London and New York.

———. 2005. *Prehistoric Figurines: Representation and Corporeality in the Neolithic*. Routledge, London.

Bakay, K. 1971. A régészeti topográfia munkálatai Békés megyében 1969-ben. *A Békés Megyei Múzeumok Közleményei* 1:135–53.

Baković, M. and B. Govedarica. 2010. Nakhodki iz "knyazheskogo" kurgana Gruda Bol'evicha v Podgoritse, Chernogoria. *Stratum plus* 2010(2):269–80.

Bălan, G. 2013. Aşezările fortificate din aria culturii Gáva din România. In: *Din preistoria Dunării de Jos. 50 de ani de la inceputul cercetărilor arheologice la Babadag (1962–2012)*, edited by S-C. Ailincăi, A. Țârlea, and C. Micu, pp. 265–310. Muzeul Brăilei, Brăila.

Bălan, G., C.P. Quinn, and G. Hodgins. 2016. The Wietenberg Culture: Periodization and Chronology. *Dacia* 60:67–92.

———. 2018. The Cultural and Chronological Context of the Bronze Age Cemetery from Sebeș–Între răstoace. In: *Bronze Age Connectivity in the Carpathian Basin*, edited by B. Rezi and R.E. Németh, pp. 183–216. Mega, Târgu Mureș.

Balcer, J.M. 1988. Persian Occupied Thrace (Skudra). *Historia: Zeitschrift für alte Geschichte* 37(1):1–21.

Baldus, B. 2017. *Origins of Inequality in Human Societies*. Routledge, New York.

Ballmer, A. 2010. Zur Topologie des bronzezeitlichen Deponierens: Von der Handlungstheorie zur Raumanalyse. *Praehistorische Zeitschrift* 85:120–31.

———. 2015. *Topografie bronzezeitlicher Deponierungen: Fallstudie Alpenrheintal*. Universitätforschungen zur prähistorischen Archäologie 278. Dr. Rudolf Habelt, Bonn.

Bandy, M.S. 2004. Fissioning, Scalar Stress, and Social Evolution in Early Village Societies. *American Anthropologist* 106(2):322–33.

Bandy, M.S. and J.R. Fox. 2010. Becoming Villagers: The Evolution of Early Village Societies. In: *Becoming Villagers: Comparing Early Village Societies*, edited by M.S. Bandy and J.R. Fox, pp. 1–16. University of Arizona Press, Tucson.

Bánffy, E. and I. Bognár-Kutzián. 2007. *The Late Neolithic Tell Settlement at Polgár-Csőszhalom, Hungary: The 1957 Excavation*. BAR International Series 1730. Archaeolingua Central European Series 4. Archaeopress, Oxford.

Banner, J. 1939. A hódmezővásárhelyi Nagytatársánc. *Dolgozatok a Magyar Királyi Ferencz József Tudományegyetem Archaeologiai Intézetéből* 15:93–114.

Barras, C. 2019. Story of Most Murderous People of All Time Revealed in Ancient DNA. *New Scientist*, March 27, 2019, https://www.newscientist.com/article/mg24132230-200-story-of-most-murderous-people-of-all-time-revealed-in-ancient-dna/#ixzz6EvkzHGD2

Bartík, J. 2009. Bronzezeitliche Gegenstände aus einer Privatsammlung II. *Zborník Slovenského Národného Múzea 103—Archeológia* 19:37–52.

Bátora, J. 2002. Contribution to the Problem of "Craftsmen" Graves at the End of Aeneolithic and in the Early Bronze Age in Central, Western and Eastern Europe. *Slovenská Arheológia* 50(2):179–228.

———. 2016. The Question of the Presence of Yamnaya and Catacomb Culture in the Area of the Middle Danube and North Carpathians. In: *Mensch, Kultur und Gesellschaft von der Kupferzeit bis zur frühen Eisenzeit im Nördlichen Eurasien: Beiträge zu Ehren zum 60. Geburtstag von Eugen Sava*, edited by A. Zanoci, E. Kaiser, M. Kashuba, E. Izbitser, and M. Bâț, pp. 103–15. Tyragetia International I. National Museum of History, Chișinău.

Bayrakov, D. 2016. Planinski svetilishta v Rodopite. In: *SYMPOSION: Sbornik v pamet na prof. Dimitar Popov*, edited by P. Delev, pp. 50–75. St. Kliment Ohridski University Press, Sofia.

Beaujard, P. 2010. From Three Possible Iron-Age World-Systems to a Single Afro-Eurasian World-System. *Journal of World History* 21(1):1–43.

Bellwood, P. and M. Oxenham. 2008. The Expansion of Farming Societies and the Role of the Neolithic Demographic Transition. In: *The Neolithic Demographic Transition and Its Consequences*, edited by J.-P. Bocquet-Appel and O. Bar-Yosef, pp. 13–34. Springer, Berlin.

Benac, A. and B. Čović. 1957. *Glasinac: Željezno doba. Katalog prehistoriske zbirke Zemaljskog muzeja u Sarajevu, sveska 2*. Zemaljskog muzeja u Sarajevu, Sarajevo.

Bernard, H.R. and P.D. Killworth. 1973. On the Social Structure of an Ocean-Going Research Vessel and Other Important Things. *Social Science Research* 2(2):145–84.

Best, J.G.P. 1969. *Thracian Peltasts and Their Influence on Greek Warfare*. Wolters–Noordhoff, Groningen.

Bettencourt, L.M.A. 2013. The Origins of Scaling in Cities. *Science* 340(6139):1438–41.

Birch, J. 2013. Between Villages and Cities: Settlement Aggregation in Cross-Cultural Perspective. In: *From Villages to Cities: Settlement Aggregation and Community Transformation*, edited by J.A. Birch, pp. 1–22. Routledge, New York.

Blanco-González, A. and T.L. Kienlin (eds.). 2020. *Current Approaches to Tells in the Prehistoric Old World: A Cross-Cultural Comparison from the Neolithic to the Iron Age*. Oxbow, Oxford.

Blanton, R.E. and L.F. Fargher. 2008. *Collective Action in the Formation of Pre-Modern States*. Springer, New York.

———. 2013. Reconsidering Darwinian Anthropology: With Suggestions for a Revised Agenda for Cooperation Research. In: *Cooperation and Collective Action: Archaeological Perspectives*, edited by D.M. Carballo, pp. 93–127. University Press of Colorado, Boulder.

———. 2016. *How Humans Cooperate: Confronting the Challenges of Collective Action*. University Press of Colorado, Boulder.

Blanton, R.E., G.M. Feinman, S.A. Kowalewski, and P.N. Peregrine. 1996. A Dual-Processual Theory for the Evolution of Mesoamerican Civilization. *Current Anthropology* 37(1):1–14.

Blanton, R.E., S.A. Kowalewski, G.M. Feinman, and L.M. Finsten. 1993. *Ancient Mesoamerica: A Comparison of Change in Three Regions*. Second edition. Cambridge University Press, Cambridge.

Blavatskaya, T.V. 1952. *Zapadnopontijskie goroda v VII–I vekah do nashej èry*. Izdatel'stvo akademii nauk SSSR, Moscow.

Blečić Kavur, M. and A. Pravidur. 2012. Ilirske kacige s područja Bosne i Hercegovine. *Glasnik Zemaljskog muzeja Bosne i Hercegovine u Sarajevu* 53:35–136.

Bondár, M. 2019. *A késő rézkori fémművesség magyarországi emlékei*. Archaeolingua, Budapest.

Bonev, A. 1988. *Trakia i Egeyskiat svyat prez vtorata polovina na II hil. pr. n. e.* Razkopki i prouchvania 20. Arheologicheski institut i muzey, Sofia.

———. 1995. The Gold Treasure from Vulchitrun Village (Pleven District) and the Problems of Cultural Contacts in Southeast Europe in the Second Half of the Second Millennium BC. In: *Prehistoric Bulgaria*, edited by D.W. Bailey and I. Panayotov, pp. 277–89. Monographs in World Archaeology 22. Prehistoric Press, Madison, WI.

———. 2003. *Ranna Trakia: Formirane na trakiyskata kultura – kraya na vtoroto – nachaloto na parvoto hilyadoletie pr. Hr.* Razkopki i prouchvania 31. Arheologicheski institut i muzey, Sofia.

Borchhardt, J. 1972. *Homerische Helme: Helmformen der Ägäis in ihren Beziehungen zu orientalischen und europäischen Helmen in der Bronze- und frühen Eisenzeit*. Philipp von Zabern, Mainz am Rhein.

Borić, D. 1996. Social Dimensions of Mortuary Practices in the Neolithic: A Case Study. *Starinar* 47:67–83.

———. 2015. The End of the Vinča World: Modelling Late Neolithic to Copper Age Culture Change and the Notion of Archaeological Culture. In: *Neolithic and Copper Age between the Carpathians and the Aegean Sea: Chronologies and Technologies from the 6th to 4th Millennium B.C.E.*, edited by S. Hansen, P. Raczky, A. Anders, and A. Reingruber, pp. 157–217. Archäologie in Eurasien 31. Dr. Rudolf Habelt, Bonn.

Borić, D. and S. Stefanović. 2004. Birth and Death: Infant Burials from Vlasac and Lepenski Vir. *Antiquity* 78(301):526–46.

Boroffka, N. 1991. *Die Verwendung von Eisen in Rumänien von den Anfängen bis in das 8. Jahrhundert v. Chr. Bemerkungen.* Self published, Berlin.

———. 1994. *Die Wietenberg-Kultur: Ein Beitrag zur Erforschung der Bronzezeit in Südosteuropa*. Dr. Rudolf Habelt, Bonn.

Borş, C., L. Rumega-Irimuş, and V. Rumega-Irimuş. 2017. Cercetări arheologice sistematice în cuprinsul sitului hallstattian Tărtăria-Podu Tărtăriei vest. Raport preliminar al campaniilor 2016–2017. *Cercetări Arheologice* 24:17–82.

Bourgeois, Q. and E. Kroon. 2017. The Impact of Male Burials on the Construction of Corded Ware Identity: Reconstructing Networks of Information in the 3rd Millennium BC. *PLoS ONE* 12(10):e0185971, DOI: 10.1371/journal.pone.0185971.

Bousquet, J. 1952. Dropionroi des Peones. *Bulletin de correspondance hellénique* 76:136–40.

Bouzek, J. 1974. Macedonian Bronzes: Their Origins, Distribution and Relation to Other Cultural Groups of the Early Iron Age. *Památky Archeologické* 65.

———. 1983. *Caucasus and Europe and the Cimmerian Problem.* Národní muzeum v Praze v nakladatelství a vydavatelství Panoram, Prague.

———. 1994. Late Bronze Age Greece and the Balkans: A Review of the Present Picture. *The Annual of the British School at Athens* 89:217–34.

Bouzek, J. and D. Graninger. 2015. Geography. In: *A Companion to Ancient Thrace*, edited by J. Valeva, E. Nankov, and D. Graninger, pp. 12–21. Wiley Blackwell, Malden, MA.

Bouzek, J. and I. Ondřejová. 1988. Sindos—Trebenishte—Duvanli: Interrelations between Thrace, Macedonia, and Greece in the 6th and 5th Centuries BC. *Mediterranean Archaeology* 1:84–94.

Bozkova, A. 2016. Pits of the First Millennium B.C. in Thrace, sine ira et studio. In: *Southeast Europe and Anatolia in Prehistory: Essays in Honor of Vassil Nikolov on His 65th Anniversary*, edited by K. Bacvarov and R. Gleser, pp. 475–84. Universitätsforschungen zur prähistorischen Archäologie 293. Dr. Rudolf Habelt, Bonn.

———. 2017. *Antichna keramika mezhdu Hemus, Rodopa i Evksinskia Pont (VII–I v. pr. Hr.): Harakteristika, razprostranenie i upotreba.* Faber, Veliko Tarnovo.

Bozkova, A. and K. Nikov. 2009. La céramique monochrome en Thrace et ses prototypes anatoliens. Problèmes de chronologie. In: *Actes du colloque international « Les productions céramiques du Pont-Euxin à l'époque grecque », Bucarest, 18–23 Septembre 2004*, edited by P. Dupont and V. Lungu, pp. 47–55. Il Mar Nero 6, 2004/2006. Quazar, Rome and Éditions de la Maison des sciences de l'homme, Paris.

———. 2019. The Grey Pottery of Southern Thrace in the Classical Age. In: *Classical Pottery of the North Aegean and Its Periphery 480–323/300 BC*, edited by E. Manakidou and A. Avramidou, pp. 35–46. University Studio Press, Thessaloniki.

Bradley, K.R. 1989. *Slavery and Rebellion in the Roman World, 140 B.C. – 70 B.C.* Indiana University Press, Bloomington.

Bradley, R. 1990. *The Passage of Arms: An Archaeological Analysis of Prehistoric Hoards and Votive Deposits.* Cambridge University Press, Cambridge.

———. 2005. *Ritual and Domestic Life in Prehistoric Europe.* Routledge, Oxon.

———. 2015. Hoards and the Deposition of Metalwork. In: *The Oxford Handbook of European Bronze Age*, edited by H. Fokkens and A. Harding, pp. 121–39. Oxford University Press, Oxford.

Brami, M., B. Horejs, and F. Ostmann. 2016. The Ground beneath Their Feet: Building Continuity at Neolithic Çukuriçi Höyük. *Anatolian Studies* 66:1–16.

Brück, J. 2006. Fragmentation, Personhood and the Social Construction of Technology in Middle and Late Bronze Age Britain. *Cambridge Archaeological Journal* 16(3):297–315.

Brück, J. and D. Fontijn. 2013. The Myth of the Chief: Prestige Goods, Power and Personhood in the European Bronze Age. In: *The Oxford Handbook of the European Bronze Age*, edited by H. Fokkens and A. Harding, pp. 193–211. Oxford University Press, Oxford.

Burmeister, S. 2016. Archaeological Research on Migration as a Multidisciplinary Challenge. *Medieval Worlds* 4:42–64.

———. 2017. The Archaeology of Migration: What Can and Should It Accomplish? In: *Migration und Integration von der Urgeschichte bis zum Mittelalter/Migration and Integration from Prehistory to the Middle Ages*, edited by H. Meller, F. Daim, J. Krause, and R. Risch, pp. 57–68. Tagungen des Landesmuseums für Vorgeschichte Halle 17. Landesmuseums für Vorgeschichte, Halle.

Buyukliev, H. 1985. Trakiyski varhove na kopia ot rannozhelyaznata epoha v bulgarskite zemi. *Arheologia* 27(2):27–35.

Cabanes, P. 2008. Greek Colonization in the Adriatic. In: *Greek Colonisation: An Account of Greek Colonies and Other Settlements Overseas*, Volume 2, edited by G.R. Tsetskhladzhe, pp. 155–85. Brill, Leiden.

Carballo, D.M. 2013. Cultural and Evolutionary Dynamics of Cooperation in Archaeological Perspectives. In: *Cooperation and Collective Action: Archaeological Perspectives*, edited by D.M. Carballo, pp. 3–33. University Press of Colorado, Boulder.

Carballo, D.M., P. Roscoe, and G.M. Feinman. 2014. Cooperation and Collective Action in the Cultural Evolution of Complex Societies. *Journal of Archaeological Method and Theory* 21(1):98–133.

Carneiro, R.L. 1967. On the Relationship between Size of Population and Complexity of Social Organization. *Southwestern Journal of Anthropology* 23(3):234–43.

Cary, F. 1752. *Histoire des rois de Thrace et de ceux du Bosphore Cimmérien éclaircie par les médailles.* Desaint & Saillant, Paris.

Cashdan, E. 1980. Egalitarianism among Hunters and Gatherers. *American Anthropologist* 82(1):116–20.

Casson, S. 1926. *Macedonia, Thrace and Illyria: Their Relations to Greece from the Earliest Times Down to the Time of Philip, Son of Amyntas.* Oxford University Press, Oxford.

Chapman, J. 1989. The Early Balkan Village. In: *Neolithic of South-Eastern Europe and Its Near Eastern Connections*, edited by S. Bökönyi, pp. 33–53. Varia Archaeologica Hungarica 2. Pytheas, Budapest.

———. 1991. The Creation of Social Arenas in the Neolithic and Copper Age of South East Europe: The Case of Varna. In: *Sacred and Profane*, edited by P. Garwood, P. Jennings, R. Skeates, and J. Toms, pp. 152–71. Oxford Committee for Archaeology Monograph 32. Oxbow, Oxford.

———. 2000. *Tensions at Funerals: Micro-Tradition Analysis in Later Hungarian Prehistory.* Archaeolingua, Budapest.

———. 2012. The Negotiation of Place Value in the Landscape. In: *The Construction of Value in the Ancient World*, edited by J.K. Papadopoulos and G. Urton, pp. 66–89. UCLA Cotsen Institute of Archaeology Press, Los Angeles.

Chapman, J. and B. Gaydarska. 2015. Spondylus Gaederopus/Glycymeris Exchange Networks in the European Neolithic and Chalcolithic. In: *The Oxford Handbook of Neolithic Europe*, edited by J. Fowler, A. Harding, and D. Hofmann, pp. 639–56. Oxford University Press, Oxford.

Chapman, J., T. Higham, V. Slavchev, B. Gaydarska, and N. Honch. 2007. Social Context of the Emergence, Development and Abandonment of the Varna Cemetery, Bulgaria. *European Journal of Archaeology* 9(2):157–81.

Chausidis, N. 2010. Neolithic Ceramic Figurines in the Shape of a Woman–House from the Republic of Macedonia. In: *Anthropomorphic and Zoomorphic Miniature Figures in Eurasia, Africa and Meso-America: Morphology, Materiality, Technology, Function and Context*, edited by D. Gheorghiu and A. Cyphers, pp. 25–35. BAR International Series 2138. Archaeopress, Oxford.

———. 2017. *Makedonskite bronzi i religijata i mitologijata na železnodobnite zaednici od Sredniot Balkan/Macedonian Bronzes and the Religion and Mythology of Iron Age Communities in the Central Balkans.* Center for Prehistoric Research, Skopje.

Chernakov, D. 2018. A New-Found Hoard of Chalcolithic Heavy Copper Tools from Northeastern Bulgaria. *Archaeologia Bulgarica* 22(2):1–14.

Chernykh, E.N., L.I. Avilova, and L.B. Orlovskaya. 2002. Metallurgy of the Circumpontic Area: From Unity to Disintegration. In: *Anatolian Metal II*, edited by Ü. Yalçin, pp. 83–100. Bergbau Museum, Bochum.

Chichikova, M. 1965. La céramique thrace. In: *Le rayonnement des civilisations grecque et romaine sur les cultures périphériques:*

Huitième congrès international d'archéologie classique (Paris, 1963), pp. 341–44. Boccard, Paris.

———. 1968. Keramika ot starata zhelyazna epoha v Trakia. *Arheologia* 10(4):15–27.

———. 1974a. Prouchvania varhu trakiyskata kultura prez starozhelyaznata epoha. *Arheologia* 16(4):19–27.

——— [Čičikova]. 1974b. Habitats et forteresses thraces du Ier millénaire av. n. ère. *Pulpudeva* 1:15–33.

——— [Čičikova]. 1981. Maedica à l'époque classique et hellénistique. In: *Spartacus: Symposium rebus Spartaci gestis dedicatum 2050 a*, edited by C.M. Danov, pp. 56–59. Académie Bulgare des Sciences, Sofia.

———. 2004. Trakiyskata keramika, rabotena na kolelo (VI–IV v. pr. Hr.). *Godishnik na Arheologicheskia muzey v Plovdiv* 9:194–203.

Chichikova, M. and K. Dimitrov. 2016. *Sevtopolis, gradat na Sevt III.* Letera, Plovdiv.

Chichikova, M., D. Stoyanova, and T. Stoyanov. 2012. *The Caryatids Royal Tomb near the Village of Sveshtari.* Historical Museum, Isperih.

Chukalev, K. and Y. Dimitrova. 2018. Valchitran Treasure. In: *Gold and Bronze: Metals, Technologies and Interregional Contacts in the Eastern Balkans during the Bronze Age*, edited by S. Alexandrov, Y. Dimitrova, H. Popov, B. Horejs, and K. Chukalev, pp. 378–82. National Archaeological Institute with Museum, Sofia.

Ciugudean, H. 2011. Mounds and Mountains: Burial Rituals in Early Bronze Age Transylvania. In: *Bronze Age Rites and Rituals in the Carpathian Basin*, edited by S. Berecki, R.E. Németh, and B. Rezi, pp. 21–57. Mega, Târgu Mureș.

Ciugudean, H., S.A. Luca, and A. Georgescu. 2008. *Depozite de bronzuri preistorice din colecția Brukenthal (I).* Bibliotheca Brukenthal 31. Altip, Alba Iulia.

Čivilyté, A. 2009. *Wahl der Waffen. Studien zur Deutung der bronzezeitlichen Waffendeponierungen im nördlichen Mitteleuropa.* Universitätsforschungen zur prähistorischen Archäologie 167. Dr. Rudolf Habelt, Bonn.

Čižmář-Salaš, M. and M. Salaš. 2009. Nové hradiště v Moravské bráně. *Archeologické Rozhledy* 61:63–76.

Clastres, P. 1987. *Society Against the State: Essays in Political Anthropology.* Zone Books, New York.

Clausing, C. 2001. Spätbronze- und eisenzeitliche Helme mit einteiliger Kalotte. *Jahrbuch des Römisch-Germanischen Zentralmuseums* 48:199–225.

———. 2002. Geschnürte Beinschienen der späten Bronze- und älteren Eisenzeit. *Jahrbuch des Römisch-Germanischen Zentralmuseums* 49:149–87.

———. 2005. *Untersuchungen zu den urnenfelderzeitlichen Gräbern mit Waffenbeigaben vom Alpenkamm bis zur Südzone des Nordischen*

Kreises: Eine Analyse ihrer Grabinventare und Grabformen. BAR International Series 1375. Archaeopress, Oxford.

Cole, S. 1970. *The Neolithic Revolution.* British Museum, London.

Collis, J. 1984. *The European Iron Age.* Routledge, London.

Colson, E. and M. Gluckman (eds.). 1951. *Seven Tribes of British Central Africa.* Oxford University Press, Oxford.

Cook, B.F. (ed.). 1989. *The Rogozen Treasure: Papers of the Anglo-Bulgarian Conference, 12 March 1987.* British Museum, London.

Čović, B. 1961. *Donja Dolina, necropole de l'âge du fer.* Inventaria Archaeologica, Corpus des Ensembles Archeologiques, Fascicule 3. Dr. Rudolf Habelt, Bonn.

———. 1979. Kneževski grobovi glasinačkog područja. In: *Sahranjivanje kod Ilira,* edited by M. Garašanin, pp. 143–69. Srpska akademija nauka i umetnosti, Belgrade.

———. 1983. Importation of Bronze Vessels in the Western Balkans (7th to 5th Century). In: *L'Adriatico tra Mediterraneo e penisola balcanica nell'antichita,* edited by G.P. Carratelli, pp. 147–54. Instituto per la storia e l'archeologia della Magna Grecia, Taranto.

———. 1984. Praistorijsko rudarstvo i metalurgija u Bosni i Hercegovini: stanje i problem istraživanja. *Godišnjak* 23:111–44.

———. 1987a. Grupa Donja Dolina–Sanski Most. In: *Praistorija jugoslavenskih zemalja V—željezno doba,* edited by A. Benac, pp. 232–86. Centar za balkanološka ispitivanja, Akademija nauka i umjetnosti Bosne i Hercegovine, Sarajevo.

———. 1987b. Glasinačka kultura. In: *Praistorija jugoslavenskih zemalja V—željezno doba,* edited by A. Benac, pp. 575–643. Centar za balkanološka ispitivanja, Akademija nauka i umjetnosti Bosne i Hercegovine, Sarajevo.

Coward, F. and R.I.M. Dunbar. 2014. Communities on the Edge of Civilization. In: *Lucy to Language: The Benchmark Papers,* edited by R.I.M. Dunbar, C. Gamble, and J.A.J. Gowlett, pp. 380–404. Oxford University Press, Oxford.

Coward, F. and C. Gamble. 2008. Big Brains, Small Worlds: Material Culture and the Evolution of the Mind. *Philosophical Transactions of the Royal Society B, Biological Sciences* 363(1499):1969–79.

Crişan, I.H. 1978. *Burebista and His Time.* Bibliotheca Historica Romaniae 20. Academiei Republicii Socialiste România, Bucharest.

Ćurčić, V. 1909. Prähistorische Funde aus Bosnien und der Herzegowina in der Sammlungen des k. k. Naturhistorischen Hofmuseums in Wien. *Wissenschaftliche Mitteilungen aus Bosnien und der Hercegovina* 11:91–100.

Czukor, P., A. Priskin, Cs. Szalontai, and V. Szeverényi. 2017. Késő bronzkori földvárak a Dél-Alföldön. In: *A második hajdúböszörményi szitula és kapcsolatrendszere,* edited by G.V. Szabó, M. Bálint, and G. Váczi, pp. 211–30. Studia Oppidorum

Haidonicalium 13. Eötvös Loránd Tudományegyetem Régészettudományi Intézet and Hajdúsági Múzeum, Budapest and Hajdúböszörmény.

Damyanov, M. 2015. The Greek Colonists. In: *A Companion to Ancient Thrace,* edited by J. Valeva, E. Nankov, and D. Graninger, pp. 295–307. Wiley Blackwell, Malden, MA.

Dani, J. 2013. The Significance of Metallurgy at the Beginning of the Third Millennium BC in the Carpathian Basin. In: *Transitions to the Bronze Age: Interregional Interaction and Socio-Cultural Change in the Third Millennium BC Carpathian Basin and Neighbouring Regions,* edited by V. Heyd, G. Kulcsár, and V. Szeverényi, pp. 203–31. Archaeolingua, Budapest.

Dani, J. and T. Horváth. 2012. *Őskori kurgánok a magyar Alföldön: A Gödörsíros (Yamnaja) entitás magyarországi kutatása az elmúlt 30 év során. Áttekintés és revízió.* Archaeolingua, Budapest.

Dani, J., A. Lantos, and R. Andrási. Forthcoming. Yamnaya Elite in the Carpathian Basin with Special Overview to the Sárrétudvari-Őrhalom Kurgan. In: *Princely Graves between the Caucasus and Atlantic, 3500–2500 BCE,* edited by S. Hansen and B. Govedarica. German Archaeological Institute, Eurasia Department, Frankfurt.

Dani, J. and V. Szeverényi. 2021. Archaeological Evidence for Steppe and Caucasian Connections in the Carpathian Basin between the Fourth and Mid-Third Millennium BC: Is There a 'Yamnaya Package'? In: *The Caucasus: Bridge between the Urban Centres in Mesopotamia and the Pontic Steppes in the 4th and 3rd Millennium BCE: The Transfer of Knowledge and Technologies between East and West in the Bronze Age,* edited by L. Giemsch and S. Hansen, pp. 251–64. Schnell & Steiner, Frankfurt am Main.

Danov, C. 1947. *Zapadniat bryag na Cherno more v drevnostta.* Universitetska biblioteka 358. Universitetska pechatnitsa, Sofia.

———. 1968. *Drevna Trakia.* Nauka i izkustvo, Sofia.

———. 1979. Die Thraker auf dem Ostbalkan von der hellenistischen Zeit bis zur Gründung Konstantinopels. In: *Aufstieg und Niedergang der Römischen Welt,* Part II (Principat) 7.1:241–300. Walter de Gruyter, Berlin and New York.

David-Elbiali, M. 2006. L'Âge du bronze. In: *Des Alpes au Léman: Images de la préhistoire,* edited by A. Gallay, pp. 191–259. Infolio, Gollion.

Delev, P. 1983. Les Odryses et les Kikones. Problèmes de géographie historique. *Pulpudeva* 4:220–26.

———. 1984. Megalithic Thracian Tombs in South-Eastern Bulgaria. *Anatolica* 11:17–45.

———. 1997. Filip II i zalezat na "golyamoto" Odrisko tsarstvo v Trakia. *Shumenski universitet "Episkop Konstantin Preslavski," Trudove na katedrite po istoria i bogoslovie* 1:7–40.

———. 2000. Lysimachus, the Getae, and Archaeology. *The Classical Quarterly* 50(2):384–401.

———. 2003. From Corupedion towards Pydna: Thrace in the Third Century. *Thracia* 15:107–20.

———. 2004. *Lizimah*. Universitetska Biblioteka 435. St. Kliment Ohridski University Press, Sofia.

———. 2007. The Edonians. *Thracia* 17:85–106.

———. 2010. Nyakoi problemi na etnonimiata v Tsentralna i Yugoiztochna Trakia. In: *Yugoiztochna Bulgaria prez II–I hilyadoletie pr. Hr.*, edited by R. Georgieva, T. Stoyanov, and D. Momchilov, pp. 96–111. Zograf, Varna.

———. 2012a. The Thracian Bessi. *Annuaire de l'Université de Sofia "St. Kliment Ohridski", Faculté d'histoire* 100:6–64.

———. 2012b. Getae. In: *The Encyclopedia of Ancient History*, Volume 10, edited by R.S. Bagnall et al., pp. 2911–12. Wiley Blackwell, Malden, MA.

———. 2013. The Tribal World of Ancient Thrace. In: *The Thracians and Their Neighbors in the Bronze and Iron Ages: Proceedings of the 12th International Congress of Thracology*, Volume 1, edited by C. Schuster, O. Cîrstina, M. Cosac, and G. Murătoreanu, pp. 123–34. Cetatea de Scaun, Târgoviște.

———. 2014. *Istoria na plemenata v Yugozapadna Trakia prez parvoto hilyadoletie pr. Hr.* St. Kliment Ohridski University Press, Sofia.

———. 2015a. From Koroupedion to the Beginning of the Third Mithridatic War (281–73 BCE). In: *A Companion to Ancient Thrace*, edited by J. Valeva, E. Nankov, and D. Graninger, pp. 59–74. Wiley Blackwell, Malden, MA.

———. 2015b. Thrace from the Assassination of Kotys I to Koroupedion (360–281 BCE). In: *A Companion to Ancient Thrace*, edited by J. Valeva, E. Nankov, and D. Graninger, pp. 48–58. Wiley Blackwell, Malden, MA.

———. 2016. Za genealogiata na Sapeyskata dinastia. In: *SYMPOSION: Shornik v pamet ma prof. Dimitar Popov*, edited by P. Delev, pp. 148–72. St. Kliment Ohridski University Press, Sofia.

———. 2018. The Romans in the Balkans and the Communities of the Thracian Interior. Actions and Reactions (2nd–1st c. BC). In: *Les communautés du Nord Égéen au temps de l'hégémonie Romaine: Entre ruptures et continuités*, edited by J. Fournier and M.-G. Parissaki, pp. 19–27. ΜΕΛΕΤΗΜΑΤΑ 77. Fondation nationale de la recherche scientifique, Athens.

Dergachev, V.A. and V.L. Sorokin. 1986. O zoomorfnom skipetre iz Moldavii i proniknovenii stepnykh eneoliticheskikh plemen v Karpato-Dunaiskie zemli. *Izvestiia Akademii Nauk MSSR, seriia Obshchestvennykh nauk* I:54–65.

Despini, A. 2016. *SINDOS: To necrotapheio, anascaphikes ereunes 1980–1982 (I–III)*. The Archaeological Society at Athens Library, Nos. 307, 308, 309. Archaeological Society, Athens.

Dessau, H. (ed.). 1887. *Corpus inscriptionum latinarum*, Volume 14: *Inscriptiones Latii veteris latinae*. Apud Georgium Reimerum, Berlin.

Diaconescu, D., V. Bunoiu, D. Vlase, and A. Hegyi. 2017. Cartarea movilelor de pământ din Banatul de Câmpie: Studiu de caz: Sânpetru Mare (comuna Sânpetru Mare, jud. Timiș). *Patrimonium Banaticum* 7:37–97.

Die Thraker: Das goldene Reich des Orpheus. 2004. Exhibition Catalog. Phillip von Zabern, Mainz am Rhein.

Dillian, G.D. and G.C. White (eds.). 2010. *Trade and Exchange: Archaeological Studies from History and Prehistory*. Springer, New York.

Dimitrijević, V., G. Naumov, L. Fidanoski, and S. Stefanović. 2021. A String of Marine Shells from the Neolithic Site of Vršnik (Tarinci, Ovće Pole) and Other Marine Shell Ornaments in the Neolithic of North Macedonia. *Anthropozoologica* 56(4):57–70.

Dimitrijević, V., B. Tripković, and G. Jovanović. 2010. Dentalium Beads: Shells of Fossilised Sea Molluscs at the Vinča-Belo Brdo Site. *Starinar* 60:7–18.

Dimitrov, D.P. 1971. Troja VIIb2 und die thrakischen und moesischen Stämme auf dem Balkan. *Studia Balcanica* 5:63–78.

Dimitrova, D. 2015. *The Tomb of King Seuthes III in Golyama Kosmatka Tumulus*. Aros, Sofia.

Dimo, V., P. Lenhardt, and F. Quantin (eds.). 2007. *Apollonia d'Illyrie 1. Atlas archéologique et historique*. Collection de l'École française de Rome 391. École française d'Athène and École française de Rome, Paris and Rome.

Dittenberger, W. 1924. *Sylloge Inscriptionum Graecorum (1915–1924)*. S. Hirzel, Leipzig.

Dizdar, M. 2015. Late Hallstatt Female Grave from Belišće: A Group of Late Hallstatt Finds in the Lower Drava Valey. In: *Beiträge zur Hallstattzeit am Rande der Südostalpen*, edited by Ch. Gutjahr and G. Tiefengraber, pp. 45–60. Internationale Archäologie, Arbeitsgemeinschaft, Symposium, Tagung, Kongress, Band 19, Heingst-Studien Band 3. Marie Leidorf, Rahden/Westfalen.

Dizdar, M. and A. Tonc. 2018. Not Just a Belt: Late Iron Age Female Costume in the South-Eastern Carpathian Basin. *Starinar* 68:47–63.

Dobruski, V. 1897. Istoricheski pogled varhu numizmatikata na trakiyskite tsare. *Shornik za narodni umotvorenia, nauka i knizhnina* 14:555–633.

Domaradzki, M. 1984. *Keltite na Balkanskia poluostrov, IV–I v. pr. n. e.* Nauka i izkustvo, Sofia.

———. 1994. Les lieux de culte thraces (deuxième moitié du IIe–Ier millénaire av. J.-C.). *Helis* 3:69–108.

———. 2003. Trakiyskite kultovi mesta (vtorata polovina na II–I hilyadoletie pr. Hr.). In: *Sbornik izsledvania v chest na prof. A. Milchev. Studia Archaeologica*, Suppl. 2, pp. 57–85. St. Kliment Ohridski University Press, Sofia.

Douzougli, A. and J.K. Papadopoulos. 2010. Liatovouni: A Molossian Cemetery and Settlement in Epirus. *Jahrbuch des Deutschen Archäologischen Instituts* 125:1–87.

Draganov, D. 2000. *Monetite na makedonskite tsare. Chast I. Ot Alexander I do Alexander Veliki.* Izdatelstvo Ya, Yambol.

Draşovean, F. 2007. The Neolithic Tells from Parţa and Uivar: Similarities and Differences of the Social Space. *Analele Banatului* 15:19–32.

Đuknić, M. and B. Jovanović. 1965. Illyrian Princely Necropolis at Atenica. *Archaeologia Iugoslavica* 6:1–35.

———. 1966. *Ilirska kneževska nekropola u Atenici.* Narodni Muzej Čačak, Čačak.

Dumanov, B. 2015. Thrace in Late Antiquity. In: *A Companion to Ancient Thrace*, edited by J. Valeva, E. Nankov, and D. Graninger, pp. 91–105. Wiley Blackwell, Malden, MA.

Dunbar, R.I.M. 2011. Constraints on the Evolution of Social Institutions and Their Implications for Information Flow. *Journal of Institutional Economics* 7(3):345–71.

———. 2013. What Makes the Neolithic So Special? *Neo-Lithics* 2/13:25–29.

Düring, B.S. 2013. The Anatomy of a Prehistoric Community: Reconsidering Çatalhöyuk. In: *From Prehistoric Villages to Cities: Settlement Aggregation and Community Transformation*, edited by J.A. Birch, pp. 23–43. Routledge, New York.

Earle, T. 1997. *How Chiefs Come to Power: The Political Economy in Prehistory.* Stanford University Press, Stanford.

———. 2002. *Bronze Age Economics: The Beginnings of Political Economies.* Westview Press, Boulder, CO.

Earle, T. and K. Kristiansen. 2010. *Organizing Bronze Age Societies: The Mediterranean, Central Europe, and Scandinavia Compared.* Cambridge University Press, Cambridge.

Egg, M. 1996. Einige Bemerkungen zum hallstattzeitlichen Wagengrab von Somlóvásárhely, Kom. Veszprém in Westungarn. *Jahrbuch des Römisch-Germanischen Zentralmuseums* 43:327–53.

Ehrenreich, R.M., C.L. Crumley, and J.E. Levy (eds.). 1995. *Heterarchy and the Analysis of Complex Societies.* Archaeological Papers of the American Anthropological Association Number 6. American Anthropological Association, Arlington, VA.

Ember, M. 1963. The Relationship between Economic and Political Development in Nonindustrialized Societies. *Ethnology* 2(2): 228–48.

Emilov, J. 2015. Celts. In: *A Companion to Ancient Thrace*, edited by J. Valeva, E. Nankov, and D. Graninger, pp. 366–82. Wiley Blackwell, Malden, MA.

Endrődi, A. 1995. Erscheinung in Steleerrichtung in Ungarn. *Notizie Archeologiche Bergomensi* 3:305–17.

Ersfeld, J. 1990. *Formen und Giessen.* Restaurierung und Museumstechnik 3. Museum für Ur- und Frühgeschichte Thübingens, Weimar.

Fages, A., K. Hanghøj, N. Khan, + 117 authors, and L. Orlando. 2019. Tracking Five Millennia of Horse Management with Extensive Ancient Genome Time Series. *Cell* 177(6):1419–35.

Falkenstein, F., S. Falkenstein, F. Herzig, and H. Emberger. 2017. Eine bronzene Lanzenspitze aus dem Main bei Volkach. Archäologische und holzanatomische Anmerkungen zu einem neuen Flussfund aus der Hügelgräberbronzezeit. *Jahrbuch für den Landkreis Kitzingen. Im Bannkreis des Schwanbergs* 2017:67–82.

Faragó, N. 2017. Differences in the Selection of Raw Materials at the Site of Polgár-Csőszhalom, Northeast Hungary. *Bulgarian e-Journal of Archaeology* 7:85–115.

Fazecaş, G. and M. Lie. 2018. Determinarea suprafeţei sitului de epoca bronzului de la Toboliu: Dâmbu Zănăcanului. *Crisia* 46:29–38.

Feinman, G.M. 1995. The Emergence of Inequality: A Focus on Strategies and Processes. In: *Foundations of Social Inequality*, edited by T.D. Price and G.M. Feinman, pp. 255–79. Plenum, New York.

———. 1998. Scale and Social Organization: Perspectives on the Archaic State. In: *Archaic States*, edited by G.M. Feinman and J. Marcus, pp. 95–133. School of American Research Press, Santa Fe, NM.

———. 2011. Size, Complexity, and Organizational Variation: A Comparative Approach. *Cross-Cultural Research* 45(1):37–58.

———. 2012. Comparative Frames for the Diachronic Analysis of Complex Societies: Next Steps. In: *The Comparative Archaeology of Complex Societies*, edited by M.E. Smith, pp. 21–43. Cambridge University Press, Cambridge.

———. 2013. The Emergence of Social Complexity: Why More than Population Size Matters. In: *Cooperation and Collective Action: Archaeological Perspectives*, edited by D.M. Carballo, pp. 35–56. University Press of Colorado, Boulder.

———. 2016. Variation and Change in Archaic States: Ritual as a Mechanism of Sociopolitical Integration. In: *Ritual and Archaic States*, edited by J.M.A. Murphy, pp. 1–22. University Press of Florida, Gainesville.

Feinman, G.M. and D.M. Carballo. 2018. Collaborative and Competitive Strategies in the Variability and Resiliency of Large-Scale Societies in Mesoamerica. *Economic Anthropology* 5(1):7–19.

Feinman, G.M. and J.E. Neitzel. 1984. Too Many Types: An Overview of Sedentary Prestate Societies in the Americas. *Advances in Archaeological Method and Theory* 7:39–102.

———. 2019. Deflating the Myth of Isolated Communities. *Science* 366(6466):682–83.

Feinman, G.M. and L.M. Nicholas. 2016. Framing the Rise and Variability of Past Complex Societies. In: *Alternative Pathways to Complexity*, edited by L.F. Fargher and V.Y. Heredia Espinoza, pp. 271–89. University Press of Colorado, Boulder.

Fejér, E. 2017. Technologische Angaben zur Deutung der Sicheln in spätbronzezeitlichen Horten. In: *State of the Hungarian Bronze Age Research*, edited by G. Kulcsár and G.V. Szabó, pp. 337–48. Prehistoric Studies 2. Institute of Archaeology, Research Centre for the Humanities, Hungarian Academy of Sciences Institute of Archaeological Sciences, Faculty of Humanities, Eötvös Loránd University, Ősrégészeti Társaság/Prehistoric Society, Budapest.

Fekete, M. 2013. A dunántúli késő bronzkori fémművesség néhány társadalom- és gazdaságtörténeti tanulsága. *Specimina nova dissertationum ex Institutio Historiae Antiquae et Archaeologiae Universitatis Quinqueecclesiensis* 21–22:85–108.

Ferenczy, I. 1997. *Észrevételek az erdélyi rézkor keleti népi és műveltségi elemeivel kapcsolatban.* Szolnok Megyei Múzeumi Adattár 33. Damjanich Museum, Szolnok.

Fernández-Götz, M. 2018. Urbanization in Iron Age Europe: Trajectories, Patterns, and Social Dynamics. *Journal of Archaeological Research* 26(2):117–62.

Fiala, F. 1893. Die Ergebnisse der Untersuchung prähistorischer Grabhügel auf dem Glasinac im Jahre 1892. *Wissenschaftliche Mitteilungen aus Bosnien und der Hercegovina* 1:126–65.

———. 1895. Die Ergebnisse der Untersuchung prähistorischer Grabhügel auf dem Glasinac im Jahre 1893. *Wissenschaftliche Mitteilungen aus Bosnien und der Hercegovina* 3:3–38.

———. 1896. Die Ergebnisse der Untersuchung prähistorischer Grabhügel auf dem Glasinac im Jahre 1894. *Wissenschaftliche Mitteilungen aus Bosnien und der Hercegovina* 4:3–32.

———. 1897. Die Ergebnisse der Untersuchung prähistorischer Grabhügel auf dem Glasinac im Jahre 1895. *Wissenschaftliche Mitteilungen aus Bosnien und der Hercegovina* 5:3–28.

———. 1899a. Das Flachgräberfeld und die prähistorische Ansiedlung in Sanskimost. *Wissenschaftliche Mitteilungen aus Bosnien und der Hercegovina* 6:62–128.

———. 1899b. Griechische Bronzehelme aus Bosnien und der Herzegovina. *Wissenschaftliche Mitteilungen aus Bosnien und der Hercegovina* 6:148–53.

———. 1899c. Die Ergebnisse der Untersuchung prähistorischer Grabhügel auf dem Glasinac im Jahre 1896. *Wissenschaftliche Mitteilungen aus Bosnien und der Hercegovina* 6:8–32.

———. 1899d. Die Ergebnisse der Untersuchung prähistorischer Grabhügel in Südostbosnien (anschliessend an den Glasinac) im Jahre 1897. *Wissenschaftliche Mitteilungen aus Bosnien und der Hercegovina* 6:33–61.

Filipović, V. 2015a. Weapons and Warrior Equipment in the Cultures of the Late Bronze and Early Iron Age on the Territories of Serbia, Macedonia, Montenegro and Albania. Ph.D dissertation, Faculty of Philosophy, University of Belgrade, Belgrade.

———. 2015b. Prilog poznavanju bronzanih strela na centralnom Balkanu tokom perioda Br C–Ha A1. *Glasnik* 31:257–70.

———. 2018. Some Observations on Communications and Contacts in the Central Balkan and Neighbouring Regions during the 7th to 5th Century BC Based on the Distribution of Weapons. In: *Proceedings of the First PeBA Conference Perspectives on Balkan Archaeology—The Early Iron Age: Methods and Approaches*, edited by B. Govedarica, pp. 105–15. Godišnjak 47. Zentrum für Balkanforschungen, Akademie der Wissenschaften und Künste von Bosnien-Herzegowina, Sarajevo.

Filipović, V. and P. Milojević. 2015. A Minoan (?) Dagger from Lipovačko Gradište (Central Balkans). *Karadžić* 7:16–25.

Filow, B. 1937. Kupolnite grobnici pri Mezek. *Izvestia na Bulgarskia arheologicheski institut* 11:1–116.

Filow, B. and I. Welkow. 1930. Grabhügelfunde aus Duvanlii in Südbulgarien. *Jahrbuch des deutschen archäologischen Instituts* 45:281–322.

Filow, B., I. Welkow, and V. Mikow. 1934. *Die Grabhügelnekropole bei Duvanlij in Südbulgarien.* Bulgarisches archäologisches Institut/Staatsdruckerei, Sofia.

Finley, M.I. 1977. *The World of Odysseus.* Chatto and Windus, London.

Fischer, F. 1973. ΚΕΙΜΗΛΙΑ. Bemerkungen zur kulturgeschichtlichen Interpretation des sogenannten Südimports in der späten Hallstatt- und frühen Latène-Kultur des westlichen Mitteleuropa. *Germania* 51(2):436–59.

Flanagan, J.G. 1989. Hierarchy in Simple "Egalitarian" Societies. *Annual Review of Anthropology* 18:245–66.

Flannery, K. 1972. The Cultural Evolution of Civilizations. *Annual Review of Ecology and Systematics* 3:399–426.

Flannery, K. and J. Marcus. 2012. *The Creation of Inequality: How Our Prehistoric Ancestors Set the Stage for Monarchy, Slavery, and Empire.* Harvard University Press, Cambridge, MA.

Fletcher, R. 1995. *The Limits of Settlement Growth: A Theoretical Outline.* Cambridge University Press, Cambridge.

Fol, A. 1972. *Politicheska istoria na trakite: Kraya na vtoroto hilyadoletie do kraya na peti vek predi novata era.* Nauka i izkustvo, Sofia.

———. 1975a. *Trakia i Balkanite prez rannoelinisticheskata epoha.* Nauka i izkustvo, Sofia.

———. 1975b. Simvolichnoto pogrebenie ot Kazichene, Sofiysko. *Izkustvo* 3–4:11–13.

———. 1986. *Trakiyskiat orfizym.* St. Kliment Ohridski University Press, Sofia.

———. 1991. *Trakiyskiat Dionis: Kniga parva, Zagrey.* St. Kliment Ohridski University Press, Sofia.

———. 1994. *Trakiyskiat Dionis: Kniga vtora, Sabaziy.* St. Kliment Ohridski University Press, Sofia.

———. 1997. *Istoria na bulgarskite zemi v drevnostta.* Second edition. St. Kliment Ohridski University Press, Sofia.

Fol, A., M. Chichikova, T. Ivanov, and T. Teofilov. 1986. *The Thracian Tomb near the Village of Sveshtari.* Svyat, Sofia.

Fol, A. and N.G.L. Hammond. 1988. Persia in Europe, Apart from Greece. In: *The Cambridge Ancient History,* Volume 4: *Persia, Greece and the Western Mediterranean, c. 525 to 479 BC,* edited by J. Boardman, N.G.L. Hammond, D.M. Lewis, and M. Ostwald, pp. 234–53. Second edition. Cambridge University Press, Cambridge.

Fol, A., K. Jordanov, K. Porozhanov, and V. Fol. 2000. *Ancient Thrace.* International Foundation Europa Antiqua, Sofia.

Fol, A. and I. Marazov. 1977. *Thrace and the Thracians.* St. Martin's Press, New York.

Fol, A., B. Nikolov, G. Mihailov, I. Venedikov, and I. Marazov. 1989. *The Rogozen Treasure.* Bulgarian Academy of Sciences, Sofia.

Fol, A., I. Venedikov, I. Marazov, and D. Popov. 1976. *Thracian Legends.* Sofia Press, Sofia.

Fontijn, D. 2002. *Sacrificial Landscapes. Cultural Biographies of Persons, Objects and 'Natural' Places in the Bronze Age of the Southern Netherlands, c. 2300–600 BC.* Analecta Praehistorica Leidensia 33–34. University of Leiden, Leiden.

Fox, J.J. and C. Sather (eds.). 2006. *Origins, Ancestry and Alliance: Explorations in Austronesian Ethnography.* ANUE Press, Canberra.

Franco, C. 1993. *Il regno di Lisimaco: strutture amministrative e rapporti con le città.* Giardini, Pisa.

Frînculeasa, A., B. Preda, and V. Heyd. 2015. Pit-Graves, Yamnaya and Kurgans along the Lower Danube: Disentangling IVth and IIIrd Millennium BC Burial Customs, Equipment and Chronology. *Praehistorische Zeitschrift* 90(1–2):45–113.

Frînculeasa A., A. Simalcsik, B. Preda, and D. Garvăn. 2017. *Smeeni— Movila Mare: Monografia unui sit arheologic regăsit.* Biblioteca Mousaios 13. Cetatea de Scaun, Târgoviște.

Fürer-Haimendorf, Ch. von. 1969. *The Konyak Nagas: An Indian Frontier Tribe.* Holt, Rinehart and Winston, New York.

Furholt, M. 2018. Massive Migrations? The Impact of Recent aDNA Studies on Our View of Third Millennium Europe. *European Journal of Archaeology* 21(2):159–91.

———. 2019. Re-Integrating Archaeology: A Contribution to aDNA Studies and the Migration Discourse on the 3rd Millennium BC in Europe. *Proceedings of the Prehistoric Society* 85:115–29.

Füzesi, A., K. Rassmann, E. Bánffy, and P. Raczky. 2020. Human Activities on a Late Neolithic Tell-Like Settlement Complex of the Hungarian Plain (Öcsöd-Kováshalom). In: *Current Approaches to Tells in the Prehistoric Old World: A Cross-Cultural Comparison from the Neolithic to the Iron Age,* edited by A. Blanco-González and T.L. Kienlin, pp. 139–62. Oxbow, Oxford.

Gabelko, O.L. 2005. *Istoria Vifinskogo tsarstva.* Gumanitarnaya Akademia, Saint Petersburg.

Galaty, M.L. 2002. Modeling the Formation and Evolution of an Illyrian Tribal System. In: *The Archaeology of Tribal Societies,* edited by W.A. Parkinson, pp. 109–22. International Monographs in Prehistory, Ann Arbor, MI.

Gale, N.H., Z.A. Stos-Gale, A. Raduncheva, I. Panayotov, I. Ivanov, P. Lilov, and T. Todorov. 2003. Early Metallurgy in Bulgaria. In: *Mining and Metal Production through the Ages,* edited by P. Craddock and J. Lang, pp. 122–74. British Museum, London.

Garašanin, D. 1975. Ostava iz Privine Glave. In: *Praistorijske ostave i Srbiji i Vojvodini I,* edited by M. Garašanin, pp. 68–72. Fontes Archaeologiae Serbiae I/1. Srpska akademija nauka i umetnosti, Beograd.

———. 1983. Razvijeno bronzano doba i prelazni period (gvozdeno doba I) Makedonije. In: *Praistorija Jugoslavenskih Zemalja IV: Bronzano doba,* edited by A. Benac, pp. 786–98. Akademija nauka i umjetnosti Bosne i Hercegovine, Sarajevo.

Garašanin, M. and M. Bilbija. 1988. Kuća 1 vo Zelenikovo. *Macedonia Acta Archaeologica* 9:31–41.

Gaunitz, C., A. Fages, K. Hanghøj, + 43 authors, and L. Orlando. 2018. Ancient Genomes Revisit the Ancestry of Domestic and Przewalski's Horses. *Science* 360(6384):111–14.

Găvan, A. 2015. *Metal and Metalworking in the Bronze Age Tells from the Carpathian Basin.* Mega, Cluj-Napoca.

Gavranović, M. 2011. *Die Spätbronze- und Früheisenzeit in Bosnien.* Teil 2. Universitätsforschungen zur prähistorischen Archäologie 195. Dr. Rudolf Habelt, Bonn.

Georganas, I. 2018. 'Warrior Graves' vs. Warrior Graves in Bronze Age Aegean. In: *Warfare in Bronze Age Societies,* edited by C. Horn and K. Kristiansen, pp. 189–97. Cambridge University Press, Cambridge.

Georgieva, R. 2004. Predstavi za smartta, martvetsa i otvadnia svyat v drevna Trakia. *Seminarium Thracicum* 6:61–80.

———. 2015. Ritual Pits. In: *A Companion to Ancient Thrace,* edited by J. Valeva, E. Nankov, and D. Graninger, pp. 144–57. Wiley Blackwell, Malden, MA.

Georgieva, R., T. Spiridonov, and M. Reho. 1999. *Etnologia na trakite*. St. Kliment Ohridski University Press, Sofia.

Gergova, D. 1980. Genesis and Development of the Metal Ornaments in the Thracian Lands during the Early Iron Age (11th–6th Century BC). *Studia Praehistorica* 3:97–112.

———. 1986. Postizhenia i problemi v prouchvaniata na rannozhelyaznata epoha v Trakia. *Arheologia* 28(3):11–26.

———. 1987. *Früh- und ältereisenzeitliche Fibeln in Bulgarien*. Prähistorische Bronzefunde XIV/7. C.H. Beck, München.

———. 1989. Thracian Burial Rites of Late Bronze and Early Iron Age. In: *Thracians and Mycenaeans: Proceedings of the Fourth International Congress of Thracology, Rotterdam, 24–26 September 1984*, edited by J. Best and N. de Vries, pp. 231–40. Brill, Leiden.

———. 1996. *Obredat na obezsmartyavaneto v drevna Trakia*. Agato, Sofia.

Gerling, C., E. Bánffy, J. Dani, K. Köhler, G. Kulcsár, A.W.G. Pike, V. Szeverényi, and V. Heyd. 2012. Immigration and Transhumance in the Early Bronze Age Carpathian Basin: The Occupants of a Kurgan. *Antiquity* 86(334):1097–1111.

Gerloff, S. 2003. Goldkegel, Kappe und Axt: Insignien bronzezeitlichen Kultes und Macht. In: *Gold und Kult der Bronzezeit*, edited by T. Springer, pp. 190–203. Verlag des Germanischen Nationalmuseums, Nürnberg.

Gheorghiu, D. 1994. Horse Head Sceptres: First Images of Yolked Horses. *Journal of Indo-European Studies* 22(2–3):221–49.

Glodariu, I. 2005. The History and Civilization of the Dacians. In: *The History of Transylvania*, Volume 1: *Until 1541*, edited by I.A. Pop, T. Nägler, and M. Bărbulescu, pp. 67–136. Romanian Cultural Institute, Cluj-Napoca.

Gogâltan, F. 2003. Die neolithischen Tellsiedlungen im Karpatenbecken: Ein Überblick. In: *Morgenrot der Kulturen: Frühe Etappen der Menscheitsgeschichte in Mittel- und Südosteuropa, Festschrift für Nándor Kalicz zum 75. Geburstag*, edited by E. Jerem and P. Raczky, pp. 223–62. Archaeolingua, Budapest.

———. 2008. Fortified Bronze Age Tell Settlements in the Carpathian Basin: A General Overview. In: *Defensive Structures from Central Europe to the Aegean in the 3rd and 2nd Millennia BC*, edited by J. Czebreszuk, S. Kadrow, and J. Müller, pp. 39–56. Dr. Rudolf Habelt, Poznań and Bonn.

———. 2010. Die Tells und der Urbanisierungsprozess. In: *Siedlung und Handwerk. Studien zu sozialen Kontexten in der Bronzezeit*, edited by B. Horejs and T.L. Kienlin, pp. 13–46. Dr. Rudolf Habelt, Bonn.

———. 2011. Die Beziehungen zwischen Siebenbürgen und dem Schwarzmeerraum: Die ersten Kontakte (ca. 4500–3500 v. Chr.). In: *Der Schwarzmeerraum vom Äneolithikum bis in die Früheisenzeit (5000–500 v. Chr.), Band 2: Globale Entwicklung*

versus Lokalgeschehen, edited by E. Sava, B. Govedarica, and B. Hänsel, pp. 101–24. Prähistorische Archäologie in Südosteuropa 27. Leidorf, Rahden/Westfalen.

———. 2014. Bronze Age Tell, Tell-Like and Mound-Like Settlements on the Eastern Frontier of the Carpathian Basin: History of Research. In: *Bronze Age Tell, Tell-Like and Mound-Like Settlements on the Eastern Frontier of the Carpathian Basin: History of Research*, edited by F. Gogâltan, C. Cordoș, and A. Ignat, pp. 13–24. Mega, Cluj-Napoca.

———. 2016a. Die Beziehungen zwischen Siebenbürgen und dem Schwarzmeerraum in der Kupfer- und am Anfang der Bronzezeit (ca. 3500–ca. 2500 v. Chr.). In: *Der Schwarzmeerraum vom Neolithikum bis in die Früheisenzeit (6000–600 v. Chr.). Kulturelle Interferenzen in der Zirkumpontischen Zone und Kontakte mit ihren Nachbargebieten*, edited by V. Nikolov and W. Schier, pp. 417–47. Marie Leidorf, Rahden/Westfalen.

———. 2016b. Building Power without Power? Bronze Age Fortified Settlements on the Lower Mureș Basin. In: *Prehistoric Settlements: Social, Economic and Cultural Aspects. Seven Studies in the Carpathian Area*, edited by F. Gogâltan and C. Cordoș, pp. 87–113. Mega, Cluj-Napoca.

———. 2017. The Bronze Age Multilayered Settlements in the Carpathian Basin (cca. 2500–1600/1500 BC): An Old Catalogue and Some Chronological Problems. *Journal of Ancient History and Archaeology* 4(4):28–63.

———. 2019. Neuere siedlungsarchäologische Forschungen im östlichen Karpatenbecken (2800–1500 v. Chr.). In: *Siedlungsarchäologie des Endneolithikums und der frühen Bronzezeit*, edited by H. Meller, S. Friederich, M. Küßner, H. Stäuble, and R. Risch, pp. 869–91. Landesamt für Denkmalpflege und Archäologie Sachsen-Anhalt Press, Halle.

Gogâltan, F., A. Gävan, M.A. Lie, G. Fazecaș, C. Cordoș, and T.L. Kienlin. 2020. Exploring the Bronze Age Tells and Tell-Like Settlements from the Eastern Carpathian Basin: Results of a Research Project. In: *Current Approaches to Tells in the Prehistoric Old World*, edited by A. Blanco-González and T.L. Kienlin, pp. 73–95. Oxbow, Oxford.

Gogâltan, F. and G.G. Marinescu. 2018. *Aur pentru zei: O descoperire aparținând epocii bronzului de la Bistrița-Dealul Târgului (nord-estul Transilvaniei)*. Mega, Cluj-Napoca.

Gogâltan, F. and V. Sava. 2018. A Violent End: An Attack with Clay Sling Projectiles against the Late Bronze Age Fortification in Sântana, South-Western Romania. In: *Bronzezeitliche Burgen zwischen Taunus und Karpaten*, edited by S. Hansen and R. Krause, pp. 349–69. Dr. Rudolf Habelt, Bonn.

Gogâltan, F., V. Sava, and R. Krause. 2019. Sântana—Cetatea Veche: A Late Bronze Age Mega-Fort in the Lower Mureș in Southwestern Romania. In: *Materialisierung von Konflikten*, edited by S. Hansen and R. Krause, pp. 191–220.

Universitätsforschungen zur prähistorischen Archäologie 346. Dr. Rudolf Habelt, Bonn.

Goldberg, A., T. Günther, N. Rosenborg, and M. Jakobsson. 2017. Ancient X Chromosomes Reveal Contrasting Sex Bias in Neolithic and Bronze Age Eurasian Migrations. *PNAS* 114(10):2657–62.

Gori, M. 2014. Metal Hoards as Ritual Gifts: Circulation, Collection and Alienation of Bronze Artefacts in Late Bronze Age Europe. In: *Gift Giving and the 'Embedded' Economy in the Ancient World*, edited by F. Carlá and M. Gori, pp. 269–88. Universitätsverlag Winter, Heidelberg.

Gotzev, A. 1994. Decoration of the Early Iron Age Pottery from South-East Bulgaria. In: *The Early Hallstatt Period (1200–700 B.C.) in South-East Europe: Proceedings of the International Symposium from Alba Iulia, 10–12 June, 1993*, edited by H. Ciugudean and N. Boroffka, pp. 97–127. Bibliotheca Musei Apulensis 1. Muzeul Naţional al Unirii, Alba Iulia.

———. 1997. Characteristics of the Settlement System during the Early Iron Age in Ancient Thrace. In: *Urbanization in the Mediterranean in the Ninth to Sixth Centuries BC*, edited by H. Damgaard Andersen, H.W. Horsnaes, and S. Houby-Nielsen, pp. 407–21. Acta Hyperborea 7. Museum Tusculanum Press, Copenhagen.

Govedarica, B. 1979. Neki rezultati revizionih istraživanja glasinačkih tumula 1974 i 1975. godine. In: *Sahranjivanje kod Ilira (Illyrian Burial Customs)*, edited by M. Garašanin, pp. 171–80. Srpska akademija nauka i umetnosti, Balkanološki institut, Belgrade.

———. 2004. *Zepterträger, Herrscher der Steppen: Die frühen Ockergräber des älteren Äneolithikums im karpatenbalkanischen Gebiet und im Steppenraum Südost- und Osteuropas.* Balkankommission der Heidelberger Akademie der Wissenschaften 6. Philipp von Zabern, Mainz.

———. 2016a. Conflict or Coexistence: Steppe and Agricultural Societies in the Early Copper Age of the Northwest Black Sea Area. In: *Interactions, Changes and Meanings. Essays in Honour of Igor Manzura on the Occasion of His 60th Birthday*, edited by S. Ţerna and B. Govedarica, pp. 81–91. Stratum, Kishinev.

———. 2016b. The Stratigraphy of Tumulus 6 in Shtoj and the Appearance of the Violin Idols in Burial Complexes of the South Adriatic Region. *Godišnjak* 45:5–34.

———. 2017. Problem interpretacije ukrašenih brusova s Glasinačkog područja. *Vjesnik za arheologiju i historiju dalmatinsku* 110–11:37–65.

———. 2018. *Kneževski grobovi iz Crne Gore.* JU Muzeji i galerije Podgorice, Podgorica.

Govedarica, B. and E. Kaiser. 1996. Die äneolithischen abstrakten und zoomorphen Steinzepter Südost- und Osteuropas. *Eurasia Antiqua* 2:59–103.

Grammenos, D.V. and E.K. Petropoulos (eds.). 2003. *Ancient Greek Colonies in the Black Sea*, Volume 1. Archaeological Institute of Northern Greece, Thessaloniki.

——— (eds.). 2007. *Ancient Greek Colonies in the Black Sea*, Volume 2. BAR International Series 1675 I–II. Archaeopress, Oxford.

Granovetter, M.S. 1973. The Strength of Weak Ties. *American Journal of Sociology* 78(6):1360–80.

———. 1983. The Strength of Weak Ties: A Network Theory Revisited. In: *Sociological Theory*, edited by R. Collins, pp. 201–33. Jossey-Bass, San Francisco.

Grinsell, L.V. 1961. The Breaking of Objects as a Funerary Rite. *Folklore* 72(3):475–91.

Grossano, S. 2017. Plato as a Social Theorist. *The Core Journal* 23:116–20.

Grumeza, I. 2009. *Dacia: Land of Transylvania, Cornerstone of Ancient Eastern Europe.* Hamilton Books, Lanham, MD.

Guilaine, J. and J. Zammit. 2005. *The Origins of War: Violence in Prehistory.* Blackwell, Malden, MA.

György, L. 2013. Late Copper Age Animal Burials in the Carpathian Basin. In: *Moments in Time: Papers Presented to Pál Raczky on His 60th Birthday*, edited by A. Anders, G. Kulcsár, G. Kalla, V. Kiss, and G.V. Szabó, pp. 627–42. L'Harmattan, Budapest.

———. 2014. Észak-Magyarország a késő rézkorban: A Baden-kultúra leletei Borsod-Abaúj-Zemplén megyében. Ph.D dissertation, Eötvös Loránd University, Institute of Archaeology, Budapest.

Gyucha, A. 2015. *Prehistoric Village Social Dynamics: The Early Copper Age in the Körös Region.* Prehistoric Research in the Körös Region II. Archaeolingua, Budapest.

Gyucha, A., W.A. Parkinson, and R.W. Yerkes. 2019. The Development of a Neolithic Tell on the Great Hungarian Plain: Site Formation and Use at Szeghalom-Kovácshalom. *Journal of Field Archaeology* 44(7):458–79.

Gyucha, A., R.W. Yerkes, W.A. Parkinson, N. Papadopoulos, A. Sarris, P.R. Duffy, and R.B. Salisbury. 2015. Settlement Nucleation in the Neolithic: A Preliminary Report of the Körös Regional Archaeological Project's Investigations at Szeghalom-Kovácshalom and Vésztő-Mágor. In: *Neolithic and Copper Age between the Carpathians and the Aegean Sea: Chronologies and Technologies from the 6th to the 4th Millennium BCE. International Workshop, Budapest 2012*, edited by S. Hansen, P. Raczky, A. Anders, and A. Reingruber, pp. 129–42. Archäologie in Eurasien 31. Dr. Rudolf Habelt, Bonn.

Haag, S., C. Popov, B. Horejs, S. Alexandrov, and G. Plattner (eds.). 2017. *Das erste Gold: Ada Tepe: Das älteste Goldbergwerk Europas.* Kunsthistorisches Museum, Vienna.

Haak, W., I. Lazaridis, N. Patterson, + 35 authors, and D. Reich. 2015. Massive Migration from the Steppe was a Source for Indo-European Languages in Europe. *Nature* 522:207–11.

Hagl, M. 2008. *Ein urnenfelderzeitlicher Depotfund vom Bullenheimer Berg in Franken (Hort F)*. Bayerische Vorgeschichtsblätter, Beiheft 19. Beck, Munich.

———. 2009. Opium—nicht für das Volk: Ein Gefäßhort vom Bullenheimer Berg, Mainfranken. In: *Alpen, Kult und Eisenzeit. Festschrift für Amei Lang zum 65. Geburtstag*, edited by J.M. Bagley, Ch. Eggl, D. Neumann, and M. Schefzik, pp. 143–58. Internationale Archäologie. Studia Honoraria 30. Marie Leidorf, Rahden/Westfalen.

Hakenbeck, S. 2008. Migration in Archaeology: Are We Nearly There Yet? *Archaeological Review from Cambridge* 23(2):9–26.

Hall, J.M. 2007. Polis, Community and Ethnic Identity. In: *The Cambridge Companion to Archaic Greece*, edited by H.A. Shapiro, pp. 40–60. Cambridge University Press, Cambridge.

Hammond, N.G.L. 1967. Tumulus Burial in Albania: The Grave Circles of Mycenae and the Indo-Europeans. *The Annual of the British School at Athens* 62:77–105.

———. 1972. *A History of Macedonia*, Volume I: *Historical Geography and Prehistory*. Clarendon Press, Oxford.

———. 1976. Tumulus Burials in Albania and the Problem of Ethnogenesis. *Iliria* 4(1):127–32.

———. 2000. The Ethne in Epirus and Upper Macedonia. *Annual of the British School at Athens* 95:345–52.

Hänsel, B. 1976. *Beiträge zur regionalen und chronologischen Gliederung der älteren Hallstattzeit an der unteren Donau 1–2*. Beiträge zur ur- und frühgeschichtlichen Archäologie des Mittelmeer-Kulturraumes 16–17. Dr. Rudolf Habelt, Bonn.

———. 1997. Gaben an die Götter: Schätze der Bronzezeit Europas: Ein Einführung. In: *Gaben an die Götter: Schätze der Bronzezeit Europas, Ausstellungskatalog*, edited by A. Hänsel and B. Hänsel, pp. 11–22. Berlin Museum für Vor- und Frühgeschichte, Berlin.

Hansen, M.H. and T.H. Nielsen (eds.). 2004. *An Inventory of Archaic and Classical Poleis*. Oxford University Press, Oxford.

Hansen, S. 1994. *Studien zu den Metalldeponierungen während der älteren Urnenfelderzeit zwischen Rhônetal und Karpatenbecken 1*. Universitätsforschungen zur prähistorischen Archäologie 21. Dr. Rudolf Habelt, Bonn.

———. 2002. Kommentar: Über bronzezeitliche Depots, Horts und Einzelfunde: Brauchen wir neue Begriffe? *Archäologische Informationen* 25:91–97.

———. 2005. Über bronzezeitliche Horte in Ungarn: Horte als soziale Praxis. In: *Interpretationsraum Bronzezeit: Bernhard Hänsel von seinen Schülern gewidmet*, edited by B. Horejs, E. Kaiser, and R. Jung, pp. 211–30. Universitätsforschungen zur prähistorischen Archäologie 121. Dr. Rudolf Habelt, Bonn.

———. 2007. *Bilder vom Menschen der Steinzeit: Untersuchungen zur Anthropomorphen Plastik der Jungsteinzeit und Kupferzeit in Südosteuropa I und II*. Philipp von Zabern, Mainz.

———. 2008. Bronzezeitliche Horte als Indikatoren für "andere Orte." *Das Altertum* 53:291–314.

———. 2011. Metal in South-Eastern and Central Europe between 4500 and 2900 BCE. In: *Anatolian Metal V*, edited by Ü. Yalçin, pp. 137–49. Veröffentlichungen aus dem Deutschen Bergbau-Museum Bochum 180. Deutsches Bergbau-Museum, Bochum.

———. 2013a. Bronzezeitliche Deponierungen in Europa nördlich der Alpen: Weihgaben ohne Tempel. In: *Sanktuar und Ritual: Heilige Plätze im archäologischen Befund. Menschen—Kulturen—Traditionen*, edited by I. Gerlach and D. Raue, pp. 371–87. Studien aus den Forschungsclustern des Deutschen Archäologischen Instituts 4/10. Marie Leidorf, Rahden/Westf.

———. 2013b. The Birth of the Hero: The Emergence of a Social Type in the 4th Millennium BC. In: *Unconformist Archaeology: Papers in Honour of Paolo Biagi*, edited by E. Starnini, pp. 101–12. Archaeopress, Oxford.

———. 2016a. A Short History of Fragments in Hoards of the Bronze Age. In: *Materielle Kultur und Identität im Spannungsfeld zwischen mediterraner Welt und Mitteleuropa/Material Culture and Identity between the Mediterranean World and Central Europe*, edited by H. Baitinger, pp. 185–208. Römisch-Germanischen Zentralmuseums – Tagungen 27, Mainz.

———. 2016b. Gabe und Erinnerung: Heiligtum und Opfer. In: *Raum, Gabe und Erinnerung: Weihgaben und Heiligtümer in prähistorischen und antiken Gesellschaften*, edited by S. Hansen, D. Neumann, and T. Vachta, pp. 211–36. Topoi. Berlin Studies in the Ancient World 38. Humboldt-Universität zu Berlin, Berlin.

———. 2019. The Hillfort of Teleac and Early Iron in Southern Europe. In: *Materialisierung von Konflikten*, edited by S. Hansen and R. Krause, pp. 201–25. Dr. Rudolf Habelt, Bonn.

Hansen, S. and J. Müller (eds.). 2017. *Rebellion and Inequality in Archaeology*. Universitätforschungen zur prähistorischen Archäologie 308. Dr. Rudolf Habelt, Bonn.

Harding, A. 1984. *The Mycenaeans and Europe*. Academic Press, London.

———. 1995. *Die Schwerter im ehemaligen Jugoslawien*. Prähistorische Bronzefunde IV/14. Franz Steiner, Stuttgart.

———. 2000. *European Societies in the Bronze Age*. Cambridge University Press, Cambridge.

——— 2007. *Warriors and Weapons in Bronze Age Europe*. Archaeolingua, Budapest.

——— 2015. The Emergence of Elite Identities in Bronze Age Europe. *Origini* 37:111–21.

——— 2017. Corneşti-Iarcuri and the Rise of Mega-Forts in Bronze Age Europe. In: *Fortifications: The Rise and Fall of Defended Sites in Late Bronze Age and Early Iron Age of South-East Europe*, edited by B.S. Heeb, A. Szentmiklosi, R. Krause, and M. Wemhoff, pp. 9–14. Staatliche Museen zu Berlin, Berlin.

———— 2018. The Question of "Proto-Urban" Sites in Later Prehistoric Europe. *Origini* 42:317–38.

Harding, A.F., S. Sievers, and N. Venclová (eds.). 2006. *Enclosing the Past: Inside and Outside in Prehistory.* J.R. Collis, Sheffield.

Harrel, K. 2014. The Fallen and Their Swords: A New Explanation for the Rise of the Shaft Graves. *American Journal of Archaeology* 118(1):3–17.

Harrison, R. and V. Heyd. 2007. The Transformation of Europe in the Third Millennium BC: The Example of "Le Petit-Chasseur I+III" (Sion, Valais, Switzerland). *Praehistorische Zeitschrift* 82(2):129–214.

Harțuche, H. 2005. Sceptrele de piatră zoomorfe. Interpretare și cronologie. *Pontica* 37–38:71–97.

Heeb, B.S., C. Jahn, and A. Szentmiklosi. 2014. Geschlossene Gesellschaft? Zur Gestaltung und Bedeutung bronzezeitlicher Festungstore. *Acta Praehistorica et Archaeologica* 46:67–103.

Heeb, J. 2014. *Copper Shaft-Hole Axes and Early Metallurgy in South-Eastern Europe: An Integrated Approach.* Archaeopress, Oxford.

Hellebrandt, M. 2011. Bronztekercs Abaújdevecserről. *A Herman Ottó Múzeum Évkönyve* 50:131–52.

Hencken, H. 1971. *The Earliest European Helmets. Bronze Age and Early Iron Age.* American School of Prehistoric Research 28. Harvard University, Cambridge, MA.

Heurtley, W.A. 1939. *Prehistoric Macedonia: An Archaeological Reconnaisance of Greek Macedonia (West of the Struma) in the Neolithic, Bronze and Early Iron Ages.* Cambridge University Press, Cambridge.

Heyd, V. 2011. Yamnaya Groups and Tumuli West of the Black Sea. In: *Ancestral Landscape. Burial Mounds in the Copper and Bronze Ages (Central and Eastern Europe—Balkans—Adriatic—Aegean, 4th–2nd Millennium B.C.),* edited by E. Borgna and S. Müller Celka, pp. 535–55. Maison de l'Orient et de la Mediterranée, Lyon.

————. 2013. Europe at the Dawn of Bronze Age. In: *Transitions to the Bronze Age. Interregional Interaction and Socio-Cultural Change in the Third Millennium BC Carpathian Basin and Neighbouring Regions,* edited by V. Heyd, G. Kulcsár, and V. Szeverényi, pp. 9–65. Archaeolingua, Budapest.

Higham, T., J. Chapman, V. Slavchev, B. Gaydarska, N. Honch, Y. Yordanov, and B. Dimitrova. 2019. New AMS Radiocarbon Dates for the Varna Eneolithic Cemetery, Bulgarian Black Sea Coast. *Acta Musei Varnaensis* 6:81–101.

Hochstetter, F. 1881. Über einem Kesselwagen aus Bronze aus einem Hügelgrab von Glasinac in Bosnien. *Mitteilungen der Antropologischen Gesellschaft in Wien* 10, Nr. 10–12:289–98.

Höck, A. 1891. Das Odrysenreich in Thrakien im fünften und vierten Jahrhundert v. Chr. *Hermes* 26:76–117.

Hoddinott, R.F. 1981. *The Thracians.* Thames and Hudson, New York.

Hoernes, M. 1889. Grabhügelfunde von Glasinac in Bosnien. *Mitteilungen der Antropologischen Gesellschaft in Wien* 19:135–49.

Hofmánová, Z., S. Kreutzer, G. Hellenthal, +35 authors, and J. Burger. 2016. Early Farmers from across Europe Directly Descended from Neolithic Aegeans. *PNAS* 113(25):6886–91.

Horváth, A. 1969. A vaszari és somlóvásárhelyi Hallstatt-kori halomsírok. *A Veszprém Megyei Múzeumok Közleményei* 8:109–34.

Horváth, F. 1987. Hódmezővásárhely-Gorzsa: A Settlement of the Tisza Culture. In: *The Late Neolithic in the Tisza Region: A Survey of Recent Excavations and Their Findings,* edited by L. Tálas and P. Raczky, pp. 31–46. Kossuth Press and Directorate of the Szolnok County Museums, Budapest and Szolnok.

————. 2009. Comments on the Tells in the Carpathian Basin: Terminology, Classification and Formation. In: *Ten Years After: The Neolithic of the Balkans as Uncovered by the Last Decade of Research,* edited by F. Drașovean, D.L. Ciobotaru, and M. Maddison, pp. 159–65. Bibliotheca Historica et Archaeologica Banatica 49. Marineasa, Timișoara.

Horváth, T. 2006. A badeni kultúráról: rendhagyó módon. *A Jósa András Múzeum Évkönyve* 48:89–134.

————. 2015. *Die Anfänge des kontinentalen Transportwesens und seine Auswirkungen auf die Bolerázer und Badener Kulturen.* Archaeopress, Oxford.

————. 2019. Cattle Deposits of the Late Copper Age and Early Bronze Age in Hungary. *Vjesnik Arheološkog muzeja u Zagrebu* 52:9–30.

Hristova, T. 2018. Hoards and Metal Assemblages on the Lower Danube during the Late Bronze Age. In: *Gold and Bronze: Metals, Technologies and Interregional Contacts in the Eastern Balkans during the Bronze Age,* edited by S. Alexandrov, Y. Dimitrova, H. Popov, B. Horejs, and K. Chukalev, pp. 161–70. National Archaeological Institute with Museum, Sofia.

Husenovski, B. 2018. Ženski grob so kultna palka od nekropolata Milci: Gevgelija. *Patrimonium* 16:103–26.

Huth, C. 1997. *Westeuropäische Horte der Spätbronzezeit: Fundbild und Funktion.* Regensburger Beiträge zur Prähistorischen Archäologie 3. Universitätsverlag , Regensburg.

Ilie, A., L. Mecu, and M. Frînculeasa. 2010. Topoare preistorice din cadrul Complexului Național Muzeal "Curtea Domnească" Târgoviște (I). *Buridava* 8:29–47.

Isaac, B. 1986. *The Greek Settlements in Thrace until the Macedonian Conquest.* Brill, Leiden.

Ivanov, D. 1975. Srebarnoto sakrovishte ot s. Borovo. *Izkustvo* 3–4:14–21.

Ivanov, I. and M. Avramova. 2000. *Varna Necropolis: The Dawn of European Civilization*. Agato, Sofia.

Ivanova, M., B. Athanasov, V. Petrova, D. Takorova, and P.W. Stockhammer (eds.). 2018. *Social Dimensions of Food in the Prehistoric Balkans*. Oxford University Press, Oxford.

Ivanova, S.V. 2013. Connections between the Budzhak Culture and Central European Groups of the Corded Ware Culture. *Baltic–Pontic Studies* 18:86–120.

Jaeger, M. 2016. *Bronze Age Fortified Settlements in Central Europe*. Dr. Rudolf Habelt, Poznań and Bonn.

Janssen, M.A, T.A. Kohler, and M. Scheffer. 2003. Sunk-Costs Effect and Vulnerability to Collapse in Ancient Societies. *Current Anthropology* 44(5):722–28.

Jantzen, D., U. Brinker, J. Orschiedt, J. Heinemeir, J. Piek, K. Hauenstein, J. Krüger, G. Lidke, H. Lübke, R. Lampe, S. Lorenz, M. Schult, and T. Terberger. 2011. A Bronze Age Battlefield? Weapons and Trauma in the Tollense Valley, North-Eastern Germany. *Antiquity* 85(328):417–33.

Jašarević, A. 2014. Socio-ekonomska i simbolička uloga importovanih metalnih posuda s Glasinca. *Godišnjak* 43:51–99.

———. 2017. Zaboravljeni grobovi iz Donje Doline. *Glasnik Zemaljskog muzeja Bosne i Hercegovine u Sarajevu* 54:7–30.

Johnson, A. and T. Earle. 1987. *The Evolution of Human Societies from Foraging Groups to Agrarian States*. Stanford University Press, Stanford.

Johnson, G.A. 1982. Organizational Structure and Scalar Stress. In: *Theory and Explanation in Archaeology*, edited by C. Renfrew, M.J. Rowlands, and B.A. Segraves, pp. 389–412. Academic Press, New York.

Jovanović, B. 1972. Podunavska industrija bronze i ostava iz Topolnice. *Starinar* 21:1–22.

———. 1975. Bronzana ostava iz Topolnice. In: *Praistorijske ostave i Srbiji i Vojvodini I*, edited by M. Garašanin, pp. 81–86. Fontes Archaeologiae Serbiae I/1. Srpska akademija nauka i umetnosti, Belgrade.

———. 1980. The Origins of Copper Mining in Europe. *Scientific American* 242(5):152–67.

Jovanović, B. and B. Ottaway. 1976. Copper Mining and Metallurgy in the Vinča Group. *Antiquity* 50(198):104–13.

Jovanović, D.B. 2010. *Ostave Vršačkog Gorja: Markovac-Grunjac*. Gradski Muzej, Vršac.

Jung, R. 2018. Warriors and Weapons in the Central and Eastern Balkans. In: *Gold and Bronze: Metals, Technologies and Interregional Contacts in the Eastern Balkans during the Bronze Age*, edited by S. Alexandrov, Y. Dimitrova, H. Popov, B. Horejs, and K. Chukalev, pp. 241–52. National Archaeological Institute with Museum, Sofia.

Kacsó, C. 2004. *Mărturii arheologice*. Nereamia Napocae, Baia Mare.

Kaiser, E. 2010. Der Übergang zur Rinderzucht im nördlichen Schwarzmeerraum. *Godišnjak* 39:23–34.

———. 2016. Migrationen von Ost nach West: Die Archäologie von Wanderungsbewegungen in 3. Jahrtausend v. Chr. *Mitteilungen der Berliner Gesellschaft für Anthropologie, Ethnologie und Urgeschichte* 37:31–44.

———. 2017. Accessing Hard-to-Analyse People in Archaeology. In: *Mobility in Prehistoric Sedentary Societies*, edited by S. Scharl and B. Gehlen, pp. 263–76. Kölner Studien zur Prähistorischen Archäologie 8. Marie Leidorf, Rahden/Westfalen.

———. 2019. *Das dritte Jahrtausend im osteuropäischen Steppenraum: Kulturhistorische studien zu prähistorischer subsistenzwirtschaft und interaktion mit benachbarten Räumen*. Berlin Studies of the Ancient World 37. Topoi, Berlin.

Kaiser, E. and K. Winger. 2015. Pit Graves in Bulgaria and the Yamnaya Culture. *Praehistorische Zeitschrift* 90(1–2):114–40.

Karavanić, S. 2009. *The Urnfield Culture in Continental Croatia*. BAR International Series 2036. Hadrian, Oxford.

Katinčarov, R. 1974. Periodizatsia i harakteristika na kulturata prez bronzovata epoha v Yuzhna Bulgaria. *Arheologia* 16(1):1–22.

———. 1978. Les tribus à l'âge du bronze en Bulgarie (d'après les données archéologiques). *Pulpudeva* 2:270–89.

Kazarow, G. 1916. *Beiträge zur Kulturgeschichte der Thraker*. J. Studnicka & Co., Sarajevo.

———. 1919. Keltite v stara Trakia i Makedonia. *Spisanie na Bulgarskata akademia na naukite 18, klon istoriko-filologichen* 10:41–80.

———. 1926. *Bulgaria v drevnostta. Istoriko-arheologicheski ocherk*. Populyarna arheologicheska biblioteka 1. Bulgarski arheologicheski institut, Sofia.

———. 1930. Thrace. *The Cambridge Ancient History*, Volume 8: *Rome and the Mediterranean 218–133 B.C.*, edited by S.A. Cook, F.E. Adcock, and M.P. Charlesworth, pp. 534–60. Cambridge University Press, Cambridge.

———. 1933. Proizhod i prav raztsvet na odriskoto tsarstvo v drevna Trakia. *Uchilishten pregled* 32:737–54.

———. 1936. Thrake (3): 10. Thrakische Religion. *Paulys Realencyclopädie der classischen Altertumswissenschaft VI A*:472–551.

———. 1954. Prinos kam istoriata na drevna Trakia. *Izvestia na Instituta za bulgarska istoria* 5:155–76.

Keeley, L. H. 1996. *War before Civilization: The Myth of the Peaceful Savage*. First edition. Oxford University Press, Oxford.

———. 1997. *War before Civilization: The Myth of the Peaceful Savage*. Pbk. edition. Oxford University Press, Oxford.

Kelly, J.E. and J.A. Brown. 2014. Cahokia: The Processes and Principles of the Creation of an Early Mississippian City. In: *Making Ancient Cities: Space and Place in Early Urban Societies*, edited by A.T. Creekmore and K.D. Fisher, pp. 292–336. Cambridge University Press, Cambridge.

Kemenczei, T. 1988. *Die Schwerter in Ungarn I*. Prähistorische Bronzefunde IV/6. C.H. Beck, Munich.

———. 1991. *Die Schwerter in Ungarn II (Vollgriffschwerter)*. Prähistorische Bronzefunde IV/9. Franz Steiner, Stuttgart.

———. 1996. Angaben zur Frage der endbronzezeitlichen Hortfundstufen im Donau–Theißgebiet. *Communicationes Archaeologicae Hungariae* 1996:53–92.

———. 2009. *Studien zu den Denkmälern skytisch geprägter Alföld Gruppe*. Inventaria Praehistorica Hungariae 12. Magyar Nemzeti Múzeum, Budapest.

Kienlin, T.L. 2008. Tradition and Innovation in Copper Age Metallurgy: Results of a Metallographic Examination of Flat Axes from Eastern Central Europe and the Carpathian Basin. *Proceedings of the Prehistoric Society* 74:79–107.

———. 2012. Patterns of Change, or: Perceptions Deceived? Comments on the Interpretation of Late Neolithic and Bronze Age Tell Settlement in the Carpathian Basin. In: *Beyond Elites: Alternatives to Hierarchical Systems in Modelling Social Transformations*, edited by T.L. Kienlin and A. Zimmermann, pp. 251–310. Universitätsforschungen zur prähistorischen Archäologie 215. Dr. Rudolf Habelt, Bonn.

———. 2013. Copper and Bronze: Bronze Age Metalworking in Context. In: *The Oxford Handbook of the European Bronze Age*, edited by H. Fokkens and A. Harding, pp. 414–36. Oxford University Press, Oxford.

———. 2015a. *Bronze Age Tell Communities in Context. An Exploration into Culture, Society and the Study of European Prehistory. Part 1: Critique. Europe and the Mediterranean*. Archaeopress, Oxford.

———. 2015b. All Heroes in Their Armour Bright and Shining? Comments on the Bronze Age 'Other'. In: *Fremdheit: Perspektiven auf das Andere*, edited by T.L. Kienlin, pp. 153–93. Dr. Rudolf Habelt, Bonn.

Kienlin, T.L., K.P. Fischl, and L. Marta. 2017. Exploring Divergent Trajectories in Bronze Age Landscapes: Tell Settlement in the Hungarian Borsod Plain and the Romanian Ier Valley. *Ziridava* 31:93–128.

Kienlin, T.L., K.P. Fischl, and T. Pusztai. 2018. *Borsod Region Bronze Age Settlement (BORBAS): Catalogue of the Early to Middle Bronze Age Tell Sites Covered by Magnetometry and Surface Survey*. Dr. Rudolf Habelt, Bonn.

Kienlin, T.L. and A. Zimmerman (eds.). 2012. *Beyond Elites: Alternatives to Hierarchical Systems in Modelling Social Formations*. Universitätsforschungen zur prähistorischen Archäologie 215. Dr. Rudolf Habelt, Bonn.

Kilian-Dirlmeier, I. 1993. *Die Schwerter in Griechenland (außerhalb der Peloponnes), Bulgarien und Albanien*. Prähistorische Bronzefunde IV/12. Franz Steiner, Stuttgart.

Kisyov, K. 2009. *Pogrebalni praktiki v Rodopite (kraya na II–I hil. pr. n. e.)*. Avtospektar, Plovdiv.

Kitanoski, B., D. Simoska, and B. Jovanović. 1990. Der Kultplatz auf der Fundstatte Vrbjanska Cuka bei Prilep. In: *Vinča and Its World*, edited by D. Srejović and N. Tasić, pp. 107–12. Serbian Academy of Science and Arts, Centre for Archaeological Research, Faculty of Philosophy, Belgrade.

Kitov, G. 1993. Trakiyskite mogili. *Thracia* 10:39–80.

———. 2003. *Thracian Cult Center near Starossel*. Slavena, Varna.

———. 2004. Grobnitsata v Aleksandrovo. *Izvestia na Istoricheski muzey Haskovo* 2:149–75.

———. 2005. Thracian Tumular Burial with a Gold Mask near the Town of Shipka, Central Bulgaria. *Archaeologia Bulgarica* 9(3):23–37.

Klejn, L. 2017. The Steppe Hypothesis of Indo-European Origins Remains to be Proven. *Acta Archaeologica* 88(1):193–203.

Knauft, B.M. 1991. Violence and Sociality in Human Evolution. *Current Anthropology* 32(4):391–428.

———. 1993. *South Coast New Guinea Cultures: History, Comparison, Dialectic*. Cambridge Studies in Social and Cultural Anthropology 89. Cambridge University Press, Cambridge.

Knöpke, S. 2010. *Der urnenfelderzeitliche Männerfriedhof von Neckarsulm*. Forschungen und Berichte zur Vor- und Frühgeschichte in Baden-Württemberg 116. Theiss, Stuttgart.

Koledin, J., U. Bugaj, P. Jarosz, M. Novak, M. Przybyła, M. Podsiało, A. Szczepanek, M. Spašić, and P. Włodarczak. 2020. First Archaeological Investigation of Barrows in the Bačka Region and the Question of the Eneolithic/Early Bronze Age Barrows in Vojvodina. *Praehistorische Zeitschrift* 95(2):350–75.

Kolištrkoska Nasteva, I. 2005. *Praistoriskite dami od Makedonija*. Muzej na Makedonija, Skopje.

König, P. 2004. *Spätbronzezeitliche Hortfunde aus Bosnien und der Herzegowina*. Prähistorische Bronzefunde XX/11. Franz Steiner, Stuttgart.

Kontny, B. 2015. Was Tacitus Right? On the Existence of Hitting Weapons of Organic Materials amongst the Balt Tribes. In: *Waffen—Gewalt—Krieg*, edited by S. Wefers, M. Karwowski, J. Fries-Knoblach, P. Trebsche, and P.C. Ramsl, pp. 77–89. Beiträge zur Ur- und Frühgeschichte Mitteleuropas 79. Beier&Beran, Langenweissbach.

Kosse, K. 1990. Group Size and Societal Complexity: Thresholds in Long-Term Memory. *Journal of Anthropological Archaeology* 9(3):275–303.

Kostof, S. 1991. *The City Shaped: Urban Patterns and Meanings through History*. Bulfinch, Boston.

Kostov, R.I. 2007. *Archaeomineralogy of Neolithic and Chalcolithic Artefacts from Bulgaria and Their Significance to Gemmology*. St. Ivan Rilski, Sofia.

Kotsakis, K. 1999. What Tells Can Tell: Social Space and Settlement in the Greek Neolithic. In: *Neolithic Society in Greece*, edited by P. Halstead, pp. 66–76. Sheffield Studies in Aegean Archaeology 2. Sheffield Academic Press, Sheffield.

Kovács, T. 1973. Korai markolatlapos bronztőrök a Kárpát-medencében. *Archaeologiai Értesítő* 100:157–66.

Krahe, G. 1980. Beinschiene der Urnenfelderzeit von Schäftstall, Stadt Donauwörth, Landkreis Donau-Ries, Schwaben. *Das archäologische Jahr in Bayern* 1980:76–77.

Krause, R., A. Szentmiklosi, B. Heeb, R. Lehmphul, K. Teinz, A. Bălărie, C. Herbig, A. Stobbe, J. Schmid, D. Schäffler, and M. Wemhoff. 2019. Cornești-Iarcuri: Die Ausgrabungen 2013 und 2014 in der befestigten Großsiedlung der späten Bronzezeit. *Eurasia Antiqua* 22:133–184.

Krauß, R., C. Schmid, D. Ciobotaru, and V. Slavchev. 2016. Varna und die Folgen: Überlegungen zu den Ockergräbern zwischen Karpatenbecken und der nördlichen Ägäis. In: *Von Baden bis Troia: Ressourcennutzung, Metallurgie und Wissenstransfer: Eine Jubiläumsschrift für Ernst Pernicka*, edited by M. Bartelheim, B. Horejs, and R. Krauss, pp. 273–315. Marie Leidorf, Rahden/Westfalen.

Kristiansen, K. 1998. *Europe Before History*. Cambridge University Press, Cambridge.

———. 1999. The Emergence of Warrior Aristocracies in Later European Prehistory and Their Long-Term History. In: *Ancient Warfare: Archaeological Perspectives*, edited by J. Carman and A. Harding, pp. 175–89. Sutton, Stroud.

———. 2001. Rulers and Warriors: Symbolic Transmission and Social Transformation in Bronze Age Europe. In: *From Leaders to Rulers*, edited by J. Haas, pp. 85–104. Kluwer Academic/Plenum, New York.

———. 2002. The Tale of the Sword: Swords and Swordfighters in Bronze Age Europe. *Oxford Journal of Archaeology* 21(4):319–32.

———. 2018a. The Rise of Bronze Age Peripheries and the Expansion of International Trade 1950–1100 BC. In: *Trade and Civilisation: Economic Networks and Cultural Ties, from Prehistory to the Early Modern Era*, edited by K. Kristiansen, T. Lindkvist, and J. Myrdal, pp. 57–86. Cambridge University Press, Cambridge.

———. 2018b. Warfare and the Political Economy: Europe 1500–1100 BC. In: *Warfare in Bronze Age Society*, edited by C. Horn and K. Kristiansen, pp. 23–46. Cambridge University Press, Cambridge.

Kristiansen, K. M. Allentoft, K. Frei, R. Iversen, N. Johannsen, G. Kroonen, Ł. Pospieszny, T.D. Price, S. Rasmussen, K.-G. Sjögren, M. Sikora, and E. Willerslev. 2017. Re-Theorising Mobility and the Formation of Culture and Language among the Corded Ware Culture in Europe. *Antiquity* 91(356):334–47.

Kristiansen, K. and T.B. Larsson. 2005. *The Rise of Bronze Age Society: Travels, Transmissions and Transformation*. Cambridge University Press, Cambridge.

Krstić, V. 2018. Trebenishte, Valley of the Kings: Excavations by Professor Nikola Vulić. In: *100 Years of Trebenishte*, edited by P. Ardjanliev, K. Chukalev, T. Cvjetićanin, M. Damyanov, V. Krstić, A. Papazovska, and H. Popov, pp. 33–41. National Archaeological Institute with Museum and Bulgarian Academy of Sciences, Sofia.

Kulcsár, G. 2009. *The Beginnings of the Bronze Age in the Carpathian Basin: The Makó-Kosihy-Čaka and the Somogyvár-Vinkovci Cultures in Hungary*. Varia Archaeologica Hungarica 23. Archaeolingua, Budapest.

Kuzman, P. 2018. Gorna Porta (Ohrid)–Trebenishte: Connections. In: *100 years of Trebenishte*, edited by P. Ardjanliev, K. Chukalev, T. Cvjetićanin, M. Damyanov, V. Krstić, A. Papazovska, and H. Popov, pp. 209–23. National Archaeological Institute with Museum and Bulgarian Academy of Sciences, Sofia.

Kuzman, P. and P. Ardjanliev. 2018. Gold Funerary Masks and Hands from Trebenishte and Ohrid. In: *100 Years of Trebenishte*, edited by P. Ardjanliev, K. Chukalev, T. Cvjetićanin, M. Damyanov, V. Krstić, A. Papazovska, and H. Popov, pp. 58–63. National Archaeological Institute with Museum and Bulgarian Academy of Sciences, Sofia.

Kytlicová, O. 1988. Příspěvek k problematice kožených pancířů zdobených bronzem v období popelnicových polí. *Archeologické Rozhledy* 40(3):306–21.

L'Or des cavaliers Thraces: Trésors de Bulgarie 1987. Exhibiton Catalog. Éditions de l'Homme, Montréal.

L'Or des Thraces: Trésors de Bulgarie 2002. Exhibition Catalog. Snoeck, Bruxelles.

Lahtov, V. and J. Kastelic. 1957. Novi istrazuvanja na nekropolata Trebeniśte (1953–1954). *Lihnid* 1:5–58.

Landucci Gattinoni, F. 1992. *Lisimaco di Tracia: Un sovrano nella prospettiva del primo ellenismo*. Jaca Book, Milan.

Lásló, A. 1997. On the Origin, Development and Chronology of the First Iron Age at the Lower Danube. In: *Actes du Colloque International Premier âge du Fer au bouches du Danube et dans les régions autour de la Mer Noire, Tulcea 1993*, edited by G. Simion and G. Jugănaru, pp. 67–75. Arti Grafiche Giacone Romania SA, Bucureşti.

Leach, E.R. 1954. *Political Systems of Highland Burma: A Study of Kachin Social Structure.* Bell and Sons, London.

LeBlanc, A.A. 2003. *Constant Battles: Why We Fight.* St. Martin's Griffin, New York.

Lehmphul, R., B. Heeb, A. Szentmiklosi, A. Stobbe, and R. Krause. 2019. The Genesis of the Fortification of Corneşti-Iarcuri near the Mureş Lower Course (Romanian Banat): A Phase Model on the Chronology of the Settlement and Fortification Structures. In: *Bronze Age Fortresses in Europe,* edited by S. Hansen and R. Krause, pp. 253–78. Dr. Rudolf Habelt, Bonn.

Lekson, S. 1985. Largest Settlement Size and the Interpretation of Socio-Political Complexity at Chaco Canyon, New Mexico. *Haliksa'i UNM Contributions to Anthropology* 4:68–75.

Lenk, B. 1936a. Thrake (3). 2. Ausdehnung, Grenzen. 3. Das Land. *Paulys Realencyclopädie der classischen Altertumswissenschaft VIA:*394–401.

———. 1936b. Thrake (3). 8. Thrakien, Geschichte. *Paulys Realencyclopädie der classischen Altertumswissenschaft VIA:*414–72.

———. 1937. Odrysai. *Paulys Realencyclopädie der classischen Altertumswissenschaft* XVII:1900–1903.

Leshtakov, K. 2006. Bronzovata epoha v Gornotrakiyskata nizina. *Godishnik na Sofiyskia universitet, Istoricheski fakultet, Specialnost Arheologiya* 3 [2002]:141–216.

Leshtakov, L. 2015. *Tipologiya i khronologiya na bronzovite vŭrkhove za kopiya ot kŭsnata bronzova i nachaloto na rannozhelyaznata Epokha v yugoiztochna Evropa.* Ars et Technica Explicatus, Sofia.

Lesser, A. 1961. Social Fields and the Evolution of Society. *Southwestern Journal of Anthropology* 17(1):40–48.

Librado, P., N. Khan, A. Fages, + 163 authors, and L. Orlando. 2021. The Origins and Spread of Domestic Horses from the Western Eurasian Steppes. *Nature* 598:634–40.

Lichtenstein, L. and Z. Rózsa. 2008. Bronzkori csalafintaságok a középkori Kaszaper területén. *Múzeumi kutatások Csongrád megyében* 2007:43–65.

Lie, M.A., A. Găvan, C. Cordoş, T.L. Kienlin, G. Fazecaş, and F. Gogâltan. 2019. The Bronze Age Tell Settlement at Toboliu (Bihor County, Romania): A Brief Outline of Recent Investigations. In: *Beyond Divides: The Otomani-Füzesabony Phenomenon: Current Approaches to Settlement and Burial in the North-Eastern Carpathian Basin and Adjacent Area,* edited by K.P. Fischl and T.L. Kienlin, pp. 351–68. Dr. Rudolf Habelt, Bonn.

Lilčić, V. 1995. Antika. In: *Makedonija Kulturno Nasledstvo,* pp. 46–89. Misla, Skopje.

Ling, J., E. Hjarthner-Holdar, L. Grandin, Z. Stos-Gale, K. Kristiansen, A. Lene Melheim, G. Artioli, I. Angelini, R. Krause, and C. Canovaro. 2019. Moving Metals IV: Swords, Metal Sources and Trade Networks in Bronze Age Europe. *Journal of Archaeological Science: Reports* 26:1–34.

Lipp, V. 1885. Őskori kőkamra-sír Keszthelyen. *Archaeologiai Értesítő* 5:369–73.

Lloyd, M. 2015. Death of a Swordsman, Death of a Sword: The Killing of Swords in the Early Iron Age Aegean ca. 1050 – ca. 690 B.C.E. In: *Ancient Warfare: Introducing Current Research,* edited by G. Lee, H. Whittaker, and G. Wrightson, pp. 14–31. Cambridge Scholars Publishing, Cambridge.

Lobo, J., T. Whitelaw, L.M.A. Bettencourt, P. Wiessner, M.E. Smith, and S. Ortman. 2019. *Scaling of Hunter Gatherer Camp Size and Human Sociality.* https://papers.ssrn.com/sol3/papers. cfm?abstract_id=3399729.

Longacre, W.A. (ed.). 1970. *Reconstructing Prehistoric Pueblo Societies.* School of American Research, Santa Fe.

Loukopoulou, L. 2002. The 'Prosodos' of the Thracian Kings. In: *Thrace and the Aegean, Proceedings of the Eighth International Congress of Thracology,* Volume 1, edited by A. Fol, pp. 345–53. International Foundation Europa Antiqua and Institute of Thracology, Sofia.

Lozanov, I. 2015. Roman Thrace. In: *A Companion to Ancient Thrace,* edited by J. Valeva, E. Nankov, and D. Graninger, pp. 75–90. Wiley Blackwell, Malden, MA.

Lucentini, N. 1981. Sulla cronologia della necropoli di Glasinac nell' età del ferro. In: *Studi di protostoria adriatica 1,* edited by R. Peroni, pp. 67–171. Quaderni di cultura materiale 2. L'Erma di Bretschneider, Rome.

Lund, H.S. 1992. *Lysimachus: A Study in Early Hellenistic Kingship.* Routledge, London and New York.

Majnarić-Pandžić, N. 2002. Multi-Headed "Pins" of the Donja Dolina Type Revisited. *Godišnjak* 32:283–91.

Mano-Zisi, Đ. and L. Popović. 1969. *Novi Pazar, grčko-ilirski nalaz.* Narodni Muzej Beograd, Belgrade.

Marazov, I. 1989. *The Rogozen Treasure.* Svyat, Sofia.

———. (ed.). 1998. *Ancient Gold: The Wealth of the Thracians: Treasures from the Republic of Bulgaria.* Harry N. Abrams, New York.

Marcsik, A. 1974. Data of the Copper Age Anthropological Find of Bárdos-Farmstead at Csongrád-Kettőshalom. *A Móra Ferenc Múzeum Évkönyve* 1971(2):19–27.

———. 1979. The Anthropological Finds of the Pit-Grave Kurgans in Hungary. In: *The People of the Pit-Grave Kurgans in Eastern Hungary,* edited by I. Ecsedy, pp. 87–98. Akadémiai, Budapest.

Marić, Z. 1963. Keltski elementi u mlađem željeznom dobu Bosne i Hercegovine. *Glasnik Zemaljskog muzeja Bosne i Hercegovine u Sarajevu* 18:63–83.

———. 1964. Donja Dolina. *Glasnik Zemaljskog muzeja Bosne i Hercegovine u Sarajevu* 19:5–128.

Martinez, J.-L., A. Baralis, N. Mathieux, T. Stoyanov, and M. Tonkova (eds.). 2015. *L'Épopée des rois thraces, des guerres médiques aux invasions celtes, 479–278 av. J.-C. Découvertes archéologiques en Bulgarie*. Somogy éditions d'art, Paris.

Mason, A.H., W.G. Powell, H.A. Bankoff, R. Mathur, A. Bulatović, V. Filipović, and J. Ruiz. 2016. Tin Isotope Characterization of Bronze Artifacts of the Central Balkans. *Journal of Archaeological Science* 69:110–17.

Mathieson, I., S. Alpaslan-Roodenberg, C. Posth, + 113 authors, and D. Reich. 2018. The Genomic History of Southeastern Europe. *Nature* 555:197–203.

Matthäus, H. 1989. Mykenai. Der mittlere Donauraum während des Hajdúsámon-Horizontes und der Schatz von Vălčitran. In: *Thracians and Mycenaeans: Proceedings of the Fourth International Congress of Thracology, Rotterdam, 24–26 September 1984*, edited by J. Best and N. de Vries, pp. 86–105. Brill, Leiden.

Mauss, M. 1990. *The Gift: The Form and Reason for Exchange in Archaic Societies*. Cohen, London.

Mehmetaj, H. 2019. *The Archaeological Heritage of the Istog Municipality*. Archaeological Institute of Kosovo, Prishtina.

Melis, A.P. and D. Semmann. 2010. How is Human Cooperation Different? *Philosophical Transactions of the Royal Society B, Biological Sciences* 365:2663–74.

Mercer, R. 2006. By Other Means: The Development of Warfare in the British Isles 3000–500 B.C. *Journal of Conflict Archaeology* 2(1):119–51.

Mesterházy, G., G. Serlegi, B. Vágvölgyi, A. Füzesi, and P. Raczky. 2019. A szociális folyamatok színterei Polgár-Csőszhalom késő neolitikus településének összefüggéseiben. *Archaeologiai Értesítő* 144:1–32.

Meyboom, P. 2014. The Tomb of Kazanlak Reconsidered. In: *Antike Malerei zwischen Lokalstil und Zeitstil: Akten des XI. Internationalen Kolloquiums der AIPMA, 13.–17. September 2010*, edited by N. Zimmermann, pp. 391–94. Österreichischen Akademie der Wissenschaften, Wien.

Mihailov, G. 1964. *Inscriptiones graecae in Bulgaria repertae*, Volume III: *Inscriptiones inter Haemum et Rhodopem repertae. Fasciculus posterior: A territorio Philippopolitano usque ad oram Ponticam*. In aedibus Academiae litterarum bulgaricae, Serdicae.

———. 1972. *Trakite*. Darzhavno voenno izdatelstvo, Sofia.

———. 1997. *Inscriptiones graecae in Bulgaria repertae*, Volume V: *Inscriptiones novae, addenda et corrigenda*. In aedibus typographicis Rivae, Serdicae.

Mikov, V. 1942. Proizhod na nadgrobnite mogili v Bulgaria. *Godishnik na Narodnia muzey* 7:15–31.

———. 1954. *Le tombeau antique près de Kazanlăk*. Académie bulgare des sciences, Sofia.

———. 1955. Proizhod na kupolnite grobnitsi v Trakia. *Izvestia na arheologicheskia institut* 19 (*Serta Kazaroviana*, part 2):15–48.

———. 1957. Nadgrobnite mogili v Bulgaria. In: *Arheologicheski otkritia v Bulgaria*, pp. 217–41. Nauka i izkustvo, Sofia.

———. 1958. *Zlatnoto sakrovishte ot Valchitran*. Bulgarska akademia na naukite, Sofia.

———. 1971. La Bulgarie à l'âge du bronze. *Studia Balcanica* 5:51–61.

Mikulčić, I. 1966. *Pelagonija u svetlosti arheoloških nalaza: od Egejske seobe do Avgusta*. Arheološko društvo Jugoslavije, Belgrade.

Milojčić, V. 1955. Einige "mitteleuropäische" Fremdlinge auf Kreta. *Jahrbuch des Römisch-Germanischen Zentralmuseums* 2:153–69.

Mitkoski, A. 2005. Vrbjanska Čuka kaj seloto Slavej, Prilepsko. *Zbornik na Muzejot na Makedonija* 2:33–46.

Mitovski, M. 2018. The Beginning of Prehistoric Metallurgy in Republic of Macedonia. In: *Neolithic in Macedonia: Challenges for New Discoveries*, edited by L. Fidanoski and G. Naumov, pp. 185–200. Center for Prehistoric Research, Skopje.

Mitrevski, D. 1995. Praistoriska nekropola Klučka-Hipodrom. *Zbornik na arheološkiot muzej—Arheologija* 1:61–89.

———. 1997. *Protoistoriskite zaednici vo Makedonija*. Republički zavod za zaštita na spomenicite na kulturata, Skopje.

———. 1999. Grobot na pajonskata sveštenička od Marvinci. *Macedoniae Acta Archaeologica* 15:69–89.

Mittnik, A., K. Massy, C. Knipper, +20 authors, and J. Krause. 2019. Kinship-Based Social Inequality in Bronze Age Europe. *Science* 366(6466):731–34.

Mödlinger, M. 2011. *Herstellung und Verwendung bronzezeitlicher Schwerter Mitteleuropas: Eine vertiefende Studie zur mittelbronze- und urnenfelderzeitlichen Bewaffnung und Sozialstruktur*. Universitätsforschungen zur prähistorischen Archäologie 193. Dr. Rudolf Habelt, Bonn.

———. 2013. From Greek Boar Tusk Helmets to the First European Metal Helmets: New Approaches on Development and Date. *Oxford Journal of Archaeology* 34(2):391–412.

———. 2017. *Protecting the Body in War and Combat: Metal Body Armour in Bronze Age Europe*. Oriental and European Archaeology 6. Austrian Academy of Sciences, Vienna.

Molloy, B. 2009. For Gods or Men? A Reappraisal of the Function of European Bronze Age Shields. *Antiquity* 83(322):1052–64.

———. 2010. Swords and Swordsmanship in the Aegean Bronze Age. *American Journal of Archaeology* 114(3):403–28.

———. 2018. Conflict at Europe's Crossroads: Analysing the Social Life of Metal Weaponry in the Bronze Age Balkans. In: *Prehistoric Warfare and Violence. Quantitative and Qualitative*

Approaches, edited by A. Dolfini, R.J. Crellin, C. Horn, and M. Uckelman, pp. 199–224. Springer, Cham.

Molloy, B. and C. Horn. 2020. Weapons, Warriors and Warfare in Bronze Age Europe. In: *The Cambridge World History of Violence*, Volume 1: *The Prehistoric and Ancient Worlds*, edited by G.G. Fagan, L. Fibiger, M. Hudson, and M. Trundle, pp. 117–41. Cambridge University Press, Cambridge.

Molloy, B., D. Jovanović, C. Bruyère, M. Marić, J. Bulatović, P. Mertl, C. Horn, L. Milašinović, and N. Mirković-Marić. 2020. A New Bronze Age Mega-Fort in Southeastern Europe: Recent Archaeological Investigations at Gradište Iđoš and Their Regional Significance. *Journal of Field Archaeology* 45(4):1–22.

Molnár, Z. and B. Ciută. 2017. Aspects Regarding the Economy of the Otomani Communities in North-Western Transylvania: Data Concerning the Middle Bronze Age Agriculture in Light of the Investigations Carried Out in the Carei-Bobald Tell. *Analele Banatului* 25:57–90.

Mozsolics, A. 1973. *Bronze- und Goldfunde des Karpatenbeckens: Depotfundhorizonte von Forró und Ópályi*. Akadémiai, Budapest.

———. 1984. Rekonstruktion des Depots von Hajdúböszörmény. *Praehistorische Zeitschrift* 59(1):81–93.

———. 1985. *Bronzefunde aus Ungarn: Depotfundhorizonte von Aranyos, Kurd und Gyermely*. Akadémiai, Budapest.

———. 2000. *Bronzefunde aus Ungarn: Depotfundhorizonte Hajdúböszörmény, Románd und Bükkszentlászló*. Prähistorische Archäologie in Südosteuropa 17. Oetker, Kiel.

Müller, J. 2012. Tells, Fire, and Copper as Social Technologies. In: *Tells: Social and Environmental Space*, edited by R. Hofmann, F.-K. Moetz, and J. Müller, pp. 47–52. Universitätsforschungen zur prähistorischen Archäologie 207. Dr. Rudolf Habelt, Bonn.

———. 2015. 8 Million Neolithic Europeans: Social Demography and Social Archaeology on the Scope of Change: From the Near East to Scandinavia. In: *Paradigm Found: Archaeological Theory—Present, Past and Future: Essays in Honour of Evžen Neustupný*, edited by K. Kristiansen, L. Šmejda, and J. Turek, pp. 200–14. Oxbow, Oxford.

Müller, J., V.P.J. Arponen, R. Hoffman, and R. Ohlrau. 2015. The Appearance of Social Inequalities: Cases of Neolithic and Chalcolithic Societies. *Origini* 38(2):65–86.

Nankov, E. 2015. Urbanization. In: *A Companion to Ancient Thrace*, edited by J. Valeva, E. Nankov, and D. Graninger, pp. 399–411. Wiley Blackwell, Malden, MA.

Nanoglou, S. 2001. Social and Monumental Space in Neolithic Thessaly, Greece. *European Journal of Archaeology* 4(3):303–22.

Naroll, R. 1956. A Preliminary Index of Social Development. *American Anthropologist* 58(4):687–715.

Naumov, G. 2011. Visual and Conceptual Dynamism of the Neolithic Altars in the Republic of Macedonia. In: *Interdisziplinäre Forschungen der Kulturerbe auf dem Balkan*, edited by V. Nikolov, K. Bacvarov, and H. Popov, pp. 89–129. Nice, Sofia.

———. 2013. Embodied Houses: Social and Symbolic Agency of Neolithic Architecture in the Republic of Macedonia. In: *Tracking the Neolithic House in Europe: Sedentism, Architecture and Practice*, edited by D. Hoffman and J. Smyth, pp. 65–94. Springer, New York.

———. 2014. Neolithic Privileges: The Selection within Burials and Corporeality in the Balkans. *European Journal of Archaeology* 17(2):184–207.

———. 2015a. Early Neolithic Communities in the Republic of Macedonia. *Archeologické Rozhledy* 67(3):331–55.

———. 2015b. The Neolithic Bodies: Intramural Burials and Anthropomorphic Representations in the Republic of Macedonia. *Folia Archaeologica* 3:31–54.

———. 2020. Tells of Domestication: Early Neolithic Farming Settlements in Pelagonia: Vrbjanska Čuka (Macedonia) as a Case Study. In: *Current Approaches to Tells in the Prehistoric Old World: A Cross-Cultural Comparison from the Neolithic to the Iron Age*, edited by A. Blanco-González and T.L. Kienlin, pp. 111–24. Oxbow, Oxford.

Naumov, G., J. Gulevska, F. Antolin, A. Sabanov, R. Soteras, and K. Penezić. 2020. A Multidisciplinary Research on Veluška Tumba at Porodin (Pelagonia) in 2020. In: *The Neolithic of Macedonia: In Honor of Dragica Simoska*, edited by L. Fidanoski and G. Naumov, pp. 29–61. Center for Prehistoric Research, Skopje.

Naumov, G., A. Mitkoski, H. Talevski, +14 authors, and J. Bumerl. 2018a. Research on the Vrbjanska Čuka Site in 2017. *Balcanoslavica* 47(1):253–85.

Naumov, G., A. Mitkoski, A. Murgoski, J. Beneš, Đ. Milevski, M. Przybyla, V. Komarkova, M. Vychronova, and I. Stoimanovski. 2018b. Multidisciplinary Research at the Vrbjanska Čuka Site near Slavej in Pelagonia, 2016. *Archaeologia Adriatica* 12:99–141.

Naumov, G., A. Mitkoski, H. Talevski, I. Živaljević, J. Pendić, F. Antolin, D. Stojanoski, F.J. Gibaja, M. Nicollo, M. Przybyla, Đ. Milevski, V. Dimitrijević, Z. Blažeska, and S. Stefanović. 2021. Early Neolithic Tell of Vrbjanska Čuka in Pelagonia. *Praehistorische Zeitschrift* 96(2):345–81.

Needham, S.P., P. Northover, M. Uckelmann, and R. Tabor. 2012. South Cadbury: The Last of the Bronze Shields? *Archäologisches Korrespondenzblatt* 42(4):473–91.

Nekhrizov, G. 2005. Cult Places of the Thracians in the Eastern Rhodope Mountains (End of the 2nd–1st Millennium B.C.). In: *The Culture of Thracians and Their Neighbours: Proceedings of the International Symposium in Memory of Prof. Mieczyslaw Domaradszki, with a Round Table "Archaeological Map of Bulgaria,"* edited by J. Bouzek and L. Domaradzka, pp. 153–58. BAR International Series 1350. Archaeopress, Oxford.

———. 2008. Klasifikacionna shema na trapeznata keramika ot rannata zhelyazna epoha v Iztochnite Rodopi. In: *Phosphorion. Studia in Honorem Mariae Čičikova*, edited by D. Gergova, pp. 114–31. Akademichno izdatelstvo Prof. Marin Drinov, Sofia.

———. 2015. Dolmens and Rock-Cut Monuments. In: *A Companion to Ancient Thrace*, edited by J. Valeva, E. Nankov, and D. Graninger, pp. 126–43. Wiley Blackwell, Malden, MA.

Nekhrizov, G. and J. Tzvetkova. 2018. Contributions to the Periodization and Absolute Chronology of the Early Iron Age in South Thrace. *Archaeologia Bulgarica* 22(1):17–44.

Nemeskéri, J. and L. Lengyel. 1976. Neolithic Skeletal Finds. In: *Neolithic Macedonia: As Reflected by Excavation at Anza, Southeast Yugoslavia*, edited by M. Gimbutas, pp. 375–410. The Regents of the University of California, Los Angeles.

Nettle, D. and R.I.M. Dunbar. 1997. Social Markers and the Evolution of Reciprocal Exchange. *Current Anthropology* 38(1):93–99.

Neumann, D. 2009. Bemerkungen zu den Schwertern der Typenfamilie Sauerbrunn-Boiu-Keszthely. In: *Apen, Kult und Eisenzeit. Festschrift für Amei Lang zum 65. Geburtstag*, edited by J.M. Bagley, C. Eggl, D. Neumann, and M. Schefzik, pp. 97–114. Marie Leidorf, Rahden/Westfalen.

———. 2014. *Landschaften der Ritualisierung. Die Fundplätze kupfer- und bronzezeitlicher Metalldeponierungen zwischen Donau und Po*. De Gruyter, Berlin and Boston.

Nikolov, V. 1989. Das frühneolithische Haus von Sofia-Slatina: Eine Untersuchung zur vorgeschichtlichen Bautechnik. *Germania* 67:1–49.

———. 1991. Zur Interpretation der späteneolithischen Nekropole von Varna. In: *Die Kupferzeit als historische Epoche*, edited by J. Lichardus, pp. 157–66. Saarbrücker Beiträge zur Altertumskunde 55. Dr. Rudolf Habelt, Bonn.

———. 2010. Salt and Gold: Provadia-Solnitsata and the Varna Chalcolithic Cemetery. *Archäologisches Korrespondenzblatt* 40(4):487–501.

Nikolov, V. and K. Bacvarov (eds.). 2012. *Salt and Gold: The Role of Salt in Prehistoric Europe*. Faber, Veliko Tarnovo.

Nikov, K. 1999. "Aeolian" Bucchero in Thrace? *Archaeologia Bulgarica* 3(2):31–41.

———. 2011. The Meaning of the Regionalism in the Early Iron Age Pottery Decoration in South Thrace. In: *Interdisziplinäre Forschungen zum Kulturerbe auf der Balkanhalbinsel*, edited by V. Nikolov, K. Bacvarov, and H. Popov, pp. 209–27. Humboldt-Union in Bulgarien, Sofia.

———. 2012. *Monochrome Pottery from Apollonia Pontica: On Its Origin and Initial Distribution (Late VIIth–VIth Century BC)*. Faber, Veliko Tarnovo.

———. 2016. The Origin of the Early Iron Age Pottery Decoration in Southern Thrace. In: *Southeast Europe and Anatolia in Prehistory: Essays in Honour of Vassil Nikolov on His 65th Anniversary*, edited by K. Bacvarov and R. Gleser, pp. 457–64. Universitätsforschungen zur prähistorischen Archäologie 293. Dr. Rudolf Habelt, Bonn.

Novotná, M. 2014. *Die Vollgriffschwerter in der Slowakei*. Prähistorische Bronzefunde IV/18. Franz Steiner, Stuttgart.

Olalde, I., S. Brace, M.E. Allentoft, + 140 authors, and D. Reich. 2018. The Beaker Phenomenon and the Genomic Transformation of Northwest Europe. *Nature* 555:190–96.

Oltean, I.A. 2007. *Dacia: Landscape, Colonization and Romanization*. Routledge, London and New York.

Ortman, S.G. and G.D. Coffey. 2017. Settlement Scaling in Middle-Range Societies. *American Antiquity* 82(4):662–82.

Osgood, R. 1998. *Warfare in the LBA of North Europe*. BAR International Series 694. Archaeopress, Oxford.

O'Shea, J.M. and A. Nicodemus. 2019. '…the nearest run thing…': The Genesis and Collapse of a Bronze Age Polity in the Maros Valley of Southeastern Europe. In: *Coming Together: Comparative Approaches to Population Aggregation and Early Urbanization*, edited by A. Gyucha, pp. 61–80. State University of New York Press, Albany.

Otto, T., H. Thrane, and H. Vandkilde. 2006. Warfare and Society: Archaeological and Anthropological Perspectives. In: *Warfare and Society: Archaeological and Social Anthropological Perspectives*, edited by T. Otto, H. Thrane, and H. Vandkilde, pp. 9–19. Aarhus University Press, Aarhus.

Oxfam Annual Report. 2018. https://www.oxfam.org/sites/www.oxfam.org/files/file_attachments/bp-reward-work-not-wealth-220118-summ-en.pdf

Özdogan, M. 1998. Early Iron Age in Eastern Thrace and the Megalithic Monuments. In: *Thracians and Phrygians: Problems of Parallelism. Proceedings of an International Symposium on the Archaeology, History and Ancient Languages of Thrace and Phrygia, Ankara, 3–4 June 1995*, edited by N. Tuna, Z. Aktüre, and M. Lynch, pp. 29–40. Middle East Technical University, Faculty of Architecture, Ankara.

Pabst, S. 2013. Naue II-Schwerter mit Knaufzunge und die Aussenbeziehungen der Mykenischen Kriegerelite in Postpalatialer Zeit. *Jahrbuch des Römisch-Germanischen Zentralmuseums* 60:105–52.

Palavestra, A. 1984. *Kneževski grobovi starijeg gvozdenog doba na centralnom Balkanu*. Srpska akademija nauka i umetnosti, Balkanološki institut, Belgrade.

———. 1998. Landmarks of Power: Princely Tombs in the Central Balkan Iron Age. In: *The Archaeology of Value: Essays in Prestige and Processes of Valuation*, edited by D. Bailey, pp. 55–69. BAR International Series 730. Hedges, Oxford.

Panayotov, I. 1989. *Jamnata kulitura v bolgarskite zemi*. Razkopki i prouchvania 21. Arheologicheski institut i muzey, Sofia.

———. 1995. The Bronze Age in Bulgaria: Studies and Problems. In: *Prehistoric Bulgaria*, edited by D. Bailey and I. Panayotov, pp. 243–52. Monographs in World Archaeology 22. Prehistory Press, Madison, WI.

Papadopoulos, T.J. 1998. *The LBA Daggers of the Aegean I. The Greek Mainland*. Prähistorische Bronzefunde VI/11. Franz Steiner, Stuttgart.

Papazoglu, F. 1978. *The Central Balkan Tribes in Pre-Roman Times: Triballi, Autariatae, Dardanians, Scordisci and Moesians*. Adolf M. Hakkert, Amsterdam.

Pare, C.F.E. 2017. Frühes Eisen in Südeuropa: Die Ausbreitung einer technologischen Innovation am Übergang vom 2. zum 1. Jahrtausend v. Chr. in das nördliche Karpatenbecken in der Hallstattzeit. In: *Wirtschaft, Handel und Gesellschaften zwischen Ostalpen und Westpannonien*, edited by E. Miroššayová, C. Pare, and S. Stegmann-Rajtár, pp. 11–116. Archaeolingua, Budapest.

———. 2019. Rhetoric and Redundancy: Aspects of Hoard Deposition at the End of the Bronze Age. In: *Hallstatt und Italien. Festschrift für Markus Egg*, edited by H. Baitinger and M. Schönfelder, pp. 67–80. Römisch-Germanischen Zentralmuseums Press, Mainz.

———. (ed.). 2000. *Metals Make the World Go Round: The Supply and Circulation of Metals in Bronze Age Europe*. Oxbow, Oxford.

Parker Pearson, M. 2003. *The Archaeology of Death and Burial*. The History Press, Stroud.

———. 2005. Warfare, Violence and Slavery in Later Prehistory: An Introduction. In: *Warfare, Violence and Slavery in Prehistory*, edited by M. Parker Pearson and I.J.N. Thorpe, pp. 19–33. BAR International Series 1374. Archaeopress, Oxford.

Parkinson, W.A. 2006. *The Social Organization of the Early Copper Age Tribes on the Great Hungarian Plain*. Archaeopress, Oxford.

Parkinson, W.A., A. Gyucha, P. Karkanas, N. Papadopoulos, G. Tsartsidou, A. Sarris, P.R. Duffy, and R.W. Yerkes. 2018. A Landscape of Tells: Geophysics and Microstratigraphy at Two Neolithic Tell Sites on the Great Hungarian Plain. *Journal of Archaeological Science: Reports* 19:903–24.

Parović-Pešikan, M. 1986. Neki novi aspekti širenja egejske i grčke kulture na centralni Balkan. *Starinar* 36:19–47.

———. 1995. Zapažanja o mikenskom uticaju na području centralnog Balkana. *Starinar* 45–46:3–26.

Pârvan, V. 1926. *Getica: O protoistorie a Daciei*. Cultura Nationala, Bucharest.

———. 1928. *Dacia: An Outline of the Early Civilisation of the Carpatho-Danubian Countries*. Cambridge University Press, Cambridge.

Patay, P. 1968. Urnenfelderzeitliche Bronzeschilde im Karpatenbecken. *Germania* 46:241–48.

Pawn, I. 2012. Negotiating Identities during the Copper Age: A Bioarchaeological Study of Burial and Social Networks on the Hungarian Plain (5400–3500 BC). Ph.D dissertation, Department of Anthropology, Florida State University, Tallahassee.

Paynter, R.W. and R.H. McGuire. 1991. The Archaeology of Inequality: Material Culture, Domination, and Resistance. In: *The Archaeology of Inequality*, edited by R. McGuire and R. Paynter, pp. 1–27. Blackwell, Oxford.

Pearce, M. 2013. The Spirit of the Sword and Spear. *Cambridge Archaeological Journal* 23(1):55–67.

Penkova, P. and M. Mehofer. 2018. The Treasure of Valchitran: Production Technique. In: *Gold and Bronze: Metals, Technologies and Interregional Contacts in the Eastern Balkans during the Bronze Age*, edited by S. Alexandrov, Y. Dimitrova, H. Popov, B. Horejs, and K. Chukalev, pp. 208–14. National Archaeological Institute with Museum, Sofia.

Pernicka, E. 2018. The Chemical Composition of the Gold Finds from Valchitran Treasure. In: *Gold and Bronze: Metals, Technologies and Interregional Contacts in the Eastern Balkans during the Bronze Age*, edited by S. Alexandrov, Y. Dimitrova, H. Popov, B. Horejs, and K. Chukalev, pp. 215–22. National Archaeological Institute with Museum, Sofia.

Pernicka, E., B. Nessel, M. Mehofer, and E. Safta. 2016. Lead Isotope Analyses of Metal Objects from the Apa Hoard and Other Early and Middle Bronze Age Items from Romania. *Archaeologia Austriaca* 100:57–86.

Peroni, R. 1956. Zur Gruppierung mitteleuropäischer Griffzungendolche der späten Bronzezeit. *Badische Fundberichte* 20:69–92.

Peter, U. 1997. *Die Münzen der thrakischen Dynasten (5.–3. Jahrhundert v. Chr.): Hintergründe ihrer Prägung*. Akademie, Berlin.

Petres, É. and K. Jankovits. 2014. Der spätbronzezeitliche zweiteilige Bronzebrustpanzeraus der Donau in Ungarn. *Acta Archaeologica Academiae Scientiarum Hungaricae* 65:43–71.

Petrescu-Dîmbovița, M. 1978. *Die Sicheln in Rumänien*. Prähistorische Bronzefunde XVIII/1. C.H. Beck, München.

Petrova, E. 1991. Payonskite pleminya i payonskoto kralstvo vo II i I milenium pred n. e. *Macedoniae Acta Archaeologica* 12:1–128.

———. 1996. *Bryges in the Central Balkans in the 2nd and 1st Millennia BC*. Museum of Macedonia, Skopje.

———. 1999. *Paeonia in the 2nd and the 1st Millennia BC*. Monumenta Macedoniae 3. Museum of Macedonia, Skopje.

Pippidi, D.M. 1971. *I Greci nel basso Danubio dall'età arcaica alla conquista romana*. Il Saggiatore, Milano.

Pippidi, D.M. and D. Berciu. 1965. *Din istoria Dobrogei 1: Geti și Greci la Dunarea de jos din cele mai vechi timpuri pina la cucerirea romana*. Academiei Republicii Socialiste România, Bucharest.

Pool, C.A. 2012. The Formation of Complex Societies in Mesoamerica. In: *The Oxford Handbook of Mesoamerican Archaeology*, edited by D.L. Nichols and C.A. Pool, pp. 169–87. Oxford University Press, Oxford.

Popa, C.I. 2016. Territory, Subsistence Strategies and Mobility Patterns in the Coțofeni Communities. Case Study: The Hilly Area of the Sebeș Valley. In: *Prehistoric Settlements: Social, Economic and Cultural Aspects. Seven Studies in the Carpathian Area*, edited by F. Gogâltan and C. Cordoș, pp. 33–72. Mega, Cluj-Napoca.

Popov, D. 1999. *Trakologia*. Izdatelstvo LIK, Sofia.

Popov, H. 2002. *Urbanizatsia vav vatreshnite rayoni na Trakia i Iliria prez VI–I vek predi Hrista*. NOUS, Sofia.

———. 2015. Settlements. In: *A Companion to Ancient Thrace*, edited by J. Valeva, E. Nankov, and D. Graninger, pp. 109–25. Wiley Blackwell, Malden, MA.

———. 2018. Trebenishte: Elites, Luxury, and Resources. In: *100 Years of Trebenishte*, edited by P. Ardjanliev, K. Chukalev, T. Cvjetićanin, M. Damyanov, V. Krstić, A. Papazovska, and H. Popov, pp. 202–207. National Archaeological Institute with Museum and Bulgarian Academy of Sciences, Sofia.

Popović, P. 1996. Early La Tène between Pannonia and the Balkans. *Starinar* 47:105–25.

Popović, V. 1964. Les masques funéraires de la nécropole archaïque de Trebenište. *Archaeologia Iugoslavica* 5:33–44.

Porčić, M. 2012. Social Complexity and Inequality in the Late Neolithic of the Central Balkans: Reviewing the Evidence. *Documenta Praehistorica* 39:167–83.

———. 2019. Evaluating Social Complexity and Inequality in the Balkans between 6500 and 4200 BC. *Journal of Archaeological Research* 27(3):335–90.

Potrebica, H. 1998. Some Remarks on the Contacts between the Greek and the Hallstatt Culture Considering the Area of Northern Croatia in the Early Iron Age. In: *Papers from the 3rd Annual Meeting of EAA at Ravenna 1997*, Volume 1: *Pre- and Protohistory*, edited by M. Pearce and M. Tosi, pp. 241–49. BAR International Series 717. Archaeopress, Oxford.

———. 2003. Požeška kotlina i Donja Dolina u komunikacijskoj mreži starijeg željeznog doba. *Opuscula Archaeologica* 27:217–42.

———. 2008. Contacts between Greece and Pannonia in the Early Iron Age with Special Concern to the Area of Thessalonica. In: *Import and Imitation in Archaeology*, edited by P. Biehl

and Y. Rassamakin, pp. 187–212. Schriften des Zentrums für Archäologie und Kulturgeschichte des Schwartzmeerraumes 11. Beier&Beran, Langenweissbach.

———. 2010. Religijski aspekti keramičkih nalaza u pogrebnom ritualu starijeg željeznog doba. *Histria Antiqua* 18(1):163–72.

———. 2012a. Kaptol: A Centre on the Periphery of the Hallstatt World. In: *Wege und Transport*, edited by C. Tappert, Ch. Later, J. Fries-Knoblach, P.C. Ramsl, P. Trebsche, S. Wefers, and J. Wiethold, pp. 235–45. Beiträge zur Ur- und Frühgeschichte Mitteleuropas 6. Beier&Beran, Langenweissbach.

———. 2012b. Religious Phenomena of the Hallstatt Communities of Southern Pannonia. In: *Iron Age Rites and Rituals in the Carpathian Basin*, edited by S. Berecki, pp. 9–30. Bibliotheca Mvsei Marisiensis, Seria Archaeologica 5. Mega, Târgu Mureș.

———. 2013. *Kneževi željeznoga doba. Arheološke studije halštatske kulture*. Meridijani, Samobor.

———. 2016. The Princes of the Crossroads: The Early Iron Age in Northern Croatia. In: *Croatia at the Crossroads. A Consideration of Archaeological and Historical Connectivity*, edited by D. Davison, V. Gaffney, P. Miracle, and J. Sofaer, pp. 109–22. Archaeopress, London.

———. 2019. The Kaptol Group and the Požega Valley. *Arheološki Vestnik* 70:487–515.

Potrebica, H. and J.K. Fileš Kramberger. 2021. Early Iron Age Textile Production Tools from the Požega Valley in Croatia. *Archaeological Textiles Review* 62:83–100.

Potrebica, H. and J. Mavrović Mokos. 2016. The Kaptol Group in the Early Iron Age Communication Network. In: *Cultural Encounters in Iron Age Europe*, edited by I. Armit, H. Potrebica, M. Črešnar, P. Mason, and L. Büster, pp. 39–65. Archaeolingua, Budapest.

Potrebica, H. and M. Rakvin. 2019. Tumulus IV on the Kaptol-Čemernica Cemetery: Revision Excavation. *Vjesnik Arheološkog muzeja u Zagrebu* 52:31–81.

Pouilloux, J. 1950. Dropionroi des Peones. *Bulletin de correspondance hellénique* 74:22–32.

Prendi, F. 2018. *The Prehistoric Settlement of Maliq*. Academy for Albanological Studies, Tirana.

Prendi, F. and S. Aliu. 1971. Vendbanimi neolitik në fshatin Kamnik të rrethit të Kolonjës (Gërmime të vitit 1970). *Iliria* 1:13–30.

Prien, R. 2005. *Archäologie und Migration: Vergleichende Studien zur archäologischen Nachweisbarkeit von Wanderungsbewegungen*. Universitätsforschungen zur prähistorischen Archäologie 120. Dr. Rudolf Habelt, Bonn.

Puskás, J. 2018. Middle Bronze Age Settlement Patterns and Metal Discoveries in the Valley of the Black River. In: *Bronze Age Connectivity in the Carpathian Basin*, edited by B. Rezi and R.E. Németh, pp. 217–78. Mega, Târgu Mureș.

Rabadjiev, K. 2015. Religion. In: *A Companion to Ancient Thrace*, edited by J. Valeva, E. Nankov, and D. Graninger, pp. 443–56. Wiley Blackwell, Malden, MA.

Raczky, P. 2015. Settlement in South-East Europe. In: *The Oxford Handbook of Neolithic Europe*, edited by C. Fowler, J. Harding, and D. Hofmann, pp. 235–54. Oxford University Press, Oxford.

———. 2018. A Complex Monument in the Making at the Late Neolithic Site of Polgár-Csőszhalom (Hungary). In: *Across the Mediterranean–Along the Nile: Studies in Egyptology, Nubiology and Late Antiquity Dedicated to László Török on the Occasion of His 75th Birthday*, edited by A.T. Bács, Á. Bollók, and T. Vida, pp. 15–60. Archaeolingua, Budapest.

Raczky, P. and A. Anders. 2008. Late Neolithic Spatial Differentiation at Polgár-Csőszhalom, Eastern Hungary. In: *Living Well Together? Settlement and Materiality in the Neolithic of South-East and Central Europe*, edited by D. Bailey, A. Whittle, and D. Hofmann, pp. 35–53. Oxbow, Oxford.

———. 2010. Activity Loci and Data for Spatial Division at a Late Neolithic Site-Complex (Polgár-Csőszhalom: A Case Study). In: *Leben auf dem Tell als soziale Praxis*, edited by S. Hansen, pp. 143–63. Eurasien-Abteilung des Deutschen Archäologischen Instituts, Kolloquien zur Vor- und Frühgeschichte 14. Dr. Rudolf Habelt, Bonn.

———. 2017. The Chosen Ones: Unconventional Burials at Polgár-Csőszhalom (North-East Hungary) from the Fifth Millennium Cal BC. In: *The Neolithic of Europe. Papers in Honour of Alasdair Whittle*, edited by P. Bickle, V. Cummings, D. Hofmann, and J. Pollard, pp. 63–81. Oxbow, Oxford.

Raczky, P., A. Anders, and L. Bartosiewicz. 2011. The Enclosure System of Polgár-Csőszhalom and Its Interpretation. In: *Sozialarchäologische Perspektiven: Gesellshaftlicher Wandel 5000–1500 v. Chr. Zwischen Atlantik und Kaukasus*, edited by S. Hansen and J. Müller, pp. 57–79. Archäologie in Eurasien 24. Philipp von Zabern, Darmstadt.

Raczky, P., L. Domboróczki, and Zs. Hajdú. 2007. The Site of Polgár-Csőszhalom and Its Cultural and Chronological Connections with the Lengyel Culture. In: *The Lengyel, Polgár and Related Cultures in the Middle/Late Neolithic in Central Europe*, edited by J.K. Kozłowski and P. Raczky, pp. 49–70. Polska Akademia Umiejętności, Kraków.

Raczky, P. and A. Füzesi. 2016. Öcsöd-Kováshalom: A Retrospective Look at the Interpretations of a Late Neolithic Site. *Dissertationes Archaeologicae ex Instituto Archaeologico Universitatis de Rolando Eötvös Nominatae* Ser. 3., Vol. 4:9–42.

Raczky, P., A. Füzesi, and A. Anders. 2018. Domestic and Symbolic Activities on a Tell-Like Settlement at Öcsöd-Kováshalom in the Tisza Region. In: *The Image of Divinity in the Neolithic and Eneolithic: Ways of Communication*, edited by S.A. Luca, pp. 117–40. Karl A. Romstorfer, Suceava.

Raczky, P. and K. Sebők. 2014. The Outset of Polgár-Csőszhalom Tell and the Archaeological Context of a Special Central Building. In: *Archeovest II: In Honorem Gheorghe Lazarovici*, edited by S. Forțiu and A. Cîntar, pp. 51–100. JatePress, Szeged.

Radivojević, M. and T. Rehren. 2016. Paint It Black: The Rise of Metallurgy in the Balkans. *Journal of Archaeological Method and Theory* 22(1):200–37.

Radivojević, M., T. Rehren, E. Pernicka, D. Šljivar, M. Brauns, and D. Borić. 2010. On the Origins of Extractive Metallurgy: New Evidence from Europe. *Journal of Archaeological Science* 37(11):2775–87.

Randsborg, K. 2002. Wetlands Hoards. *Oxford Journal of Archaeology* 21(4):415–18.

Rappaport, R. 1971. The Sacred in Human Evolution. *Annual Review of Ecology and Systematics* 2:23–44.

Rascovan, N., K.G. Sjögren, K. Kristiansen, R. Nielsen, E. Willerslev, C. Desnues, and S. Rasmussen. 2019. Emergence and Spread of Basal Lineages of Yersinia Pestis during the Neolithic Decline. *Cell* 176(1–2):295–305.

Rasmussen, S., M.E. Allentoft, K. Nielsen, + 27 authors, and E. Willerslev. 2015. Early Divergent Strains of *Yersinia pestis* in Eurasia 5000 Years Ago. *Cell* 163(3):571–82.

Rassamakin, Y.Y. 2011. Eneolithic Burial Mounds in the Black Sea Steppe: From the First Burial Symbols to Monumental Ritual Architecture. In: *Ancestral Landscape. Burial Mounds in the Copper and Bronze Ages (Central and Eastern Europe – Balkans – Adriatic – Aegean, 4th–2nd Millennium B.C.)*, edited by E. Borgna and S. Müller Celka, pp. 293–306. Maison de l'Orient et de la Mediterranée, Lyon.

Renfrew, C. 1974. Beyond a Subsistence Economy: The Evolution of Social Organization in Prehistoric Europe. In: *Reconstructing Complex Societies: An Archaeological Colloquium*, edited by C.B. Moore, pp. 69–85. American Schools of Oriental Research, Cambridge, MA.

———. 1986. Varna and the Emergence of Wealth in Prehistoric Europe. In: *The Social Life of Things: Commodities in Cultural Perspective*, edited by A. Appadurai, pp. 141–68. Cambridge University Press, Cambridge.

Rezi, B. 2011. Voluntary Destruction and Fragmentation in Late Bronze Age Hoards from Central Transylvania. In: *Bronze Age Rites and Rituals in the Carpathian Basin*, edited by S. Berecki, R.E. Németh, and B. Rezi, pp. 303–34. Bibliotheca Mvsei Marisiensis, Seria Archaeologica 4. Mega, Târgu Mureș.

———. 2017. Újabb bográcslelet Erdőszentgyörgyről (Sângeorgiu de Pădure, Ro). *Archaeologiai Értesítő* 142:35–73.

Richerson, P.J. and R. Boyd. 2005. *Not by Genes Alone: How Culture Transformed Human Evolution*. University of Chicago Press, Chicago.

Rișcuța, N.C. 2001. O nouă descoperire arheologică la Baia de Criș (jud. Hunedoara). *Thraco-Dacica* 22(1–2):139–72.

Roberts, S.G.B. 2010. Constraints on Social Networks. In: *Social Brain, Distributed Mind*, edited by R. Dunbar, C. Gamble, and J. Gowlett, pp. 115–34. Oxford University Press, Oxford.

Robson, J. 1857. Thracia. In: *Dictionary of Greek and Roman Geography*, Volume II, edited by W. Smith, pp. 1176–90. Walton and Baberly, London.

Rosenstock, E. 2009. *Tells in Südwestasien und Südosteuropa: Verbreitung, Entstehung und Definition eines Siedlungsphänomens.* Urgeschichtliche Studien 2. Greiner, Remshalden.

Roska, M. 1933. Le dépôt de haches en cuivré de Baniabic, département de Turda-Arieș. *Dacia* 3–4:352–55.

———. 1959. A bányabükki rézlelet. *Folia Archaeologica* 11:25–35.

Rotea, M. 2009. *Pagini din preistoria Transilvaniei: Epoca bronzului.* Mega, Cluj-Napoca.

Rousseau, J.J. 1754. *Discourse on the Origin and Basis of Inequality Among Men.*

Rousseva, M. 2000. *Thracian Cult Architecture in Bulgaria.* Izdatelstvo Ya, Yambol.

———. 2002. *Trakiyska grobnichna arhitektura v bulgarskite zemi prez V–III v. pr. n. e.* Izdatelstvo Ya, Yambol.

Rustoiu, A. 2012. The Celts and Indigenous Populations from the Southern Carpathian Basin: Intercommunity Communication Strategies. In: *Iron Age Rites and Rituals in the Carpathian Basin*, edited by S. Berecki, pp. 357–90. Bibliotheca Mvsei Marisiensis, Seria Archaeologica 5. Mega, Târgu Mureș.

Rusu, M. 1963. Die Verbreitung der Bronzehorte in Transsilvanien vom Ende der Bronzezeit bis in die mittlere Hallstattzeit. *Dacia* 7:177–210.

———. 1981. Bemerkungen zu den Grossen Werkstätten- und Giessereifunden aus Siebenbürgen. In: *Studien zur Bronzezeit: Festschrift für Wilhelm Albert v. Brunn*, edited by H. Lorenz, pp. 375–402. Philipp von Zabern, Mainz am Rhein.

Salzani, L. 1986. Gli schinieri di Desmontá (Verona). *Aquileia Nostra* 57:386–91.

Sandars, N.K. 1974. Thracians, Phrygians and Iron. *Thracia* 3:195–202.

———. 1961. The First Aegean Swords and Their Ancestry. *American Journal of Archaeology* 65(1):17–29.

Sanev, D. 2006. Anthropomorphic Cult Plastic of Anzabegovo-Vršnik Cultural Groups of the Republic of Macedonia. In: *Homage to Milutin Garašanin*, edited by N. Tasić and C. Grozdanov, pp. 71–192. Serbian Academy of Sciences and Arts and Macedonian Academy of Sciences and Arts, Belgrade.

Sarafov, T. 1974. Trakiyskite satri. Prinos kam etnogenezisa na trakiyskite plemena. *Godishnik na Sofiyskia universitet, Fakultet zapadni filologii* 67(1):119–91.

Sastre, I. 2008. Community, Identity, and Conflict: Iron Age Warfare in the Iberian Northwest. *Current Anthropology* 49(6):1021–51.

Sava, V. and F. Gogâltan. 2017. The Bronze Age Fortifications in Munar "Wolfsberg," Arad County. The 2014 and 2017 Archaeological Researches. *Analecta Archaeologica Ressoviensia* 12:75–100.

Sava, V., F. Gogâltan, and R. Krause. 2019. First Steps in the Dating of the Bronze Age Mega-Fort in Sântana-Cetatea Veche (Southwestern Romania). In: *Bronze Age Fortresses in Europe*, edited by S. Hansen and R. Krause, pp. 161–76. Dr. Rudolf Habelt, Bonn.

Schauer, P. 1979. Eine urnenfelderzeitliche Kampfweise. *Archäologisches Korrespondenzblatt* 9:69–80.

———. 1982a. Deutungs- und Rekonstruktionsversuche Bronzezeitlicher Kompositpanzer. *Archäologisches Korrespondenzblatt* 12:335–49.

———. 1982b. Die Beinschinen der späten Bronze- und frühen Eisenzeit. *Jahrbuch des Römisch-Germanischen Zentralmuseums* 29:100–55.

———. 1986. *Die Goldblechkegel der Bronzezeit: Ein Beitrag zur Kulturverbindung zwischen Orient und Mitteleuropa.* Monographien, Römisch-Germanisches Zentralmuseum, Forschungsinstitut für Vor- und Frühgeschichte 8. Dr. Rudolf Habelt, Bonn.

Scheidel, W. and S.J. Freisen. 2009. The Size of the Economy and the Distribution of Income in the Roman Empire. *Journal of Roman Studies* 99:61–91.

Schulting, R.J. and L. Fibiger (eds.). 2012. *Sticks, Stones, and Broken Bones: Neolithic Violence in a European Perspective.* Oxford University Press, Oxford.

Schwenzer, S. 2004. *Frühbronzezeitliche Vollgriffdolche: Typologische, chronologische und technische Studien auf der Grundlage einer Materialaufnahme von Hans-Jürgen Hundt.* Kataloge Vor- und Frühgeschichtlicher Altertümer 36. Römisch-Germanischen Zentralmuseums, Mainz.

Scott, J. 2010. *The Art of Not Being Governed: An Anarchist History of Upland Southeast Asia.* Yale University Press, New Haven, CT.

Šemrov, A. and P. Turk (eds.). 2009. *Neolithic Art in the Republic of Macedonia.* Narodni Muzej Slovenije, Ljubljana.

Shalganova, T. and A. Gotzev. 1995. Problems of Research on the Early Iron Age. In: *Prehistoric Bulgaria*, edited by D. Bailey and I. Panayotov, pp. 327–43. Monographs in World Archaeology 22. Prehistory Press, Madison, WI.

Sherratt, A. 1987. Warriors and Traders: Bronze Age Chiefdoms in Central Europe. In: *Origins: The Roots of European Civilisation*, edited by B.W. Cunliffe, pp. 54–66. BBC Books, London.

———. 1993. What Would a Bronze Age World System Look Like? Relations between Temperate Europe and the Mediterranean in Later Prehistory. *European Journal of Archaeology* 1(2):1–58.

———. 1994. The Emergence of Elites: Earlier Bronze Age Europe, 2500–1300 BC. In: *The Oxford Illustrated Prehistory of Europe*, edited by B. Cunliffe, pp. 244–76. Oxford University Press, Oxford.

Sherratt, A. and T. Taylor. 1989. Metal Vessels in Bronze Age Europe and the Context of Vulchetrun. In: *Thracians and Mycenaeans: Proceedings of the Fourth International Congress of Thracology, Rotterdam, 24–26 September 1984*, edited by J. Best and N. de Vries, pp. 107–34. Brill, Leiden.

Shishlina, N. 2008. *Reconstruction of the Bronze Age of the Caspian Steppes: Life Styles and Life Ways of Pastoral Nomads*. BAR International Series 1876. Archaeopress, Oxford.

———. 2013. The Steppe and the Caucasus during the Bronze Age: Mutual Relationships and Mutual Enrichments. In: *Counterpoint: Essays in Archaeology and Heritage Studies in Honour of Professor Kristian Kristiansen*, edited by S. Bergerant and S. Sabatini, pp. 53–60. BAR International Series 2508. Oxford University Press, Oxford and New York.

Shishlina, N., E.P. Zazovskaya, J. van der Plicht, R.E.M. Hedges, V.S. Sevastyanov, and O.A. Chichagova. 2009. Paleoecology, Subsistence and 14C Chronology of the Eurasian Caspian Steppe Bronze Age. *Radiocarbon* 51(2):481–99.

Shishlina, N., E.P. Zazovskaya, J. van der Plicht, and V.S. Sevastyanov. 2012. Isotopes, Plants, and Reservoir Effects: Case Study from the Caspian Steppe Bronze Age. *Radiocarbon* 54(3–4):749–60.

Siedlaczek, M. 2011. Der experimentelle Nachguss von bronzezeitlichen Schwertern. *Experimentelle Archäologie in Europa* 10:109–19.

Siklósi, Zs. 2013. *Traces of Social Inequality during the Late Neolithic in the Eastern Carpathian Basin*. Dissertationes Pannonicae Ser. 4., Vol. 3. Eötvös Loránd University, Institute of Archaeology, Budapest.

Šimek, M. 2004. Grupa Martijanec–Kaptol. In: *Ratnici na rezmeđu istoka i zapada – starije željezno doba u kontinentalnoj Hrvatskoj*, edited by D. Balen-Letunić, pp. 79–129. Exhibition Catalog. Arheološki muzej u Zagrebu, Zagreb.

Simon, E. 1960. Der Goldschatz von Panagjuriste: Eine Schöpfung der Alexanderzeit. *Antike Kunst* 3:3–29.

Simoska, D. and V. Sanev. 1976. *Praistorija vo Centralna Pelagonija*. Naroden Muzej, Bitola.

Sîrbu, V. 2003. Funerary Practices in the Iron Age between the Carpathians and the Danube. In: *Burial Customs in the Bronze and Iron Age: Symposium Čačak, 4–8 September 2002*, edited by R. Vasić, pp. 139–70. Narodni Muzej, Čačak.

Sîrbu, V. and R. Ştefănescu (eds.). 2007. *Iron Age Sanctuaries and Cult Places in the Thracian World: Proceedings of the International Colloquium Braşov, 19–21 October 2006*. C2 Design, Braşov.

Škorpil, H. and K. Škorpil. 1898. *Mogili: Pametnitsi iz Bulgarsko*. Pchela, Plovdiv.

Slavchev, V. (ed.). 2008. *The Varna Eneolithic Necropolis and Problems of Prehistory in Southeast Europe*. Acta Musei Varnaensis 6. Regionalen Istoričeski Muzej, Varna.

Šljivar, D. 2006. The Earliest Copper Metallurgy in the Central Balkans. *Journal of Mining and Metallurgy* 12(2–3):93–104.

Smith, M.E. 2019. Energized Crowding and the Generative Role of Settlement Aggregation and Urbanization. In: *Coming Together: Comparative Approaches to Population Aggregation and Early Urbanization*, edited by A. Gyucha, pp. 37–58. State University of New York Press, Albany.

Smith, M.E., T.A. Kohler, and G.M. Feinman. 2018. Studying Inequality's Deep Past. In: *Ten Thousand Years of Inequality: The Archaeology of Wealth Differences*, edited by M.E. Smith and T.A. Kohler, pp. 3–38. University of Arizona Press, Tucson.

Snodgrass, A. 1964. *Early Greek Armour and Weapons*. University Press, Edinburgh.

———. 1982. *Arms and Armours of the Greeks*. Cornell University Press, Ithaca, NY.

Sokolovska, V. 1990. Payonskoto pleme agriyani i vrskite so Damastion. *Macedoniae Acta Archaeologica* 11:9–34.

Soroceanu, T. 1995. Die Fundumstände bronzezeitlicher Deponierungen: Ein Beitrag zur Hortdeutung beiderseits der Karpaten. In: *Bronzefunde aus Rumänien I*, edited by T. Soroceanu, pp. 15–80. Prähistorische Archäologie in Südosteuropa 10. V. Spiess, Berlin.

———. 2005. Zu den Fundumständen der europäischen Metallgefäße bis in das 8. Jh. v. Chr. Ein Beitrag zu deren religiongeschichtlicher Deutung. In: *Bronzefunde aus Rumänien II. Beiträge zur Veröffentlichung und Deutung bronze- und älterhallstattzeitlicher Metallfunde in europäischem Zusammenhang*, edited by T. Soroceanu, pp. 387–428. Biblioteca Muzeului Bistriţa, Seria Historica 11. Accent, Cluj-Napoca.

———. 2008. *Bronzefunde aus Rumänien. III. Die vorskythenzeitlichen Metallgefäße im Gebiet des heutigen Rumänien*. Accent, Bistriţa and Cluj-Napoca.

———. 2011a. Le guerrier des Carpates à l'âge du Bronze: Particularités régionales et traits communs continentaux. In: *L'armement et l'image du guerrier dans les sociétés anciennes: De l'objet à la tombe*, edited by L. Baray, M. Honegger, and M.-H. Dias-Meirinho, pp. 227–72. Universitaires de Dijon Press, Dijon.

———. 2011b. "GLADIUS BARBARICO RITU HUMI FIGITUR NUDUS": Schriftliches, Bildliches und Ethnologisches zur Bedeutung der Schwerter und der

Schwertdeponierungen außerhalb des militärischen Verwendungsbereiches. *Tyragetia* 5(1):39–116.

———. 2012. *Die Kupfer- und Bronzedepots der frühen und mittleren Bronzezeit in Rumänien. Depozitele de obiecte din cupru și bronz din România: Epoca timpurie și mijlocie a bronzului*. Accent, Cluj-Napoca and Bistrița.

Soroceanu, T., B. Rezi, and R. Németh. 2017. *Der Bronzedepotfund von Bandul de Câmpie, jud. Mures/Mezőbánd, Maros-Megye: Beiträge zur Erforschung der spätbronzezeitlichen Metallindustrie in Siebenbürgen*. Universitätsforschungen zur prähistorischen Archäologie 307. Dr. Rudolf Habelt, Bonn.

Sperber, L. 1999. Zu den Schwertträgern im Westlichenkreis der Urnenfelderkultur: Profane und religiöse Aspekte. In: *Eliten in der Bronzezeit*, edited by V.L. Aravantinos, J.A. Barceló, and Ch. Bockisch-Bräuer, pp. 605–59. Römisch-Germanischen Zentralmuseum Monographien 43. Dr. Rudolf Habelt, Mainz.

———. 2003. Wer trug den goldenen Hut? Überlegungen zur gesellschaftlichen Einbindung der Goldkegel vom Typus Schifferstadt. In: *Gold und Kult der Bronzezeit*, edited by T. Springer, pp. 204–19. Germanisches Nationalmuseum, Nürnberg.

Spiridonov, T. 1979. Selishtnata sistema v drevna Trakia prez I hil. pr. n. e. *Thracia Antiqua* 5:67–92.

Stancheva, M. 1973. Trakiyskiat zlaten sad ot Sofia. *Muzei i pametnitsi na kulturata* 3:59–63.

Stapleton, L. 2014. The Prehistoric Burial Customs. In: *The Excavation of a Prehistoric Burial Tumulus at Löfkend, Albania*. Volume I: *Text*, edited by J.K. Papadopoulos, S.P. Morris, L. Bejko, and L.A. Schepartz, pp. 193–226. Cotsen Institute of Archaeology Press, University of California, Los Angeles.

Stare, F. 1957. *Inventaria Archaeologica: Corpus des Ensembles Archeologiques. Jugoslavija 1 (feuilles Y1–Y10)*. Société Archéologique de Yougoslavie, Beograd.

Starnini E., Gy. Szakmány, S. Józsa, Zs. Kasztovszky, V. Szilágyi, B. Maróti, B. Voytek, and F. Horváth. 2015. Lithics from the Tell Site Hódmezővásárhely-Gorzsa (Southeast Hungary): Typology, Technology, Use and Raw Material Strategies during the Late Neolithic (Tisza Culture). In: *Neolithic and Copper Age between the Carpathians and the Aegean Sea. Chronologies and Technologies from the 6th to the 4th Millennium B.C.E.*, edited by S. Hansen, P. Raczky, A. Anders, and A. Reingruber, pp. 105–28. Dr. Rudolf Habelt, Bonn.

Sterelny, K. 2019. The Origins of Multi-Level Society. *Topoi* 40:207–20.

Sterelny, K. and T. Watkins. 2015. Neolithization in Southwest Asia in a Context of Niche Construction Theory. *Cambridge Archaeological Journal* 25(3):673–705.

Stocker, S.R. and J. Davis. 2006. The Earliest History of Apollonia: Heroic Reflections from Beyond the Acropolis. In: *New*

Directions in Albanian Archaeology, edited by L. Bejko and R. Hodges, pp. 85–93. ICAA, Tirana.

Stoia, A. 1989. The Beginning of Iron Technology in Romania (1200–700 BC). In: *The Bronze Age–Iron Age Transition in Europe*, edited by M.L. Stig-Sorenson and R. Thomas, pp. 43–67. BAR International Series 483. Archaeopress, Oxford.

Stoyanov, T. 1990. Grobnichnata arhitektura v Severoiztochna Trakia v svetlinata na kontaktite s Mala Azia (VI–III v. pr. n. e.). *Terra Antiqua Balcanica* 4:122–33.

———. 1992. Pogrebalnite obichai v Severoiztochna Trakia prez rannozhelyaznata epoha v svetlinata na novite prouchvania. In: *Helis I. Getskite zemi prez bronzovata i zhelyaznata epoha*, edited by D. Gergova, pp. 82–96. Arheologicheski institut s muzey, Sofia.

———. 1997. *Sboryanovo I. Mogilen nekropol ot rannozhelyaznata epoha*. Svyat Nauka, Sofia.

———. 1998a. Sakrovishteto ot Borovo v arheologicheski i istoricheski kontekst. *Seminarium Thracicum* 3 (*Parvi akademichni chetenia v pamet na akademik Gavril Kazarow*):65–90.

———. 1998b. Who was Buried in the Caryatids' Tomb at Sveshtari? *Thracia* 12:103–7.

———. 2004. Panagyurskoto sakrovishte: izobrazitelna programa i prinadlezhnost. In: *Dokladi ot Vtori mexhdunaroden simpozium "Panagyurskoto sakrovishte i trakiyskata kultura," Panagyurishte, 8–9 dekemvri 1999*, edited by D. Agre and G. Kitov, pp. 11–30. Fondatsia Trakiyska drevnost, Sofia.

———. 2015a. Borovo: un cadeau royal. In: *L'Épopée des rois thraces, des guerres médiques aux invasions celtes, 479–278 av. J.-C. Découvertes archéologiques en Bulgarie*, edited by J.-L. Martinez, A. Baralis, N. Mathieux, T. Stoyanov, and M. Tonkova, pp. 212–19. Somogy éditions d'art, Paris.

———. 2015b. Le trésor de Panagyurishte. In: *L'Épopée des rois thraces, des guerres médiques aux invasions celtes, 479–278 av. J.-C. Découvertes archéologiques en Bulgarie*, edited by J.-L. Martinez, A. Baralis, N. Mathieux, T. Stoyanov, and M. Tonkova, pp. 220–29. Somogy éditions d'art, Paris.

——— (ed.). 2015c. *Sboryanovo, Volume III: The Thracian City: City Planning, Fortification System, Architecture*. History Museum Isperih and University St. Kliment Ohridski, Sofia.

———. 2015d. Warfare. In: *A Companion to Ancient Thrace*, edited by J. Valeva, E. Nankov, and D. Graninger, pp. 426–42. Wiley Blackwell, Malden, MA.

Stoyanov, T., Z. Mihaylova, K. Nikov, M. Nikolaeva, and D. Stoyanova. 2006. *The Getic Capital in Sboryanovo: 20 Years of Investigations*. Studio DADA, Sofia.

Stoyanov, T. and D. Stoyanova. 2011. Problemi na hronologiata i kulturnia kontekst na nyakoi ranni grobnitsi ot Kazanlashkata dolina. In: *Problemi i izsledvania na trakiyskata kultura* 5:106–26. Irita, Kazanlak.

———. 2016. Early Tombs of Thrace: Questions of the Chronology and the Cultural Context. In: *Tumulus as Sema: Space, Politics, Culture and Religion in the First Millennium BC,* Volume 1, edited by O. Henry and U. Kelp, pp. 313–37. De Gruyter, Berlin.

Stoyanova, D. 2015. Tomb Architecture. In: *A Companion to Ancient Thrace,* edited by J. Valeva, E. Nankov, and D. Graninger, pp. 158–79. Wiley Blackwell, Malden, MA.

Stratimirović, G. 1893. Ausgrabungen auf der Hochebene Glasinac im Jahre 1891. *Mitteilungen der Antropologischen Gesellschaft in Wien* 1:113–25.

Strauss, B. 2009. *The Spartacus War.* Simon&Schuster, New York.

Sutcliffe, A., R. Dunbar, J. Binder, and H. Arrow. 2012. Relationships and the Social Brain: Integrating Psychological and Evolutionary Perspectives. *British Journal of Psychology* 103(2):149–68.

Suttles, W. (ed.). 1990. *Handbook of North American Indians*, Volume 7: *Northwest Coast.* Smithsonian Institute, Washington, D.C.

Svoronos, J.N. 1919. *L'hellénisme primitif de la Macédoine prouvé par la numismatique et l'or du Pangée (extrait de JIAN 19).* Ernest Leroux and M. Eleftheroudakis, Paris and Athens.

Szabó, G. 1994. A Kárpát-medencei késő bronzkori sisakok készítésének problémái egy újabb lelet alapján. In: *A kőkortól a középkorig. Tanulmányok Trogmayer Ottó 60. születésnapjára,* edited by G. Lőrinczy, pp. 219–27. Csongrád Megyei Múzeumok Igazgatósága, Szeged.

Szabó, G.V. 2013. Late Bronze Age Stolen: New Data on the Illegal Acquisition and Trade of Bronze Age Artefacts in the Carpathian Basin. In: *Moments in Time. Papers Presented to Pál Raczky on His 60th Birthday,* edited by A. Anders and G. Kulcsár, pp. 793–815. Prehistoric Studies 1. L'Harmattan, Budapest.

———. 2019a. *Bronze Age Treasures in Hungary: The Quest for Buried Weapons, Tools and Jewellery.* Archaeolingua, Budapest.

———. 2019b. *Bronzkori kincsek Magyarországon: Földbe rejtett fegyverek, eszközök, ékszerek nyomában.* Archaeolingua, Budapest.

Szabó, G.V. and M. Bálint. 2016. Hajdúböszörmény 2.0: An Old Hoard in a New Perspective. *Hungarian Archaeology, E-Journal,* Summer 2016:1–10.

Szabó, G.V. and P. Czukor. 2017. Late Bronze Age Golden Greave from the Outskirts of Szeged. *Hungarian Archaeology, E-Journal,* Summer 2017:1–9.

Szakmány, Gy., E. Starnini, F. Horváth, V. Szilágyi, and Zs. Kasztovszky. 2009. Investigating Trade and Exchange Patterns during the Late Neolithic: First Results of the Archaeometric Analyses of the Raw Materials for the Polished and Ground Stone Tools from Tell Gorzsa (SE Hungary). In: *MOMOSZ VI,* edited by G. Ilon, pp. 369–83. Field Service for Cultural Heritage and Vas County's Museum Directorate, Budapest and Szombathely.

Szathmári, I. 2005. Folyókból előkerült bronzkori kardleletek a Magyar Nemzeti Múzeum gyűjteményében. *Communicationes Archaeologicae Hungariae* 2005:143–66.

Szentmiklosi, A., B.S. Heeb, J. Heeb, A. Harding, R. Krause, and H. Becker. 2011. Corneşti-Iarcuri: A Bronze Age Town in the Romanian Banat? *Antiquity* 85(329):819–38.

Szeverényi, V. 2013. The Earliest Copper Shaft-Hole Axes in the Carpathian Basin: Interaction, Chronology and Transformations of Meaning. In: *Moments in Time: Papers Presented to Pál Raczky on His 60th Birthday,* edited by A. Anders, G. Kulcsár, G. Kalla, V. Kiss, and G.V. Szabó, pp. 661–69. L'Harmattan, Budapest.

Tacheva, M. 1997. *Istoria na bulgarskite zemi v drevnostta prez elinisticheskata i rimskata epoha.* Second edition. St. Kliment Ohridski University Press, Sofia.

——— [Tatscheva]. 1998. Getas Ēdoneon Basileus. In: *Stephanos nomismatikos: Edith Schönert-Geiss zum 65. Geburtstag,* edited by U. Peter, pp. 613–26. Akademie Verlag, Berlin.

———. 2006. *Tsarete na drevna Trakia, kniga parva.* Agato, Sofia.

Tálas, L. and P. Raczky (eds.). 1987. *The Late Neolithic of the Tisza Region: A Survey of Recent Excavations and Their Findings.* Kossuth Press and Directorate of the Szolnok County Museums, Budapest and Szolnok.

Tarbay, J.G. 2015. A New Late Bronze Age Warrior Equipment from East Central Europe. *Archaeologiai Értesítő* 140:29–70.

———. 2016. Kopott markolatú kardok… A gyopárosfürdői későbronzkori kardlelet a legújabb kutatások tükrében. *Mozaikok Orosháza és vidéke múltjából* 17:3–26.

———. 2019. A késő bronzkori kard útja. In: *Régészeti nyomozások Magyarországon 2,* edited by G. Ilon, pp. 135–50. Martin Opitz, Budapest.

———. 2020. Melted Swords and Broken Metal Vessels: A Late Bronze Age Assemblage from Tatabánya-Bánhida and the Selection of Melted Bronzes. *Dissertationes Archaeologicae ex Instituto Archaeologico Universitatis de Rolando Eötvös Nominatae* Ser. 3, Vol. 7:29–99.

Tarbay, J.G., B. Maróti, and Z. Kis. 2018. Introducing the Spear Project: The Tale of the LBA Spearhead with Wooden Shaft from the Marshland of Kikinda, Serbia. *Journal of Archaeological Science: Reports* 21:268–74.

Tarot, J. 2000. *Die bronzezeitliche Lanzenspitzen der Schweiz unter Einbeziehung von Lichtenstein und Vorarlberg.* Universitätsforschungen zur prähistorischen Archäologie 66. Dr. Rudolf Habelt, Bonn.

Taylor, R.J. 1993. *Hoards of the Bronze Age in Southern Britain: Analysis and Interpretation.* BAR British Series 228. Tempus Reparatum, Oxford.

Telegin, D.Y. and J.P. Mallory. 1994. *The Anthropomorphic Stelae of the Ukraine: The Early Iconography of the Indo-Europeans.* Institute for the Study of Man, Washington, D.C.

Teržan, B. 1987. The Early Iron Age Chronology of the Central Balkans. *Archaeologia Iugoslavica* 24:3–27.

Theodossiev, N. 2000. *North-Western Thrace from the Fifth to First Centuries BC.* BAR International Series 859. Archaeopress, Oxford.

———. 2007a. The Beehive Tombs in Thrace and Their Connection with Funerary Monuments in Thessaly, Macedonia and Other Parts of the Ancient World. In: *Ancient Macedonia 7: Macedonia from the Iron Age to the Death of Philip II: Papers Read at the Seventh International Symposium Held in Thessaloniki, October 14–18, 2002,* pp. 423–44. Institute for Balkan Studies, Thessaloniki.

———. 2007b. The Lantern-Roofed Tombs in Thrace and Anatolia: Some Evidence about Cultural Relations and Interaction in the East Mediterranean. In: *Thrace in the Graeco-Roman World: Proceedings of the 10th International Congress of Thracology, Komotini–Alexandeoupolis, 18–23 October 2005,* edited by A. Iakovidou, pp. 602–13. National Hellenic Research Foundation, Athens.

———. 2011. Ancient Thrace during the First Millennium BC. In: *The Black Sea, Greece, Anatolia and Europe in the First Millennium BC,* edited by G. Tsetskhladze, pp. 1–60. Peeters, Leuven.

Thevenot, J.-P. 1998. Un outillage de bronzier: le dépôt de La Petite Laugère, à Génelard (Saône-et-Loire, France). In: *L'atelier du bronzier en Europe du XXe au VIIIe siècle avant notre ère,* edited by C. Mordant, M. Pernot, and V. Rychner, pp. 123–44. Éditions du Comité des travaux historiques et scientifiques, Paris.

Thorpe, N. 2013. Warfare in the European Bronze Age. In: *The Oxford Handbook of the European Bronze Age,* edited by H. Fokkens and A. Harding, pp. 234–47. Oxford University Press, Oxford.

Tiverios, M. 2008. Greek Colonisation of the Northern Aegean. In: *Greek Colonisation: An Account of Greek Colonies and Other Settlements Overseas,* Volume 2, edited by G. Tsetskhladze, pp. 1–154. Brill, Leiden and Boston.

Točik, A. and J. Paulík. 1960. Výskum mohyly v Čaka v Rokoch 1950–51. *Slovenská Archeológia* 8(1):59–124.

Tod, M.N. 1968. *A Selection of Greek Historical Inscriptions,* Volume II. Clarendon Press, Oxford.

Todorov, Y. 1933. Trakiyskite tsare. *Godishnik na Sodiyskia universitet, Istoriko-filologicheski fakultet* 29(7):3–80.

Tomaschek, W. 1893–94. Die alten Thraker. *SB Akad. Wien* 128:1–130; 130:1–70; 131:1–104.

Tonev, M. 1942. Prinosi kam istoriata na trakite. *Belomorski pregled* 1:179–228.

Tonkova, M. 2015. Adornments. In: *A Companion to Ancient Thrace,* edited by J. Valeva, E. Nankov, and D. Graninger, pp. 212–28. Wiley Blackwell, Malden, MA.

Torbov, N. 2005. *Mogilanskata mogila vav Vratsa.* Mayobo, Vratsa.

Traci. Arte e cultura nelle terre di Bulgaria dalle origini alla tarda romanità. 1989. Exhibition Catalog. Art World Media, Venezia.

Treherne, P. 1995. The Warrior's Beauty: The Masculine Body and Self-Identity in Bronze-Age Europe. *Journal of European Archaeology* 3(1):105–44.

Tringham, R. 2000. Southeastern Europe in the Transition to Agriculture in Europe: Bridge, Buffer, or Mosaic. In: *Europe's First Farmers,* edited by T.D. Price, pp. 19–56. Cambridge University Press, Cambridge.

Trigger, B.G. 2006. *A History of Archaeological Thought.* Second edition. Cambridge University Press, Cambridge.

Trommer, F. and T. Bader. 2013. Lanzenspitzenherstellung. In: *Bronze Age Crafts and Craftsmen in the Carpathian Basin,* edited by B. Rezi, R. Németh, and S. Berecki, pp. 313–40. Mega, Târgu Mureş.

Truhelka, Ć. 1893. Hügelgräber und Ringwälle auf Hochebene Glasinac. *Wissenschaftliche Mitteilungen aus Bosnien und der Herzegowina* 1:61–112.

———. 1904. Der vorgeschichtliche Pfahlbau im Savebette bei Donja Dolina (Bezirk Bosnisch-Gradiška): Bericht über die Ausgrabungen bis 1904. *Wissenschaftliche Mitteilungen aus Bosnien und der Herzegowina* 9:3–170.

Tsonchev, D. 1959. Sivata trakiyska keramika v Bulgaria. *Godishnik na Narodnia arheologicheski muzey v Plovdiv* 3:93–131.

Turchin, P. 2011. Warfare and the Evolution of Social Complexity: A Multilevel-Selection Approach. *Structure and Dynamics* 4(3):1–37.

Turk, P. 1996. Datacija poznobronastodobnih depojev. In: *Depojske in posamezne kovinske najdbe bakrene in bronaste dobe na Slovenskem,* edited by B. Teržan, pp. 89–124. Katalogi in monografije 30. Narodni muzej Slovenije, Ljubljana.

Uckelmann, M. 2012. *Die Schilde der Bronzezeit in Nord-, West- und Zentraleuropa.* Prähistorische Bronzefunde III/4. Franz Steiner, Stuttgart.

Uhlár, V. 1959. Poklad šiestich bronzových mečov z Vyšného Sliača. *Slovenská Archeológia* 7(1):71–78.

Uhnér, C., H. Ciugudean, G. Bălan, R. Burlacu-Timofte, S. Hansen, and G. Rustoiu. 2018. Settlement Structure and Demography in Teleac: A Late Bronze Age – Early Iron Age Hillfort in Transylvania. In: *Bronzezeitliche Burgen zwischen Taunus und Karpaten,* edited by S. Hansen and R. Krause, pp. 371–93. Dr. Rudolf Habelt, Bonn.

Uhnér, C., H. Ciugudean, S. Hansen, F. Becker, G. Bălan, and R. Burlacu-Timofte. 2019. The Teleac Hillfort in Southwestern

Transylvania: The Role of the Settlement, War and the Destruction of the Fortification System. In: *Bronze Age Fortresses in Europe*, edited by S. Hansen and R. Krause, pp. 177–200. Dr. Rudolf Habelt, Bonn.

Ur, J.A. 2014. Households and the Emergence of Cities in Ancient Mesopotamia. *Cambridge Archaeological Journal* 24(2):249–68.

Urban, B. 1991. Spanschäftung für Lanzen und Pfeile. *Fundberichte aus Baden-Württemberg* 16:127–31.

Vachta, T. 2008. *Studien zu den bronzezeitliche Hortfunden des oberen Theissgebietes*. Universitätsforschungen zur prähistorischen Archäologie 159. Dr. Rudolf Habelt, Bonn.

———. 2016. *Bronzezeitliche Hortfunde und ihre Fundorte in Böhmen*. Berlin Studies of the Ancient World 33. Topoi, Berlin.

Váczi, G. 2014. A hálózatelemzés régészeti alkalmazásának lehetőségei a későbronzkori fémművesség tükrében. *Archaeologiai Értesítő* 139:261–91.

Valeva, J. 2015. The Decoration of Thracian Chamber Tombs. In: *A Companion to Ancient Thrace*, edited by J. Valeva, E. Nankov, and D. Graninger, pp. 180–96. Wiley Blackwell, Malden, MA.

Valeva, J., E. Nankov, and D. Graninger (eds.). 2015. *A Companion to Ancient Thrace*. Wiley Blackwell, Malden, MA.

Vandkilde, H. 2011. Bronze Age Warfare in Temperate Europe. In: *Sozialarchäologische Perspektiven: Gesellschaftlicher Wandel 5000-1500 v. Chr. zwischen Atlantik und Kaukasus*, edited by S. Hansen and J. Müller, pp. 365–80. Philipp von Zabern, Berlin.

Vasić, R. 1982. Spätbronzezeitliche und älterhallstattzeitliche Hortfunde im östlichen Jugoslawien. In: *Südosteuropa zwischen 1600 und 1000 v. Chr*, edited by B. Hänsel, pp. 267–85. Prähistorische Archäologie in Südosteuropa 1. Moreland, Berlin.

———. 1987a. Centralnobalkanska regija: Uvod. In: *Praistorija jugoslavenskih zemalja V—željezno doba*, edited by A. Benac, pp. 571–73. Centar za balkanološka ispitivanja, Akademija nauka i umjetnosti Bosne i Hercegovine, Sarajevo.

———. 1987b. Kneževski grobovi iz Novog Pazara i Atenice. In: *Praistorija Jugoslavenskih Zemalja V: Željezno doba*, edited by A. Benac, pp. 644–50. Akademija nauke i umetnosti Bosne i Hercegovine, Sarajevo.

———. 1991. Cultural Groups of the Early Iron Age in the West and Central Balkan and the Possibilities of Their Ethnical Identification. In: *I. Iliro–trački simpozijum–Paleobalkanska plemena između Jadran skog i Crnog mora od eneolita do helenističkoga doba*, edited by A. Benac, pp. 73–82. Posebna izdanja XCIV/14. Akademija nauka i umjetnosti Bosne i Hercegovine, Centra za Balkanološka ispitivanja & Srpska akademija nauka i umetnosti, Sarajevo and Belgrade.

———. 1996. Trebenište i Sindos. *Zbornik Narodnog muzeja* 16(1):143–48.

———. 2001. Prilog proučavanju bronzanih kopalja u Srbiji. *Zbornik radova Narodnog muzeja* 17(1):95–99.

———. 2003. To the North of Trebenishte. In: *Trebenishte: The Fortunes of an Unusual Excavation*, edited by C. Stibbe, pp. 111–33. Studia Archaeologica 121. L'Erma di Bretschneider, Roma.

———. 2015. *Die Lanzen- und Pfeilspitzen im Zentralbalkan (Vojvodina, Serbien, Kosovo, Mazedonien)*. Prähistorische Bronzefunde V/8. Franz Steiner, Stuttgart.

Vasilev, M. 2015. *The Policy of Darius and Xerxes towards Thrace and Macedonia*. Brill, Leiden and Boston.

Vassileva, M. 2015. Persia. In: *A Companion to Ancient Thrace*, edited by J. Valeva, E. Nankov, and D. Graninger, pp. 320–36. Wiley Blackwell, Malden, MA.

Vasileva, Z. 2017. The Early Bronze Age Rings of Type Leukas: New Considerations Regarding Their Origin, Distribution and Function. *Archaeologia Bulgarica* 21(1):1–13.

Vassiliev, A. 1958. *Kazanlashkata grobnitsa*. Bulgarski hudozhnik, Sofia.

Veligianni-Terzi, C. 2004. *Oi Hellēnides poleis kai to basileio tōn Odrusōn apo Abdērōn poleōs mechri Istrou potamou*. Ekdotikos Oikos Adelphōn Kuriakidē, Thessaloniki.

Velkov, V., G. Georgiev, H. Danov, T. Ivanov, and A. Fol (eds.). 1979. *Istoria na Bulgaria, tom 1: Parvobitno-obshtinen i robovladelski stroy: Traki*. Izdatelstvo na Bulgarskata akademia na naukite, Sofia.

Venedikov, I. 1961. *The Panagiurishte Treasure*. Bulgarski Houdozhnik, Sofia.

———. 1976. The Thracian Horseman. In: *Thracian Legends*, edited by A. Fol, I. Venedikov, I. Marazov, and D. Popov, pp. 9–37. Sofia Press, Sofia.

———. 1978. Les migrations en Thrace. *Pulpudeva* 2:162–80.

———. 1987. *The Vulchetrun Treasure*. Svyat, Sofia.

———. 1996. *Trakiyskoto sakrovishte ot Letnitsa*. St. Kliment Ohridski University Press, Sofia.

Venedikov, I. and T. Gerassimov. 1979. *Thracian Art Treasures*. Caxton, London.

Verdelis, N.M. 1967. Neue Funde von Dendra. *Mitteilungen des Deutschen Archäologischen Instituts Athenische Abteilung* 82:1–53.

Videski, Z. 1999. Lisićin Dol-Marvinci. *Macedoniae Acta Archaeologica* 15:91–111.

Vinski-Gasparini, K. 1973. *Kultura polja sa žarama u sjevernoj Hrvatskoj*. Monografije 1/1. Sveučilište u Zagrebu Filozofski Fakultet, Zadar.

Vitucci, G. 1953. *Il regno di Bitinia*. A. Signorelli, Roma.

Vlachopoulos A., Y. Lolos, R. Laffineur, and M. Fotiadis (eds.). 2017. *Hesperos: The Aegean Seen from the West*. Peeters, Leuven.

Vokotopoulou, I. 1985. *Sindos: katalogos tes ekthes*. Arhaiologiko Mouseio Thessalonikes. Tameio Archaiologikōn Porōn kai Apallotriōseōn, Athens.

von Brunn, W.A. 1968. *Mitteldeutsche Hortfunde der jüngeren Bronzezeit*. Römisch-Germanische Forschungen 29. De Gruyter, Berlin.

Vulpe, A. 1990. *Die Kurzschwerter, Dolche und Streitmesser der Hallstattzeit in Rumänien*. Prähistorische Bronzefunde VI/9. C.H. Beck, Munich.

Vulpe, R. 1938. Histoire ancienne de la Dobroudja. In: *La Dobroudja*, edited by R. Vulpe, pp. 35–416. Académie Roumaine, Bucharest.

Walbank, F.W. 1981. Prelude to Spartacus: The Romans in Southern Thrace, 150–70 B.C. In: *Spartacus: Symposium rebus Spartaci gestis dedicatum 2050 a., Blagoevgrad, 20–24.IX.1977*, edited by K.M. Danov, pp. 14–27. Académie Bulgare des Sciences, Sofia.

Wason, P. 1994. *The Archaeology of Rank*. Cambridge University Press, Cambridge.

Webber, C. 2011. *The Gods of Battle: The Thracians at War 1500 BC–150 AD*. Pen and Sword Military, Barnsley.

Weiss, P. and R. Taruskin. 1984. *Music in the Western World: A History in Documents*. Schrimer Books, New York.

Wellman, B. 2012. Is Dunbar's Number Up? *British Journal of Psychology* 103(2):174–76.

Whiteley, P.M. 1988. *Deliberate Acts: Changing Hopi Culture through the Oraibi Split*. University of Arizona Press, Tucson.

Whitley, J. 2002. Objects with Attitude: Biographical Facts and Fallacies in the Study of Late Bronze Age and Early Iron Age Warrior Graves. *Cambridge Archaeological Journal* 12(2):217–32.

Whittle, A. 1996. *Europe in the Neolithic: The Creation of New Worlds*. Cambridge, University Press, Cambridge.

———. 2018. *The Times of Their Lives: Hunting History in the Archaeology of Neolithic Europe*. Oxbow, Oxford.

Wiesner, J. 1963. *Die Thraker: Studien zu einem versunkenen Volk des Balkanraumes*. Kohlhammer, Stuttgart.

Wilkes, J.J. 1992. *The Illyrians*. Blackwell, Oxford.

———. 1996. The Danubian and Balkan Provinces. In: *The Cambridge Ancient History*, Volume 10: *The Augustan Empire 43 B.C.–A.D. 69*, edited by A. Bowman, E. Champlin, and A. Lintott, pp. 545–85. Second edition. Cambridge University Press, Cambridge.

———. 2000. The Danube Provinces. In: *The Cambridge Ancient History*, Volume 11: *The High Empire, A.D. 70–192*, edited by P. Garnsey, D. Rathbone, and A.K. Bowman, pp. 577–603. Cambridge University Press, Cambridge.

Wilkin, S., A. Ventresca Miller, R. Fernandes, + 16 authors, and N. Boivin. 2021. Dairying Enabled Early Bronze Age Yamnaya Steppe Expansions. *Nature* 598:629–33.

Windholz-Konrad, M. 2012. Das Deponierungsareal bei der Rabenwand im steirischen Kainischtal, Österreich: Zum ausgeprägten Hortphänomen entlang der Traun im Alpendurchgang zwischen Zinkenkogel und Hohem Sarstein. In: *Hort und Raum. Aktuelle Forschungen zu bronzezeitlichen Deponierungen in Mitteleuropa*, edited by S. Hansen, D. Neumann, and T. Vachta, pp. 117–49. Topoi. Berlin Studies of the Ancient World 10. De Gruyter, Berlin and Boston.

Wirth, M. 2003. *Rekonstruktion bronzezeitlicher Gießereitechniken mittels numerischer Simulation, gießtechnologischer Experimente und werkstofftechnischer Untersuchungen an Nachguss und Original*. Forschung, Entwicklung, Ergebnisse 40. Gießerei-Institut, Aachen.

Yordanov, K. 1998. *Politicheski otnoshenia mezhdu Makedonia i trakiyskite darzhavi (359–281 g. pr. Hr.)*. Studia Thracica 7. Bulgarska akademia na naukite, Institut po trakologia, Sofia.

———. 2011. Dobrudja prez I-oto hil. pr. Hr. Geti. In: *Istoria na Dobrudja, tom 1: Vtoro preraboteno i dopalneno izdanie*, edited by H. Todorova, K. Yordanov, V. Velkov, and S. Torbatov, pp. 131–236. Faber, Veliko Tarnovo.

Youroukova, Y. 1992. *Monetite na trakijskite plemena i vladeteli*. Izdatelstvo Petar Beron, Sofia.

Zalai-Gaál, I. 2010. *Die soziale Differenzierung im Spätneolithikum Südtransdanubiens: die Funde and Befunde aus den Altgrabungen der Lengyel-Kultur*. Archaeolingua, Budapest.

Žeravica, Z. 1993. *Äxte und Beile aus Dalmatien und anderen Teilen Kroatiens, Montenegro, Bosnien und Herzegowina*. Prähistorische Bronzefunde IX/18. Franz Steiner, Stuttgart.

Zhivkova, L. 1975. *The Kazanlak Tomb*. Bongers, Recklinghausen.

Zoffmann, Zs.K. 1978. Das anthropologische Material der Ockergräber-Bestattung von Szentes-Besenyőhalom. *A Móra Ferenc Múzeum Évkönyve* 1976–1977(1):39–40.

———. 2000. Anthropological Sketch of the Prehistoric Population of the Carpathian Basin. *Acta Biologica Szegediensis* 44(1–4):75–79.

———. 2006. Anthropological Finds of the Pit Grave Culture from the Sárrétudvari-Őrhalom Site. In: Sárrétudvari-Őrhalom Tumulus Grave from the Beginning of the EBA in Eastern Hungary, edited by J. Dani and I.M. Nepper. *Communicationes Archaeologicae Hungariae* 2006:51–58.

———. 2011. Human Remains from the Kurgan at Hajdúnánás-Tedej-Lyukashalom and an Anthropological Outline of the Pit-Grave Ethnic Groups. In: *Kurgan Studies: An Environmental and Archaeological Multiproxy Study of Burial Mounds in the Eurasian Steppe Zone*, edited by Á. Pető and A. Barczi, pp. 173–81. BAR International Series 2238. Archaeopress, Oxford.

Index